RELIGION AND MENTAL HEALTH

Research and Clinical Applications

HAROLD G. KOENIG, MD

Professor of Psychiatry & Behavioral Sciences
Associate Professor of Medicine
Director, Center for Spirituality, Theology and Health
Duke University Medical Center, Durham, North Carolina, United States
Adjunct Professor, Department of Medicine, King Abdulaziz University, Jeddah, Saudi Arabia
Adjunct Professor of Public Health, Ningxia Medical University, Yinchuan, People's Republic of China

ELSEVIER

ACADEMIC PRESS
An imprint of Elsevier

Academic Press is an imprint of Elsevier
125 London Wall, London EC2Y 5AS, United Kingdom
525 B Street, Suite 1800, San Diego, CA 92101-4495, United States
50 Hampshire Street, 5th Floor, Cambridge, MA 02139, United States
The Boulevard, Langford Lane, Kidlington, Oxford OX5 1GB, United Kingdom

Library of Congress Cataloging-in-Publication Data
A catalog record for this book is available from the Library of Congress

British Library Cataloguing-in-Publication Data
A catalogue record for this book is available from the British Library

ISBN: 978-0-12-811282-3

For information on all Academic Press publications visit our website at https://www.elsevier.com/books-and-journals

Publisher: Nikki Levy
Acquisition Editor: Nikki Levy
Editorial Project Manager: Barbara Makinster
Production Project Manager: Priya Kumaraguruparan
Designer: Matthew Limbert

Typeset by Thomson Digital

To my wife, Charmin, and our three beautiful children,
Jordan, Rebekah, and son-in-law, Enrique.

Contents

I
RESEARCH

II

CLINICAL APPLICATIONS

Preface

I first came to know Dr. Harold G. Koenig as the leading authority on research into religion, spirituality, and health. His books, *Handbook of Religion and Health* and *Handbook of Religion and Mental Health*, remain comprehensive and authoritative volumes; his summer research workshops and fellowships train professionals in a variety of disciplines; and his monthly eNewsletter *Crossroads* of The Center for Spirituality, Theology and Health provides current, as well as critical information about this growing field.

Only more recently have I come to appreciate Dr. Koenig as a committed clinician. This should not have been a surprise considering that during medical school he took time to also become an RN, trained as a family physician before entering psychiatry and later geriatric psychiatry, and continues to treat patients.

The organization and focus of this book reflect its author's longstanding dedication and unique ability to clearly summarize the results of research in a broad and complex area, to engage directly the questions that both researchers and clinicians face, and then to discuss practical applications of what we know.

This book fills an important gap. Although psychiatry's historical mistrust of religion has lessened, many clinicians continue to neglect religion because they lack background and training in using what patients tell them about the positive and/or negative role of faith in their lives. In the first part, readers can find empirical justification for addressing religion to enhance mental health, as well as the distilled wisdom of the author on questions central to the religion/psychiatry interface. In the second part, they will find many ways to be effective in doing so, as well as guidance in approaching the ethical challenges raised by engaging these issues with patients.

Many others have now written thoughtfully about these questions, but usually in specialized journals or multi-authored texts. I know of no more comprehensive, accessible resource than this book for those interested in taking better care of the whole patient.

John R. Peteet, MD

Associate Professor of Psychiatry,
Harvard Medical School, Dana-Farber Cancer Institute,
Brigham and Women's Hospital, Boston, MA, United States

Acknowledgments

A sincere thanks to Ken Pargament, PhD, for his advice, knowledge, and support in writing this book, and to my publisher Nikki Levy, senior editorial project manager Barbara Makinster, and production manager Priya Kumaraguruparan.

Introduction

This volume is for people in the business of helping those who are suffering from emotional problems adversely affecting their lives and relationships. The focus here is on the role, both positive and negative, that religion can play. The premise is that religious beliefs and practices can be a great source of comfort for many, but for some, may seem to exacerbate distress or make life more difficult. Based on systematic research and common sense, how can mental health and religious professionals use a person's religious faith to help them feel better in the short-term and grow mentally healthier over the long-term? Much research remains to be done to fully understand this connection between religion and mental health, although much research has already been done that demands application. This volume comprehensively addresses both of these subjects.

First, research findings from the late 1800s up to the present day are summarized and citations of seminal and more recent studies are provided. Based on this information, advice is offered on how to better care for religious (and nonreligious) persons by taking a religious history, supporting beliefs, challenging beliefs, and sometimes utilizing beliefs to produce more rapid and complete healing. Attention is paid to both religious interventions that are simple and to more complex religiously integrated treatments. Information is provided on how to identify those who might benefit most from such interventions, how to effectively apply them, the training necessary to do so, and educational resources that will help in this regard.

CONTENT

The text is divided into two major sections: research and clinical applications. The first section begins by defining and distinguishing religion and spirituality, and then proceeds to describe how to quantitatively measure religiosity so as to assess its relationship to various mental health outcomes. The role of religion in coping with stress is then examined as a key mechanism explaining why one might expect a relationship between religion and mental health. Research is then reviewed that explores associations between religious beliefs/practices and emotional disorders, such as depression, suicide, anxiety, PTSD, substance abuse, schizophrenia, bipolar disorder, and neurocognitive disorders, such as dementia. Next examined are relationships with positive emotional states, such as well-being, life satisfaction, hope, optimism, and purpose/meaning in life. Considerable space is given to the precise mechanisms that may help to clarify how religious involvement affects mental health, including genetic, biological, psychological, social, environmental, and individual factors (i.e., personal decision-making). Religious struggles and doubt are then investigated and relationships to negative emotional states examined, paying particular attention to the question of causality (chicken vs. egg dilemma). Finally, research questions that have been answered and those that remain to be answered are discussed, and directions for future research are proposed.

The second section describes applications to clinical practice for mental health professionals and religious professionals. Case vignettes are provided throughout this section to illustrate the points being made. First, general clinical applications are examined that are relevant to all clients, regardless of the client's religious or spiritual orientation. Described here are attitudes of mental health professionals (and professional organizations) toward assessing, addressing, and integrating religion/spirituality. Guidelines are provided on how to take a *mental health* spiritual history, as well as how to sensibly implement more controversial practices, such as praying with clients, sharing personal religious beliefs during client sessions, and encouraging clients to be more active in their own religious faith for mental health reasons. Next, religious interventions for depression, anxiety, and other distressing emotional states are reviewed; and the evidence for their use presented. The focus here is on randomized clinical trials and single group experimental studies, the results of which will be examined by examining individual studies and summarized through systematic reviews and metaanalyses. Religious interventions are divided into simple religious practices (e.g., meditation, prayer, scripture reading, scripture recitation, religious support, and discussions) and interventions that explicitly integrate religious/spiritual beliefs and practices into psychotherapy. The latter types of therapies utilize clients' religious resources to achieve therapeutic goals by altering dysfunctional thoughts, challenging underlying assumptions, pointing out defeating behaviors, and when necessary, targeting religious struggles that may be blocking recovery.

Next, guidelines are provided on how to identify clients who might benefit from religious psychotherapy, and how to distinguish these individuals from clients who would do better with standard secular therapy. As part of this discussion, the attitudes of clients toward therapists bringing up religious/spiritual issues in therapy are examined, as well as the training that providers need to competently administer this form of integrated therapy. The final chapter of this section discusses situations where religion is the problem, not the solution, to the client's mental health difficulties. How to identify the neurotic use of religion is illustrated by a series of cases, and suggestions are made on how to sensitively manage these clients (which may sometimes involve delicately challenging strongly held sacred beliefs). In contrast to neurotic religion, a description is provided of a "healthy" religion that fosters both psychological and spiritual growth, as well as increases social capital. This volume concludes with a summary of what is known about the relationship between religion and mental health, what needs to be known in the future, and how to apply this information when working with religious and nonreligious clients. In addition, a special section on resources for researchers, clinicians, educators, and clergy is provided that includes recommended measures of religiosity and their psychometric characteristics, books, classic review articles, and Internet sites, where more information on religion and mental health can be found. In summary, this extensively referenced book presents the latest research, integrates it into clinical practice, makes recommendations for next steps, and provides further information should the reader wish to know more.

SPECIAL FEATURES

Religion and Mental Health has several special features that mark it as unique. Most books on religion, psychology, and mental health are multi-authored or edited texts with a range of different perspectives, which is of course a positive (in terms of breadth and range of views), but also a negative (not having a common "story line" that follows from beginning to end). The present volume is a single authored text with a common voice that carries throughout, where each chapter builds on the other and repetition is minimized. Second, most books published in this area are primarily clinician-oriented and experience-based, rather than firmly research-based. This one, written by a researcher and clinician, cannot be anything, but evidence-based (although admittedly may present a particular view of the evidence that carries its own bias). Third, much of the recent literature has emphasized spirituality—an often broad and conceptually nebulous construct. Books on spirituality are necessary and helpful, but in a laudable effort to make spirituality as inclusive as possible, the concept has become common to all and relevant to none, a toothless tiger without any real bite. This book is different. It focuses squarely on religion. The view taken here is that the real power of religion for good or for evil lies in the details, that is, the specific teachings of faith traditions that have persisted for thousands of years. Passed down from generation to generation, religious beliefs and practices have filled a vital human need, a need related to how trauma, tragedy, uncertainty, success, and joy are experienced and interpreted.

WRITING STYLE AND LANGUAGE

The writing here is conversational in style, rather than strictly academic, making the text easy to read and the content easy to understand (with the possible exception of some sections that contain specific scientific terminology for researchers). The use of simple language makes this volume readily accessible to a wide range of professional and nonprofessional readers. While the primary audience of this book is mental health professionals (psychiatrists, psychologists, counselors, social workers, nurses) and religious professionals (chaplains, pastoral counselors, and community clergy), anyone interested in the intersection between mental health and religion will likely benefit from the information provided here.

In order to be politically correct and as ecumenical as possible, the word "God" is frequently avoided in academic writing, since not all world religions emphasize a personal divinity that is separate from the physical world and universe (or any divinity at all, whether separate from or part of creation). In the present text, however, the word God will be used frequently and without censure. The reason is that only 2% to 13% of the world's population indicates that they are convinced atheists, most of who live in East Asian countries that have outlawed religion for decades (e.g., China). According to Wave 6 of the World Values Survey (2010–14), 5.4% of a random sample of 84,751 persons representing 57 countries indicated they were atheist (latest available data). In fact, the average annual global change in atheism from 2000 to 2010 was −0.17% (Encyclopedia Britannica, 2010; Gallup International, 2012), indicating that despite global secularization, atheism is actually decreasing worldwide. The term "God" for referring to divinity, then, is central to most major world religions. This does not mean that space will not be given to religions that do not emphasize God, nor does it mean the exclusion of atheists or agnostics in the discussions here.

Please join me now in a journey where we will discover how religious involvement is related to mental health and how this information can be utilized (in and out of the clinic) to maximize well-being and promote healing.

References

Encyclopedia Britannica (2010). *Worldwide adherents of all religions by six Continental areas mid–2010.* Available from: https://www.britannica.com/topic/religion-Year-In-Review-2010/Worldwide-Adherents-of-All-Religions.

Gallup International (2012). *Global index of religiosity and atheism*. Available from: http://www.wingia.com/web/files/news/14/file/14.pdf.

World Values Survey (2010). *Results: "Independently of whether you attend religious services or not would you say you are…,"* 147, 349. Available from: http://www.worldvaluessurvey.org/WVSDocumentationWV6.jsp.

PART I

RESEARCH

CHAPTER

1

Religion vs. Spirituality

This book is specifically about *religion* and mental health. Although many applications to clinical practice will be addressed here, the primary research questions that will be asked throughout this text are the following: *Do religious beliefs and practices affect mental health; what is the nature of that effect (positive or negative); what is the direction of the effect (in terms of causality)*; and *how does this effect come about (etiology and mechanisms)?* Yet there is another seemingly related term, *spirituality*, which has recently become the focus of many books in the mental health field. How do these two terms relate to each other? Are they the same or different concepts? There is a growing consensus that religion and spirituality are different (Zinnbauer et al., 1997; Hill et al., 2000; Worthington, Hook, Davis, & McDaniel, 2011; Oman, 2013; Pargament, Mahoney, Exline, Jones, & Shafranske, 2013; Klein, Hood, Silver, Keller, & Streib, 2016). But are they?

The first mention of the word *spirit* is in the book of Genesis 1:2 ("And the Spirit of God moved upon the face of the waters" [KJV]), and so is a distinctively religious term. The traditional use of the term spirituality (until the past 25 years or so), in fact, has been to describe the core of what it means to be religious (Sheldrake, 2010). In that traditional understanding, many persons might consider themselves religious, but only deeply religious persons could call themselves spiritual. Being spiritual meant that life was centered on and directed by one's religious beliefs. Such persons were considered exemplars of their faith tradition. Spiritual was often used to describe the clergy or other devout religious leaders such as Jesus, Moses, Gandhi, Mother Teresa, the Prophet Mohammad, the Buddha, and other saints and prophets. There was no such thing as being spiritual, but not religious. This would have been a contradiction in terms.

That has all changed. Reflecting on this trend, Smith and Denton (2005) note that "The very idea and language of 'spirituality,' originally grounded in the self-disciplining faith practices of religious believers, including ascetics and monks, then becomes detached from its moorings in historical religious traditions and is redefined in terms of subjective self-fulfillment" (p. 175). The term spirituality among many mental health

Religion and Mental Health. http://dx.doi.org/10.1016/B978-0-12-811282-3.00001-X

professionals and those in the social and behavioral sciences has become a popular one, a descriptor that now expands far beyond religion. One can be spiritual but not religious, or even completely secular and still consider oneself spiritual (Walach, 2015). While academics argue fiercely that spirituality is different from religion, research has now examined how people in the general population feel about the terms religion and spirituality (Smith & Denton, 2005; Ammerman, 2013; Klein et al., 2016). These studies report considerable overlap in how most people understand spirituality and religion, even those who are less religious and more religiously diverse than in the United States (Ammerman, 2013; Klein et al., 2016).

Efforts to broaden the definition of spirituality make perfect sense. Given the differences in belief between world religions that have created strife, division, wars, terrorist activities, coercion, etc., and the need to address the healthcare needs of all regardless of belief, many have sought a less divisive language that includes everyone. Enter the term spirituality. Spirituality has rapidly gained popularity as a way to talk about "something" that is common to all, both the religious and the nonreligious. That something, though, has become difficult to define in a way that everyone can agree on (Rose, 2001; Koenig, 2008). Most agree that it is more than simply humanism, but what that "more" involves is controversial. The efforts to redefine spirituality have resulted in a broad and diffuse concept that has lost almost everything that distinguishes it as a unique term that is different from everything else (Bash, 2004; Popp-Baier, 2010; Streib & Hood, 2011; Westerink, 2012; La Cour, Ausker, & Hvidt, 2012; Salander, 2012).

Of course, this has created a problem when conducting research that requires universal agreement on a concept so that (1) clear communication can occur about it; (2) it can be measured, quantified, and related to mental health (which is the goal here); and (3) the resulting research findings can be replicated by others. When discussing the research in this area, then, the term *religion* will be used throughout the text. The scientific rationale for doing so will now be further developed.

CONSTRUCTS FOR RESEARCH

To conduct quantitative research on a construct, that construct must have at least three characteristics. Admittedly, these characteristics are less important for qualitative research, but for quantitative studies in the social, psychological, and behavioral sciences, they are essential.

First, there must be agreement in the research community on what the construct is (i.e., a common definition) for the reasons noted above.

Second, the construct must be clear and unambiguous, distinct and unique, and must not overlap with similar constructs. In psychometric terms, this is called discriminant validity. The construct must be distinguishable from other constructs like it, particularly those that it might influence (i.e., mental health). In this respect, the construct must not be confused with its "outcome" (psychological states which result from the construct). This is important, as interventions are usually directed at the beginning of a causal pathway to affect the eventual outcome. Using an example from the field of medicine, if a person has a fever and that fever is being caused by a bacterial pneumonia, then it is important to distinguish between the fever and the bacterial infection that is causing the fever. The fever results from the bacterial infection. Treating only the fever will result in the death of the patient; treating the bacterial infection, however, will result in the elimination of the fever and improvement in the patient's condition. Therefore it is important to identify the original cause and distinguish it from the effects that result from that original cause.

Third, the construct must be measurable and quantifiable, especially if the goal is to examine relationships with other constructs that are likewise quantifiable. In the mental health field the latter means negative states characterized by depressive symptoms, anxiety symptoms, psychotic symptoms, symptoms of substance abuse, etc., and positive states characterized by feeling happy, satisfied with life, optimistic about the future, and feeling that life has purpose and meaning. Many psychometrically valid scales now exist to quantify these constructs.

In mental health research, the goal is to identify risk factors for emotional and mental disorders, and determine characteristics that promote and improve mental health, with the ultimate intention of developing interventions to treat disorders and enhance well-being and functioning.

RELIGION

How do the three characteristics for a researchable construct relate to religion and its measurement when examining relationships with mental health?

Agreed Upon Definition

While the term itself has come under disfavor within academia, there is consistent agreement on the definition of religion. This term has been used for centuries, long accepted as characterizing certain types of beliefs and behaviors (see definition below). Thus, mental health, social, and behavioral scientists can communicate with each other about religion (as long as the particular religion is specified) and everyone knows what the other is talking about. There is also general agreement between academics and the general population on what is meant by religion. Admittedly, disagreement occurs when religion is viewed as institutional only or is equated with rules and laws, rather than when it is understood as involving a connection to the transcendent that encompasses personal beliefs along with communal and private devotional practices.

Overlap With Mental Health

There is very little overlap between religion and mental health, an important point that requires further examination. Religion and mental health are two quite distinct and separate constructs. Religious beliefs, rituals, practices, importance, motivation, and centrality in life are different from emotional states, which religion may or may not affect. As noted earlier, good mental health is usually characterized by low levels of negative emotions, high levels of positive emotions, and the ability to function in social, recreational, and occupational settings.

Although both positive and negative emotions can occur at the same time, this is not often the case. When people are happy, they are not also typically sad at the same time; when individuals are at peace, they are not usually anxious; suicidal thoughts are not present in those who are hopeful and experience meaning and purpose in life; and so forth. Negative mental states include feelings of sadness, hopelessness, fear, anxiety, distress, loneliness, distrust, or alienation from others, whereas positive mental states are characterized by happiness, well-being, satisfaction with life, optimism, peacefulness, harmony with others, having purpose and meaning in life, and being hopeful about the future. A good example of poor mental health is major depressive disorder. Major depression, according to the Diagnostic and Statistical Manual of Mental Disorders, is characterized by the presence of a sad mood (the opposite of feeling happy or satisfied with life) or loss of interest along with at least four other symptoms, such as feeling worthless (lack of meaning and purpose), being social withdrawn (not feeling connected to others), exhibiting psychomotor agitation or restlessness (lack of harmony and peace), and so forth.

Religious involvement may lead to major depression by enhancing guilt, shame, and lowering self-esteem for failure to live up to religious values or standards. In that case, challenging religious beliefs and discouraging religious behaviors (as mental health professions, particularly psychoanalysts, once did) would improve mental health and well-being. In contrast, religious beliefs and behaviors may protect against depression by giving meaning to life events, providing hope, surrounding persons with a community of support, and providing beliefs and practices that generate feelings of being loved and care for. In that case, interventions that support and encourage religion would result in a decrease or resolution of depression. Therefore, there is little likelihood that "what it means to be religious" would overlap with "what it means to be depressed," and

TABLE 1.1 Religion in the United States: 1938–2016 (Gallup Poll, December 23, 2016)

	1938	1944	1950	1962	1974	1986	1998	2010	2016
Characteristics expressed as percentage (%)									
Membership[a]	73	75	73	73	71	71	70	63	56
Attendance (past 7 days)	41	37	39	46	40	40	44	37	36
Importance (very)	—	—	—	70	52	54	57	55	53
Influence on American life									
Increasing	—	—	—	69	44	48	36	25	22
Decreasing	—	—	—	14	45	38	59	73	75

[a] *In church, synagogue, or mosque.*

researchers can examine the relationship between the two and try to determine whether and how one influences the other.

Measurable and Quantifiable

Religious beliefs, behaviors, and commitments (Table 1.1) can be measured, quantified, and examined in their relationships with mental states that can also be measured and quantified. Many scales now exist that assess whether people are religious, how important religion is to them (level of religious motivation or commitment), frequency of engagement in religious activities or rituals (such as religious attendance), and frequency of other behaviors that are religiously motivated. There scales assess religion with Likert-type responses similar to scales used to measure symptoms of depression, anxiety, or stress. Indeed, there are hundreds of psychometrically reliable and valid measures of religiosity that allow for the quantification of this construct without including indicators of mental health in the measure.

Since religion fulfills each of the three criteria above (agreed upon definition, distinct from mental health, quantifiable), research can be conducted that meets the objectives described earlier (i.e., examine the relationship between religion and mental health, determine casual direction, and develop interventions that target religion).

SPIRITUALITY

What about spirituality? How do the three characteristics necessary for quantitative research apply to spirituality and its measurement in mental health research?

Agreed Upon Definition

There is no widespread agreement on what the term "spirituality" means, particularly among mental health, social, and behavioral scientists. Many gatherings of health professionals and even international conferences have struggled with the definition of spirituality, particularly in the palliative care setting (Puchalski et al., 2009; Nolan, Saltmarsh, & Leget, 2011; Puchalski, Vitillo, Hull, & Reller, 2014). The definitions proposed, however, have not received widespread acceptance within the research community because of the strong overlap these definitions have with mental health constructs. Some of the confusion comes from trying to come up with a definition that is appropriate for both clinicians and researchers. The broad and overlapping definitions proposed by Puchalski et al. primarily apply to definitions of spirituality for use in *clinical practice* (see below).

With regard to research, there has been considerable progress in attempting to define spirituality as a more distinctive construct, tying it to what has been called "the sacred" in a person's life (Pargament & Mahoney, 2002; Hill & Pargament, 2003; Pargament 2013). Nevertheless, one might argue that this progress is not far enough. What is sacred for one person may be quite different from what is sacred for another, making this benchmark highly individualized. Some persons view (or actually treat) as "sacred" their savings, stock market investments, cars, homes, jobs, hobbies, sports teams, friends, family, and lovers. Some even hold sacred their desires for revenge against those who have hurt them or their need to dominate and control others. These objects of affection and desire may be highly valued, protected, revered, and pursued with great zeal and devotion, exclusive of other goals or pursuits in life. The sacred may have little or nothing to do with the transcendent, i.e., that which is outside of the person or separate from one's own particular ego needs. Spirituality, then, even if anchored in the "sacred" may be different for every person, making the actual content of the definition highly variable.

Overlap With Mental Health

To make spirituality more inclusive and distinguish it from religion, efforts have often sought to exclude religious beliefs, practices, and motivations, minimize them, or refer to them broadly in the definition of spirituality. However, if spirituality is not defined by engagement in religious beliefs and practices, then how does one define it? The resulting search to identify descriptors of spirituality separate from religion has presented academics with a dilemma. How do you characterize a historically religious term (spirituality) by attributes that are not religious? This has created a vacuum in the definition, a vacuum that has drawn in what?

Yes, indeed, the vacuum has drawn in indicators of positive psychological and emotional states: for example, having meaning and purpose in life, feeling connected to others, experiencing inner peace and harmony, and so forth (i.e., indicators that reflect the exact opposite of emotional illness or pathology). This tendency ends up contaminating definitions of spirituality with good mental health.

Measurable and Quantifiable

As ways to assess spirituality are necessarily grounded on the definition of spirituality, the contamination of the definition with mental health content has found its way into instruments to measure spirituality. A recent systematic review reported that nearly 50% of all studies reporting positive relationships between spirituality and mental health used measures contaminated by mental health indicators (Garssen, Visser, & de Jager Meezenbroek, 2015). Consider the spirituality measures most often used today to examine relationships with mental health listed in Table 1.2. To get a sense of how often these measures are being used, number of citations to the original articles where psychometrics of the scale were reported are listed here. Table 1.2 provides these citation numbers by three different time periods: 1929–16, 2011–16, and 2016. This provides a comparison over time on how frequently these scales have been used. For a comparison to religiosity scales uncontaminated with mental health indicators, see the scales and citation numbers listed in Tables 2.1 and 2.2 in the next chapter.

TABLE 1.2 Most Commonly Used Measures of Spirituality[a]

1929–2016		
Scales	**Cites**	**Authors**
1. Spiritual Well-Being Scale[b]	1245	Paloutzian and Ellison (1982)
2. FACIT-Sp[c]	925	Peterman, Fitchett, Brady, Hernandez, & Cella (2002)
3. Spiritual Transcendence Scale (Piedmont)	805	Piedmont (1999)
4. Daily Spiritual Experiences Scale	713	Underwood and Teresi (2002)
5. Spiritual Involvement and Beliefs Scale	328	Hatch et al. (1998)
6. WHOQOL-SRPB[d]	274	Saxena (2006)
7. Spirituality Assessment Scale	218	Howden (1992)
8. Spirituality Index of Well-Being[e]	170	Daaleman and Frey (2004)
9. JAREL Spiritual Well-Being Scale	153	Hungelmann, Kenkel-Rossi, Klassen, & Stollenwerk (1996)
10. Spiritual Transcendence Scale (Reed)	131	Reed (1986)

(Continued)

TABLE 1.2 Most Commonly Used Measures of Spirituality[a] (*Cont.*)

Scales	Cites	Authors
2011–16		
1. FACIT-Sp	584	Peterman et al. (2002)
2. Spiritual Well-Being Scale	495	Paloutzian and Ellison (1982)
3. Daily Spiritual Experiences Scale	429	Underwood and Teresi (2002)
4. Spiritual Transcendence Scale	433	Piedmont (1999)
5. WHOQOL-SRPB	191	Saxena (2006)
6. Spiritual Involvement and Beliefs Scale	124	Hatch et al. (1998)
7. Spirituality Assessment Scale	108	Howden (1992)
8. Spirituality Index of Well-Being	107	Daaleman and Frey (2004)
9. JAREL Spiritual Well-Being Scale	65	Hungelmann et al. (1996)
10. Spiritual Transcendence Scale (Reed)	38	Reed (1986)
2016		
1. FACIT-Sp	92	Peterman et al. (2002)
2. Daily Spiritual Experiences Scale	82	Underwood and Teresi (2002)
3. Spiritual Transcendence Scale	81	Piedmont (1999)
4. Spiritual Well-Being Scale	75	Paloutzian and Ellison (1982)
5. WHOQOL-SRPB	33	Saxena (2006)
6. Spirituality Index of Well-Being	28	Daaleman and Frey (2004)
7. JAREL Spiritual Well-Being Scale	13	Hungelmann et al. (1996)
8. Spiritual Involvement and Beliefs Scale	12	Hatch et al. (1998)
9. Spirituality Assessment Scale	10	Howden (1992)
10. Spiritual Transcendence Scale (Reed)	7	Reed (1986)

[a] *Based on citations of the original report of the scale in Google Scholar on December 17, 2016.*
[b] *Applies to existential well-being subscale only; citation source in this case was: Paloutzian and Ellison (1982). Spiritual well-being scale. Hill P., Hood R. (Eds.), (1999).* Measures of Religiosity *(pp. 382–385). Birmingham, AL: Religious Education Press.*
[c] *Functional Assessment of Chronic Illness Therapy: Spiritual Well-Being Scale.*
[d] *World Health Organization's Quality of Life-Spirituality, Religion, and Personal Beliefs.*
[e] *Particularly the existential well-being subscale that is often considered the "spirituality" portion of the measure.*

All of these measures include one or more items that assess purpose and meaning in life, experiences of inner peace and harmony, feelings of fulfillment and satisfaction, having a sense of well-being, and feeling connected with others. Positive responses to these items indicate good mental health, the exact opposite of the kinds of feelings that depressed, anxious, distressed, or people with emotional disorders have (i.e., restless, anxious, dissatisfied, unfulfilled, socially withdrawn, alienated from others, etc.). Is it really that surprising that these measures of spirituality are related to good mental health when spirituality is defined and measured a priori as good mental health? When such measures are used to assess spirituality, those with mental illness or emotional problems not surprisingly score low on them. This excludes a very large proportion of this population from being spiritual. Does that sound right? Just because a person has a mental illness, does this automatically mean they are not spiritual? Furthermore, adding the descriptor "well-being" to create a category called "spiritual well-being" makes it nearly impossible to distinguish measures of this construct from similar measures of psychological well-being (Tsuang, Simpson, Koenen, Kremen, & Lyons, 2007).

Defining spirituality as good mental health ensures that a positive correlation will be found with good mental health. This practice predetermines the outcome before a single study participant completes a survey. The results of such research produce what are called tautological findings, where a construct is correlated with itself. Such meaningless associations do little to further scientific knowledge. The evidence base on mental health risk factors is not advanced by finding that people with greater meaning and purpose in life (higher scores on spirituality) have fewer suicidal thoughts or commit suicide less often (as reported in one of the world's leading medical journals) (McClain, Rosenfeld, & Breithart, 2003). Similarly, not useful to mental health practitioners is the finding that spirituality measured by feelings of peace and deep inner harmony is inversely related to anxiety or depression (as reported in one of the world's top mental health journals) (Mofidi et al., 2007). Is research really needed to conclude that a major reason why people commit suicide is because they believe their lives have lost meaning and purpose, or that people who are anxious or depressed are less likely to feel deep inner peace and harmony? This author doesn't think so.

Hundreds and hundreds of studies have now been published in academic mental health journals reporting positive connections between spirituality and mental health using measures of spirituality that are simply assessing mental health itself. This trend has prompted researchers to challenge the validity of the findings between measures of spirituality and mental health outcomes when contaminated scales like this are used (Salandar, 2006; Tsuang et al., 2007; Koenig, 2008; Tsuang & Simpson, 2008; Krause, 2008; Reinert & Koenig, 2013). One very practical reason for challenging such findings is that measuring spirituality as good mental health often interferes with efforts to examine the relationship between religion and mental health. When spirituality is measured by scales containing mental health indicators and included in statistical models that also contain measures of religiosity, religiosity often loses statistical significance as a predictor of the mental health outcome once "spirituality" is controlled. The reason is because religiosity often has its effects on mental health by increasing meaning and purpose in life, peace and harmony, and social connections with others, and when these factors under the guise of "spirituality" are controlled for, the positive relationship between religiosity and the mental health is weakened or disappears (Koenig, 2011).

A major purpose of epidemiological research is to identify factors that influence mental health and can be targeted in future interventions. Measuring spirituality in the way described above confuses cause and effect, and therefore provides little information on what mental health professionals should direct their interventions at. People who are suicidal often lack a sense of meaning and purpose in life. Mental health professionals already know that; what they need to know is where the patient can *find* sources of meaning and purpose, which can then be supported or enhanced. Conceptualizing spirituality as the state of having meaning and purpose puts the cart before the horse. For mental health professionals from a Christian faith tradition, the following may help to clarify the issue. St. Paul talks about the "fruit of the spirit" being "love, joy, peace, forbearance, kindness, goodness, faithfulness, gentleness and self-control" (Galatians 5:22–23). These are the *fruit* of the spirit (the results of living a spiritual life), not the spirit itself. Most of the Christian scriptures are aimed at nourishing a distinctively religious "spirit," and their claim is that doing so will produce the fruit of mental health.

SUMMARY OF DEFINITIONS FOR RESEARCH PURPOSES

When spirituality is conceptualized and defined by positive emotions and healthy psychological states, this produces nothing but confusion. Why use the *religious* term "spirituality" to describe psychological concepts such as meaning and purpose, peacefulness, and social bonding, when there is already a secular language and descriptor terms that distinguish them from religion. Spirituality, then, simply becomes synonymous with having good mental health, and its relationship to mental health can no longer be examined using the scientific method. The result is that research reporting positive correlations between spirituality and mental health becomes subject to serious criticism (i.e., tautological findings), and provides little useful information for mental health professionals who are looking for characteristics that can be addressed to enhance mental health (since spirituality in these cases is the mental health outcome being sought, not the underlying etiologic factor that can be targeted).

Religion, in contrast to spirituality, is a distinct construct that is separate from psychological, social and mental health concepts, and therefore can be examined as a predictor of mental health and a potential target for intervention. This is not to suggest that mental health professionals should try to make clients religious. They don't need to. A very large proportion (if not the majority) of patients seen by mental health professions are *already religious*. Rather than discourage religious involvement as grandfathers of psychiatry and psychology sometimes did assuming it was pathologic (Freud, 1927; Ellis, 1980; Watters, 1992), religious beliefs and activities can be assessed and if present, considered a resource for improving mental health and reducing emotional distress. This, of course, assumes that religion is generally non-pathologic, that there is a positive correlation between religious involvement and good mental health, and that the direction of causality is from religion to mental health, all of which will soon be examined here by reviewing findings from systematic research.

DEFINING RELIGION

Having discussed the benefits and perils of religion and spirituality, the task now is to define these terms as they are used by the author of this text. With regard to religion, the following definition describes its use here:

> Beliefs, practices, and rituals related to the 'transcendent," where the transcendent is that which relates to the mystical, supernatural, or God in Western religious traditions, or to Brahman, Ultimate Truth, Ultimate Reality, or practices leading to Enlightenment, in Eastern traditions. Religion may also involve beliefs about spirits, angels, or demons. Usually religion involves specific beliefs about the life after death and rules to guide personal behaviors and interactions with others during this life. Religion is often organized and practiced within a community, but it can also be practiced alone and in private, outside of an institution, such as personal beliefs about and commitment to the transcendent and private activities such as prayer, meditation, and scripture study. Thus, the term religion is not limited to organized religion, religious affiliation or religious attendance. Central to its definition, though, is that religion is rooted in an established tradition that arises out of a group of people with common beliefs and practices concerning the transcendent (also see Koenig, 2011, p. 196, and Koenig, King, & Carson, 2012, p. 37).

Dimensions of Religion

Religion defined in this way has many distinct dimensions that can and have been measured (some of these dimensions have either been called "spirituality" or included in measures of spirituality). Charles Glock and Rodney Stark at the University of California at Berkeley were one of the first academics to break down religion into its dimensions. Five dimensions were described in their classic *Religion and Society in Tension* (Glock &

Stark, 1965, pp. 18–38): religious belief (ideological dimension), religious practice (ritualistic dimension), religious feeling (experiential dimension), religious knowledge (intellectual dimension), and religious effects (consequential dimension).

More recently, at a meeting sponsored by the National Institute on Aging and Fetzer Institute, the dimensions of religion were more briefly categorized into three major groupings: organizational, nonorganizational, and subjective or intrinsic religiosity (Futterman & Koenig, 1995). Organizational religiosity involves religious practices in a community or social setting, such as attending religious services, participating in a prayer or Scripture study group, or participating in other religious activities with fellow congregants. Nonorganizational religiosity consists of personal religious activities, such as prayer, meditation, Scripture reading, watching or listening to religious media, and other religious activities and rituals that are done alone and in private. Subjective or intrinsic religiosity, rather than based on religious activities or practices, is the cognitive dimension of religious involvement having to do with self-perceived importance of religion in daily life or the degree to which religion is the object of a person's ultimate concern, with other aspects of life guided and directed by religious doctrines. Level of religious engagement or commitment is often assessed by a combination of measures assessing organizational, nonorganizational, and subjective or intrinsic religiosity (Koenig, Meador, & Parkerson, 1997; Koenig et al., 2015; see Chapter 2).

A more detailed list of religious dimensions that might be assessed when doing research is the following:

1. Religious denomination or affiliation
2. Religious belief or orthodoxy
3. Religious practices (public)
4. Religious practices (private)
5. Religious salience (or importance of religion)
6. Religious motivation (intrinsic vs. extrinsic)
7. Religious well-being
8. Religious coping (general vs. specific)
9. Religious history
10. Religious support (church/synagogue related)
11. Religious experience (conversion, mystical, and daily experiences of God)
12. Religious attachment (love of God)
13. Religious giving (either giving money or donating time to religious causes)
14. Religious knowledge (scripture)
15. Religious quest
16. Religious development (growth and maturity)
17. Religious commitment (overall)

Only 3 of the 17 dimensions above focus on institutional forms of religion (see Koenig, 2011, pp. 210–215, for a detailed description of most of these dimensions). Thus, religion conceptualized in this way is much more than just institutional religion.

DEFINING SPIRITUALITY

As noted earlier, the definition of spirituality proposed by Pargament and coworkers moves the term beyond simply a state of good mental health to something more distinctive in its own right: *the sacred* (Pargament & Mahoney, 2002; Hill & Pargament, 2003; Pargament 2013). However, it is the opinion of the present author that we need to go further in defining spirituality as a distinct and clear concept. Rather than grounding spirituality on the "sacred," what is proposed here grounds it on: *the transcendent*. Doing so, however, makes the definition of spirituality very similar to that of religion, which may cause some uneasiness among those who believe that spirituality and religion are different.

> Spirituality is distinguished from its consequences – human values, morals, meaning, purpose, peace, connectedness to others, feelings of awe and wonder – by its link to the transcendent. The transcendent is that which is outside of the self, and yet also within the self – and in Western traditions is called God, Allah, HaShem, or a Higher Power, and in Eastern traditions is called Ultimate Truth or Reality, Brahman, the Dharma or Buddha. Spirituality is intimately connected to religion, and in fact, lies at its core. Spirituality is a process that involves traveling along the path that leads from non-consideration of the transcendent, to a decision not to believe, to the struggle of questioning, to a decision to believe, to the struggle of conforming life to that belief, to devotion and worship of the transcendent, and ultimately, to surrender of the person's will to the will of the transcendent as understood by the individual and their religious community.

Definitions for Clinical Purposes

In contrast to definitions of religion and spirituality intended for research, a more gentle approach is necessary when interacting with patients about this topic. Granted, some may take issue with using a different definition for conducting research than the definition used in clinical settings. However, the author thinks this is justified based on the sensitive nature of the subject and the need to be inclusive. Spirituality as currently defined in palliative and other clinical settings (and criticized above because of its broad, inclusive, and nebulous nature) is actually ideal for clinical settings (Puchalski et al., 2009, 2014; Nolan et al., 2011). Terminology here must be inclusive so that everyone has a "seat at the table," including those with and without religious beliefs. Thus, the mental health professional is encouraged to take a "spiritual history," identify "spiritual needs," make efforts to identify "spiritual resources," and perhaps provide "spiritually integrated" therapy. The goal of the clinician is not quite the same as the goal of the researcher (i.e., to compare, identify relationships, and seek causal inferences). Rather, the clinician seeks to engage patients in conversation, establish a safe and caring relationship, and ultimately neutralize negative unhealthy emotions, cognitions, and behaviors. Using the broad language of spirituality, which enables the patient to determine its definition and meaning, firmly anchors the discussion in the patient's camp. This will often involve religion, but not always, and so using a concept that extends beyond religion and overlaps to some degree with mental health is less problematic than when conducting research.

SUMMARY AND CONCLUSIONS

When discussing research, the term "religion" not spirituality will be used here (except when spirituality has been specifically measured, when the term religion/spirituality will be used). The reason is that religion as presented here is a distinct construct that (1) has a definition that can be agreed upon, (2) avoids conceptual overlap with mental health, and (3) can be measured and quantified, allowing for research that can examine connections with mental health that produces meaningful and interpretable results. Ordinarily, when the term "spirituality" is used to discuss the research, the traditional understanding of the term should be assumed, that is, it is either synonymous with religion or refers to a subset of deeply religious individuals whose lives are centered on their religious faith. When assessing spirituality in future research, measures should not be contaminated with positive psychological states or character traits. This will help to avoid defining spirituality a priori as good mental health (and the tautological relationships with mental health that will result). In clinical settings, the use of a broadly inclusive and nebulous term such as spirituality is ideal. In this case, spirituality can be defined by clients themselves to maximize connection, engagement, and conversation.

References

Ammerman, N. T. (2013). Spiritual but not religious? Beyond binary choices in the study of religion. *Journal for the Scientific Study of Religion*, *52*(2), 258–278.

Bash, A. (2004). Spirituality: the emperor's new clothes? *Journal of Clinical Nursing*, *13*(1), 11–16.

Daaleman, T. P., & Frey, B. B. (2004). The Spirituality Index of Well-Being: a new instrument for health-related quality-of-life research. *Annals of Family Medicine*, *2*, 499–503.

Ellis, A. (1980). *Case against religion: A psychotherapists view and the case against religiosity*. Austin, TX: American Atheist Press.

Freud, S., & Strachey, J. (1927). Future of an Illusion. In J. Strachey (Ed.), *Standard edition of the complete psychological works of Sigmund Freud*. London: Hogarth Press [Translator, 1962].

Futterman, A. & Koenig, H. G., (1995). Measuring religiosity in later life: what can gerontology learn from the sociology and psychology of religion? Background paper. *Proceedings of Conference on Methodological Approaches to the Study of Religion, Aging, and Health*. Bethesda, Maryland: NIA and Fetzer Institute [March 16–17].

Garssen, B., Visser, A., & de Jager Meezenbroek, E. (2015). Examining whether spirituality predicts subjective well-being: how to avoid tautology. *Psychology of Religion and Spirituality*, *8*(2), 141–148.

Glock, C. Y., & Stark, R. (1965). *Religion and Society in Tension*. Chicago: Rand McNally & Company.

Hatch, R. L., Burg, M. A., Naberhaus, D. S., & Hellmich, L. K. (1998). The spiritual involvement and beliefs scale: development and testing of a new instrument. *Journal of Family Practice*, *46*(6), 476–487.

Hill, P. C., & Pargament, K. I. (2003). Advances in the conceptualization and measurement of religion and spirituality: Implications for physical and mental health research. *American Psychologist*, *58*(1), 64–74.

Hill, P. C., Pargament, K. I., Hood, R. W., Jr., McCullough, M. E., Swyers, J. P., Larson, D. B., & Zinnbauer, B. J. (2000). Conceptualizing religion and spirituality: points of commonality, points of departure. *Journal for the Theory of Social Behavior*, *30*, 51–77.

Howden, J. (1992). *Development and psychometric characteristics of the Spirituality Assessment Scale [thesis]*. Houston, TX: Texas Women's University.

Hungelmann, J., Kenkel-Rossi, E., Klassen, L., & Stollenwerk, R. (1996). Focus on Spiritual Well-Being: Harmonious interconnectedness of mind-body-spirit—use of the JAREL Spiritual Well-Being Scale: assessment of spiritual well-being is essential to the health of individuals. *Geriatric Nursing*, *17*(6).

Klein, C., Hood, R. W., Silver, C. F., Keller, B., & Streib, H. (2016). Is "spirituality" nothing but "religion"? An indirect measurement approach. In H. Streib, & R. W. Hood (Eds.), *Semantics and psychology of spirituality* (pp. 71–85). Cham, Switzerland: Springer International.

Koenig, H. G. (2008). Concerns about measuring "spirituality" in research. *Journal of Nervous and Mental Disease*, *196*(5), 349–355.

Koenig, H. G. (2011). *Spirituality and health research: Methods, measurement, statistics & resources*. Conshohocken: Templeton Foundation Press.

Koenig, H. G., King, D. E., & Carson, V. B. (2012). *Handbook of Religion and Health* (2nd ed.). New York, NY: Oxford University Press.

Koenig, H. G., Meador, K. G., & Parkerson, G. (1997). Religion index for psychiatric research. *American Journal of Psychiatry*, *154*(6), 885–886.

Koenig, H. G., Nelson, B., Shaw, S. F., Al Zaben, F., Wang, Z., & Saxena, S (2015). Belief into Action scale: a brief but comprehensive measure of religious commitment. *Open Journal of Psychiatry*, *5*(1), 66–77.

Krause, N. M. (2008). *Aging in the church: How social relationships affect health*. Conshohocken, Pennsylvania: Templeton Foundation Press.

La Cour, P., Ausker, N. H., & Hvidt, N. C. (2012). Six understandings of the word 'spirituality' in a secular country. *Archive for the Psychology of Religion*, *34*(1), 63–81.

McClain, C. S., Rosenfeld, B., & Breithart, W. (2003). Effect of spiritual well-being on end-of-life despair in terminally ill cancer patients. *Lancet*, *361*, 1603–1607.

Mofidi, M., DeVellis, R. F., DeVellis, B. M., Blazer, D. G., Panter, A. T., & Jordan, J. M. (2007). The relationship between spirituality and depressive symptoms: testing psychosocial mechanisms. *Journal of Nervous and Mental Disease*, *195*, 681–688.

Nolan, S., Saltmarsh, P., & Leget, C. (2011). Spiritual care in palliative care: working towards an EAPC Task Force. *European Journal of Palliative Care*, *18*, 86–89.

Oman, D. (2013). Defining religion and spirituality. In R. Palouzian, & C. Park (Eds.), *Handbook of the psychology of religion and spirituality* (2nd ed., pp. 23–47). New York, NY: Guilford Press.

Paloutzian, R. F., & Ellison, C. W. (1982). Loneliness, spiritual well-being, and the quality of life. In L. A. Peplau, & D. Perlman (Eds.), *Loneliness: A sourcebook of current theory research and therapy* (pp. 224–236). New York, NY: John Wiley & Sons.

Pargament, K. I. (2013). Searching for the sacred: Toward a nonreductionistic theory of spirituality. In K. I. Pargament, J. J. Exline, & J. James (Eds.), *APA handbook of psychology, religion, and spirituality (volume 1): Context, theory, and research* (pp. 257–293). Washington, DC: American Psychological Association.

Pargament, K. I., & Mahoney, A. (2002). Spirituality: discovering and conserving the sacred. In C. R. Snyder, & S. J. m Lopez (Eds.), *Handbook of positive psychology* (pp. 646–659). New York, NY: Oxford University Press.

Pargament, K. I., Mahoney, N., Exline, J. J., Jones, J. W., & Shafranske, E. P. (2013). Envisioning an integrative paradigm for the psychology of religion and spirituality. In K. I. Pargament (Ed.), *APA handbook of psychology, religion, and spirituality* (pp. 3–19). Washington, DC: American Psychological Association.

Peterman, A. H., Fitchett, G., Brady, M. J., Hernandez, L., & Cella, D. (2002). Measuring spiritual wellbeing in people with cancer: the functional assessment of chronic illness therapy—Spiritual Well-being Scale (FACIT-Sp). *Annals of Behavioral Medicine, 24*, 49–58.

Piedmont, R. L. (1999). Does spirituality represent the sixth factor of personality? Spiritual transcendence and the five-factor model. *Journal of Personality, 67*, 985–1013.

Popp-Baier, U. (2010). From religion to spirituality—megatrend in contemporary society or methodological artefact? A contribution to the secularization debate from psychology of religion. *Journal of Religion in Europe, 3*(1), 34–67.

Puchalski, C., Ferrell, B., Virani, R., Otis-Green, S., Baird, P., Bull, J., Chochinov, H., Handzo, G., Nelson-Becker, H., Prince-Paul, M., & Pugliese, K. (2009). Improving the quality of spiritual care as a dimension of palliative care: the report of the Consensus Conference. *Journal of Palliative Medicine, 12*(10), 885–904.

Puchalski, C. M., Vitillo, R., Hull, S. K., & Reller, N. (2014). Improving the spiritual dimension of whole person care: reaching national and international consensus. *Journal of Palliative Medicine, 17*(6), 642–656.

Reed, P. G. (1986). Developmental resources and depression in the elderly. *Nursing Research, 35*(6), 368–374.

Reinert, K. G., & Koenig, H. G. (2013). Re-examining definitions of spirituality in nursing research. *Journal of Advanced Nursing, 69*(12), 2622–2634.

Rose F.S. (2001). Is the term 'spirituality' a word that everyone uses, but nobody knows what anyone means by it? *Journal of Contemporary Religion, 16*(2), 193–207.

Salandar F.P. (2006). Who needs the concept of 'spirituality'? *Psycho-Oncology, 15*, 647–649.

Salander, P. (2012). The emperor's new clothes: spirituality. A concept based on questionable ontology and circular findings. *Archive for the Psychology of Religion, 34*(1), 17–32.

Saxena, S. (2006). A cross-cultural study of spirituality, religion, and personal beliefs as components of quality of life. *Social Science and Medicine, 62*, 1486–1497.

Sheldrake, P. (2010). *A brief history of spirituality*. Boston, MA: Blackwell Publishing.

Smith, C., & Denton, M. L. (2005). *Soul searching: The religious and spiritual lives of American teenagers*. New York, NY: Oxford University Press.

Streib, H., & Hood, R. W. (2011). "Spirituality" as privatized experience-oriented religion: empirical and conceptual perspectives. *Implicit Religion, 14*(4), 433–453.

Tsuang, M. T., & Simpson, J. C. (2008). Commentary on Koenig (2008): "Concerns about measuring 'spirituality' in research". *Journal of Nervous and Mental Disease, 196*, 647–649.

Tsuang, M. T., Simpson, J. C., Koenen, K. C., Kremen, W. S., & Lyons, M. J. (2007). Spiritual well-being and health. *Journal of Nervous and Mental Disease, 195*(8), 673–680.

Underwood, L. G., & Teresi, J. A. (2002). The daily spiritual experiences scale: development, theoretical description, reliability, exploratory factor analysis, and preliminary construct validity using health-related data. *Annals of Behavioral Medicine, 24*, 22–33.

Walach, H. (2015). *Secular spirituality: The next step towards enlightenment*. New York, NY: Springer.
Watters, W. (1992). *Deadly doctrine: Health, illness and Christian God-talk*. Buffalo, NY: Prometheus Books.
Westerink, H. (2012). Spirituality in psychology of religion: a concept in search of its meaning. *Archive for the Psychology of Religion*, *34*(1), 3–15.
Worthington, E. L., Hook, J. N., Davis, D. E., & McDaniel, M. A. (2011). Religion and spirituality. *Journal of Clinical Psychology*, *67*, 204–214.
Zinnbauer, B. J., Pargament, K. I., Cole, B., Rye, M. S., Butter, E. M., Belavich, T. G., Hipp, K. M., Scott, A. B., & Kadar, J. L. (1997). Religion and spirituality: unfuzzying the fuzzy. *Journal for the Scientific Study of Religion*, *36*, 549–564.

CHAPTER

2

Measurement of Religiosity

This chapter focuses on the quantitative measurement of religious involvement, religiousness, and religiosity. The importance of quantitative measurement will be discussed, the necessity of establishing the reliability and validity of measures will be emphasized, and both single and multi-item scales will be described. How to choose a scale will be discussed, commonly used scales will be examined, and recommendations made on the best scales to use depending on the researcher's needs. Finally, we will briefly review statistical considerations when choosing a measure, including the need to visually inspect the form of the relationship between religiosity and mental health to determine whether it is linear or nonlinear.

MEASUREMENT AND QUANTIFICATION

Qualitative Research

Although the focus here will be on quantitative measurement, it is necessary to underscore the importance of qualitative approaches. Qualitative research involves descriptive, nonquantitative methods that provide in-depth information about participants. Qualitative methods are ideal for examining the role that religion plays in maintaining, enhancing, or worsening mental health. The details of individual stories and experiences often provide some of the best evidence of the impact that religion can have on people's lives. Such information is crucial in the design of quantitative observational studies and clinical trials, and is also essential for interpreting the results of such studies. Unfortunately, in the quantitative world of psychology and psychiatry, qualitative research is not given the credit and value that it deserves. Nevertheless, qualitative methods play a pivotal role in understanding the relationship between religion and

Religion and Mental Health. http://dx.doi.org/10.1016/B978-0-12-811282-3.00002-1

mental health, and provide information that quantitative research cannot. As qualitative methods will not be discussed here, the reader is referred to other sources (Cheek, 1996; Streubert Speziale & Carpenter, 2003; Ulin, Robinson, & Tolley, 2005).

Quantitative Research

Quantitative research involves numbers and counting. The measurement of mental health has long involved the count of symptoms and their severity to determine the presence or absence of mental conditions that impact functioning. When examining risk factors for mental/emotional illness or preventative factors that protect against or alleviate symptoms, quantitative statistical methods are commonly used. These methods help to determine whether associations are significant and beyond simple chance, and contribute to their clinical significance that will determine whether those risk or protective factors are worthy of attention. Quantitative methods determine not only whether significant associations are present, but can also say something about the direction of causation and identify effective interventions that warrant clinical implementation. The healthcare system depends heavily on quantitative methods, since both clinical and administrative decisions are often based on numbers.

Quality of Measures

When assessing religiosity, the psychometric characteristics of the measure need to be established in the population being studied. This means that reliability and validity statistics for the measure have been identified and published in the literature.

Reliability

Two types of reliability need to be established for a multi-item measure or scale. This will determine whether (1) items on a scale are all measuring the same construct and (2) the likelihood that responses to items on the scale will be the same when administered on different occasions, assuring their stability over time. The first type of reliability is called internal consistency reliability (degree to which all items on a scale are measuring the same thing), which is measured by a Cronbach's alpha. The second type of reliability is called test–retest reliability, which is determined by administering the scale at two time points 1 or 2 weeks apart. Cronbach's alphas of 0.70 or higher are considered adequate internal reliability (Cronbach, 1951). Test–retest reliability is measured by the intraclass correlation coefficient (ICC), where ICCs of 0.70 or higher are considered acceptable (Shrout & Fleiss, 1979). Reliability can be illustrated by an archer shooting an arrow at a target; reliability is how accurate the archer is in hitting the same target every time. Although the archer may be very accurate in hitting the same target every time, however, the target may be the wrong one.

Validity

Validity is the degree to which the target is the right one. In other words, to what extent is the scale assessing what it claims to be measuring? There are three types of validity for a scale that need to be established to demonstrate that it is measuring what it claims to be measuring: content validity, construct validity, and criterion validity. When comparing a new measure to an existing measure, there is also a fourth type called incremental validity.

Content validity (also called "face" validity) is the extent to which it makes rational sense on the surface that items on a scale are assessing what the scale claims to be measuring. For example, if a researcher wants to know if religion is used to cope with the loss of a loved one, participants in the study may simply be asked to what extent they use religion to cope, perhaps rating the degree to which they do so on a scale from 0 (not at all) to 10 (very much). It makes logical sense that if participants circle 10 on this scale, then they are more likely to use religion to cope than those who circle 0 on the scale. A reasonable person by simply examining the content of the question would likely agree that the item is assessing the degree to which the person uses religion to cope. This is called content validity.

Construct validity is the degree to which a measure is related to constructs that one would expect the measure to be related to and not related to constructs one would expect it to be independent of. The three components of construct validity are convergent, discriminant, and factor analytic validity, each of which must be established for a measure to be valid. First, convergent validity is how strongly the new scale correlates with existing measures of the construct. For example, how strong is the correlation between a new measure of religiosity with existing measures that already have established reliability and validity? Second, discriminant validity is the extent to which the measure is unrelated to constructs it is expected to be unrelated to. For example, are there only weak correlations between a religiosity measure and measures of other psychosocial constructs that are distinct from religion (such as measures of mental health or social support)? Third, factor analytic validity is the extent to which the structure of a measure is consistent with underlying theory. This is often established by factor analysis. For example, if a measure claims to assess a single underlying construct then factor analysis should reveal a single factor that explains most of the variance in the scale. If underlying theory suggests the scale is assessing three dimensions of a construct, then factor analysis should reveal three factors.

Criterion validity is the extent to which a measure is related to a "gold standard," which is a firmly established and widely accepted measure of the construct, particularly an objective standard, such as clinical evaluation by an expert in the area. Unfortunately, there is no widely recognized gold standard for religiosity (subjective or objective), making this difficult to establish. However, one could ask clergy (i.e., experts in religiosity) to identify deeply religious persons and also identify completely nonreligious persons, and then have them complete the religiosity measure to determine if scores on the measure differentiate the religious from the nonreligious. Criterion validity for the Intrinsic Religiosity Scale was determined by asking clergy to answer the scale items in a way they would predict an intrinsically religious person to answer them (Hoge, 1972; Koenig, Smiley, & Gonzales, 1988c, p. 175). In this case, the resulting clergy-rated scores were near the maximum score for the measure, which helped to establish the scale's criterion validity.

Predictive validity is a component of criterion validity that examines to what extent a measure predicts important outcomes over time that one would expect it to predict based on theoretical considerations. For example, a measure of religious coping might be expected to predict better adaptation to stress and lower levels of depression over time, indicating successful adjustment. This assumes, however, that religion is a healthy coping behavior that leads to better coping and adaptation, which must be established by research (it could also lead to worse psychological adjustment, as forefathers of psychiatry have claimed). Predictive validity, then, may not be so easy to establish, as a weak or absent correlation between a religiosity measure and mental health may indicate the absence of a relationship with mental health or simply a poor measure of the construct.

Finally, *incremental validity* is the extent to which a new measure is a better predictor of an outcome than an existing measure. For example, the Belief Into Action Scale (BIAC) has been shown to predict mental and social health outcomes incrementally better than the Duke Religion Index (DUREL) by 75%–300% (Koenig, Wang, Al Zaben, & Adi, 2015a).

Multi-Item vs. Single-Item Scales

Multi-item scales are preferred over single item scales for a number of reasons. First, a single-item scale assumes a single underlying dimension for the construct. Given that religiosity is likely to be a multidimensional construct, the use of single-item measures to assess it may not be appropriate

(Oshagbemi, 1999; Loo, 2002). A multi-item religiosity scale allows for the assessment of these multiple dimensions. Second, even if religiosity were a single dimensional construct, a single-item scale would necessarily assess it in a global, relatively superficial fashion. In contrast, a multi-item measure of even a single dimension is able to assess that dimension in greater detail from various perspectives. Third, there is no way to determine the reliability of a single-item measure, as respondents may answer the single item differently depending on their mood at the moment, how rapidly they are trying to complete the survey, etc. Rather than depending on response to a single item, a multi-item scale asks several questions in different ways to get at the construct so that dependency on the respondent's fickleness in response to any single item is less of an issue. This increases the stability and precision of responses. Fourth, a single-item scale usually has only a few response options. An example is self-rated importance of religion, where responses might be "not at all," "somewhat," and "very." If the population being studied is very religious, then most participants will fall into the "very religious" category and there will be very little range in responses (called response *variability*). With multi-item scales, there are other questions that can assess importance of religion from various perspectives that would allow a much greater range of responses. Greater variability in responses increases the ability to identify significant correlations with mental health outcomes to which it might be related (increases sensitivity in detection). Finally, as religiosity is likely a multidimensional construct, there is the possibility that each dimension of religiosity is related to mental health in different ways, some dimensions associated with better mental health and others with worse mental health. A single-item measure aggregates all of these different effects into one. This prevents the identification of significant effects that may be in opposite directions.

Each of the above five considerations favor the use of multi-item religiosity scales rather than single-item scales. There are others, however, who have argued the contrary. Assuming that religiosity is a single dimensional construct, as these investigators have claimed (similar to "happiness"), then single-item measures may have as good reliability (test–retest) and validity as multi-item measures (Abdel-Khalek, 2007; Dollinger & Malmquist, 2009). For a more nuanced discussion of the advantages of single-item versus multi-item scales of religiosity, see Gorsuch and McFarland (1972).

MEASURES OF RELIGIOSITY BY DIMENSION

In chapter 1, it was proposed that religion is a multidimensional construct consisting of at least 17 distinct dimensions. Here, these dimensions of religiosity are presented again, this time with measures to assess them.

Religious Affiliation

There are at least two options for identifying religious affiliation in a detailed and comprehensive fashion. First is the categorization developed by Christopher Ellison (1999) in the Brief Multidimensional Measure of Religiosity and Spirituality (BMMRS) (Fetzer Institute, 1999, pp. 81–84), which covers Christian, nontraditional Christian, Jewish, Muslim, Hindu, and Buddhist affiliations (with considerable differentiation by subcategory). The second measure is that described by Roof and McKinney (1987) (p. 255) that assesses mainline American religious traditions, breaking them down into simpler categories of liberal Protestants, moderate Protestants, Black Protestants, Catholics, Jews, others, and none (with additional subcategories). The measure chosen should depend on the likely distribution of religious affiliations in the population under study.

Religious Belief

Religious belief or orthodoxy of belief can be assessed either globally with a single-item scale or in a more nuanced fashion using a multi-item scale specific to a particular religion. A single-item scale might consist of the question "Do you have any religious beliefs?" Response categories may be "yes" or "no" or may consist of more graded responses ranging, for example, from "none whatsoever" to "yes, very much." Alternatively, for a specific religion such as Christianity, a multi-item scale, such as the 4-item Orthodoxy Index, might be used. This scale was developed by the famous sociologists of religion, Charles Glock and Rodney Stark at University of California, Berkeley in the 1960s. The Orthodoxy Index assesses belief in the existence of God, the divinity of Jesus Christ, the authenticity of Biblical miracles, and the existence of the Devil (Glock & Stark, 1966, see pp. 5 and 7 for examples of response options and p. 11 for the index). There are at least 21 other measures of religious belief listed in *Measures of Religiosity* (Hill & Hood, 1999), including a 26-item measure by Thouless (1935), which assesses not only particular beliefs, but also the "certainty" of belief. Almost all of these scales were meant for Christians. Orthodoxy of belief scales also exist for Muslims (8-item Islamic Orthodoxy Scale by Abou El Azayem and Hedayat-Diba (1994)), Jews (6-item subscale of the 20-item Jewish Religiosity Scale by Ben-Meir and Kedem (1979)), Buddhists (11-item Buddhist Beliefs and Practices Scale by Emavardhana and Tori (1997)), and Hindus (19-item Santosh–Frances Attitude toward Hinduism Scale by Francis, Santosh, Robbins, and Vij (2008)).

Public Religious Practices

Communal religious practices include attending religious services and engaging in other religious communal activities, such as prayer or scripture study groups. Perhaps the most common way of assessing this dimension of religiosity is by a single-item scale that asks about frequency of attending religious services, with responses ranging from "not at all" to "every day." Ellen Idler (1999) has developed a 2-item scale assessing this dimension with a 9-level response option for each item [see Fetzer Institute's (1999) BMMRS, p. 79]. Related to religious attendance, though distinctively different from it, is *attitude* toward religious institutions. The 45-item Attitude toward the Church Scale was one of the first measures designed for this purpose and used widely by sociologists of religion in the early 1900's, but not so much today (Thurstone & Chave, 1929).

Private Religious Practices

Private religious practices can be quite specific to a particular faith tradition, although practices such as prayer or meditation are common across most major world religions. The DUREL has a single item that assesses private religious practices in a global manner: "How often do you spend time in private religious activities, such as prayer, meditation or Bible [Qu'ran, Bhaghavad Gita, Dhammapada] study?" with six response options from "rarely or never" to "more than once/day" (Koenig, Meador, & Parkerson, 1997). Jeff Levin (1999) has developed a 4-item private religious practices scale (again, largely nonspecific in terms of religion) that assesses frequency of private prayer, watching or listening to religious programs on TV or radio, reading religious literature, and frequency of prayers said before or after meals (see Fetzer Institute's (1999) BMMRS, pp. 41–42). There are no measures of private religious activities that cover Hindu or Buddhist practices very well.

Religious Salience

Importance of religion in daily life (sometimes called subjective religiousness or religious salience) is typically measured with a single-item scale: "How important is religion in your daily life?" with four or five response options, such as "not at all important," "somewhat important," "moderately important," and "very important" (sometimes "extremely important" is added to expand the range). This dimension includes self-rated religiosity, which may be assessed by a single-item such as: "How religious would you say you are?" with responses ranging from "not religious at all" to "very religious" (Chatters, Levin, & Taylor, 1992). Such single items are often included in large epidemiological studies where there is little space in questionnaires to ask questions about religion or investigators don't have much interest in religion.

Religious Motivation

The construct of religious motivation has long been one of the most important dimensions of religiosity and as a result has received much attention. The work of Harvard psychologist Gordon Allport (1950) on this construct resulted in the classic 21-item Religious Orientation Scale (ROS) with two subscales, one assessing intrinsic religiosity (IR) and the other assessing extrinsic religiosity (ER) (Allport & Ross, 1967). The purpose of the 9-item IR subscale is to assess the degree to which religious belief is central to a person's life and considered an "end in itself." In contrast, the 12-item ER subscale assesses the degree to which religion is used as a "means to an end" (social position or standing, financial gain, etc.). Several versions of the ROS have been developed by other investigators including the 10-item Intrinsic Religiosity Scale (Hoge, 1972), the 20-item Age Universal Religious Orientation Scale (Gorsuch & Venable, 1983), and the 14-item Religious Orientation Scale-Revised (ROS-R) (Gorsuch & McPherson, 1989). The ROS-R assesses IR and breaks down ER into personally oriented (Ep) and socially oriented (Es) subscales. One version of the ROS-R is a 3-item scale that assesses IR, Ep, and Es with single items. Those single items are: "My whole approach to life is based upon my religion" (IR); "What religion offers me most is comfort in times of trouble and sorrow" (Ep); and "I go to church mainly because I enjoy seeing people I know there" (Es).

Religious Well-Being

Religious well-being (RWB) assesses the quality of a person's relationship with God. One way to measure RWB is by the 10-item subscale of the Spiritual Well-Being Scale, which also has a 10-item existential well-being subscale (EWB) (Paloutzian & Ellison, 1982). While the EWB subscale is simply a measure of psychological well-being focused on meaning and purpose in life, the RWB is a valid scale uncontaminated by psychological well-being. Items on the RWB subscale include "I believe that God loves me and cares about me"; "I believe that God is concerned about my problems"; and "I feel most fulfilled when I'm in close communion with God." RWB tends to be strongly related to EWB and often has its effects on mental health through EWB (EWB mediating the effect of RWB on mental health).

Religious Coping

Although thoroughly covered in the next chapter, religious coping can be assessed in a number of ways. Frequently, a single-item scale may be used with a question such as: "To what extent do you depend on your religious beliefs to provide you with comfort during times of stress?" ("not at all" to "very much"). Multi-item scales have also been developed to assess this dimension in greater detail. Religious coping can be assessed using either global measures or measures that specify exactly how a person uses religion to cope. The 3-item Religious Coping Index (RCI) is an example of a multi-item scale that assesses global religious coping with a score range from 0 to 30 (Koenig et al., 1992). Instead of assessing religious coping globally, Ken Pargament et al. have identified specific ways that people use religion to cope with stress (Pargament et al., 1988; Pargament et al., 1990; Pargament, Smith, Koenig, & Perez, 1998; Pargament, 1999; Pargament, Koenig, & Perez, 2000). Measures used to assess specific coping behaviors, which range in length from 3 to over 100 items, include the 14-item Brief RCOPE (Pargament et al., 1998). The Brief RCOPE assesses both positive and negative ways of coping, and is probably the most widely used measure of this construct by researchers. There are also scales now available for assessing Hindu (Hindu COPE), Buddhist (BCOPE), Jewish (JCOPE), and Muslim forms of coping (Tarakeshwar, Pargament, & Mahoney, 2003; Phillips, Michelle Cheng, Oemig, Hietbrink, & Vonnegut, 2012; Rosmarin, Pargament, Krumrei, & Flannelly, 2009a; Abu Raiya, Pargament, Mahoney, & Stein, 2008).

Religious History

Most epidemiological studies that examine risk or protective factors that influence health assess exposure to that factor over a person's lifetime. In the physical health arena, cigarette smoking as a risk factor for lung cancer is measured by number of cigarette packs smoked per day × years smoking (called pack-years). In contrast, religious beliefs and practices are almost always measured in terms of the present. Frequency of religious activities is usually assessed without reference to timeframe, and is almost never assessed by how many years a person has been engaged in those activities. This notion of lifetime exposure to religion is called religious history, that is, the number of years that a person has been engaged in religious beliefs and practices and the intensity of that activity. Of the few measures developed to assess this dimension, perhaps the best is that described by Linda George (1999) in the Fetzer Institute's (1999)'s BMMRS (see pp. 68–69).

Religious Support

This dimension is measured by the amount of supportive interactions (and negative interactions) with members of one's faith community. The dimension covers support received from or given to members of one's congregation, as well as negative interactions involving conflict with other congregants.

An 8-item Religious Support Scale (short form) has been developed by Neal Krause (1999) that assesses emotional support received, emotional support given, negative interactions, and anticipated support if needed (see Fetzer Institute's (1999)'s BMMRS, p. 62). Given that involvement in religious community activity is one of the strongest predictors of mental health, this measure may be used to help understand these effects better.

Religious Experience

Religious experiences vary widely. These include daily spiritual experiences involving God or other supernatural entities, dramatic religious conversion experiences, or mystical experiences that are other worldly and difficult to explain. A variety of scales have been developed to capture these experiences. The 12-item Religious Experience Questionnaire asks about the frequency of experiences of feeling God's love, God's forgiveness, feelings of closeness to God, and feelings of anger and resentment toward God (Edwards, 1976). The 10-item Religious Experience Episodes Measure contains short vignettes based on William James (1902) account of religious experiences, where respondents rate the degree to which they have had these experiences (Hood, 1970; Rosegrant, 1976). Ralph Hood has also developed the 32-item Mysticism Scale (M Scale), which is composed of a 20-item general mysticism subscale and a 12-item religious interpretation subscale (Hood, 1975). Kass, Friedman, Leserman, Zuttermeister, and Benson (1991) have developed the 7-item Index of Core Spiritual Experiences (ICSE), which assesses religious/spiritual beliefs and experiences related to God or a Higher Power.

Religious Attachment

Attachment theory is growing in importance as a developmental model for explaining experiences during childhood that lead to relationship problems during adulthood. Secure attachments during childhood appear crucial for the formation of trust and close adult relationships (Groh, Fearon, Ijzendoorn, Bakermans-Kranenburg, & Roisman, 2017). This raises the question of whether attachment to God might influence mental health and social relationships (and vice-versa) (Granqvist, 2016). The most commonly used measures to assess attachment to God are the 28-item Attachment to God Inventory (Beck & McDonald, 2004) and the 9-item Attachment to God Scale (Rowatt & Kirkpatrick, 2002). Both scales assess problems in a person's relationship with God with a focus on avoidance, anxious, and distant forms of attachment. Other scales that measure more positive aspects of this dimension are love of God and trust in God scales. A 4- and 8-item Love of God Scale seeks to capture the extent to which an individual has a loving relationship with God (Levin & Kaplan, 2010). Rosmarin et al.'s 6- and 16-item Trust in God Scale serves the same purpose (Rosmarin, Pargament, & Mahoney, 2009b; Rosmarin, Pirutinsky, & Pargament, 2011). Scales assessing images of God are also in this category. An example of such a scale is the 10-item Loving and Controlling God Scale (Benson and Spilka, 1973).

Religious Giving

Religious giving has to do with spending one's money and time on religious endeavors. Percentage of gross income given each year to religious causes is one way to quantify religious giving (ranging from 0% to 15% or greater). Another way is hours spent volunteering in religious organizations or for religious causes. To the author's knowledge, no standard question or specific multi-item scale currently exists that assesses this dimension (although there are items on existing scales that do so; see "Religious Commitment" below).

Religious Knowledge

This dimension is religion specific and based on knowledge about one's religious teachings and core scriptures. Glock and Stark (1970) developed a Religious Knowledge Index applicable to adherents of the Judeo–Christian tradition. It consists of two questions: (1) the identification of scriptures contained in the Bible and (2) knowledge of Old Testament prophets (Glock & Stark, 1970, pp. 147–162). The question on Biblical scriptures asks: "Now would you please read each of the following statements…decide whether the statement is from the Bible or not" (e.g., "Blessed are the strong: for they shall be the sword of God;" "Thou shalt not suffer a witch to live"; and so forth). The second question asks: "Which of the following were Old Testament Prophets?" The possibilities listed are: (1) Elijah, (2) Deuteronomy, (3) Jeremiah, (4) Paul, (5) Leviticus, (6) Ezekiel, and (7) None of these were prophets. Responses for each question are coded from 0 (low) to 2 (high), with a total score ranging from 0 to 4. In Glock and Stark's survey of church members in the 1960s, 51% of Southern Baptists and 69% of small sects scored a 4 on this measure (i.e., named each of the prophets correctly). However, in a 1954 survey of the national US population by Gallup that assessed religious knowledge, only 36% of Protestants and 25% of Catholics knew who delivered the Sermon on the Mount (Glock & Stark, 1970, p. 161). It would be interesting to re-administer these measures to a national sample in 2018.

Religious Seeking, Striving, or Quest

Seeking for religious truth is the core of this dimension. A person may not be very religious, but is open and hungry to learn more about religion and may struggle with belief in the transcendent and their relationship to the transcendent. Religious "quest" is a term used to characterize individuals who "view religion as an endless process of probing and questioning generated by the tensions, contradictions, and tragedies in their own lives and in society" (Batson, 1976, p. 32). The "spiritual but not religious" person may also fit into this category. Religious quest is assessed using the 12-item Quest Scale (Batson & Schoenrade, 1991a; Batson & Schoenrade, 1991b). Studies using the Quest Scale have seldom found a positive relationship between this dimension and good mental health.

Religious Development

Assessment of this dimension involves the extent to which a person is growing in their religious faith, developing toward maturity. This often includes a progressive deepening of faith that may end in surrender or union with the transcendent. This is different from religious seeking or religious quest, which assesses ambivalence about religion among those trying to sort out their feelings and beliefs. Rather, religious maturity involves a flexible confidence in one's own religious faith and openness to the religious faith of others. Religious maturity is often assessed within a particular faith tradition, as different religions (and denominations within those religions) define maturity based on beliefs, attitudes, practices, and experiences specific to the tradition, although general measures do exist. Morton King (1967) developed a 5-item subscale (one of the nine dimensions of religiosity he proposed) that globally assesses "openness to religious growth." This subscale has been used by numerous investigators and involves questions that ask about interest in moral growth and degree to which a person is trying to understand their religious faith better. Benson's 38-item Faith Maturity Scale assesses the "priorities, commitments, and perspectives characteristic of a vibrant and life transforming faith" (Benson, Donahue, & Erickson, 1993, p. 3). Ellison's 30-item Spiritual Maturity Index assesses spiritual maturity within a conservative Christian framework, and presupposes that maturity involves beliefs and commitments that are independently held with conviction and maintained without the support or consensus of others (Ellison, 1984).

Religious Commitment

Religious commitment is a measure of religious devotion that is often reflected by high scores on several dimensions of religion, although it is presented here as a separate, more comprehensive dimension of religiosity. The 10-item Religious Commitment Inventory is one commonly used scale to assess overall level of religious engagement (Worthington et al., 2003), although there are several others. Religious commitment is closely related to IR and seeks to assess the degree to which a person is focused on living out their religious beliefs. This is often reflected by devout adherence to religious doctrines, frequent public and private religious practices, and engagement in nonreligious activities (such as volunteering) for religious reasons. Religious commitment is best assessed by measuring the degree to which an individual has decided to conform their life to the teachings of their religious faith, how much value the person places on religion in comparison to other priorities in life, the amount of time spent on religious activities, and the amount of money given to support religious causes. A new measure, the 10-item Belief into Action Scale (BIAC), was designed to capture these aspects of religious commitment on a scale ranging from 10 to 100 (see Resources for full measure and scoring) (Koenig, Wang, Al Zaben, & Adi, 2015; Koenig et al., 2015a). Arabic, Farsi, Spanish, and Chinese translations of the scale are also available and psychometric properties published for all except the Spanish version (Alakhdhair, Sheets, Geib, Alkhuwaildi, & Koenig, 2016; Hafizi, Tabatabaei, Memari, Saghazadeh, & Koenig, 2016; Wang, Ma, Rong, & Koenig, 2016).

MULTIDIMENSIONAL SCALES

There are also numerous scales that assess several dimensions of religiosity in one instrument. Briefly reviewed here will be six such measures: Dimensions of Religiosity; Religious Variables: 10 Scales; Springfield Religiosity Scale; DUREL; BMMRS; and Muslim Religiosity Scale.

Dimensions of Religiosity

This measure assesses four dimensions: belief (orthodoxy index, salvation beliefs, and beliefs about relations with others), ritual (public religious practices and devotional practices), experience (personal contact with the supernatural), and religious knowledge (Biblical content) (Glock & Stark, 1966). The measure consists of 48 items, many items with subsections that increase the length considerably. While the length of the measure has limited its use in religion–mental health research, specific subscales have often been used by researchers.

Religious Variables: 10 Scales

During their time, the King and Hunt scales were widely utilized by sociologists of religion, although they are seldom used today

(King & Hunt, 1972). The 10 scales they developed focus on six dimensions: Christian beliefs, private religious practices (devotion, including prayer and other forms of communication with God), communal religious participation (congregational involvement, including financial support), religious knowledge (biblical and church history knowledge), orientation to religion (growth and striving, vs. extrinsic religiosity), and importance of religious beliefs (assessed by behavior and cognition). A total of 59 items make up the 10 scales.

Springfield Religiosity Scale (SRS)

The 15-item short version of the SRS assesses organizational (ORA), nonorganizational (NORA), and IR (two items for ORA; three items for NORA; and 10 items for IR from the Hoge scale) (Koenig, Kvale, & Ferrel, 1988a, pp. 171–187; Koenig, Al-Zaben, Khalifa, & Al Shohaib, 2014, pp. 545–548). The 34-item long version of the SRS assesses ORA, NORA, and IR, plus items that measure orthodoxy of Christian belief, religious coping, religious well-being, private prayer importance, religious knowledge, preferences for physician-led prayer, and other items from existing scales. This measure was originally used in early studies of religion and health (Koenig et al., 1988a; Koenig, Moberg, & Kvale, 1988c), although is rarely used today.

Duke Religion Index (DUREL)

The 5-item DUREL assesses the three major dimensions of religiosity: ORA (single item on frequency of religious attendance), NORA (single item on private prayer, meditation, and scripture reading), and IR (three items from the Hoge scale) (Koenig et al., 1997; Koenig & Bussing, 2010; Koenig et al., 2014, pp. 544–545). This brief and comprehensive measure of religiosity is now used widely, and has been translated into many languages (Spanish, Portuguese, Chinese, Romanian, Japanese, Thai, Persian/Arabic, Hebrew, Russian, Ukrainian, German, Italian, Norwegian, Dutch, Danish, Malaysian, Filipino, Serbian, and others). See Resources for full measure and scoring.

Brief Multidimensional Measure of Religiosity and Spirituality (BMMRS)

The BMMRS is made up of short and long subscales assessing daily spiritual experiences, meaning, values, beliefs, forgiveness, private religious activities, religious coping, religious support, religious/spiritual history, religious commitment, organizational religiosity, self-rated religiosity and spirituality, and religious preference (Idler, 1999). National norms exist for the 40-item version of the scale, since it was included in the 1997–98 US General Social Survey. Several subscales assess outcomes of religion/spirituality (forgiveness, values, meaning), not religion/spirituality itself. Removing the three items on forgiveness, the one item on values, and the two items on meaning, as well as questions #2, #3, and #6 on the 6-item Daily Spiritual Experiences subscale (items assessing mental health itself) reduces the number of BMMRS items from 40 to 31, and decreases the likelihood of contamination. Researchers seldom use the full scale (given its length), but often choose subscales to include in surveys.

Muslim Religiosity Scale (MRS)

This 14-item scale assesses the three major dimensions of religiosity (ORA, NORA, and IR) in Muslim populations (Koenig et al., 2014, pp. 551–553). The reliability and validity of the scale has been established in an Arabic-speaking Muslim population of patients with end-stage renal disease receiving dialysis (Al Zaben et al., 2015a; Al Zaben, Sehlo, Khalifa, & Koenig, 2015a). Factor analysis of the scale reveals two major factors (eigenvalues > 1.0) corresponding to a religious practices subscale (ORA and NORA) and an IR subscale. This relatively new scale is increasingly being used in Arabic-speaking Muslim populations in the Middle East. Other multidimensional measures of Muslim religiosity with solid psychometric characteristics also exist in the literature (Ghorbani, Watson, Ghramaleki, Morris, & Hood, 2000; Abu Raiya et al., 2008; Alakhdhair et al., 2016).

MOST COMMONLY USED MEASURES

As relationships with mental health may be different for *religiosity* (religious engagement or commitment) as a "trait" measure and *religious coping* as a "state" measure (see next chapter), measures in each category are presented separately.

Religiosity

To give a sense of the most commonly used measures today for assessing religiosity, multi-item scales most often cited in the literature are listed in Table 2.1. Several factors likely affect the rankings provided here. First, the ranking is based on the number of citations of the original article introducing the scale. This means that those scales developed many years ago will be more highly ranked than more recent measures,

TABLE 2.1 Most Commonly Used Measures of Religiosity[a]

Scales	Cites	Authors
1929–2016		
1. Religious Orientation Scale	3889	Allport and Ross (1967)
2. Attitude Toward Church Scale	1645	Thurstone and Chave (1929)
3. Religious Orientation Scale-Revised	920	Gorsuch and McPherson (1989)
4. Intrinsic Religiosity Scale	617	Hoge (1972)
5. Duke Religion Index	574	Koenig et al. (1997)
6. Religious Commitment Inventory	535	Worthington et al. (2003)
7. Mysticism Scale	499	Hood (1975)
8. Brief Multidimensional Measure of R/S	491	Idler et al. (2003)
9. Index of Core Spiritual Experiences	477	Kass et al. (1991)
10. Loving and Controlling God Scales	425	Benson and Spilka (1973)
2011–16		
1. Religious Orientation Scale	1630	Allport and Ross (1967)
2. Religious Orientation Scale-Revised	422	Gorsuch and McPherson (1989)
3. Religious Commitment Inventory	378	Worthington et al. (2003)
4. Duke Religion Index	326	Koenig et al. (1997)
5. Brief Multidimensional Measure of R/S	261	Idler et al. (2003)
6. Attitude Toward Church Scale	246	Thurstone and Chave (1929)
7. Intrinsic Religiosity Scale	223	Hoge (1972)
8. Mysticism Scale	194	Hood (1975)
9. Loving and Controlling God Scales	151	Benson and Spilka (1973)
10. Index of Core Spiritual Experiences	144	Kass et al. (1991)
2016		
1. Religious Orientation Scale	232	Allport and Ross (1967)
2. Religious Commitment Inventory	78	Worthington et al. (2003)
3. Religious Orientation Scale-Revised	49	Gorsuch and McPherson (1989)
4. Duke Religion Index	41	Koenig et al. (1997)
5. Brief Multidimensional Measure of R/S	37	Idler et al. (2003)
6. Mysticism Scale	36	Hood (1975)
7. Attitude Toward Church Scale	33	Thurstone and Chave (1929)
8. Intrinsic Religiosity Scale	31	Hoge (1972)
9. Loving and Controlling God Scales	20	Benson and Spilka (1973)
10. Index of Core Spiritual Experiences	16	Kass et al. (1991)

R/S, Religiosity/spirituality.

[a] *Based on citations of the original report of the scale in Google Scholar on December 17, 2016.*

as earlier-developed measures have had more time to be cited by researchers. Second, number of citations was only included for the original article, which may or may not contain the psychometric properties of the measure (the usual reason for citation). For example, only a few psychometric properties of the DUREL were published in the original Koenig et al. (1997) report. The full psychometric properties of the measure were not reported until over a decade later in Koenig and Bussing (2010). Researchers, then, may often cite the more recent paper instead of the original report, decreasing the latter's citation count. Third, the original article may be cited for reasons other than to conduct research using the scale. Instead, it may be cited for the research findings reported in the article or cited to critique the scale (e.g., hundreds of articles were written to critique the Allport and Ross's Religious Orientation Scale). Each of these factors, then, will influence a scale's ranking. To address the time delay issue, rankings are provided for three periods: 1929–2016, 2011–16, and 2016.

Based on these rankings, the five most commonly cited measures of religiosity since the Attitude Toward Church Scale (Thurstone & Chave, 1929) are the Religious Orientation Scale (ROS) (sometimes called the Intrinsic–Extrinsic Religiosity Scale) (Allport & Ross, 1967), the Religious Orientation Scale-Revised (ROS-R) (Gorsuch & McPherson, 1989), the Intrinsic Religiosity Scale (Hoge, 1972), and the DUREL (Koenig et al., 1997). The most recently cited scales (2011–16) were the ROS, ROS-R, and DUREL. However, due to their increasing use, the Religious Commitment Inventory (Worthington et al., 2003) and the BMMRS (Idler et al., 2003) are now included in the top five.

Religious Coping

The same procedure for ranking religiosity scales was repeated for multi-item measures of religious coping (Table 2.2). Pargament's RCOPE scales are the most commonly cited religious coping scales regardless of time frame, especially the Brief RCOPE (Pargament et al., 1998). The only other scale used to assess specific ways of religious coping is the 60-item COPE scale by Carver, Scheier, and Weintraub (1989), which contains a 4-item subscale on religious coping: "I put my trust in God"; "I seek God's help"; "I try to find comfort in my religion;" and "I pray more than usual." The COPE, however, is most often used for assessing nonreligious coping behaviors, and of the over 8000 articles that cite the original study, less than one-eighth of these even mentions the phrase "religious coping." The 3-item RCI, as noted earlier, assesses religious coping from a global perspective (Koenig et al., 1992). As it must be interviewer administered, the RCI is seldom used today, although single items (particularly the self-rated item) have been chosen from the scale and used more often.

TABLE 2.2 Most Commonly Used Measures of Religious Coping[a]

Scales	Cites	Authors
1929–2016		
1. Brief RCOPE	1541	Pargament et al. (1998)
2. RCOPE	1402	Pargament et al. (2000)
3. Religious coping subscale of COPE	967	Carver et al., 1989
4. Religious Coping Activities Scale	685	Pargament et al. (1990)
5. Religious Coping Index	630	Koenig et al. (1992)
2011–16		
1. Brief RCOPE	856	Pargament et al. (1998)
2. RCOPE	807	Pargament et al. (2000)
3. Religious coping subscale of COPE	530	Carver et al., 1989
4. Religious Coping Activities Scale	229	Pargament et al. (1990)
5. Religious Coping Index	179	Koenig et al. (1992)
2016		
1. Brief RCOPE	128	Pargament et al. (1998)
2. RCOPE	120	Pargament et al. (2000)
3. Religious coping subscale of COPE	88	Carver et al., 1989
4. Religious Coping Activities Scale	26	Pargament et al. (1990)
5. Religious Coping Index	14	Koenig et al. (1992)

[a] *Based on citations of the original report of the scale in Google Scholar on December 17, 2016.*

CHOOSING A MEASURE

CASE VIGNETTE

Sally is a graduate student working on her doctoral thesis. She wishes to identify a measure of religiosity for her study on religious involvement and eating disorders. Her hypothesis is that greater religious involvement is related to fewer symptoms of eating disorder in teenage girls hospitalized in a psychiatric unit. She is looking for a relatively brief measure that captures the major dimensions of religious involvement. Given that many of her potential participants are severely ill, the entire questionnaire can only take about 15 minutes. The questionnaire already has 30 questions assessing demographics and eating disorder symptoms. Participants are a mixture of Christians, Jews, and Muslims, and she wants a measure that will quantify religiousness across these faith traditions. She asks her advisor, "Do you know of two or three short measures of religiosity that I could use in my study?"

First, choosing a measure to assess religiosity will depend on the mental health outcome being studied and the logic behind why this mental health outcome ought to be related to the particular dimension of religiosity the researcher wishes to measure. A solid rationale is needed for choosing a particular dimension of religiosity based on underlying theory that explains why it ought to be related to the particular aspect of mental health being studied. Multidimensional measures provide a more comprehensive assessment of religiosity, and so are preferred in many cases. In other instances, choosing a particular dimension to focus on and measuring it comprehensively may be preferred. The measure chosen should be sensitive in assessing the full range of religious involvement likely to be encountered in the population being studied (in order to obtain a wide range of responses, increase response variability, and reduce likelihood of ceiling or floor effects). This maximizes the likelihood of detecting an association between the religious measure and mental health.

The second factor influencing choice of measure is amount of space available in the questionnaire. Most persons are unlikely to complete questionnaires that are much longer than 30 minutes, unless they are receiving compensation for their participation. The highest completion rates are for questionnaires that are about 10–15 minutes long. When items on questionnaires are short and written clearly, most participants can thoughtfully complete about five to seven questions per minute. This means that there is usually room for only about 75–100 questions in a self-completed survey. In addition to the measure of religiosity, there must be room for demographic information, covariates (mediators and moderators), and measures of the mental health outcome. If questionnaire space is an issue, then brief measures of religiosity are preferred.

Recommended Measures

For assessing overall religiosity as a "trait" (see Chapter 3) when there is little space available in the questionnaire, the 5-item DUREL is recommended, as it covers the three major dimensions of religious involvement (ORA, NORA, and IR). If there is room for 10 items, either the BIAC (Koenig et al., 2015a,b) or the Religious Commitment Inventory (Worthington et al., 2003) is recommended. When space is not a concern, then the 31-item version of the Brief BMMRS should be considered (i.e., the version without the forgiveness, values, and meaning subscales). Due to its strong relationship with mental health, frequency of religious attendance should always be included in whatever measure is used (or added as a separate item to the questionnaire).

For assessing religious coping, either the 3- or 14-item Brief RCOPE that assesses positive and negative religious coping (NRC) (as a "state" measure) is recommended (Pargament, 1999, p. 48; Pargament et al., 1998). NRC is almost always associated with poor mental health, so the 7-item NRC subscale of the Brief RCOPE should be included if there is adequate questionnaire space. Religious or spiritual struggles (another term for NRC) can also be assessed more comprehensively using the 26-item Religious/Spiritual Struggles Scale (Exline, Pargament, Grubbs, & Yali, 2014). Finally, if a short scale is needed for assessing positive forms of religious coping, the 4-item religious coping subscale of the COPE is an option (Carver et al., 1989).

RECOMMENDED MEASURES OF "SPIRITUALITY"

Since most measures of spirituality are contaminated by indicators of mental health, making them inappropriate for studying relationships between religion/spirituality and mental health (Table 1.2), it is difficult to recommend any particular instrument. However, among the least contaminated spirituality scales are the 16-item Daily Spiritual Experiences Scale (DSES) (Underwood & Teresi, 2002), the Index of Core Spiritual Experiences (ICSE) (Kass, Friedman, Leserman, Zuttermeister, & Benson, 1991), and the 10-item Religious Well-Being (RWB) subscale of the Spiritual Well-Being Scale (Paloutzian & Ellison, 1982). Given that the 16-item DSES has several items that bias scores toward good mental health, if investigators decide to use this scale, then results should be analyzed with and without the items contaminating the measure (#2, #3, #5, #6, #11–14). If results are similar, then this should be noted and results from the full scale reported. The ICSE is recommended because most items assess experiences related to the transcendent, measuring spirituality in a distinctive (and largely traditional) manner. The RWB subscale of the Spiritual Well-Being Scale also assesses spirituality in a way that is distinctive and separate from psychological well-being. Native American spirituality (Greenfield et al., 2015) and New Age spirituality (Granqvist & Hagekull, 2001) scales are also available.

STATISTICAL CONSIDERATIONS

Quantitative research involves analyzing data using statistical methods that rely on mathematical calculations, and so is heavily dependent on statistical tests used to analyze information collected by scales and measures. The structure of response options provided for the items that make up the scale, then, is an important consideration when choosing a scale. Since most questions making up religious and mental health scales depend on subjective responses and do not involve physical measurement (such as blood pressure, weight, blood glucose, or levels of other substances measured in laboratories), the response options to those questions will be either categorical or ordinal.

Examples of questions with "categorical" responses are the participant's religious affiliation, marital status, or gender, where a higher number is irrelevant, as each category has its own distinct meaning. Responses are "ordinal" in nature if some responses indicate less of something (assigned a lower number) and other responses indicate more of something (assigned a higher number). There is not, however, an equal distance between response categories as would be the case for "continuous" responses. Both individual item scores and the total scores that result when summing responses to items making up a scale are also considered ordinal, ordered from low to high, but again not continuous. Examples of single items with ordinal response options are self-rated health (poor, fair, good, etc.), severity of depressive symptoms (none, mild, moderate, severe, etc.), importance of religiosity (none, somewhat, moderate, very, etc.), and frequency of religious attendance (none, monthly, weekly, etc.). Again, because responses are ordered from low to high the "distance" between responses is not equal as is the case for increments of blood pressure, weight, or height where response categories are continuous.

The choice of statistical test depends on the form of the response options, that is, whether they are categorical, ordinal, or continuous. Thus, attention must be paid to the type of response options for questions that make up a scale. Questions with response options that involve single categories, such as gender or race, will need to be handled using nonparametric categorical statistics (when both predictor and outcome are categorical). Data collected from single- or multi-item scales with ordinal response options will need to be handled by nonparametric ordinal statistics (if both predictor and outcome are ordinal). Data collected that are continuous in nature are analyzed using parametric statistics (if either the predictor or the outcome is continuous). Parametric statistics are much more powerful than nonparametric methods in detecting associations between religiosity and mental health, although certain assumptions are required (i.e., that the data are normally distributed).

Since almost all measures of religious involvement and mental health depend on subjective responses (beliefs, attitudes, behaviors, experiences, and feelings), these data are considered "ordinal." Unfortunately, this limits the power of statistical tests to identify associations between religion and mental health, as these data require nonparametric methods to analyze the data. However, statisticians have argued that parametric statistical methods may be used with ordinal data if there are five or more response categories for a single-item scale or for the total score of a multi-item scale (Borgatta & Bohrnstedt, 1980; Myers & Well, 2003; Newsom, 2011; Koenig, 2011, p. 258). This allows researchers to analyze ordinal scores obtained from religious and mental health measures using parametric statistics (typically reserved for continuous data). This behooves the researcher to choose single-item scales with five or more response options or a multi-item scale. For more discussion of statistical methods used to analyze data from religious measures, see Koenig (2011).

Another consideration is the form of the relationship between religiosity and mental health. Is the relationship linear, U-shaped, or inverted U-shaped? As both mental health and religious involvement are dynamic constructs that change over time and likely influence each other in bidirectional ways, the association with mental health may be different at very high or very low levels of religiosity. This will likely depend on the particular measure, the population in which it is used, the measure of mental health, and the variables controlled for in the analysis. The relationship between mental health and dimensions of religiosity can be examined by graphing average levels of mental health across categories of religiosity. Fig. 2.1 illustrates several such graphs of the cross-sectional relationship between caregiver distress (assessed by a combined measure of caregiver burden, received stress, and depression) and scores on several dimensions of religiosity (overall religious commitment, religious attendance, and frequency of private prayer). These data are from a study of persons caring for severely disabled family members living in the Southeastern and Southwestern United States (unpublished data; also see Koenig, Nelson, Shaw, Saxena, & Cohen, 2016). Note how the relationship with caregiver distress changes with each religious dimension (almost reversing in parts of the curve for prayer, a "state" measure, which likely increases during emotional distress as individuals try to cope with it). Discovering how mental health is related to religious involvement across the entire spectrum of religiosity may help uncover dynamics of the association that would otherwise be hidden. Consequently, investigators are encouraged to visually inspect the form of the relationship with mental health, which may also influence their statistical approach to the data.

SUMMARY AND CONCLUSIONS

There are many measures of religiosity and religious coping. These measures are important for quantifying religious involvement so that its relationship with mental health (similarly quantified) can be examined. Measures for 17 different dimensions of religiosity have been described, a list of the most commonly used measures provided, and advice given on how to choose a scale. Unlike most measures of spirituality, these measures are not contaminated with indicators of mental health. Measures of religiosity (and spirituality) have been recommended here depending on the purposes of the researcher and the amount of space she or he has in their questionnaire. Statistical considerations when analyzing the data have also been discussed, including the use of parametric statistics with single-item and multi-item measures of religiosity with ordinal response categories and the need to visually inspect the form of the relationship between religiosity and

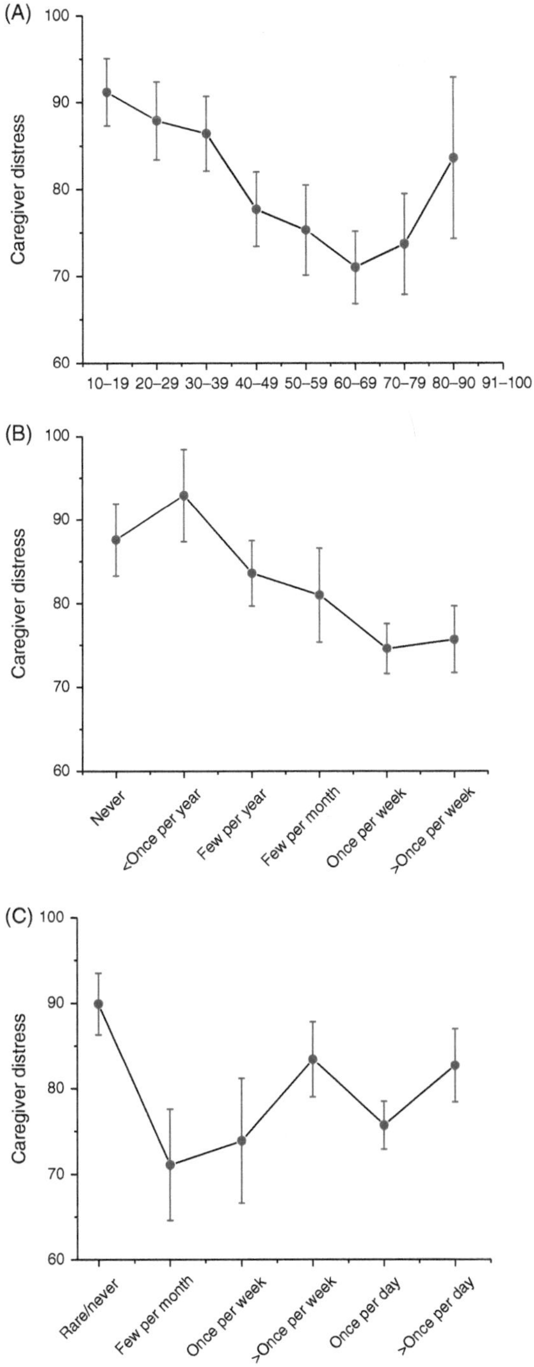

FIGURE 2.1 **Religiosity by caregiver distress (mean ± standard error) (*n* = 245),** where (A) Belief Into Action (BIAC) Scale scores, (B) religious attendance, and (C) frequency of prayer.

mental health that may not always be linear. The measures described here are useful for conducting research, not for taking a clinical spiritual history. However, an example of a structured spiritual history for assessing clients in clinical settings has been included in the Resources section of this book.

References

Abdel-Khalek, A. M. (2007). Assessment of intrinsic religiosity with a single-item measure in a sample of Arab Muslims. *Journal of Muslim Mental Health, 2*(2), 211–215.

Abou El Azayem, G., & Hedayat-Diba, Z. (1994). The psychological aspects of Islam: basic principles of Islam and their psychological corollary. *International Journal for the Psychology of Religion, 4*, 41–50.

Abu Raiya, H., Pargament, K. I., Mahoney, A., & Stein, C. (2008). A psychological measure of Islamic religiousness: development and evidence for reliability and validity. *The International Journal for the Psychology of Religion, 18*(4), 291–315.

Al Zaben, F., Khalifa, D. A., Sehlo, M. G., Al Shohaib, S., Binzaqr, S. A., Badreg, A. M., & Koenig, H. G. (2015a). Religious involvement and health in dialysis patients in Saudi Arabia. *Journal of Religion and Health, 54*(2), 713–730.

Al Zaben, F., Sehlo, M., Khalifa, D., & Koenig, H. G. (2015b). Test-retest reliability of the Muslim Religiosity Scale: follow-up to "religious involvement and health among dialysis patients in Saudi Arabia". *Journal of Religion and Health, 54*(3), 1144–1147.

Alakhdhair, S., Sheets, V., Geib, R., Alkhuwaildi, A., & Koenig, H. G. (2016). Psychometric properties of the Arabic version of the Belief Into Action Scale. *Mental Health Religion and Culture, 19*, 846–857.

Allport, G. W. (1950). *The individual and his religion: A psychological interpretation*. Oxford: Macmillan.

Allport, G. W., & Ross, J. M. (1967). Personal religious orientation and prejudice. *Journal of Personality and Social Psychology, 5*, 432–443.

Batson, C. D., & Schoenrade, P. (1991a). Measuring religion as quest: 1. Validity concerns. *Journal for the Scientific Study of Religion, 30*, 416–429.

Batson, C. D., & Schoenrade, P. (1991b). Measuring religion as quest: 2. Reliability concerns. *Journal for the Scientific Study of Religion, 30*, 430–447.

Batson, C. D. (1976). Religion as prosocial agent or double agent? *Journal for the Scientific Study of Religion, 15*, 29–45.

Beck, R., & McDonald, A. (2004). Attachment to God: The Attachment to God Inventory, tests of working model correspondence, and an exploration of faith group differences. *Journal of Psychology and Theology, 32*(2), 92–103.

Ben-Meir, Y., & Kedem, P. (1979). Index of religiosity of the Jewish population of Israel. *Megamot, 24*, 353–362.

Benson, P. L., Donahue, M. J., & Erickson, J. A. (1993). The Faith Maturity Scale: conceptualization, measurement, and empirical validation. In M. L. Lynn, & D. O. Moberg (Eds.), *Research in the Social Scientific Study of Religion* (pp. 1–26). Greenwich, CT: JAI Press [Full scale can be found in Hill, P. C. & Hood, R. W. (1999). *Measures of religiosity* (pp. 172–173). Birmingham, AL: Religious Education Press].

Benson, P., & Spilka, B. (1973). God image as a function of self-esteem and locus of control. *Journal for the Scientific Study of Religion*, 297–310.

Borgatta, E. F., & Bohrnstedt, G. W. (1980). Level of measurement: once over again. *Sociological Methods and Research, 9*(2), 147–160.

Carver, C. S., Scheier, M. F., & Weintraub, J. K. (1989). Assessing coping strategies: a theoretically based approach. *Journal of Personality and Social Psychology, 56*(2), 267–283.

Chatters, L. M., Levin, J. S., & Taylor, R. J. (1992). Antecedents and dimensions of religious involvement among older black adults. *Journal of Gerontology, 47*, S269–S278.

Cheek, J. (1996). Taking a view: qualitative research as representation. *Qualitative Health Research, 6*(4), 492–505.

Cronbach, L. J. (1951). Coefficient alpha and the internal structure of tests. *Psychometrika, 16*, 297–334.

Dollinger, S. J., & Malmquist, D. (2009). Reliability and validity of single-item self-reports: with special relevance to college students' alcohol use, religiosity, study, and social life. *The Journal of General Psychology, 136*(3), 231–242.

Edwards, K. J. (1976). Sex-role behavior and religious experience. In W. J. Donaldson (Ed.), *Research and mental health in religious behavior: An introduction to research in the integration of Christianity and the behavioral sciences* (pp. 224–238). Atlanta: Psychological Studies Institute [Full scale can be found in Hill, P. C. & Hood, R. W. (1999). *Measures of religiosity* (p. 220). Birmingham, AL: Religious Education Press].

Ellison, C. W. (1984). Personality, religious orientation, and spiritual well-being. *Unpublished manuscript*. Nyack, NY: Alliance Theological Seminary [Full scale can be found in Hill, P. C. & Hood, R. W. (1999). *Measures of religiosity* (pp. 203–204). Birmingham, AL: Religious Education Press].

Ellison, C. E. (1999). Religious preference. *Multidimensional measurement of religiousness/spirituality for use in health research: A report of the Fetzer Institute/National Institute on Aging Workshop Group*. Kalamazoo, MI: Fetzer Foundation [pp. 81–84; Available from http://fetzer.org/resources/multidimensional-measurement-religiousnessspirituality-use-health-research].

Emavardhana, T., & Tori, C. D. (1997). Changes in self-concept, ego defense mechanisms, and religiosity following seven-day Vipassana meditation retreats. *Journal for the Scientific Study of Religion, 36*, 194–206.

Exline, J. J., Pargament, K. I., Grubbs, J. B., & Yali, A. M. (2014). The Religious and Spiritual Struggles Scale: development and initial validation. *Psychology of Religion and Spirituality, 6*(3), 208–222.

Fetzer Institute. (1999). *Multidimensional measurement of religiousness/spirituality for use in health research: A report of the Fetzer Institute/National Institute on Aging Workshop Group*. Kalamazoo, MI: Fetzer Foundation [Available from http://fetzer.org/resources/multi-dimensional-measurement-religiousnessspirituality-use-health-research].

Francis, L. J., Santosh, R., Robbins, M., & Vij, S. (2008). Assessing attitude toward Hinduism: the Santosh-Francis Scale. *Mental Health, Religion and Culture, 11*, 609–621.

George, L. K. (1999). Religious/spiritual history. *Multidimensional measurement of religiousness/spirituality for use in health research: A report of the Fetzer Institute/National Institute on Aging Workshop Group*. Kalamazoo, MI: Fetzer Foundation [pp. 65–69; Available from http://fetzer.org/resources/multidimensional-measurement-religiousnessspirituality-use-health-research].

Ghorbani, N., Watson, P. J., Ghramaleki, A. F., Morris, R. J., & Hood, R. W., Jr. (2000). Muslim attitudes towards religion scale: factors, validity and complexity of relationships with mental health in Iran. *Mental Health Religion and Culture, 3*(2), 125–132.

Glock, C. Y., & Stark, R. (1966). *Christian beliefs and anti-Semitism*. New York, NY: Harper and Row.

Glock, C. Y., & Stark, R. (1970). *American piety: The nature of religious commitment*. Berkeley, CA: University of California Press.

Gorsuch, R. L., & McFarland, S. G. (1972). Single vs. multiple-item scales for measuring religious values. *Journal for the Scientific Study of Religion*, 53–64.

Gorsuch, R. L., & McPherson, S. E. (1989). Intrinsic/extrinsic measurement: I/E-revised and single-item scales. *Journal for the Scientific Study of Religion, 28*(3), 348–354.

Gorsuch, R. L., & Venable, G. D. (1983). Development of the "Age Universal" I-E scale. *Journal for the Scientific Study of Religion, 22*, 181–187.

Granqvist, P. (2016). Attachment, emotion, and religion. In D. Evers, M. Fuller, A. Runehov, & K. -W. Sæther (Eds.), *Issues in science and theology: Do emotions shape the world?* (pp. 9 26). New York, NY: Springer International Publishing.

Granqvist, P., & Hagekull, B. (2001). Seeking security in the New Age: on attachment and emotional compensation. *Journal for the Scientific Study of Religion*, *40*(3), 527–545.

Greenfield, B. L., Hallgren, K. A., Venner, K. L., Hagler, K. J., Simmons, J. D., Sheche, J. N., Homer, E., & Lupee, D. (2015). Cultural adaptation, psychometric properties, and outcomes of the Native American Spirituality Scale. *Psychological Services*, *12*(2), 123–133.

Groh, A. M., Fearon, R. M., IJzendoorn, M. H., Bakermans-Kranenburg, M. J., & Roisman, G. I. (2017). Attachment in the early life course: metaanalytic evidence for its role in socioemotional development. *Child Development Perspectives*, *11*(1), 70–76.

Hafizi, S., Tabatabaei, D., Memari, A. H., Saghazadeh, A., & Koenig, H. G. (2016). Belief Into Action Scale: psychometric properties of the Farsi version. *Mental Health, Religion and Culture*, *19*(5), 440–447.

Hill, P. C., & Hood, R. W. (Eds.). (1999). *Measures of religiosity*. Birmingham, AL: Religious Education Press.

Hoge, D. R. (1972). A validated intrinsic religious motivation scale. *Journal for the Scientific Study of Religion*, *11*, 369–376.

Hood, R. W. (1970). Religious orientation and the report of religious experience. *Journal for the Scientific Study of Religion*, *9*, 285–291.

Hood, R. W. (1975). The construction and preliminary validation of a measure of reported mystical experience. *Journal for the Scientific Study of Religion*, *14*, 29–41.

Idler, E. (1999). Organizational religiousness. *Multidimensional measurement of religiousness/spirituality for use in health research: A report of the Fetzer Institute/National Institute on Aging Workshop Group*. Kalamazoo, MI: Fetzer Foundation [pp. 75–80; Available from http://fetzer.org/resources/multidimensional-measurement-religiousnessspirituality-use-health-research].

Idler, E. L., Musick, M. A., Ellison, C. G., George, L. K., Krause, N., Ory, M. G., Pargament, K. I., Powell, L. H., Underwood, L., & Williams, D. R. (2003). Measuring multiple dimensions of religion and spirituality for health research conceptual background and findings from the 1998 General Social Survey. *Research on Aging*, *25*(4), 327–365.

James, W. (1902). *The varieties of religious experience: A study in human nature*. Cambridge, MA: Harvard University Press.

Kass, J. D., Friedman, R., Leserman, J., Zuttermeister, P. C., & Benson, H. (1991). Health outcomes and a new index of spiritual experience. *Journal for the Scientific Study of Religion*, *30*(2), 203–211.

King, M. B. (1967). Measuring the religious variable: nine proposed dimensions. *Journal for the Scientific Study of Religion*, *6*, 173–185.

King, M. B., & Hunt, R. A. (1972). Measuring the religious variable: replication. *Journal for the Scientific Study of Religion*, *11*, 240–251.

Koenig, H. G. (2011). *Spirituality and health research: Methods, measurement, statistics, & resources*. Conshohocken, PA: Templeton Foundation Press.

Koenig, H. G., Al-Zaben, F., Khalifa, D. A., & Al Shohaib, S. (2014). Measures of religiosity. In G. J. Boyle, D. H. Saklofske, & G. Mathews (Eds.), *Measures of personality and social psychological constructs*. San Diego, CA: Academic Press [Chapter 19].

Koenig, H. G., & Bussing, A. (2010). The Duke Religion Index: a brief measure for use in epidemiological studies. *Religions*, *1*(1), 78–85.

Koenig, H. G., Cohen, H. J., Blazer, D. G., Pieper, C., Meador, K. G., Shelp, F., Goli, V., & DiPasquale, R. (1992). Religious coping and depression in elderly hospitalized medically ill men. *American Journal of Psychiatry*, *149*, 1693–1700.

Koenig, H. G., Kvale, J. N., & Ferrel, C. (1988a). Religion and well-being in later life. *The Gerontologist*, *28*, 18–28.

Koenig, H. G., Meador, K., & Parkerson, G. (1997). Religion index for psychiatric research: a 5-item measure for use in health outcome studies. *American Journal of Psychiatry, 154*, 885–886.

Koenig, H. G., Moberg, D. O., & Kvale, J. N. (1988b). Religious activities and attitudes of older adults in a geriatric assessment clinic. *Journal of the American Geriatrics Society, 36*, 362–374.

Koenig, H. G., Nelson, B., Shaw, S. F., Al Zaben, F., Wang, Z., & Saxena, S. (2015b). Belief Into Action Scale: a brief but comprehensive measure of religious commitment. *Open Journal of Psychiatry, 5*(1), 66–77.

Koenig, H. G., Nelson, B., Shaw, S. F., Saxena, S., & Cohen, H. J. (2016). Religious involvement and adaptation in female family caregivers. *Journal of the American Geriatrics Society, 64*(3), 578–583.

Koenig, H. G., Smiley, M., & Gonzales, J. (1988c). *Religion, health and aging*. Westport, CT: Greenwood Press.

Koenig, H. G., Wang, Z., Al Zaben, F., & Adi, A. (2015a). Belief Into Action Scale: a comprehensive and sensitive measure of religious involvement. *Religions, 6*(3), 1006–1016.

Krause, N. (1999). Religious support. *Multidimensional measurement of religiousness/spirituality for use in health research: A report of the Fetzer Institute/National Institute on Aging Workshop Group*. Kalamazoo, MI: Fetzer Foundation [pp. 57–63; Available from http://fetzer.org/resources/multidimensional-measurement-religiousnessspirituality-use-health-research].

Levin, J. S. (1999). Private religious practices. *Multidimensional measurement of religiousness/spirituality for use in health research: A report of the Fetzer Institute/National Institute on Aging Workshop Group*. Kalamazoo, MI: Fetzer Foundation [pp. 39–42; Available from http://fetzer.org/resources/multidimensional-measurement-religiousnessspirituality-use-health-research].

Levin, J. S., & Kaplan, B. (2010). The Sorokin multidimensional inventory of love experience (SMILE): development, validation, and religious determinants. *Review of Religious Research, 42*(3), 277–293.

Loo, R. (2002). A caveat on using single-item versus multiple-item scales. *Journal of Managerial Psychology, 17*, 68–75.

Myers, J. L., & Well, A. D. (2003). *Research design and statistical analysis* (2nd ed.). Mahwah, NJ: Lawrence Erlbaum Associates.

Newsom, J. T. (2011). Basic longitudinal analysis approaches for continuous and categorical variables. In J. T. Newsom, R. N. Jones, & S. M. Hofer (Eds.), *Longitudinal data analysis: A practical guide for researchers in aging, health, and social sciences* (pp. 144). New York, NY: Routledge.

Oshagbemi, T. (1999). Overall job satisfaction: how good are the single versus the multiple-item measures? *Journal of Managerial Psychology, 14*(5), 388–403.

Paloutzian, R. F., & Ellison, C. W. (1982). Loneliness, spiritual well-being, and the quality of life. In L. A. Peplau, & D. Perlman (Eds.), *Loneliness: A sourcebook of current theory, research and therapy* (pp. 224–236). New York, NY: John Wiley & Sons.

Pargament, K. I. (1999). Religious/spiritual coping. *Multidimensional measurement of religiousness/spirituality for use in health research: A report of the Fetzer Institute/National Institute on Aging Workshop Group*. Kalamazoo, MI: Fetzer Foundation [pp. 43–56; Available from http://fetzer.org/resources/multidimensional-measurement-religiousnessspirituality-use-health-research].

Pargament, K. I., Ensing, D. S., Falgout, K., Olsen, H., Reilly, B., Van Haitsma, K., & Warren, R. (1990). God help me:(I): religious coping efforts as predictors of the outcomes to significant negative life events. *American Journal of Community Psychology, 18*(6), 793–824.

Pargament, K. I., Kennell, J., Hathaway, W., Grevengoed, N., Newman, J., & Jones, W. (1988). Religion and the problem-solving process: three styles of coping. *Journal for the Scientific Study of Religion, 27*, 90–104.

Pargament, K. I., Koenig, H. G., & Perez, L. M. (2000). Comprehensive measure of religious coping: development and initial validation of the RCOPE. *Journal of Clinical Psychology, 56*, 519–543.

Pargament, K. I., Smith, B. W., Koenig, H. G., & Perez, L. (1998). Patterns of positive and negative religious coping with major life stressors. *Journal for the Scientific Study of Religion, 37*(4), 710–724.

Phillips, R. E., Michelle Cheng, C., Oemig, C., Hietbrink, L., & Vonnegut, E. (2012). Validation of a Buddhist coping measure among primarily non-Asian Buddhists in the United States. *Journal for the Scientific Study of Religion, 51*(1), 156–172.

Roof, W. C., & McKinney, W. (1987). *American mainline religion: Its changing shape and future.* New Brunswick, NJ: Rutgers University Press.

Rosegrant, J. (1976). The impact of set and setting on religious experience in nature. *Journal for the Scientific Study of Religion, 15*, 301–310.

Rosmarin, D. H., Pargament, K. I., Krumrei, E. J., & Flannelly, K. J. (2009a). Religious coping among Jews: development and initial validation of the JCOPE. *Journal of Clinical Psychology, 65*(7), 670–683.

Rosmarin, D. H., Pargament, K. I., & Mahoney, A. (2009b). The role of religiousness in anxiety, depression and happiness in a Jewish community sample: a preliminary investigation. *Mental Health Religion and Culture, 12*, 97–113.

Rosmarin, D. H., Pirutinsky, S., & Pargament, K. I. (2011). A brief measure of core religious beliefs for use in psychiatric settings. *International Journal of Psychiatry in Medicine, 41*, 253–261.

Rowatt, W. C., & Kirkpatrick, L. A. (2002). Two dimensions of attachment to God and their relation to affect, religiosity, and personality constructs. *Journal for the Scientific Study of Religion, 41*(4), 637–651.

Shrout, P. E., & Fleiss, J. L. (1979). Intraclass correlations: uses in assessing rater reliability. *Psychological Bulletin, 86*, 420–428.

Streubert Speziale, H. J., & Carpenter, D. R. (2003). *Qualitative research in nursing: Advancing the humanistic perspective* (3rd ed.). Philadelphia, PA: Lippincott.

Tarakeshwar, N., Pargament, K. I., & Mahoney, A. (2003). Initial development of a measure of religious coping among Hindus. *Journal of Community Psychology, 31*(6), 607–628.

Thouless, R. (1935). The tendency to certainty in religious belief. *British Journal of Psychology, 26*, 16–31.

Thurstone, L. L., & Chave, E. J. (1929). *The measurement of attitude: A psychophysical method and some experiments with a scale for measuring attitude toward the church*. Chicago, IL: University of Chicago Press [Full scale can be found in Hill, P. C. & Hood, R. W. (1999). *Measures of religiosity* (pp. 470–471). Birmingham, AL: Religious Education Press].

Ulin, P. R., Robinson, E. T., & Tolley, E. E. (2005). *Qualitative Methods in Public Health*. San Francisco, CA: Josey-Bass.

Underwood, L. G., & Teresi, J. A. (2002). The daily spiritual experience scale: development, theoretical description, reliability, exploratory factor analysis, and preliminary construct validity using health-related data. *Annals of Behavioral Medicine, 24*(1), 22–33.

Wang, Z., Ma, H., Rong, Y., & Koenig, H. G. (2016). Psychometric properties of Belief Into Action Scale among university students in China. *International Journal of Social Science Studies, 4*(3), 83–93.

Worthington, E. L., Jr., Wade, N. G., Hight, T. L., Ripley, J. S., McCullough, M. E., Berry, J. W., Schmitt, M. M., Bursley, K. H., & O'Connor, L. (2003). The Religious Commitment Inventory-10: development, refinement, and validation of a brief scale for research and counseling. *Journal of Counseling Psychology, 50*(1), 84–96.

CHAPTER

3

Religion and Coping

The use of religion to cope with emotional, social, and physical distress is one of the most important functions that religion serves, and from an evolutionary perspective, may be one reason contributing to the development, flourishing, and persistence of religious groups over time, along with their ability to enhance cooperation and cohesion within groups (Beit-Hallahmi & Argyle, 1997; Gould, 1991; Pals, 1996). Religion as a coping strategy has been utilized for thousands of years and until present times, despite an increasing emphasis on objective verification and rationality within the scientific worldview. Freud (1927) called religious belief delusional. Ellis (1980) called it irrational. Is religion really delusional and irrational, incompatible with the reasoning of a healthy mind? Is it really irrational for the monotheist to believe that God exists, that God is behind everything that happens, and that things happen—even bad things—for a reason? Is it irrational for the pantheist to believe that God is everything and everywhere, and that all of reality is identical with divinity? Exact beliefs differ between religions, but they all have one thing in common—devout adherents say that religious beliefs provide comfort and meaning when tragedy strikes.

Religion is not only for the masses, the simple, and the uneducated. Some of the most famous scientists of the 21st century have been quite religious. There was Charles Townes, physicist at the University of California at Berkeley, who was awarded the Nobel Prize for inventing the laser. There is Francis Collins, the current (2018) director of the National Institutes of Health and former director of the US National Human Genome Research Institute. There is Martin Nowak, an evolutionary biologist and mathematician at Harvard. In fact, at least two-thirds of all Nobel Prizes awarded between 1901 and 2000 were to scientists with religious beliefs (Shalev, 2002). Thus, despite the claim that religion is delusional and irrational, religious belief has been and continues to be held by some of the greatest minds in recent times, does not appear to be decreasing very quickly (despite movements toward secularization), and for the vast majority of humanity, is still how most make sense of and cope with the events that happen around them.

Religion and Mental Health. http://dx.doi.org/10.1016/B978-0-12-811282-3.00003-3

That includes the amazingly complex physiological processes within the body that makes survival even possible. How much control does a person have over these internal activities (beating of the heart, digestion within the gastrointestinal tract, intracellular processes, etc.) and the external events that occur during a typical day? Indeed, there is much that is unknown, and therefore saying with certainty that religious beliefs are delusional or irrational may be itself a giant leap of faith.

It is proposed here that religious coping represents a *gateway* to many of the mental and physical health benefits that religion provides. While religious beliefs and values have validity in their own right, separate from their functional nature, the fact is that most religious persons use their religious beliefs and practices to make sense of, manage, and adapt to unwanted change, loss, and everyday disturbances. There are many colloquial expressions among the religious and non-religious alike as they react spontaneously to bad news: "Oh my God!," "God forbid," "for God's sake," and so forth. Religious beliefs provide meaning to life experiences that allow persons to understand and process them more easily. Religious dogmas provide guidelines on behavior when responding to negative life events and stressful circumstances. These doctrines direct people away from actions that might otherwise lead to long-term problems (drug abuse, alcohol misuse, promiscuous sexual activity, cheating in business, aggression and violence toward others in retaliation, etc.). Finally, religious beliefs and commitments affect both the amount and the quality of social engagement, and provide guidelines for making decisions that affect relationships at home and with colleagues at work, individuals who may be needed for support when trauma and tragedy strike.

How a person uses religion to cope will depend on many things, including their personality (formed early in life during interactions with caregivers), genetic predispositions, and degree of environmental stress in early and later life. It is often adverse circumstances that drive people toward religion, which as noted above, helps them make sense of difficult situations, provides a sense of control, and gives hope for better circumstances in the future. Traumatic life events, however, do not always drive people toward religion. Sometimes, adverse circumstances can derail religion, wounding an individual so deeply that he or she is unable to access religious resources for comfort or meaning. In some cases, such events may cause a person to turn completely away from religion and/or cause rage and anger toward it. Finally, genetically vulnerable individuals who have been severely traumatized early in life may find no need for religion because of psychological defense mechanisms or biological changes in the brain that reduce their ability to experience anxiety, feel pain, become attached to others, or experience emotions of guilt or shame when causing harm to others (Wall, Wygant, & Sellbom, 2015).

These are bold, calm, covertly, and sometimes overtly aggressive individuals who calculate carefully as they manipulate others in search of personal gain and pleasure. Such persons are often given the diagnosis of antisocial personality disorder, psychopathic subtype. These unfortunate individuals are often difficult to treat because they experience little of the distress or emotional pain necessary for motivation to change (Salekin, 2002).

Of course, there are many mentally healthy and stable individuals who find no need for religion, and cope with stress by use of rational cognitive processes (analyzing and verbally articulating whatever is stressful or causing grief), and/or by sharing these thoughts and feelings with family or friends. These individuals may seek wisdom through non-religious sources such as Marcus Aurelius' *Meditations* or the writings of other philosophers and sages (Aristotle, Seneca, Descartes, Sartre, Twain, Russell, and Hitchens), engage in non-religious meditation and relaxation exercises, or involve themselves in activities close to nature such as gardening, fishing, or an absorbing hobby. They may participate in stress-relieving vigorous exercise such as running, swimming, or other physical activity. Others may cope by reading books, or becoming involved in altruistic activities that contribute in a meaningful way to the lives of others. These approaches to coping may provide great comfort (or at least distraction) that rivals the support others obtain from religion.

DEFINITION

Stepping back a bit, what exactly is meant here by religious coping? A formal definition will help clarify this terminology. Here is a definition that will describe what the author means by religious coping in this context.

> Religious coping is the use of religious beliefs or practices to deal with and make sense of negative life experiences (and sometimes positive ones). In Western religious traditions, this may include behaviors such as praying during emotionally trying times; reading religious writings for inspiration and guidance; attending religious services to be uplifted by singing and worshiping together with others; seeking support from members of one's congregation; and/or giving support to others for religious reasons. In Eastern traditions, coping behaviors may include meditation; rituals involving prayer, worship, reverence, making sacrificial offerings at the temple or at home; visiting the grave sites of ancestors; showing compassion to others; and/or study of sacred Hindu or Buddhist texts. Religious coping may also involve cognitive processes, including beliefs about a better life after death when pain and suffering will cease, reincarnation and progression toward Nirvana, or beliefs in a loving, caring God who is in control, has a purpose for the world and individuals in it, and has the power to transform difficult circumstances so that good outcomes are possible. Thus, both behaviors and beliefs are involved in religious coping.

HOW DOES RELIGION HELP?

How exactly might religious beliefs and behaviors help people to cope? There are many potential pathways and mechanisms, some of which will now be summarized. While this list is by no means exhaustive, it does provide some of the major ways that religious beliefs and practices help people to deal with traumatic stressors.

First, religious beliefs provide a generally optimistic and positive view of the world. In the Judeo–Christian–Islamic traditions, for example, there is belief in a loving, merciful, and compassionate God; belief that the world and universe is not a result of random chance, but rather arises out of divine purpose; belief that God is in ultimate control of everything (with perhaps the exception of human choice); belief that humans can communicate with and influence God; and belief that this life is not the end, but only a brief existence before their eternal destination in heaven, where there is no pain or suffering or separation from loved ones. This worldview is arguably more positive than the scientific worldview that sees all events as random and meaningless, and considers humans a product of a heartless evolutionary process that favors survival of the fittest only. Of course, some religions also have beliefs about hell and damnation that may evoke excessive guilt or obsessive ruminations in those who are vulnerable to such tendencies.

Second, religious beliefs provide people's lives with meaning and purpose. A common religious belief is that every person's life is meaningful and has a specific purpose that fits into the divine purpose. Individuals in Western religious traditions, for example, see events and circumstances, including (and perhaps especially) painful experiences, as being used by God to achieve something good in the person's life. According to this view, all pain and suffering has purpose and meaning. When suffering has meaning, it is much easier to deal with. When suffering has no meaning and is senseless, random, and uncontrollable, it increases suffering and reduces the ability to tolerate it. This view has been well articulated in Viktor Frankl's *Man's Search for Meaning* (Frankl, 1946).

Third, religious beliefs enable a person to psychologically integrate and process loss, trauma, and unwanted change. A severe trauma may challenge a person's worldview about predictability and safety, which often causes anxiety due to loss of control. Until those events can be integrated, the person may be unable to move on with life and instead remains stuck in the trauma. Religious beliefs give explanations for why things happen and provide behaviors that may reduce or prevent the trauma from happening again (it doesn't matter whether those behaviors actually prevent the trauma or not, as long as the person believes they will). Religions also provide rituals for dealing with distressing events, rituals that may be practiced alone or in community settings with the support of like-minded believers.

Fourth, religion provides hope for better times ahead. There is hope that the situation will resolve in a positive manner and things will get better. There is also the hope that goes beyond this life, such that if things don't get better here, then they will be better after this life ends. Indeed, *only* religion can provide this hope that transcends death. Hope is what motivates people to improve their lives and to push on when the going gets tough. Without hope, few people will strive to make the painful changes necessary to maintain or enhance their health, recover from a disabling illness or painful surgery, excel on their job (striving to do their best to meet the goals of the team), and improve their relationships with family or friends.

Fifth, religion empowers individuals by providing activities they can do to improve their situation with or without the aid of others. No longer are they helpless and dependent on others' whims, but now have behaviors they can engage in that will address their problems (and do so in a manner that does not have long-term negative consequences). For example, a person may volunteer for religious reasons to help others, actions that they believe will be rewarded either now or later. The Catholic may go to confession to ask forgiveness and be given penance to compensate for real or perceived wrongs that have been committed.

Sixth, related to this empowerment, religion provides a sense of control. For example, the Judeo–Christian–Islamic traditions teach that one can pray to God and that God cares and answers prayer. The sick person, then, is not totally dependent on health professionals to meet all their needs. Instead, he or she can pray to God for healing or for the strength to cope with the illness, whether or not it is treatable by conventional medicine. This reduces dependency and gives people a sense that they can control their fate without necessarily depending on others in powerful positions.

Seventh, religion provides role models to help individuals persist during periods of suffering. Such role models facilitate acceptance of the situation for now and endurance to make it through. A classic example is Job in the Hebrew Bible. Job lost everything—his finances, property, children, and health. Yet he persisted, even when getting bad advice from his counselors. Eventually, Job's patience was rewarded by God answering him. The end of the story is that Job once again prospered and lived a full and complete life. Religious figures such as Job, Abraham, Moses, David, Jesus the Christ, and the Prophet Mohammad provide role models in the Judeo–Christian–Islamic traditions that people can relate to and emulate.

Eighth, religion provides guidance for decision-making in difficult situations where one might be tempted to reduce stress in ways that might create more problems in the long term. For example, those suffering a major financial loss may be tempted to increase their intake of alcohol, use drugs, overeat, engage in sexually promiscuous behaviors as a way to sooth themselves and reduce the pain, or may steal or cheat others to compensate for their losses. Religious beliefs discourage such behavior and provide alternative ways to cope that do not have long-term consequences, but rather may lead to psychological or spiritual growth.

Ninth, religion provides *answers* to ultimate questions. Why am I here? Where do I come from? Where am I going after I die? Science and medicine have no answers to these questions, which lie solely in the province of religion. The great world religions provide answers that provide many with meaning and comfort during difficult circumstances that give rise to the asking of such questions (such as during illness or severe trauma or loss).

Finally, religion provides a community of believers to support, encourage, comfort, and advise during difficult times. Besides other members of the congregation with whom friendships may develop, the clergy are also a major source of mental health care for people having emotional problems, marital conflicts, or problems with children. Weaver (1995) notes that clergy are on the front lines delivering community mental health services, providing nearly as much counseling to people in terms of hours per week as the entire membership of the American Psychological Association. Help from clergy has no cost, no stigma, and is readily available. Is it surprising, then, that many people seek support from this source before going to mental health professionals?

Not only does religion provide human support, but many faith traditions also emphasize divine support, particularly when humans are not around or not cooperating. This is particularly true in faith traditions that believe in a powerful personal God who cares about people, is involved in the world, and is responsive to human need. In the middle of the night when no one else is around, a mentally or physically ill person may begin to dwell on problems and worry about the future. For members of faith traditions who believe in a personal deity, they can always talk to God. In these traditions, God serves as an attachment figure from whom one can readily obtain nurturance and support when needed (Koenig, 2016).

Attachment and Suffering

In the Buddhist tradition, emphasis is placed on the root cause of all suffering (*dukkha*). According to the second of the Four Noble Truths, the origin of suffering is attachment—attachment to the things of this world. The Buddha taught that clinging to, having desire, or craving for the objects of attachment was the cause of suffering (see Dhammacakkappavattana Sutta, the first teaching of the Buddha after he reached enlightenment [Thera, 1993]). Because all things in this world are fleeting, impermanent, and subject to change, it is the sense of loss or inability to obtain and possess the objects of attachment that is the cause of emotional pain. The third of the Four Noble Truths says that to reduce or end suffering, individuals must practice nonattachment, avoid clinging, and eliminate or control sensual desires ("The dissolution of craving subdues all suffering... Through craving for possessions, one deficient in wisdom strikes himself down as one would the others" – The Dhammapada 354–355; see also 40, 91, 93, 171, 214, 352–353, 367, 396–397, 411, 421). Strictly speaking, this includes avoiding excessive attachments to other people ("Therefore, let one not make endearment...For one set free from endearment, there is no grief..."—The Dhammapada 211–212) (Carter and Palihawadana, 2000).

In the monotheistic religious traditions of Judaism, Christianity, and Islam, a similar teaching exists. The teaching involves belief in, attachment to, love of and submission to God, who is to be the central and primary object of worship and devotion (based on the First Commandment). A primary attachment to God means that all other things and people that are desired and craved for are secondary. If all other things and people are secondary and of less importance than God, then loss or change of possessions, relationships, or personal goals will cause less suffering since the primary attachment remains intact. If true, then those with a strong attachment to God will experience less suffering, less emotional distress, and greater well-being.

CASE VIGNETTE

The following is a case described in the July 24, 2002 issue of the *Journal of the American Medical Association*, and provides a good example of a form of religious coping that involves attachment to God (Koenig, 2002). Mrs. A is an 83-year-old African–American woman with multiple serious medical problems (hypertension, diabetes, polymotor and sensory neuropathy, goiter, spinal stenosis, and multiple joint bursitis). She has chronic, progressive, unrelenting neuropathic pain that is unresponsive to antiinflammatory drugs, anticonvulsants, and narcotic analgesics (including tramadol, codeine, oxycodone, and fentanyl). Both standard medical treatments and alternative medical treatments (acupuncture, massage, etc.) have been ineffective. Neurological consultation has not been helpful. She has limited material resources and lives alone, yet is able to perform all activities of daily living independently and requires no outside assistance. When her physician sees her in clinic, the doctor does not know how to relieve her symptoms. However, the physician notices that Mrs. A is doing well psychologically despite severe chronic pain and disability. She is positive, hopeful, and optimistic. The doctor asks her how she does it. How does she maintain her positive emotional state? Mrs. A consistently responds that her faith in God has enabled her to endure the pain. The following quote is taken from the JAMA article.

> I don't dwell on the pain, you know. Some people are sick and have pain, and it gets the best of them. Not me. Praying eases the pain, it takes it away. Sometimes I pray when I am in deep, serious pain; I pray, and all at once the pain gets easy. Praying helps me a lot. I feel that has helped me more than the medication.
>
> A doctor is a doctor. Not everybody is bound to believe in God. It's your own mind, your thoughts, and your belief. The doctor gives you the medicine. God works through the doctor. He is a great physician and he heals, but you have to believe. I believe in God. He's my guide and my protector.
>
> Whenever you pray, you will get healing from God. You will. But you must have that belief. Because if you don't believe in God and turn your life over to him, it's nothing doing. You can't just pray, "God, I'm suffering, and I ask you to heal my body." It don't work like that. You have to really be a child of God. (p. 487)

The way Mrs. A uses religion to cope, at least for her, is a pathway to resilience and adaptability. She says that the really devout—those who are completely and wholly committed to their religious faith—derive substantial benefit from religious beliefs. Is genuine and whole-hearted belief, where religion is central in a person's life, the only kind of faith that works? Is this the only kind of faith capable of affecting everyday attitudes, perceptions, and responses to events and circumstances, especially of the magnitude that Mrs. A must confront? What about individuals with more moderate levels of religious commitment? Will persons not also benefit to some degree? The "graded benefits" hypothesis holds that any amount of religious involvement helps compared to no religious involvement, and that the benefit increases stepwise with increasing religiosity. The "threshold" hypothesis holds that religious belief and activity are helpful only after they have reached a certain level of religious commitment. Systematic research can examine and help to answer such questions. Those answers are important for understanding how religious coping affects mental health. Before moving onto that research, however, something needs to be said about how religious belief in some circumstances might hinder successful coping.

RELIGION AS A BARRIER TO COPING

How might religion stand in the way of successful coping? Could strong religious beliefs sometimes make a person's emotional state worse? Anecdotes abound of cases where people who relied on religious beliefs to cope experienced increased emotional distress. Here is one of them.

> Mrs. Z is a 52-year-old married Caucasian woman who suffers from an autoimmune disorder that causes chronic pain. She is devoutly religious and attends religious services several times a week and is a volunteer in her church. During healing services at the church, which are frequent in her denomination, she prays for healing. Likewise,

other members pray and "lay hands on" her for healing. She has been doing this for many months. She has now become discouraged because pain and disability have increased. She wonders what she has done to deserve this and why her prayers (and the prayers of others on her behalf) have not been answered. She wonders whether God loves her. Other members seem to be healed when they pray or are prayed for during these services, but this has not happened in her case. After several more months of prayer without relief, she begins to feel that God is punishing her for activities in the past when she was a youth. She stops going to healing services at the church and stops volunteering. Consequently, she has become socially withdrawn and more and more discouraged. Despite increasing depression, she is reluctant to seek mental health care because of what she heard years ago about how people often lose their faith after seeing a psychiatrist who places them on medications that turn them into zombies.

When bad things happen despite religious attempts to cope, people may turn away from religion, become discouraged, and sometimes lose their faith entirely (as noted earlier). This can occur not only for individuals but also for entire faith communities (Blazer, Cohen, George, Koenig, & Verhey, 2011). Even in the absence of major life stress, failure to live up to high religious ethical and moral standards (love your neighbor, forgive those who hurt you, don't lie or cheat, etc.) may result in "religious strains" (Exline, Yali, & Sanderson, 2000). Religious strains, while helping to motivate people to behave in a prosocial manner, may also cause emotional distress in those who are vulnerable. Such strains may even interfere with a person's ability to access religious resources for support. Having God as the primary attachment figure, then, raises the possibility that one can perceive oneself as disappointing God, and this may create guilt, shame, and anxiety.

RESEARCH ON RELIGIOUS COPING

A number of claims have been made by the author above. Is there any evidence to back up such musings? Systematic observation and experiment research is how claims like these are tested. This helps to separate the wheat from the chaff, the proclamations of charlatans from the truth of reality that can be observed and measured. Some of what has been said above, admittedly, is merely opinion (although arguably reasonable and rational). No research method exists that can test truth claims about that which exists outside of nature (i.e., the supernatural). Other statements made above, however, have been examined, and the next section summarizes some of that research, presenting results from an earlier systematic review completed in 2010 and examples of more recent studies conducted since then.

In discussing the research, however, it is first important to describe how religious coping has been quantified. Although the measurement of religious coping was examined in chapter 2, the points made there will be summarized and elaborated on here. A common method of assessment is to ask a single or several questions to determine whether a person uses religion to cope and how much. The question/s may assess religious coping more generally or anchor it to a specific situation (i.e., when upset, stressed, etc.). Alternatively, researchers may present the person with a series of specific statements about how people cope and ask to what extent the person engages in such activity.

With regard to general religious coping, a 3-item measure has been validated for use in medically ill populations and examined in relationship to depressive symptoms (Koenig et al., 1992; Koenig, Al-Zaben, Khalifa, & Al Shohaib, 2014). This measure, called the Religious Coping Index (RCI), consists of the following items. First, the participant is asked an open-ended question on what enables her/him to cope with life stress. No mention of religion is made in order not to bias the participant (given concern over social desirability, i.e., that people often respond in ways they think the examiner wants them to). Whatever the person says in response to the open-ended coping question is then documented by the interviewer on the form. If the coping described is religious in nature, the item receives a score of 10; if not, the item receives a score of 0. In the second question, the participant rates on a 0–10 scale the extent to which religion is used to cope (where 0 = "not at all" and 10 = "the most important factor that keeps me going"). In the third question, the interviewer asks the participant how she/he uses religion to cope, encouraging specific details about the last time religion was used to cope and what the person did in this regard. The participant's response is then documented on the form, and the interviewer then rates the response on a 0–10 scale to indicate the extent to which the person relies on religion to cope. That judgment is made on how quick the participant responds to the question (vs. a delay that indicates the person is searching for a response), how detailed the response is, and how sincere and animated the person is in their response. The RCI, then, is a combination of both quantitative and qualitative questions, and total score ranges from 0 to 30. The downside is that it must be interviewer-administered (at least the last question).

The second way that religious coping is measured is by asking questions about specific ways that people use religion to deal with adversity (RCOPE). This method, developed by Ken Pargament, assesses both positive and negative ways that people use religion to cope. Although a variety of RCOPE measures exist, ranging from a 3-item version (Pargament, 1999) to a 100-item version (Pargament, Koenig, & Perez, 2000), the most common is the 14-item brief RCOPE that includes seven positive religious coping statements and seven negative religious coping statements (Pargament, Smith, Koenig, & Perez, 1998). The RCOPE has been used widely in hundreds of research studies (Ano & Vasconcelles, 2005; Pargament, Feuille, & Burdzy, 2011). Research using questions that assess general religious coping and more specific types of religious coping is now reviewed below.

Early Research

Based on a systematic review of research published in the first and second editions of the *Handbook of Religion and Health* (Koenig, McCullough, & Larson, 2001; Koenig, King, & Carson, 2012), rates of religious coping from studies conducted around the world are listed in Table 3.1. The research conducted prior to 2010 found that religious coping was most prevalent in the Middle East, Africa, and the Americas, and least prevalent in Northern Europe and East Asia. In the United States, based on 33 studies that provided prevalence rates (unpublished data), use of religion to cope was reported by 20%–80% depending on the geographical location, population (clinical vs. community), gender, race, and how the question was asked (spontaneous report vs. explicitly inquired about). The average percentage of those using religion to cope in those studies was 68.4% (standard deviation = 19.1, 95% confidence interval = 61.6%–75.1%). Thus, at least in the U.S., the majority of the population uses their religious faith to cope with life problems.

But, does religious coping really help? What is the relationship, then, with mental health? In the first edition of the *Handbook*, 110 studies were published in or prior to the year 2000; in the second edition, 344 studies were published between 2000 and 2010, yielding a total of 454 studies. The majority of these studies reported a positive relationship between reliance on religion to cope and better mental health, particularly for general religious coping and those measuring "positive" religious coping (as in the Pargament approach). Likewise, a majority of the studies examining "negative" religious coping (also called religious or spiritual struggles) found this type of coping associated with worse mental health.

TABLE 3.1 Rates of Religious Coping Around the World (excluding the United States)

Countries	Samples	Rates	Citations
CANADA AND AUSTRALIA			
Canada	Lung cancer patients	44%	Ginsburg, Quirt, and Ginsburg (1995)
Australia	Medical patients	56%	Parker and Brown (1982)
Australia	Psychiatric patients	67%	D'Souza (2002)
EUROPE			
Switzerland	Cancer patients	38%	Kesselring, Dodd, Lindsey, and Strauss (1986)
Switzerland	Medical patients and children	61%–73%	Landolt, Vollrath, and Ribi (2002)
Switzerland	Patients with schizophrenia	58%	Huguelet, Mohr, Borras, Gillieron, and Brand (2006)

(Continued)

TABLE 3.1 Rates of Religious Coping Around the World (excluding the United States) (Cont.)

Countries	Samples	Rates	Citations
Switzerland	Patients with schizophrenia	71%	Mohr, Brandt, Borras, Gillieron, and Huguelet (2006)
Germany	Patients with schizophrenia	0%	Conrad et al. (2007)
Germany	Older adults with dentures	29%	Heydecke, Tedesco, Kowalski, and Inglehart (2004)
Germany	Medical patients (ALS)	57%	Hecht et al. (2002)
United Kingdom	Relatives of terminally ill patients	43%	Walsh, King, Jones, Tookman, and Blizard (2002)
United Kingdom	College students	Low	Loewenthal, Cinnirella, Evdoka, and Murphy (2001)
United Kingdom	Young adults in community	Low	Maltby and Day (2004)
United Kingdom	Young adults in community	Low	Lewis et al. (2005)
Europe	Depressed adults in community	13%–18%	Angst et al. (2002)
NORTHERN EUROPE			
Sweden	Adults at risk for mental disorder	1%	Cederblad, Dahlin, and Hagnell (1995)
Sweden	GI cancer patients and spouses	Very low	Nordin, Wasteson, Hoffman, Glimelius, and Sjoden (2001)
Sweden	GI cancer patients	Very low	Wasteson, Nordin, Hoffman, Glimelius, and Sjoden (2002)
Sweden	Terminal brain cancer patients	10%	Strang and Strang (2001)
Norway	Terminal cancer patients	55%	Ringdal, Gotestam, Kaasa, Kvinnslaud, and Ringdal (1995)
EASTERN ASIA			
China	Caregivers of stroke patients	Very low	Qiu and Li (2008)
China (Taiwan)	Medical patients	75%	Tzeng and Yin (2008)

TABLE 3.1 Rates of Religious Coping Around the World (excluding the United States) (*Cont.*)

Countries	Samples	Rates	Citations
Central Asia			
India	Tibetan refugees (Buddhists)	>90%	Sachs, Rosenfeld, Lhewa, Rasmussen, and Keller (2008)
India	Caregivers of schizophrenia	50%	Rammohan, Rao, and Subbakrishna (2002)
Sri Lanka	Adults exposed to tsunami	53%	Hollifield et al. (2008)
Pakistan	Psychology students	84%	Khan and Watson (2006)
MIDDLE EAST			
United Arab Emirates	Parents of child with cancer	100%	Eapen, Revesz, and Revesz (2003)
Afghanistan	Community adults in war zone	98%	Scholte et al. (2004)
Egypt	Patients with cancer	92%	Kesselring et al. (1986)
Jordan	Medical students	66%–77%	Bataineh, Hijazi, and Hijleh (2006)
Jordan	Patients with schizophrenia	29%	Conrad et al. (2007)
Israel	Terminally ill patients and caregivers	Very low	Rokach, Matalon, Safarov, and Bercovitch (2007)
AFRICA			
Sudan	Sudan refugees in Australia	Very high	Schweitzer, Greenslade, and Kagee (2007)
South Africa	Families after divorce	51%	Greeff and Van Der Merwe (2004)
South Africa	Senior high and sociology students	64%	Peltzer (2002)
Morocco	Cancer patients (Muslim)	95%	Errihani et al. (2008)
SOUTH AMERICA			
Chile	Breast cancer patients	96%	Choumanova, Wanat, Barrett, and Koopman (2006)
Brazil	Young, 1st episode psychosis	Very high	Redko (2003)

Recent Research

Table 3.2 provides a sampling of more recent studies published since 2010. These were chosen to give the reader a sense of the breadth and range of this research across different illnesses and stressful life experiences. Not based on a systematic review (like the research reported prior to 2010), these studies were selected based on their quality (in the author's opinion). While an attempt has been made to provide a balance of studies reporting positive and negative associations, even this cursory review indicates that studies finding positive relationships with mental health published since 2010 far outnumbered those reporting negative relationships. This reflects the findings reported prior to 2010. Of course, the "file drawer phenomenon" remains a problem in that studies finding no association often do not get published.

The findings from studies listed in Table 3.2 indicate that religious coping is common in many diseases and stressful circumstances. A positive relationship between religious coping and mental health is especially likely among those with higher levels of religious commitment (Ellison, Bradshaw, Flannelly, & Galek, 2014). Religious interventions also appear to be more effective in relieving distress among more highly religious individuals (Koenig et al., 2015). Some studies have found that attachment to God moderates the relationship between stressful live events and psychological distress (Ellison, Bradshaw, Kuyel, & Marcum, 2012) and is generally associated with better mental health (Bradshaw, Ellison, & Marcum, 2010; Granqvist, 2014). In contrast, negative religious coping (religious struggles involving anger at or alienation from God) has been uniformly related to worse mental health in both early and more recent research.

Now back to the question of whether there is a threshold for religious coping above which it is significantly more effective in relieving distress (threshold hypothesis), or whether the relationship with mental health increases in magnitude gradually across the entire spectrum of religious coping (graded benefits hypothesis). When one examines the relationship between mental health and religious involvement (where religiosity is assessed with a "trait" measure rather than a "state" measure, as religious coping might be considered, see below), the evidence supports both the threshold hypothesis and the graded benefits hypothesis. For example, with regard to religious attendance and suicide, while the greatest benefits occur for those attending weekly or more often, there is also a "gradient of effect," such that there is a stepwise increase in the benefits of attendance that goes from no attendance up to weekly attendance or more (VanderWeele, Li, Tsai, & Kawachi, 2016). The inverse relationship between religious attendance and depression also shows a gradient of increasing effect from less than weekly attendance to weekly to more than weekly (Li, Okereke, Chang, Kawachi, & VanderWeele, 2016). With regard

TABLE 3.2 Recent Research on Religious Coping, Mental and Physical Health Since 2010

Circumstances	Locations	Authors/citations
Adverse life situations	USA	Burke, Neimeyer, McDevitt-Murphy, Ippolito, and Roberts (2011) (homicide)
	USA	Leaman and Gee (2012) (torture)
	USA	Hamilton, Sandelowski, Moore, Agarwal, and Koenig (2013)
	USA	Bradshaw, Ellison, Fang, and Mueller (2014)
	Zimbabwe	Mhizha (2014) (poverty)
Bereavement	USA	Burke et al. (2011)
	USA	Kelley and Chan (2012)
	USA	Boulware and Bui (2016)
Blood disorders	USA	Bediako et al. (2011)
	USA	Cotton, Grossoehme, & McGrady (2012)
	USA	Clayton-Jones, Haglund, Belknap, Schaefer, and Thompson (2016)
Cancer	Israel	Hasson-Ohayon, Goldzweig, Braun, and Galinsky (2010)
	USA	Trevino, Archambault, Schuster, Richardson, and Moye (2012)
	Greece	Kaliampos and Roussi (2015)
	—	Salsman et al. (2015)[a]
	USA	Hamilton, Worthy, Kurtz, Cudjoe, and Johnstone (2016)
Cancer surgery	USA	Biegler et al. (2012)
Caregiver burden	USA	Merritt and McCallum (2013)
	USA	Heo and Koeske (2013)
	USA	Rathier, Davis, Papandonatos, Grover, and Tremont (2015)
	USA	Pearce, Medoff, Lawrence, and Dixon (2016)
	USA	Koenig, Nelson, Shaw, Saxena, and Cohen (2016)
Chronic medical illness	USA	Assari (2014)
	—	Cummings and Pargament (2010)[a]
	Northern Israel	Keshet and Liberman (2013)
	USA	Reynolds, Mrug, Hensler, Guion, and Madan-Swain (2014)
	—	Reynolds et al. (2016)[a]

(Continued)

TABLE 3.2 Recent Research on Religious Coping, Mental and Physical Health Since 2010 (*Cont.*)

Circumstances	Locations	Authors/citations
Chronic mental disorder	Malaysia	Nurasikin et al. (2013)
	USA	Pearce et al. (2016)
Chronic pain	Belgium	Dezutter, Robertson, Luyckx, and Hutsebaut (2010)
	USA	Parenteau et al. (2011)
Diabetes	USA	Dzivakwe and Guarnaccia (2014)
	Nigeria	Amadi et al. (2016)
	Iran	Shamsalinia, Pourghaznein, and Parsa (2016)
Early life trauma	USA	Reinert, Campbell, Bandeen-Roche, Sharps, and Lee (2015)
End-of-life issues	USA	Vallurupalli et al. (2012)
	USA	Maciejewski et al. (2012)
Eating disorders	Israel	Latzer et al. (2014)
	USA	Rider, Terrell, Sisemore, and Hecht (2014)
	Lebanon	Doumit et al. (2017)
Heart/ cardiovascular	USA	Park, Sacco, and Edmondson (2012)
	USA	Ai, Hopp, Tice, & Koenig (2013)
	USA	Trevino and McConnell (2014)
HIV/AIDS	USA	Trevino et al. (2010)
	USA	Lee, Nezu, and Nezu (2014)
	USA	Kremer and Ironson (2014)
	USA	Kremer et al. (2014)
	USA	Henry, Ironson, Gonzalez, and Schneiderman (2014)
	USA	Ironson, Kremer, and Lucette (2016)
Inflammatory bowel disease	Brazil	Freitas et al. (2015)
Interpersonal violence	USA	Bryant-Davis and Wong (2013)
Kidney disease	Brazil	Ramirez et al. (2012)
	Iran	Saffari et al. (2013)
Loneliness	Israel	Rokach, Chin, and Sha'ked (2012)
Musculoskeletal disease	Brazil	Pizutti, Taborda, and Tourinho (2012)
	Poland	Stecz and Kocur (2015)

TABLE 3.2 Recent Research on Religious Coping, Mental and Physical Health Since 2010 (*Cont.*)

Circumstances	Locations	Authors/citations
Natural disasters	USA	Chan and Rhodes (2013)
	Pakistan	Feder et al. (2013)
	Chile	García et al. (2014)
	USA	Henslee et al. (2015)
Neurological disorders	Italy	Giaquinto, Sarno, Dall'Armi, and Spiridigliozzi (2010)
	Brazil	Tedrus, Fonseca, Magri, and Mendes (2013)
	Germany	Büssing et al. (2013)
	Iran	Rahnama et al. (2015)
Obesity	USA	Pirutinsky, Rosmarin, and Holt (2012)
Pregnancy/neonatal loss	USA	Cowchock, Lasker, Toedter, Skumanich, and Koenig (2010)
	USA	Hawthorne, Youngblut, and Brooten (2016)
Posttraumatic stress disorder	USA	Greenawalt et al. (2011)
	Pakistan	Feder et al. (2013)
	USA	Bryant-Davis et al. (2015)
	USA	Kopacz, Currier, Dresher, and Pigeon (2016)
Traumatic events	USA	Thomas and Savoy (2014)
Prison	France	Mandhouf, Aubin, Amirouche, Perroud, and Huguelet (2013)
	USA	Aday, Krabillb, and Deaton-Owensc (2014)
Psychosis/schizophrenia	USA	Nolan et al. (2012)
	USA	Rosmarin, Bigda-Peyton, Öngur, Pargament, and Björgvinsson (2013)
Pulmonary disease	USA	Green, Emery, Kozora, Diaz, and Make (2011)
	Denmark	Pedersen, Pargament, Pedersen, and Zachariae (2013)
	USA	Reynolds, Mrug, Britton, et al. (2014)
Racism	USA	Kim, Kendall, and Webb (2015)

(*Continued*)

TABLE 3.2 Recent Research on Religious Coping, Mental and Physical Health Since 2010 (*Cont.*)

Circumstances	Locations	Authors/citations
Secular society	China	Wang, Michaels, and Day (2011) (Autism)
	China	Zhang, Wang, Shi, Wang, and Zhang (2012) (Earthquake)
	Norway	Sørensen et al. (2012) (cancer)
	Denmark	Hvidtjorn, Hjelmborg, Skytthe, Christensen, and Hvidt (2014)
	Sweden	Granqvist and Moström (2014)
	Norway	Kvande, Klöckner, Moksnes, and Espnes (2015)
Substance abuse	USA	Martin, Ellingsen, Tzilos, and Rohsenow (2015)
Terrorism	Jerusalem	Ankri, Bachar, and Shalev (2010)
	Pakistan	Khan, Watson, and Chen, (2016)
Visual impairment	United Kingdom	Marqués-Brocksopp (2014)
	Iran	Abarghouei, Sorbi, Abarghouei, and Bidaki (2016)
War	Croatia	Mihaljević, Aukst-Margetić, Vuksan-Ćusa, Koić, and Milošević (2012)
	Palestine	Thabet, El Buhaisi, and Vostanis (2014)
	USA	Sterner and Jackson-Cherry (2015)
	USA	Tsai, E, Sledge, Southwick, and Pietrzak (2015)

[a] *Review of original research.*

to religious coping, however, the question of whether benefits are seen only above a certain threshold of devout religious coping or whether benefits are more graded depending on degree of religious coping has yet to be determined. The possibility that the relationship between religiosity and mental health is U-shaped has also been raised, such that those with very low religiosity and those with very high religiosity have the best mental health (King et al., 2007; Wei & Liu, 2013). Whether this is also true for religious coping is not known.

A consistent finding, however, is that relationships between religious coping and mental health are weaker (or even negative) in areas of the world that are more secular. This is especially true in regions where religious involvement is in disfavor, discouraged politically, or not supported by the majority of the populace. These regions tend to be East Asia (China, etc.), Northern Europe (Scandinavian countries), former communist countries in Eastern Europe, and to some extent Israel. As noted above, when religion is not supported within a society, people tend to turn to religion only when they become very desperate and have exhausted other coping resources. This dynamic, that is, turning to religion when in severe emotional or physical distress, creates an artificial positive correlation between religious coping and mental distress. This is true for cross-sectional studies and also to some extent for longitudinal studies where follow-up is relatively short (due to carryover effects) (Bekke-Hansen et al., 2014; Sørensen et al., 2012). In this case, even if religious coping is beneficial (as both qualitative and quantitative research suggests it is in religious areas of the world), such benefits may be hidden or disguised by such a dynamic in non-religious regions. Thus, religious involvement in secular populations ends up being a marker for mental distress, and beneficial effects are difficult to demonstrate without careful follow-up over long periods of time.

An analogy is found in studies of depression and antidepressant use. Not surprisingly, researchers usually find a positive correlation between antidepressant use and depressive symptoms. The reason is that these drugs are only used in persons with depression (not those who are mentally healthy and happy). The use of antidepressants in those with serious depression, then, creates an artificial positive correlation between antidepressant use and depressive symptoms. This doesn't mean that antidepressants cause depression. The same dynamics may be true for religious coping and emotional distress in secular countries.

There is some evidence to support this reasoning in Northern Europe. Consider a study that examined religious involvement and physical illness in a sample of 3000 young Danish twins (Hvidt, Hvidtjorn, Christensen, Nielsen, & Sondergaard, 2016). All religiosity measures were positively correlated with medical disease severity. The presence of life-threatening diseases and poor health was uniformly associated with belief in God, importance of God, praying to God, and finding strength and comfort in religion. One possibility is that these severe life-threatening diseases were *caused by* praying or depending on religion to cope (which frankly doesn't make much sense). A more likely explanation is that distressing physical illness leads to religious involvement in an attempt to cope with the health problem. Longitudinal data and randomized clinical trials, however, will be necessary to prove this hypothesis (VanderWeele, Jackson, & Li, 2016). Nevertheless, there is already some evidence (at least in religious populations) that cognitive–behavioral religious interventions in those with depression and chronic medical illness result in a reduction, not an increase, in depressive symptoms (Koenig et al., 2015). Perhaps reports of a positive relationship between religious coping and worse mental or physical health in secular areas of the world should be interpreted in this light. In religious countries, in contrast to secular ones, people are more likely to turn to religion before the emotional distress becomes too severe. Religious beliefs and practices may then help to prevent or lessen the progression of the distress, which is then easier to detect in cross-sectional and longitudinal studies.

When conducting research on religion and mental health, religious coping scales (including scales assessing private religious activities) should be considered "state" measures, where the particular situation or state may determine scores on these scales. In contrast, measures of religious attendance and intrinsic religiosity should be considered "trait" measures, since they are more stable and tend to reflect the religiousness of the person across time, rather than only during stressful circumstances. While state and trait measures of religious involvement are highly correlated, there is a much greater chance of detecting relationships between religion and mental health when using trait measures of religiosity.

While relationships have generally been positive between religious coping and mental health in religious areas of the world, religion may hinder coping efforts when religious beliefs conflict with behavior or lifestyle. For example, one early study found that frequency of religious attendance was associated with more depressive symptoms among unwed Catholic teenagers shortly after delivery (Sorenson, Grindstaff, & Turner, 1995). Other more recent studies have found that religiosity is associated with worse mental health in gay, homosexual, or bisexual populations (Meanley, Pingel, & Bauermeister, 2016; Watkins et al., 2016), although that finding is not always consistent (Dalmida, Koenig, Holstad, & Thomas, 2015; Walker & Longmire-Avital, 2013).

SUMMARY AND CONCLUSIONS

The use of religion to cope with difficult life situations is prevalent around the world. Both research prior to the year 2010 and more recent studies suggest that religious coping is often associated with better mental health. There are numerous reasons why, and some of those reasons have been described in this chapter. Level of religious commitment or attachment to God may influence the effectiveness of religious coping. Studies in secular areas of the world where religious beliefs and practices are uncommon or discouraged may report positive relationships between religious coping and mental distress or physical illness. The direction of causation in such reports needs further study, although at least in cases of physical illness, it is likely that the distress caused by the illness increases religious coping (not vice versa). In religious areas of the world, the threshold for religious coping is lower than in secular regions, and so religion may be turned to for comfort before distress becomes too severe, thus helping to resolve it more quickly. This is not always the case, however, depending on the particular population. Religious coping in populations where behaviors such as sexual practices conflict with religious beliefs is sometimes associated with worse mental health. Greater religiosity in those circumstances may result in psychological distress or strain.

References

Abarghouei, M., Sorbi, M. H., Abarghouei, M. R., & Bidaki, R. (2016). The relationship between religious coping strategies and happiness with meaning in life in blind people. *Global Journal of Health Science, 9*(1), 130.

Aday, R. H., Krabillb, J. J., & Deaton-Owensc, D. (2014). Religion in the lives of older women serving life in prison. *Journal of Women and Aging, 26*, 238–256.

Ai, A. L., Hopp, F., Tice, T. N., & Koenig, H. (2013). Existential relatedness in light of eudemonic well-being and religious coping among middle-aged and older cardiac patients. *Journal of Health Psychology, 18*(3), 368–382.

Amadi, K. U., Uwakwe, R., Odinka, P. C., Ndukuba, A. C., Muomah, C. R., & Ohaeri, J. U. (2016). Religion, coping and outcome in out-patients with depression or diabetes mellitus. *Acta Psychiatrica Scandinavica, 133*(6), 489–496.

Angst, J., Gamma, A., Gastpar, M., Lepine, J. P., Mendlewicz, J., & Tylee, A. (2002). Gender differences in depression: Epidemiological findings from the European DEPRES I and II studies. *European Archives of Psychiatry and Clinical Neurosciences, 252*, 201–209.

Ankri, Y. L., Bachar, E., & Shalev, A. Y. (2010). Reactions to terror attacks in ultra-Orthodox Jews: The cost of maintaining strict identity. *Psychiatry, 73*(2), 190–197.

Ano, G. G., & Vasconcelles, E. B. (2005). Religious coping and psychological adjustment to stress: A meta-analysis. *Journal of Clinical Psychology, 61*(4), 461–480.

Bataineh, Z. M., Hijazi, T. A., & Hijleh, M. F. (2006). Attitudes and reactions of Jordanian medical students to the dissecting room. *Surgical and Radiologic Anatomy, 28*(4), 416–421.

Bediako, S. M., Lattimer, L., Haywood, C., Jr., Ratanawongsa, N., Lanzkron, S., & Beach, M. C. (2011). Religious coping and hospital admissions among adults with sickle cell disease. *Journal of Behavioral Medicine, 34*(2), 120–127.

Beit-Hallahmi, B., & Argyle, M. (1997). *The psychology of religious behavior, belief and experience*. London and New York: Routledge.

Bekke-Hansen, S., Pedersen, C. G., Thygesen, K., Christensen, S., Waelde, L. C., & Zachariae, R. (2014). The role of religious faith, spirituality and existential considerations among heart patients in a secular society: Relation to depressive symptoms 6 months post acute coronary syndrome. *Journal of Health Psychology, 19*(6), 740–753.

Biegler, K., Cohen, L., Scott, S., Hitzhusen, K., Parker, P., Gilts, C. D., Canada, A., & Pisters, L. (2012). The role of religion and spirituality in psychological distress prior to surgery for urologic cancer. *Integrative Cancer Therapies, 11*(3), 212–220.

Blazer, D. G., Cohen, H. J., George, L. K., Koenig, H. G., & Verhey, A. (2011). Why John wasn't healed by prayer. *International Journal of Psychiatry in Medicine, 42*(4), 379–393.

Boulware, D. L., & Bui, N. H. (2016). Bereaved African American adults: the role of social support, religious coping, and continuing bonds. *Journal of Loss and Trauma, 21*(3), 192–202.

Bradshaw, M., Ellison, C. G., Fang, Q., & Mueller, C. (2014). Listening to religious music and mental health in later life. *The Gerontologist, 55*(6), 961–971.

Bradshaw, M., Ellison, C. G., & Marcum, J. P. (2010). Attachment to God, images of God, and psychological distress in a nationwide sample of Presbyterians. *International Journal for the Psychology of Religion, 20*(2), 130–147.

Bryant-Davis, T., Ullman, S., Tsong, Y., Anderson, G., Counts, P., Tillman, S., Bhang, C., & Gray, A. (2015). Healing pathways: Longitudinal effects of religious coping and social support on PTSD symptoms in African American sexual assault survivors. *Journal of Trauma and Dissociation, 16*(1), 114–128.

Bryant-Davis, T., & Wong, E. C. (2013). Faith to move mountains: Religious coping, spirituality, and interpersonal trauma recovery. *American Psychologist, 68*(8), 675–684.

Burke, L. A., Neimeyer, R. A., McDevitt-Murphy, M. E., Ippolito, M. R., & Roberts, J. M. (2011). Faith in the wake of homicide: Religious coping and bereavement distress in an African American sample. *International Journal for the Psychology of Religion, 21*(4), 289–307.

Büssing, A., Wirth, A. G., Humbroich, K., Gerbershagen, K., Schimrigk, S., Haupts, M., & Heusser, P. (2013). Faith as a resource in patients with multiple sclerosis is associated with a positive interpretation of illness and experience of gratitude/awe. *Evidence-Based Complementary and Alternative Medicine*, 128575. doi: 10.1155/2013/128575.

Carter, J. R., & Palihawadana, M. (2000). *The Dhammapada: The sayings of the Buddha (Oxford World's Classics)*. Oxford, UK: Oxford University Press.

Cederblad, M., Dahlin, L., Hagnell, O., et al. (1995). Coping with life span crises in a group at risk of mental and behavioral disorders: From the Lundby study. *Acta Psychiatrica Scandinavia, 91*, 322–330.

Chan, C. S., & Rhodes, J. E. (2013). Religious coping, posttraumatic stress, psychological distress, and posttraumatic growth among female survivors four years after Hurricane Katrina. *Journal of Traumatic Stress, 26*, 257–265.

Choumanova, I., Wanat, S., Barrett, R., & Koopman, C. (2006). Religion and spirituality in coping with breast cancer: Perspectives of Chilean women. *Breast Journal, 12*(4), 349–352.

Clayton-Jones, D., Haglund, K., Belknap, R. A., Schaefer, J., & Thompson, A. A. (2016). Spirituality and religiosity in adolescents living with sickle cell disease. *Western Journal of Nursing Research, 38*(6), 686–703.

Conrad, R., Schilling, G., Najjar, D., Geiser, F., Sharif, M., Liedtke, R., et al. (2007). Cross-cultural comparison of explanatory models of illness in schizophrenic patients in Jordan and Germany. *Psychological Reports, 101*(2), 531–546.

Cotton, S., Grossoehme, D., & McGrady, M. E. (2012). Religious coping and the use of prayer in children with sickle cell disease. *Pediatric Blood and Cancer, 58*(2), 244–249.

Cowchock, F. S., Lasker, J. N., Toedter, L. J., Skumanich, S. A., & Koenig, H. G. (2010). Religious beliefs affect grieving after pregnancy loss. *Journal of Religion and Health, 49*(4), 485–497.

Cummings, J. P., & Pargament, K. I. (2010). Medicine for the spirit: Religious coping in individuals with medical conditions. *Religions, 1*, 28–53.

Dalmida, S. G., Koenig, H. G., Holstad, M. M., & Thomas, T. L. (2015). Religious and psychosocial covariates of health-related quality of life in people living with HIV/AIDS. *HIV/AIDS Research and Treatment, 1*(1), 1–15.

Dezutter, J., Robertson, L. A., Luyckx, K., & Hutsebaut, D. (2010). Life satisfaction in chronic pain patients: The stress-buffering role of the centrality of religion. *Journal for the Scientific Study of Religion, 49*(3), 507–516.

Doumit, R., Khazen, G., Katsounari, I., Kazandjian, C., Long, J. A., & Zeeni, N. (2017). Investigating vulnerability for developing eating disorders in a multi-confessional population. Community Mental Health *Journal, 53*(1), 107–116.

D'Souza, R. (2002). Do patients expect psychiatrists to be interested in spiritual issues? *Australasian Psychiatry, 10*(1), 44–47.

Dzivakwe, V. G., & Guarnaccia, C. (2014). Religiosity as a coping resource for depression and disease management among older diabetic patients. *Annals of Behavioral Medicine, 47*(1 Supplement, A-055), s17.

Eapen, V., Revesz, T., & Revesz, T. (2003). Psychosocial correlates of paediatric cancer in the United Arab Emirates. *Supportive Care in Cancer, 11*(3), 185–189.

Ellis, A. (1980). *Case against religion: A psychotherapists view and the case against religiosity*. Austin, TX: American Atheist Press.

Ellison, C. G., Bradshaw, M., Flannelly, K. J., & Galek, K. C. (2014). Prayer, attachment to God, and symptoms of anxiety-related disorders among US adults. *Sociology of Religion, 75*(2), 208–233.

Ellison, C. G., Bradshaw, M., Kuyel, N., & Marcum, J. P. (2012). Attachment to God, stressful life events, and changes in psychological distress. *Review of Religious Research, 53*(4), 493–511.

Errihani, H., Mrabti, H., Boutayeb, S., El Ghissassi, I., El Mesbahi, O., Hammoudi, M., Chergui, H., & Riadi, A. (2008). Impact of cancer on Moslem patients in Morocco. *Psychooncology, 17*(1), 98–100.

Exline, J. J., Yali, A. M., & Sanderson, W. C. (2000). Guilt, discord, and alienation: The role of religious strain in depression and suicidality. *Journal of Clinical Psychology*, *56*(12), 1481–1496.

Feder, A., Ahmad, S., Lee, E. J., Morgan, J. E., Singh, R., Smith, B. W., Southwick, S. M., & Charney, D. S. (2013). Coping and PTSD symptoms in Pakistani earthquake survivors: Purpose in life, religious coping and social support. *Journal of Affective Disorders*, *147*(1), 156–163.

Frankl, T. (1997). *Man's search for meaning*. New York, NY: Poket books.

Freitas, T. H., Hyphantis, T. N., Andreoulakis, E., Quevedo, J., Miranda, H. L., Alves, G. S., Souza, M. H., Braga, L. L., Pargament, K. I., Soczynska, J. K., McIntyre, R. S., & Carvalho, A. F. (2015). Religious coping and its influence on psychological distress, medication adherence, and quality of life in inflammatory bowel disease. *Revista Brasileira de Psiquiatria*, *37*(3), 219–227.

Freud, S. (1927). Future of an illusion. In J. Strachey (Ed. and Trans.), Standard edition of the complete psychological works of Sigmund Freud. London: Hogarth Press, 1962.

García, F. E., Páez-Rovira, D., Zurtia, G. C., Martel, H. N., & Reyes, A. R. (2014). Religious coping, social support and subjective severity as predictors of posttraumatic growth in people affected by the earthquake in Chile on 27/2/2010. *Religions*, *5*(4), 1132–1145.

Giaquinto, S., Sarno, S., Dall'Armi, V., & Spiridigliozzi, C. (2010). Religious and spiritual beliefs in stroke rehabilitation. *Clinical and Experimental Hypertension*, *32*(6), 329–334.

Ginsburg, M. L., Quirt, C., Ginsburg, A. D., et al. (1995). Psychiatric illness and psychosocial concerns of patients with newly diagnosed lung cancer. *Canadian Medical Association Journal*, *152*, 701–708.

Gould, S. J. (1991). Exaptation: A crucial tool for an evolutionary psychology. *Journal of Social Issues*, *47*, 43–65 (see p. 58).

Granqvist, P. (2014). Mental health and religion from an attachment viewpoint: Overview with implications for future research. *Mental Health, Religion and Culture*, *17*(8), 777–793.

Granqvist, P., & Moström, J. (2014). There are plenty of atheists in foxholes: In Sweden. *Archive for the Psychology of Religion*, *36*(2), 199–213.

Greeff, A. P., & Van Der Merwe, S. (2004). Variables associated with resilience in divorced families. *Social Indicators Research*, *68*(1), 59–75.

Green, M. R., Emery, C. F., Kozora, E., Diaz, P. T., & Make, B. J. (2011). Religious and spiritual coping and quality of life among patients with emphysema in the national emphysema treatment trial. *Respiratory Care*, *56*(10), 1514–1521.

Greenawalt, D. S., Tsan, J. Y., Kimbrel, N. A., Meyer, E. C., Kruse, M. I., Tharp, D. F., Gulliver, S. B., & Morissette, S. B. (2011). Mental health treatment involvement and religious coping among African American, Hispanic, and white veterans of the wars of Iraq and Afghanistan. *Depression Research and Treatment* 2011:192186.

Hamilton, J. B., Sandelowski, M., Moore, A. D., Agarwal, M., & Koenig, H. G. (2013). "You need a song to bring you through": The use of religious songs to manage stressful life events. *The Gerontologist*, *53*(1), 26–38.

Hamilton, J. B., Worthy, V. C., Kurtz, M. J., Cudjoe, J., & Johnstone, P. A. (2016). Using religious songs as an integrative and complementary therapy for the management of psychological symptoms among African American cancer survivors. *Cancer Nursing* (Epub ahead of print).

Hasson-Ohayon, I., Goldzweig, G., Braun, M., & Galinsky, D. (2010). Women with advanced breast cancer and their spouses: Diversity of support and psychological distress. *Psycho-Oncology*, *19*(11), 1195–1204.

Hawthorne, D. M., Youngblut, J. M., & Brooten, D. (2016). Parent spirituality, grief, and mental health at 1 and 3 months after their infant's/child's death in an intensive care unit. *Journal of Pediatric Nursing*, *31*, 73–80.

Hecht, M., Hillemacher, T., Grasel, E., Tigges, S., Winterholler, M., Heuss, D., et al. (2002). Subjective experience and coping in ALS. *Amyotrophic Lateral Sclerosis and Other Motor Neuron Disorders*, *3*(4), 225–231.

Henry, S. M., Ironson, G., Gonzalez, B., & Schneiderman, N. (2014). Buffers of impact of bereavement or divorce on viral load in HIV: Role of religious coping and social support. *Annals of Behavioral Medicine*, *47*(1 Supplement, D-064), s260.

Henslee, A. M., Coffey, S. F., Schumacher, J. A., Tracy, M. H., Norris, F., & Galea, S. (2015). Religious coping and psychological and behavioral adjustment after Hurricane Katrina. *The Journal of Psychology*, *149*(6), 630–642.

Heo, G. J., & Koeske, G. (2013). The role of religious coping and race in Alzheimer's disease caregiving. *Journal of Applied Gerontology*, *32*(5), 582–604.

Heydecke, G., Tedesco, L. A., Kowalski, C., & Inglehart, M. R. (2004). Complete dentures and oral health-related quality of life: Do coping styles matter? *Community Dentistry and Oral Epidemiology*, *32*(4), 297–306.

Hollifield, M., Hewage, C., Gunawardena, C. N., Kodituwakku, P., Bopagoda, K., Weerarathnege, K., et al. (2008). Symptoms and coping in Sri Lanka 20–21 months after the 2004 tsunami. *British Journal of Psychiatry*, *192*(1), 39–44.

Huguelet, P., Mohr, S., Borras, L., Gillieron, C., & Brandt, P. -Y. (2006). Spirituality and religious practices among outpatients with schizophrenia and their clinicians. *Psychiatric Services*, *57*(3), 366–372.

Hvidt F N.C., Hvidtjorn, D., Christensen, K., Nielsen F J.B., & Sondergaard, J. (2016). Faith moves mountains—mountains move faith: Two opposite epidemiological forces in research on religion and health. *Journal of Religion and Health*, *56*(1), 294–304.

Hvidtjorn, D., Hjelmborg, J., Skytthe, A., Christensen, K., & Hvidt, N. C. (2014). Religiousness and religious coping in a secular society. *Journal of Religion and Health*, *53*, 1329–1341.

Ironson, G., Kremer, H., & Lucette, A. (2016). Relationship between spiritual coping and survival in patients with HIV. *Journal of General Internal Medicine* May 5, E-pub ahead of print.

Kaliampos, A., & Roussi, P. (2015). Religious beliefs, coping, and psychological well-being among Greek cancer patients. *Journal of Health Psychology* Nov 26, E-pub ahead of press.

Kelley, M. M., & Chan, K. T. (2012). Assessing the role of attachment to God, meaning, and religious coping as mediators in the grief experience. *Death Studies*, *36*(3), 199–227.

Keshet, Y., & Liberman, I. (2013). Coping with illness and threat: Why non-religious Jews choose to consult rabbis on healthcare issues. *Journal of Religion and Health*, *53*(4), 1146.

Kesselring, A., Dodd, M. J., Lindsey, A. M., & Strauss, A. L. (1986). Attitudes of patients living in Switzerland about cancer and its treatment. *Cancer Nursing*, *9*, 77–85.

Khan, Z. H., & Watson, P. J. (2006). Construction of the Pakistani Religious Coping Practices Scale: Correlations with religious coping, religious orientation, and reactions to stress among Muslim university students. *International Journal for the Psychology of Religion*, *16*(2), 101–112.

Khan, Z. H., Watson, P. J., & Chen, Z. (2016). Muslim spirituality, religious coping, and reactions to terrorism among Pakistani university students. *Journal of Religion and Health* E-pub ahead of press.

Kim, P. Y., Kendall, D. L., & Webb, M. (2015). Religious coping moderates the relation between racism and psychological well-being among Christian Asian American college students. *Journal of Counseling Psychology*, *62*(1), 87–94.

King, D. A., Lyness, J. M., Duberstein, P. R., He, H., Tu, X. M., & Seaburn, D. B. (2007). Religious involvement and depressive symptoms in primary care elders. *Psychological Medicine*, *37*(12), 1807–1815.

Koenig, H. G. (2002). An 83-year-old woman with chronic illness and strong religious beliefs. *Journal of the American Medical Association (JAMA)*, *288*(4), 487–493.

Koenig, H. G. (2016). *You are my beloved really?* Amazon: CreateSpace Publishing Platform.

Koenig, H. G., Al-Zaben, F., Khalifa, D. A., & Al Shohaib, S. (2014). Measures of religiosity. In G. J. Boyle, D. H. Saklofske, & G. Mathews (Eds.), *Measures of personality and social psychological constructs* (pp. 533–564). San Diego, CA: Academic Press (Elsevier) Chapter 19 (see pp. 538–539 for RCI).

Koenig, H. G., Cohen, H. J., Blazer, D. G., Pieper, C., Meador, K. G., Shelp, F., Goli, V., & DiPasquale, R. (1992). Religious coping and depression in elderly hospitalized medically ill men. *American Journal of Psychiatry, 149*, 1693–1700.

Koenig, H. G., King, D. E., & Carson, V. B. (2012). *Handbook of religion and health* (2nd ed.). New York, NY: Oxford University Press.

Koenig, H. G., McCullough, M. E., & Larson, D. B. (2001). *Handbook of religion and health* (1st ed.). New York, NY: Oxford University Press.

Koenig, H. G., Nelson, B., Shaw, S. F., Saxena, S., & Cohen, H. J. (2016). Religious involvement and adaptation in female family caregivers. *Journal of the American Geriatric Society, 64*(3), 578–583.

Koenig, H. G., Pearce, M. J., Nelson, B., Shaw, S. F., Robins, C. J., Daher, N., Cohen, H. J., Berk, L. S., Belinger, D., Pargament, K. I., Rosmarin, D. H., Vasegh, S., Kristeller, J., Juthani, N., Nies, D., & King, M. B. (2015). Religious vs. conventional cognitive-behavioral therapy for major depression in persons with chronic medical illness. *Journal of Nervous and Mental Disease, 203*(4), 243–251.

Kopacz, M. S., Currier, J. M., Dresher, K. D., & Pigeon, W. R. (2016). Suicidal behavior and spiritual functioning in a sample of Veterans diagnosed with PTSD. *Journal of Injury and Violence Research, 8*(1), 6–14.

Kremer, H., & Ironson, G. (2014). Longitudinal spiritual coping with trauma in people with HIV: Implications for health care. *AIDS Patient Care and STDs, 28*(3), 144–154.

Kremer, H., Ironson, G., Kaplan, L., Stuetzele, R., Baker, N., & Fletcher, M. A. (2014). Spiritual coping predicts CD4-cell preservation and undetectable viral load over four years. *AIDS Care, 27*(1), 71–79.

Kvande, M. N., Klöckner, C. A., Moksnes, U. K., & Espnes, G. A. (2015). Do optimism and pessimism mediate the relationship between religious coping and existential well-being? Examining mechanisms in a Norwegian population sample. *International Journal for the Psychology of Religion, 25*(2), 130–151.

Landolt, M. A., Vollrath, M., & Ribi, K. (2002). Predictors of coping strategy selection in paediatric patients. *Acta Paediatrica, 91*, 954–960.

Latzer, Y., Weinberger-Litman, S. L., Gerson, B., Rosch, A., Mischel, R., Hinden, T., Kilstein, J., & Silver, J. (2014). Negative religious coping predicts disordered eating pathology among Orthodox Jewish adolescent girls. *Journal of Religion and Health, 54*(5), 1760–1771.

Leaman, S. C., & Gee, C. B. (2012). Religious coping and risk factors for psychological distress among African torture survivors. *Psychological Trauma, 4*(5), 457–465.

Lee, M., Nezu, A. M., & Nezu, C. M. (2014). Positive and negative religious coping, depressive symptoms, and quality of life in people with HIV. *Journal of Behavioral Medicine, 37*(5), 921–930.

Lewis, C. A., Maltby, J., & Day, L. (2005). Religious orientation, religious coping and happiness among UK adults. *Personality and Individual Differences, 38*(5), 1193–1202.

Li, S., Okereke, O. I., Chang, S. C., Kawachi, I., & VanderWeele, T. J. (2016). Religious service attendance and lower depression among women: A prospective cohort study. *Annals of Behavioral Medicine, 50*(6), 876–884.

Loewenthal, K. M., Cinnirella, M., Evdoka, G., & Murphy, P. (2001). Faith conquers all? Beliefs about the role of religious factors in coping with depression among different cultural-religious groups in the UK. *British Journal of Medical Psychology, 74*(3), 293–303.

Maciejewski, P. K., Phelps, A. C., Kacel, E. L., Balboni, T. A., Balboni, M., Wright, A. A., Pirl, W., & Prigerson, H. G. (2012). Religious coping and behavioral disengagement: Opposing influences on advance care planning and receipt of intensive care near death. *Psycho-Oncology, 21*(7), 714–723.

Maltby, J., & Day, L. (2004). Should never the twain meet? Integrating models of religious personality and religious mental health. *Personality and Individual Differences, 36*(6), 1275–1290.

Mandhouf, O., Aubin, H. J., Amirouche, A., Perroud, N. A., & Huguelet, P. (2013). Spirituality and religion among French prisoners: An effective coping resource? *International Journal of Offender Therapy and Comparative Criminology*, *58*(7), 821–834.

Marquès-Brocksopp, L. (2014). Mindfulness, spiritual well-being, and visual impairment: An exploratory study. *British Journal of Visual Impairment*, *32*(2), 108–123.

Martin, R. A., Ellingsen, V. J., Tzilos, G. K., & Rohsenow, D. J. (2015). General and religious coping predict drinking outcomes for alcohol dependent adults in treatment. *American Journal on Addictions*, *24*(3), 240–245.

Meanley, S., Pingel, E. S., & Bauermeister, J. A. (2016). Psychological well-being among religious and spiritual identified young gay and bisexual men. *Sexuality Research and Social Policy*, *13*(1), 35–45.

Merritt, M. M., & McCallum, T. J. (2013). Too much of a good thing? Positive religious coping predicts worse diurnal salivary cortisol patterns for overwhelmed African American female dementia family caregivers. *American Journal of Geriatric Psychiatry*, *21*(1), 46–56.

Mhizha, S. (2014). Religious self-beliefs and coping among vending adolescents in Harare [Zimbabwe]. *Journal of Religion and Health*, *53*, 1487–1497.

Mihaljević, S., Aukst-Margetić, B., Vuksan-Ćusa, B., Koić, E., & Milošević, M. (2012). Hopelessness, suicidality and religious coping in Croatian war veterans with PTSD. *Psychiatria Danubina*, *24*(3), 292–297.

Mohr, S., Brandt, P. Y., Borras, L., Gillieron, C., & Huguelet, P. (2006). Toward an integration of spirituality and religiousness into the psychosocial dimension of schizophrenia. *American Journal of Psychiatry*, *163*(11), 1952–1959.

Nolan, J. A., McEvoy, J. P., Koenig, H. G., Hooten, E. G., Whetten, K., & Pieper, C. F. (2012). Religious coping and quality of life among individuals living with schizophrenia. *Psychiatric Services*, *63*(10), 1051–1054.

Nordin, K., Wasteson, E., Hoffman, K., Glimelius, B., & Sjoden, P. -O. (2001). Discrepancies between attainment and importance of life values and anxiety and depression in gastrointestinal cancer patients and their spouses. *Psycho-Oncology*, *10*(6), 479–489.

Nurasikin, M. S., Khatijah, L. A., Aini, A., Ramli, M., Aida, S. A., Zainal, N. Z., & Ng, C. G. (2013). Religiousness, religious coping methods and distress level among psychiatric patients in Malaysia. *International Journal of Social Psychiatry*, *59*(4), 332–338.

Pals, D. L. (1996). *Seven theories of religion*. Oxford; New York, NY: Oxford University Press.

Parenteau, S. C., Hamilton, N. A., Wu, W., Latinis, K., Waxenberg, L. B., & Brinkmeyer, M. Y. (2011). The mediating role of secular coping strategies in the relationship between religious appraisals and adjustment to chronic pain: The middle road to Damascus. *Social Indicators Research*, *104*(3), 407–425.

Pargament, K., Feuille, M., & Burdzy, D. (2011). The Brief RCOPE: Current psychometric status of a short measure of religious coping. *Religions*, *2*(1), 51–76.

Pargament, K. I. (1999). Religious/spiritual coping. *Multidimensional measurement of religiousness/spirituality for use in health research*. Kalamazoo, MI: A Report of the Fetzer Institute/National Institute on Aging Working Group (pp. 43–56).

Pargament, K. I., Koenig, H. G., & Perez, L. M. (2000). Comprehensive measure of religious coping: Development and initial validation of the RCOPE. *Journal of Clinical Psychology*, *56*, 519–543.

Pargament, K. I., Smith, B. W., Koenig, H. G., & Perez, L. (1998). Patterns of positive and negative religious coping with major life stressors. *Journal for the Scientific Study of Religion*, *37*(4), 710–724.

Park, C. L., Sacco, S. J., & Edmondson, D. (2012). Expanding coping goodness-of-fit: Religious coping, health locus of control, and depressed affect in heart failure patients. *Anxiety, Stress and Coping*, *25*(2), 137–153.

Parker, G. B., & Brown, L. B. (1982). Coping behaviors that mediate between life events and depression. *Archives of General Psychiatry*, *39*, 1386–1391.

Pearce, M. J., Medoff, D., Lawrence, R. E., & Dixon, L. (2016). Religious coping among adults caring for family members with serious mental illness. *Community Mental Health Journal, 52*(2), 194–202.

Pedersen, H. F., Pargament, K. I., Pedersen, C. G., & Zachariae, R. (2013). Religious coping and quality of life among severely ill lung patients in a secular society. *International Journal for the Psychology of Religion, 23*(3), 188–203.

Peltzer, K. (2002). Religiosity, religious coping and health behavior among Black students in South Africa. *Studia Psychologica, 44*(1), 75–83.

Pirutinsky, S., Rosmarin, D. H., & Holt, C. L. (2012). Religious coping moderates the relationship between emotional functioning and obesity. *Health Psychology, 31*, 394–397.

Pizutti, L. T., Taborda, J. G., & Tourinho, T. F. (2012). Evaluation of religious spiritual coping in patients with fibromyalgia syndrome: A case-controlled study. *Journal of Musculoskeletal Pain, 20*(3), 194–201.

Qiu, Y., & Li, S. (2008). Stroke: Coping strategies and depression among Chinese caregivers of survivors during hospitalisation. *Journal of Clinical Nursing, 17*(12), 1563–1573.

Rahnama, P., Javidan, A. N., Saberi, H., Montazeri, A., Tavakkoli, S., Pakpour, A. H., & Hajiaghababaei, M. (2015). Does religious coping and spirituality have a moderating role on depression and anxiety in patients with spinal cord injury: A study from Iran. *Spinal Cord, 53*(12), 870–874.

Ramirez, S. P., Macêdo, D. S., Sales, P. M. G., Figueiredo, S. M., Daher, E. F., Araújo, S. M., Pargament, K. I., Hyphantis, T. N., & Carvalho, A. F. (2012). The relationship between religious coping, psychological distress and quality of life in hemodialysis patients. *Journal of Psychosomatic Research, 72*(2), 129–135.

Rammohan, A., Rao, K., & Subbakrishna, D. (2002). Religious coping and psychological wellbeing in careers of relatives with schizophrenia. *Acta Psychiatrica Scandinavica, 105*(5), 356–362.

Rathier, L. A., Davis, J. D., Papandonatos, G. D., Grover, C., & Tremont, G. (2015). Religious coping in caregivers of family members with dementia. *Journal of Applied Gerontology, 34*(8), 977–1000.

Redko, C. (2003). Religious construction of a first episode of psychosis in urban Brazil. *Transcultural Psychiatry, 40*(4), 507–530.

Reinert, K. G., Campbell, J. C., Bandeen-Roche, K., Sharps, P., & Lee, J. (2015). Gender and race variations in the intersection of religious involvement, early trauma, and adult health. *Journal of Nursing Scholarship, 47*(4), 318–327.

Reynolds, N., Mrug, S., Britton, L., Guion, K., Wolfe, K., & Gutierrez, H. (2014a). Spiritual coping predicts 5-year health outcomes in adolescents with cystic fibrosis. *Journal of Cystic Fibrosis, 13*(5), 593–600.

Reynolds, N., Mrug, S., Hensler, M., Guion, K., & Madan-Swain, A. (2014b). Spiritual coping and adjustment in adolescents with chronic illness: A 2-year prospective study. *Journal of Pediatric Psychology, 39*(5), 542–551.

Reynolds, N., Mrug, S., Wolfe, K., Schwebel, D., & Wallander, J. (2016). Spiritual coping, psychosocial adjustment, and physical health in youth with chronic illness: A meta-analytic review. *Health Psychology Review* March 22, E-pub ahead of press.

Rider, K. A., Terrell, D. J., Sisemore, T. A., & Hecht, J. E. (2014). Religious coping style as a predictor of the severity of anorectic symptomotology. *Eating Disorders, 22*(2), 163–179.

Ringdal, G., Gotestam, K., Kaasa, S., Kvinnslaud, S., & Ringdal, K. (1995). Prognostic factors and survival in a heterogeneous sample of cancer patients. *British Journal of Cancer, 73*, 1594–1599.

Rokach, A., Chin, J., & Sha'ked, A. (2012). Religiosity and coping with loneliness. *Psychological Reports, 110*(3), 731–742.

Rokach, A., Matalon, R., Safarov, A., & Bercovitch, M. (2007). The dying, those who care for them, and how they cope with loneliness. *American Journal of Hospice and Palliative Care, 24*(5), 399–407.

Rosmarin, D. H., Bigda-Peyton, J. S., Öngur, D., Pargament, K. I., & Björgvinsson, T. (2013). Religious coping among psychotic patients: Relevance to suicidality and treatment outcomes. *Psychiatry Research, 210*(1), 182–187.

Sachs, E., Rosenfeld, B., Lhewa, D., Rasmussen, A., & Keller, A. (2008). Entering exile: Trauma, mental health, and coping among Tibetan refugees arriving in Dharamsala, India. *Journal of Traumatic Stress, 21*(2), 199–208.

Saffari, M., Pakpour, A. H., Naderi, M. K., Koenig, H. G., Baldacchino, D. R., & Piper, C. N. (2013). Spiritual coping, religiosity and quality of life: A study on Muslim patients undergoing haemodialysis. *Nephrology, 18*(4), 269–275.

Salekin, R. T. (2002). Psychopathy and therapeutic pessimism: Clinical lore or clinical reality? *Clinical Psychology Review, 22*, 79–112.

Salsman, J. M., Nunoz, A. R., Pustejovsky, J. E., Jim, H. S., Park, C. L., Danhauer, S. C., Sherman, A. C., Goerge, L., Merluzzi, T. V., & Fitchett, G. (2015). A meta-analytic approach to examining the correlation between religion/spirituality and mental health in cancer. *Cancer, 121*(21), 3769–3778.

Scholte, W. F., Olff, M., Ventevogel, P., de Vries, G. -J., Jansveld, E., Lopes Cardozo, B., et al. (2004). Mental health symptoms following war and repression in Eastern Afghanistan. *Journal of the American Medical Association, 292*(5), 585–593.

Schweitzer, R., Greenslade, J., & Kagee, A. (2007). Coping and resilience in refugees from the Sudan: A narrative account. *Australian and New Zealand Journal of Psychiatry, 41*(3), 282–288.

Shalev, BA. (2002). *100 years of Nobel prizes*. Los Angeles, CA: Americas Group.

Shamsalinia, A., Pourghaznein, T., & Parsa, M. (2016). The relationship between hope and religious coping among patients with type II diabetes. *Global Journal of Health Science, 8*(1), 208–216.

Sorenson, A. M., Grindstaff, C. F., & Turner, R. J. (1995). Religious involvement among unmarried adolescent mothers: A source of emotional support? *Sociology of Religion, 56*, 71–81.

Sørensen, T., Dahl, A. A., Fosså, S. D., Holmen, J., Lien, L., & Danbolt, L. J. (2012). Is "Seeking God's Help" associated with life satisfaction and disease-specific quality of life in cancer patients? The HUNT Study. *Archive for the Psychology of Religion, 34*(2), 191–213.

Stecz, P., & Kocur, J. (2015). Religiousness, religious coping with illness, and psychological function among polish elderly patients with osteoarthritis undergoing arthroplasty. *Journal of Religion and Health, 54*(2), 554–570.

Sterner, W. R., & Jackson-Cherry, L. R. (2015). The influence of spirituality and religion on coping for combat-deployed military personnel. *Counseling and Values, 60*(1), 48–66.

Strang, S., & Strang, P. (2001). Spiritual thoughts, coping and "sense of coherence" in brain tumour patients and their spouses. *Palliative Medicine, 15*(2), 127–134.

Tedrus, G. M. A. S., Fonseca, L. C., Magri, F. D. P., & Mendes, P. H. M. (2013). Spiritual/ religious coping in patients with epilepsy: Relationship with sociodemographic and clinical aspects and quality of life. *Epilepsy and Behavior, 28*(3), 386–390.

Thabet, A., El Buhaisi, O., & Vostanis, P. (2014). Trauma, PTSD, anxiety, and coping strategies among Palestinians adolescents exposed to war on Gaza. *Arab Journal of Psychiatry, 25*(1), 71–82.

Thera, N. (1993). Dhammacakkappavattana Sutta: Setting Rolling the Wheel of Truth. Translated from sutta 11, chapter 56, of the Pali Canon's Samyutta Nikāya. Available from http://www.accesstoinsight.org/tipitaka/sn/sn56/sn56.011.nymo.html.

Thomas, E., & Savoy, S. (2014). Relationships between traumatic events, religious coping style, and posttraumatic outcomes. *Traumatology: An International Journal, 20*(2), 84–90.

Trevino, K. M., Archambault, E., Schuster, J., Richardson, P., & Moye, J. (2012). Religious coping and psychological distress in military veteran cancer survivors. *Journal of Religion and Health, 51*(1), 87–98.

Trevino, K. M., & McConnell, T. R. (2014). Religiosity and religious coping in patients with cardiovascular disease: Change over time and associations with illness adjustment. *Journal of Religion and Health, 53*(6), 1907–1917.
Trevino, K. M., Pargament, K. I., Cotton, S., Leonard, A. C., Hahn, J., Caprini-Faigin, C. A., & Tsevat, J. (2010). Religious coping and physiological, psychological, social, and spiritual outcomes in patients with HIV/AIDS: Cross-sectional and longitudinal findings. *AIDS and Behavior, 14*(2), 379–389.
Tsai, J., El-Gabalawy, Sledge, W. H., Southwick, S. M., & Pietrzak, R. H. (2015). Post-traumatic growth among veterans in the USA: Results from the National Health and Resilience in Veterans Study. *Psychological Medicine, 45*, 165–179.
Tzeng, H. M., & Yin, C. Y. (2008). Religious activities of inpatients and their family visitors in Taiwan. *Journal of Holistic Nursing, 26*(2), 98–106.
Vallurupalli, M. M., Lauderdale, M. K., Balboni, M. J., Phelps, A. C., Block, S. D., Ng, A. K., Kachnic, L. A., Vanderweele, T. J., & Balboni, T. A. (2012). The role of spirituality and religious coping in the quality of life of patients with advanced cancer receiving palliative radiation therapy. *Journal of Supportive Oncology, 10*(2), 81–87.
VanderWeele, T. J., Jackson, J. W., & Li, S. (2016a). Causal inference and longitudinal data: A case study of religion and mental health. *Social Psychiatry and Psychiatric Epidemiology, 51*(11), 1457–1466.
VanderWeele, T. J., Li, S., Tsai, A. C., & Kawachi, I. (2016b). Association between religious service attendance and lower suicide rates among US women. *JAMA Psychiatry, 73*(8), 845–851.
Walker, J. N. J., & Longmire-Avital, B. (2013). The impact of religious faith and internalized homonegativity on resiliency for black lesbian, gay, and bisexual emerging adults. *Developmental Psychology, 49*(9), 1723–1731.
Wall, T. D., Wygant, D. B., & Sellbom, M. (2015). Boldness explains a key difference between psychopathy and antisocial personality disorder. *Psychiatry, Psychology and Law, 22*, 94–105.
Walsh, K., King, M. B., Jones, L., Tookman, A., & Blizard, R. (2002). Spiritual beliefs may affect outcome of bereavement: Prospective study. *British Medical Journal, 324*(7353), 1551.
Wang, P., Michaels, C. A., & Day, M. S. (2011). Stresses and coping strategies of Chinese families with children with autism and other developmental disabilities. *Journal of Autism and Developmental Disorders, 41*(6), 783–795.
Wasteson, E., Nordin, K., Hoffman, K., Glimelius, B., & Sjoden, P. O. (2002). Daily assessment of coping in patients with gastrointestinal cancer. *Psycho-Oncology, 11*(1), 1–11.
Watkins, T. L., Simpson, C., Cofield, S. S., Davies, S., Kohler, C., & Usdan, S. (2016). The relationship of religiosity, spirituality, substance abuse, and depression among black men who have sex with men (MSM). *Journal of Religion and Health, 55*, 255–268.
Weaver, A. J. (1995). Has there been a failure to prepare and support-based clergy in their role as front-line community mental health workers? A review. *Journal of Pastoral Care, 49*, 129–149.
Wei, D., & Liu, E. Y. (2013). Religious involvement and depression: Evidence for curvilinear and stress-moderating effects among young women in rural China. *Journal for the Scientific Study of Religion, 52*(2), 349–367.
Zhang, Z., Wang, W., Shi, Z., Wang, L., & Zhang, J. (2012). Mental health problems among the survivors in the hard-hit areas of the Yushu earthquake. *PLoS One, 7*(10), e46449.

Further Reading

Assari, S. (2014). Chronic medical conditions and major depressive disorder: Differential role of positive religious coping among African Americans, Caribbean Blacks and Non-Hispanic Whites. *International Journal of Preventive Medicine, 5*(4), 405.

CHAPTER

4

Negative Emotions and Behaviors

This chapter provides the core of the evidence that makes religion relevant to the clinical setting. "Negative emotions" include feelings of depression, loss of interest, anxiety/fear, hopelessness, and loss of peace. "Negative behaviors" discussed here refer to misuse of alcohol, use of illicit drugs, and antisocial behaviors such as delinquency and crime. Such feelings and behaviors usually exist on a spectrum from mild to severe. When they reach a certain threshold where a person's social, occupational, or recreational functioning is adversely affected, then a "disorder" is said to be present. Mental disorders usually require some level of professional help to improve feelings or behaviors so that the person can once again function. Can knowledge about the religious beliefs of clients or possibly even the use of religiously-integrated interventions help clinicians care for those with clinical disorders of this type?

Discussed here are relationships between religious involvement and negative emotional symptoms that may indicate the presence of disorders such as depression, suicide, anxiety and traumatic stress, or substance use/abuse, as well as antisocial behaviors such as delinquent and criminal activities. In discussing each of these categories, the author will first present the results of a systematic review of the quantitative research literature conducted from the late 19th century up through 2010 (Koenig et al., 2001, 2012), and then discuss a number of high quality studies selected from the research literature between 2010 and 2017 to illustrate more recent findings. By "high quality," this means better research design (prospective vs. cross-sectional), larger sample size, and better statistical methods with more rigorous controls, often reflected in the quality of the journal in which the study has been published (indicated by the journal's impact factor).

Religion and Mental Health. http://dx.doi.org/10.1016/B978-0-12-811282-3.00004-5

DEPRESSION

Depression is among the most common and disabling of emotional disorders, and is by far the most common mental condition that people seek professional help for (from mental health specialists, primary care physicians, or clergy). By 2020, according to a study by the World Health Organization and Harvard School of Public Health, major depressive disorder is expected to be the world's second most debilitating illness based on "years of life lived with disability" (Murray & Lopez, 1996). Only cardiovascular disease will cause more disability. In the United States, up to one-quarter of all women and one of 10 men have met criteria for a major depressive episode (MDE) at some time in their lives, and 7% of Americans suffered from a MDE within the past 12 months (Kessler et al., 2003). The global point prevalence of major depression, after adjusting for methodological differences, has been reported to be 5%, with an annual incidence of 3% (Ferrari et al., 2013). Rates of depressive disorder are even higher among those with physical health problems requiring hospitalization, with point prevalence rates exceeding 40% depending on diagnostic method (Koenig et al., 1997). As religious beliefs and practices are often used to cope with difficult life situations including physical illness, it should not be surprising that religious involvement is related to depressive symptoms and depressive disorder.

In our systematic review of quantitative studies published prior to 2010 that examined religiosity/spirituality (R/S) and depressive disorder or symptoms, 61% (271 of 443) reported inverse relationships (including nine studies at a statistical trend level). In contrast, only 6% (28 of 443) found positive relationships between R/S and depression (including two studies at a trend level). Of 178 studies with the best methodology, 68% (119/178) reported inverse relationships between R/S and depression, whereas 7% (13/178) found positive relationships. Among the 28 clinical trial or experimental studies that examined R/S interventions for depression, 61% (17/28) reported benefits significantly greater than standard treatment or control conditions, whereas 2 studies (7%) found that R/S interventions were less effective (one of the two showing a trend in that direction only).

Smith and McCullough (2003) conducted an independent review of research on R/S and depression, identifying 147 studies involving 98,975 subjects. The average correlation between R/S and depression was −0.10, although among stressed populations, it was 50% stronger ($r = -0.15$). Although small, this effect is similar to that of gender (where depression is twice as common in women as in men). Furthermore, in a review of studies published in the top 25% of psychiatry and neurology journals based on the 2010 ISI journal citation index, Bonelli and Koenig (2013) found that 78.9% (15 of 19 studies) reported a significant inverse

TABLE 4.1 Number of Studies and Relationship Between Religious or Spiritual Involvement and Negative Emotional/Behavioral States in Different Religions

	Depression	Suicide	Anxiety	Substance use/abuse	
				Alcohol	Drugs
Number of studies					
Christians[a]	416	125	245	268	181
Jews	6	2	14	0	0
Muslims	13	8	22	6	6
Hindus	2	2	6	0	0
Buddhists	1	4[b]	3	1	—

Findings of studies

	Depression		Suicide		Anxiety		Substance use/abuse			
							Alcohol		Drugs	
	%P	%N	%P	%N	%P	%N	%P	%N	%P	%N
Christians	61	6	79	2	49	10	87	1	85	1
Jews	50	17	100	0	50	21	—	—	—	—
Muslims	92	0	75	0	68	5	100	0	100	0
Hindus	50	0	50	0	33	17	—	—	—	—
Buddhists	0	0	0	25	100	0	100	0	—	—

Based on systematic review of research published prior to 2010.
%P, percent positive studies (i.e., religiosity/spirituality related to *less* symptoms or disorder); *%N*, percent negative studies (i.e., religiosity/spirituality related to *more* symptoms or disorder).
[a] *By Christians, this means that the majority of the study sample was Christian; similar for other religions as well (i.e., majority).*
[b] *All four studies were conducted in China.*
Source: Koenig, H. G., McCollough, M. E., Larson, D. B. (2001). *Handbook of religion and health* (1st ed.). New York, NY: Oxford University Press and Koenig, H. G., King, D. E., Carson, V. B. (2012). *Handbook of religion and health* (2nd ed.). New York, NY: Oxford University Press.

relationship between religiosity and depression up through 2010. Thus, the majority of studies—particularly those published in high quality peer-review journals—found lower rates of depression among those who were more R/S or reported that a religious intervention significantly reduced depressive symptoms compared to an active control condition or standard care (see Table 4.1 for a breakdown of results by religion).

Since 2010, many studies—some with improved methodology over earlier ones—have now examined the relationship between R/S and depression. The following is a selective review of such studies that will give the reader a sense of the findings now being reported. In a 10-year prospective study of 114 adult offspring of depressed and nondepressed parents, Miller et al. (2012) from Columbia University in New York City examined the relationship between R/S and major depression at follow-up. After controlling for gender, age, history of depression, and risk status (based on parental depression), those who indicated that R/S was "very important" were 73% less likely to be depressed compared to those who indicated that religion was only somewhat important or not important at all (OR = 0.27, 95% CI = 0.07–1.08, p = 0.06). In high risk participants due to parental depression, those indicating at baseline that R/S was very important were 90% less likely to experience depression (adjusted OR = 0.10, 95% CI = 0.01–0.92, $p < 0.05$). This research group later reported the results of structural MRI scans of the brains of participants at high risk for depression. MRI results showed significant thinning of the cerebral cortex in multiple areas among those for whom R/S was only somewhat or not at all important compared to those indicating that R/S was very important; similar findings were found for religious attendance, although the effect lost significance after controlling for multiple comparisons (Miller et al., 2014).

Most studies find weaker relationships between religiosity and depression in Europe and other secular areas of the world (compared to more religious areas such as the United States or Middle East). In nonreligious regions of the world, as noted in chapter 3, religious involvement often serves as a marker for psychological distress because individuals do not turn to religion until symptoms are severe and other attempts to relieve symptoms have failed. This is because there is very little support for R/S in secular social environments. Despite this tendency, however, several observational studies in Europe have reported inverse relationships. For example, in a 4-year prospective study of 9068 persons aged 50 years or older participating in the Survey of Health, Ageing and Retirement in Europe (SHARE), Croezen et al. (2015) examined the relationship between various forms of social activity and depressive symptoms. Participants were asked if they engaged in (1) voluntary or charity work; (2) educational or training courses; (3) sports, social club, or other kinds of club activities; (4) religious organizations; and (5) political or community organizations. After controlling for education, region, marital status, household size, employment status, financial status, self-rated health, long-term health problems, activities of daily living, and physician-diagnosed illnesses, only participation in religious activities predicted a decrease in depressive symptoms over time ($B = -0.190$, 95% CI = −0.365 to −0.016). In contrast, participation in political or community organizations actually predicted an *increase* in depressive symptoms ($B = 0.222$, 95% CI = 0.018–0.428). Only 10% of participants in this study, however, were engaged in religious activities.

A question has been raised about "direction of effect" in studies of R/S and depression. This is particularly true when R/S is assessed by attendance at religious services. There is evidence from longitudinal studies that depression itself may reduce the likelihood of attending religious services due to the effect on energy, motivation, and interest in social activity (Maselko et al., 2012). However, in the largest and best designed study to date, Li, Okereke, Chang, Kawachi, and VanderWeele (2016) from the Harvard School of Public Health followed close to 50,000 participants in the Nurses' Health Study for 12 years. They found that while depression indeed predicted a reduction in religious attendance, religious attendance also predicted a reduction in depressive symptoms. They concluded that a bidirectional effect between religious attendance and depression likely exists; depression predicted a reduction in religious attendance by 26%, and religious attendance predicted a 29% reduction in depression.

Conclusions

Recent prospective epidemiological studies suggest that those who are more involved in religious activities or say R/S is very important are less likely to become depressed over time. However, depression may also affect the willingness and ability to engage in religious activities, suggesting that religious organizations need to follow up on previously active members who suddenly stop attending (to ensure that depression is not why they have stopped attending).

SUICIDE

One of the most feared consequences of depression is suicide. This is especially true when depression is combined with anger, impulsiveness, substance abuse, and social isolation (Heikkinen et al., 2007; Henriksson et al., 1993; Hawton & van Heeringen, 2009; Robins et al., 1979). The suicide rate in the United States is increasing. The Centers for Disease Control and Prevention (CDC) reported that between 1999 and 2014, the suicide rate increased from 10.5/100,000 to 13/100,000, a nearly 25% jump (Curtin et al., 2016). This trend was especially strong in white women, where the incident suicide rate increased from 4.7/100,000 in 1999 to 7.5/100,000 in 2014, a 60% increase.

Religious involvement is associated with negative attitudes toward suicide, fewer suicide attempts, and fewer completed suicides. In our systematic review of studies conducted prior to 2010, 75% of studies (106 of 141) reported significantly fewer suicidal thoughts and behaviors among those who were more R/S (Koenig et al., 2012) (Table 4.1). Several more recent high-quality studies have now confirmed these earlier findings. For example, in the NHANES-III study, which followed 20,014 US adults from 1988 to 2006, those attending religious services at least 24 times/year experienced a 94% lower risk of dying by

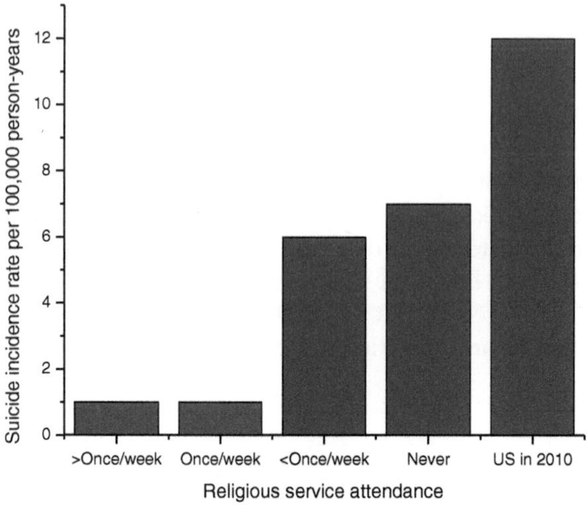

FIGURE 4.1 **Suicide incidence and religious attendance in the Nurses' Health Study from 1996 to 2010 (last column is for the United States overall in 2010, and includes men).** *Source: Nurses' Health Study; VanderWeele, T. J., Li, S., Tsai, A. C., Kawachi, I. (2016). Association between religious service attendance and lower suicide rates among US women.* JAMA Psychiatry, *73(8): 845–851.*

suicide during follow-up compared to those who attended less frequently (HR = 0.06, 95% CI = 0.01–0.54) (Kleiman & Liu, 2014). Even after controlling for gender, age, size of household, marijuana use, and previous suicide attempt, frequent attendees were still 68% less likely to die by suicide (HR = 0.32, 95% CI = 0.01–0.99).

In the latest study of suicide incidence in the United States, VanderWeele, Li, Tsai, and Kawachi (2016) at the Harvard School of Public Health analyzed data from a 14-year prospective study of 89,708 women aged 30–55 years (98% white) participating in the Nurses' Health Study. Results indicated that women who attended religious services at least once a week were 84% less likely to commit suicide than women who never attended services (HR = 0.16, 95% CI = 0.06–0.46). The incident rate for suicide decreased from 7/100,000 person-years to only 1/100,000 person-years (Figure 4.1). Results were similar when excluding women who were depressed or had chronic illness at baseline in 1996. Effects were particularly strong among Catholic women (HR = 0.05, 95% CI = 0.01–0.48). Adjustments for age, lifestyle, demography, and religious service attendance in 1992, as well as further adjustment for social integration in 1992, could not explain the effect. Sensitivity analysis indicated that unmeasured confounders would have to both increase the likelihood of religious service attendance and decrease the likelihood of suicide by 12-fold above and beyond the measured confounders to explain the effect (highly unlikely).

In an accompanying editorial, Koenig (2016) notes that social integration—previously thought to be the primary cause for a lower suicide rate among churchgoers—played a surprising small role in explaining this effect. Religious attendance was the strongest predictor of suicide incidence among all six indicators of social integration. Furthermore, controlling for social integration in the analysis had little effect on the attendance–suicide relationship for participants attending religious services weekly or more. This finding challenges the assumption that religious attendance affects suicide rate simply by increasing social support or improving social integration (an explanation often given for the effects of religion on other health outcomes as well, see Shor & Roelfs, 2013). Strong religious prohibitions against suicide are one of many other possible causes.

VanderWeele, Li, and Kawachi (2017) hypothesized further that given the 24% increase in suicide rate in the United States from 1999 to 2014 and the decrease in weekly religious attendance in the United States from 43% to 36% during this time, nearly 40% of the increase in suicide rate could be attributed to the decline in weekly religious attendance.

Conclusions

There is growing evidence that religious involvement (particularly attendance at religious services) is associated with a lower risk of suicidal thoughts and behaviors, including completed suicide. These findings have implications for clinicians when assessing suicide risk.

ANXIETY

Anxiety disorders (phobias, posttraumatic stress disorder, generalized anxiety disorder, separation anxiety disorder, panic disorder, and obsessive-compulsive disorder) are among the most common mental disorders in the United States with a combined lifetime prevalence of nearly 15% (Kessler et al., 2012). Anxiety is a powerful motivator of religious involvement, and religious involvement may help to relieve anxiety symptoms (and sometimes exacerbate them). There is an old saying (attributed to Reinhold Niebuhr) that religion "comforts the afflicted and *afflicts the comfortable.*"

Our systematic review identified 299 quantitative studies published prior to 2010 that examined this association (Koenig et al., 2012). Of those, 49% (147/299) reported inverse relationships between religiosity and anxiety or a significant decline in anxiety symptom in response to R/S interventions. Also found was that 11% (33 of 299) reported greater anxiety in those who were more religious (Table 4.1). Among the 67 best-designed studies, 57% reported lower anxiety and 10% greater anxiety among the more religious. Of the 41 experimental studies or randomized clinical trials identified in that review, 71% (29/41) reported significantly lower anxiety among those receiving R/S interventions compared to control conditions.

Since 2010, a number of additional observational studies and randomized clinical trials have examined the effects of R/S on anxiety symptoms. For example, in an observational study, Konkoly-Thege et al. (2012) surveyed a national random sample of 12,643 adults in Hungary 13 years after the overthrow of Hungary's Communist regime. Religious attendance was associated with significantly higher well-being and lower anxiety (both $p < 0.001$), whereas importance of religion was related to greater well-being but *higher levels of anxiety*. Religious attendance was also correlated with better self-rated health, fewer days spent on sick leave in past year, and less decline in work capacity (all $p < 0.001$).

King et al. (2013b) interviewed a random sample of 7,403 adults in the United Kingdom, assessing psychiatric disorders using the Clinical Interview Schedule and assessing R/S using the Royal Free Interview. Religious persons were 27% less likely to have ever used drugs (OR = 0.73, 95% CI = 0.60–0.88) and 19% less likely to be a hazardous drinker (OR = 0.81, 95% CI = 0.69–0.96). Those with a "spiritual" view of life (but not religious) were 40% more likely to be taking psychiatric medication (OR = 1.40, 95% CI = 1.05–1.86), more likely to have ever used drugs, be dependent on drugs, have abnormal eating attitudes, and have generalized anxiety, a phobia, or a neurotic disorder. Being "spiritual but not religious," then, was associated with a higher likelihood of anxiety disorder.

In a prospective study of 47 psychiatric patients with current or past psychosis receiving day treatment at the McLean Hospital in Boston, Rosmarin et al. (2013) assessed psychosis, depression, anxiety, and psychological well-being with self-rated scales at the beginning and end of a day treatment program. All patients received case management, psychopharmacology, psycho-vocational counseling, milieu therapy, and group therapy over an average length of 8 days. General religious involvement and religious coping (RC) were assessed at baseline. During the course of treatment, positive RC at baseline predicted a significant decrease in depressive symptoms ($r = 0.50$, $p < 0.005$), decrease in anxiety symptoms ($r = 0.60$, $p < 0.001$), and increase in psychological well-being ($r = 0.37$, $p = 0.05$), explaining 14% to 36% of the variance in outcomes.

King et al. (2013a) prospectively followed 170 patients with terminal illness (97% end-stage cancer) who were receiving palliative care at home in London, UK. Participants were assessed at study entry, and at 3 and 10 weeks later (81% response rate at 3 weeks and 66% at 10 weeks). Spiritual beliefs were assessed using the 20-item Beliefs and Values Scale (BVS), which included some items that measured more traditional religious concepts ("I believe there is a God") while others assessed broader spiritual concepts ("I feel most at one with the world when surrounded by nature").

Mental health was measured using the Hospital Anxiety and Depression Scale (HADS). There was little change in spiritual beliefs during this short 3–10 week follow-up period. Psychological distress at baseline was the only predictor of change in spiritual beliefs over time (increase in spiritual belief). There was no relationship between spiritual beliefs and either depression or anxiety scores. However, those with low spiritual belief scores experienced over twice the mortality compared to those with high scores during the first 6 months of follow-up (HR = 2.19, 95% CI = 1.30–3.70), a finding that remained significant after controlling for multiple predictors of survival.

Ellison et al. (2014) examined the cross-sectional association between prayer and anxiety in the presence of different levels of "attachment to God" in 1,511 US adults. Frequency of prayer was measured by asking the question: "About how often do you spend time alone praying, outside of religious services?" Attachment to God was measured using the Rowatt and Kirkpatrick 9-item scale. Anxiety was assessed using four 3-item measures: a generalized anxiety disorder scale, a social anxiety/social phobia scale, a measure of obsessions, and a measure of compulsions. Controlling for age, gender, race, marital status, education, and level of religiousness (religious attendance and self-rated religiosity), researchers found that prayer was related to fewer symptoms of anxiety disorder among those with a secure attachment to God; however, among those with an insecure attachment to God, prayer was related to more anxiety symptoms. Researchers concluded that the relationship between prayer and anxiety symptoms varied widely depending upon one's attachment to God. Thus, for those with a strong relationship with God, prayer appeared to be more effective than for those with a weaker, more superficial, or conflicted relationship.

In one of the few studies examining anxiety and religion in China, Wang et al. (2015) assessed the cross-sectional relationship between religious involvement and mental disorder in a representative sample of 2,770 community-dwelling adults in western China (8.9% Buddhist/Taoist, 39.8% Muslim, 2.0% Christian/Catholic, and 49.3% no affiliation). Mental disorders were diagnosed using the WHO's Composite International Diagnostic Interview (CIDI). Religious attendance and importance of religion in daily life were also assessed, along with affiliation. Those who frequently participated in religious services (vs. infrequent), those for whom religion was very important (vs. not important), and those with high overall religiosity (vs. low) were *more likely* to have an anxiety disorder ($p < 0.001$). After controlling for multiple demographic, socioeconomic, and physical health characteristics, researchers found that those with a religious affiliation (vs. none) were 60% more likely to have an anxiety disorder (OR = 1.6, 95% CI = 1.2–2.2, $p < 0.01$). Degree of religiosity, however, was unrelated to mental disorder after controlling for demographic and physical health characteristics. Stratifying analyses by ethnicity and age revealed that the positive relationship between religious affiliation and mental disorder was found only in those of Han ethnicity (i.e., non-Muslims), and only in those of Han ethnicity who were younger than 50 years of age.

Post-traumatic stress disorder (PTSD) is one of the most serious and difficult to treat anxiety disorders and is associated with considerable psychiatric comorbidity. Currier et al. (2015) examined the effects of R/S on PTSD symptoms in a prospective study of 532 US veterans involved in a 60–90-day residential program for the treatment of severe combat-related PTSD. R/S was assessed during the first week of the program and then again at discharge using a 6-item version of the Daily Spiritual Experiences Scale, a 3-item forgiveness scale (self, others, and God), a measure of private religious practices (prayer and meditation), scales of positive and negative religious coping, and frequency of religious attendance. PTSD severity was measured using the PTSD Checklist-Military version. Baseline spirituality predicted significantly lower PTSD symptoms at discharge, independent of baseline PTSD severity. Cross-lagged analyses indicated that the effect of baseline R/S on future PTSD severity ($B = -0.10$, $P < 0.05$) was stronger than the cross-lagged effect of baseline PTSD on future R/S ($B = 0.03$, p = ns).

Tsai, Sippel, Mota, Southwick, and Pietrzak (2016) prospectively followed a nationally representative sample of 1,838 US veterans over 24 months examining the association between post-traumatic growth (PTG) and spirituality. PTG was assessed using a standard 10-item scale that measured development of intimate relationships, recognition of new possibilities for life, increase in personal strength, increase in spiritual development, and increase in appreciation for life. Spirituality (frequency of religious attendance, private religious activities, and intrinsic religiosity) at Wave 1 predicted consistently high PTG and increasing levels of PTG over time, independent of PTSD symptoms at baseline and follow-up. The effect was particularly strong for intrinsic religiosity.

In one of the largest and best-designed studies examining associations between religious involvement, PTSD, and comorbid disorders in US veterans, Sharma et al. (2017) analyzed data from a nationally representative sample of 3,151 US military veterans. Major depressive disorder, PTSD, suicidal ideation, and alcohol use disorder were diagnosed using Diagnostic and Statistical Manual (DSM) criteria. Religiosity was assessed using the 5-item DUREL; scores were divided to form low (9%), moderate (80%), and high (12%) religiosity groups. Data were analyzed using a series of covariance (ANCOVAs) and multivariable logistic regression models. Those in the high religiosity group were significantly less likely to report lifetime PTSD (OR = 0.46), major depressive disorder (OR = 0.50), and alcohol use disorder (OR = 0.66). High levels of religiosity were also associated with greater purpose in life and with posttraumatic growth. Researchers concluded that "higher levels of R/S may help buffer risk for certain mental disorders and promote protective psychological characteristics in US military veterans" (p. 197).

R/S interventions have also been tested as a treatment for those with significant anxiety. For example, Rosmarin et al. (2010) examined the efficacy of a spiritually-integrated treatment (SIT) for stress and anxiety in a sample of Jewish patients with elevated symptom levels. A total of 126 adults were randomized to either SIT ($n = 36$), progressive muscle relaxation (PMR, $n = 42$), or a waitlist control group (WLC, $n = 47$). Participants in the SIT and PMR groups underwent Internet-based treatments on a daily basis for 2 weeks. All participants were assessed at baseline, completion of treatment, and 6–8 weeks of follow-up. Those receiving SIT experienced large improvements in stress and worry as well as improvements in secondary outcomes (depression and intolerance of uncertainty). SIT participants also reported greater treatment satisfaction than those in the PMR group. Both primary and secondary outcomes were better for those in the SIT group than those in the WLC group, whereas both PMR and WLC groups were similar on most outcomes.

Finally, Babamohammadi, Sotodehasl, Koenig, Jahani, and Ghorbani (2015) randomized 60 Iranian hemodialysis patients to either Qur'an recitation or a nontreated control group. A measure of state-trait anxiety (Spielberger) was completed by patients at baseline and one month afterward. The intervention involved listening to the Qur'an being recited in the traditional cantillation voice. Recitation of the Qur'an significantly reduced anxiety in the intervention group, decreasing State-Trait Anxiety Inventory (STAI) scores at baseline from 128.5 (SD = 13.0) to 82.1 (SD = 11.3) after the intervention, compared to members of the control group who experienced no significant change in anxiety scores (118.3, SD = 14.5, vs. 120.1, SD = 14.4, respectively). After adjusting for baseline differences, between group-comparison at follow-up indicated a significant reduction in anxiety in the intervention group compared to the control group ($F = 15.5$, $p = 0.0002$, Cohen's $d = 1.03$). This large effect size prompted researchers to conclude that listening to Qur'an recitation is an effective intervention for anxiety in Iranian hemodialysis patients.

Conclusions

While studies (particularly those from Western Europe and China) show weak or positive cross-sectional relationships between R/S involvement and greater anxiety symptoms, prospective studies (particularly in US military veterans) indicate that R/S may buffer against anxiety symptoms or increase treatment response. Furthermore, both early and more recent R/S-integrated interventions appear to be effective in reducing anxiety compared to active and nonactive control conditions.

SUBSTANCE ABUSE

Alcohol abuse and illicit drug use are widespread. Based on in-person interviews conducted with 36,309 adults in the 2012–2013 US National Epidemiologic Survey on Alcohol and Related Conditions–III (latest available data), the 12-month and lifetime prevalence of alcohol use disorders were 13.9% and 29.1%, respectively (Grant et al., 2015). For drug use disorders, comparable figures were 3.9% and 9.9%, respectively (Grant et al., 2016). According to the US Surgeon General's Report on Alcohol, Drugs and Health (DHHS, 2016), over 27 million currently use illicit drugs or misuse prescription drugs, and nearly one out of four Americans report binge drinking during the past month. The estimated yearly cost is $249 billion for alcohol misuse and $193 billion for illicit drug use.

The consequences of alcohol and drug use disorders, particularly as they usually begin during young adulthood, are manifold (DHHS, 2016). Immediate consequences include impaired judgment, driving while intoxicated (10.6% of all drivers), risk of unprotected sex (unintended pregnancy and sexually transmitted diseases), and sharing of needles or syringes (increased risk of HIV and hepatitis). Long-term health consequences for heavy drinking include liver disease, cancer, and hypertension; for regular marijuana use, long-term consequences include chronic bronchitis and exacerbation of psychotic disorders; and for stimulant use, consequences include premature heart disease. The use of alcohol and drugs during pregnancy can result in fetal alcohol syndrome (2%–5% of the population) and neonatal abstinence syndrome. Finally, in terms of societal consequences, alcohol and drug misuse can adversely affect completion of education, reduce productivity, increase healthcare costs (as above), and increase crime, interpersonal violence, and family dissolution. Indeed, over 135,000 people die prematurely every year as a result of drug overdose or alcohol abuse.

What role does religious involvement play in the prevention or cessation of alcohol and drug use/abuse? In short, the answer is *a big one*. In our systematic review of the research published prior to 2010, we identified 278 quantitative studies examining the relationship between R/S and alcohol use, abuse, or dependence (Koenig et al., 2012). Of those studies, 86% reported inverse relationships while only 4 (1%) indicated positive relationships. Among the 145 higher quality studies, 131 (90%) found inverse relationships, while only one reported a positive relationship. With regard to illicit drug use/abuse, we identified 185 quantitative studies. Of those, 84% reported inverse relationship with R/S while only two studies (1%) found positive relationships (Table 4.1). Among 112 higher quality studies, 86% reported inverse relationships, whereas only one study found a positive relationship. As the majority of these studies were conducted in adolescents or young adults attending high school or college (when addictive habits often begin), these findings suggest that R/S may have an impact on mental health throughout the life course by affecting substance use during the formative years.

A selective review of recent high-quality studies published since 2010 confirms these earlier reports. In one of the few prospective studies, Kelly, Pagano, Stout, and Johnson (2011) examined how religious practices influence participation in 12-step programs and program outcomes. Participants were 195 substance-dependent adolescents aged 14–18 years referred by the court to a 2-month residential treatment program. They were assessed at the time of admission and at the time of discharge. A religious background and behaviors questionnaire assessed lifelong religious involvement. Twelve-step program involvement was measured by frequency of meeting attendance, step work, and AA/NA-related helping of others. Outcomes were assessed using toxicology screens and various psychosocial scales. Results indicated that greater lifetime religious involvement assessed at baseline was significantly and positively related to increased step work and AA/NA-related helping, factors which in turn predicted better substance abuse outcomes, greater overall functioning, and decreased narcissistic entitlement. Similarly, in a study of 116 alcohol-dependent adults, Martin et al. (2015) followed participants from 2 weeks after entering outpatient treatment to 6 months after treatment, finding that religious coping at 6 months predicted fewer heavy alcohol use days and fewer drinks per day.

In a small study, Kulis, Hodge, Ayers, Brown, and Marsiglia (2012) surveyed 123 American Indian 7th and 8th grade youth attending middle schools in a southwestern US city, examining relationships between religion, spirituality, and substance abuse. This study is important because of the dearth of research on religion and mental health in this population, and because American Indian adults are at particularly high risk for substance abuse. Regression analyses revealed that affiliation with the Native American Church and following Christian beliefs were associated with significantly lower levels of substance use and higher anti-drug attitudes. Researchers concluded that belonging to the traditions of both Christianity and American Indian culture may help to integrate American Indian youth into society and protect against substance abuse.

One of the largest studies of American adolescents to examine relationships religious involvement across a range of alcohol, drug, and tobacco use was reported by Ford and Hill (2012). They analyzed data from a subsample of 17,727 US adolescents aged 12–17 years participating in the National Survey on Drug Use and Health, meticulously controlling for demographic factors and attitudes of parents, adolescent, and peers toward substance use. Religiosity was assessed by frequency of religious attendance, importance of religion, influence of religious beliefs on decision-making, and involvement in church or faith-based activities.

Controlling for age, gender, race, family income, and parental attitudes toward substance use, youth religiosity was inversely related to depression ($B = -0.211$, $p < 0.001$), and positively related to youth attitude toward substance use ($B = 0.156$, $p < 0.001$) and peer attitude toward substance use ($B = 0.125$, $p < 0.001$) (higher scores indicating more negative views on substance use). After controlling for depression, respondent attitude, and peer attitude toward substance use, researchers found that religiosity was inversely related to cigarette smoking ($B = -0.159$, $p < 0.001$), heavy drinking ($B = -0.190$, $p < 0.01$), prescription drug misuse ($B = -0.143$, $p < 0.01$), marijuana use ($B = -0.302$, $p < 0.001$), and other illicit drug use ($B = -0.185$, $p < 0.01$).

Gomes, de Andrade, Izbicki, Moreira-Almeida, and de Oliveira (2013) from the Department of Psychiatry at the University of Sao Paulo reported data from the first nationwide population-based survey of alcohol and drug use by college students in Brazil. Included were 12,595 university students from throughout the country. Religiosity was measured by frequency of religious attendance and divided into two categories: monthly or more (FR) versus less than monthly or never (NFR). Alcohol and drug use were assessed for the past 30 days. Analyses were adjusted for gender, age, marital status, socioeconomic status, and region of country. Results indicated that infrequent attendees (NFR) were two and one-half times more likely than FR to use alcohol (OR = 2.52, 95% CI = 2.08–3.06), nearly three times more likely to smoke cigarettes (OR = 2.83, 95% CI = 2.09–3.83), twice as likely to use marijuana (OR = 2.09, 95% CI = 1.39–3.14), and 42% more likely to use other drugs (OR = 1.42, 95% CI = 1.12–1.79).

In another study of young adults involving over 4,000 female adolescents and young adults aged 13–19 years, Haber, Grant, Jacob, Koenig, and Heath (2012) examined relationships between demographic factors, nine R/S characteristics, and five alcohol use indicators (age at initial first drink, age at first intoxication, regular use of alcohol, heavy consumption of alcohol, and alcohol dependence). Multivariate modeling revealed that R/S involvement was inversely related to these indicators of alcohol use in most cases, with the strength of associations ranging from moderate to strong. Although the last three studies above were cross-sectional, these results suggest that R/S characteristics may help to prevent alcohol use disorders in adolescents and young adults.

Similar results are reported outside the Americas. In a 15-month prospective study of 2,774 young men (average age 19 years) seen at Army recruitment centers in Switzerland, Haug, Nunez, Becker, Gmel, and Schaub (2014) examined predictors of marijuana and other drug use during follow-up in those not using substances at baseline. Religious denomination was inquired about with one question that divided respondents into Christians, Muslims, other religion, and no religion. Religiosity was measured with a single question with 5 response options: (1) "I believe in

God and practice religion," (2) "I believe in God but do not practice religion," (3) "I do not know what to believe about God," (4) "I believe we cannot really know about God" (agnostic), and (5) "I do not believe in God" (atheist). Use of 15 different drugs in the past 12 months was assessed, in addition to lifetime alcohol, tobacco, marijuana, and other drug use. After controlling for all other variables, one of 18 predictors of marijuana use onset during follow-up was the combination of lower belief in God and less practicing of religion (OR = 0.54, 95% CI = 0.31–0.96, $p < 0.05$).

In the most recent research, a web-based survey study of 5,217 students in grades 6–8 at parochial private schools in the Baltimore area by Debnam et al. (2016) at Johns Hopkins School of Public Health and Center for the Prevention of Youth Violence examined associations between stress, spirituality, and substance use using multilevel structural equation modeling. While higher stress was related to greater use of alcohol, tobacco, and other drugs as expected ($B = 0.306$, $p < 0.001$), lower spiritual beliefs was even more strongly and positively related to substance use ($B = 0.359$, $p < 0.001$).

Drabble et al. (2016) analyzed data on 11,169 women aged 18 years or older responding to the National Alcohol Survey in 2000, 2005, and 2010 comparing the effects of R/S on alcohol use among exclusively heterosexual women ($n = 10{,}723$) and (1) 184 heterosexual and same-sex partner women, (2) 140 bisexual women, and (3) 122 lesbian women (total number of sexual minority women = 446). Religiosity was measured by a single question: "How important is religion in your life?" with responses dichotomized into (1) "very important" versus (2) "somewhat important," "not really important," and "not at all important." Religiosity (very important) was more prevalent in heterosexual women (62%) than in minority women (range 31% to 43%). In heterosexual women, religiosity was associated with a 55% lower risk of lifetime alcohol use (OR = 0.45, 95% CI = 0.40–0.52), 39% lower risk of past 12-month hazardous drinking (OR = 0.61, 95% CI = 0.52–0.72), and 21% lower risk of past 12-month illicit drug use (OR = 0.79, 95% CI = 0.69–0.91). Among *sexual minority women*, religiosity was associated with a 60% lower risk of lifetime alcohol use (OR = 0.40, 95% CI = 0.19–0.86), 50% lower risk of hazardous drinking (OR = 0.50, 95% CI = 0.27–0.95), and 67% lower risk of illicit drug use (OR = 0.33, 95% CI = 0.19-0.58). This study suggests that high personal religiosity was as protective (if not more so) in sexual minority women as it was in exclusively heterosexual women.

Finally, Meyers, Brown, Grant, and Hasin (2017) analyzed data from a random national US sample of 21,965 adult alcohol drinkers (National Epidemiologic Survey of Alcohol-Related Conditions-II), to examine the relationship among religiosity, race/ethnicity, and alcohol use behaviors. Participants were 66% white, 18% Hispanic, and 16% African-American. The Alcohol Use Disorder and Associated Disability Interview Schedule,

DSM-IV version, was used to identify alcohol consumption and alcohol use disorders (AUD). Religiosity was assessed by attendance at religious services, importance of religious or spiritual beliefs in life, and size of religious social group. Structural equation modeling was used to examine the data. Results indicated that among Whites, participants indicating very important R/S beliefs used alcohol less frequently; however, this was not true in Blacks or Hispanics. Frequency of religious service attendance was also inversely related to AUD, and the association was more robust in Blacks compared to Whites and Hispanics. Among Blacks, those who participated in larger religious social groups experienced a lower risk of AUD, which was not observed in Whites or Hispanics.

Conclusions

Both cross-sectional and prospective studies indicate a moderate to strong inverse relationship between R/S involvement and substance use disorders. Many of the studies were conducted in adolescents and young adults. These findings have serious implications for mental health across the lifespan, given the well-established impact that substance use disorders have on mental health.

ANTISOCIAL BEHAVIORS

Antisocial behaviors include delinquency during childhood/adolescence and criminal activity during adulthood. Juvenile delinquency and conduct disorders are characterized by "externalizing behaviors" such as substance use, truancy, theft, selling drugs, carrying a handgun, fighting, group fighting, and other violent behaviors and displays of aggression. The prevalence of severe delinquency in American youth aged 12–17 years is estimated to be about 5% (Vaughn et al., 2014). Delinquency during youth often gradually progresses to antisocial behaviors during adulthood. Antisocial personality disorder (ASPD) and adult antisocial behavioral syndrome (AABS) are the diagnoses given to individuals who show pervasive lack of respect for the rights of others. Specifically, ASPD is the label given to those who display a pattern of irresponsible, impulsive, aggressive, and remorseless (often criminal) behaviors usually beginning by early adolescence and persisting into adulthood. This diagnosis requires the presence of conduct disorder prior to age 15 years. AABS is a similar syndrome that does not require conduct disorder before age 15 years, and is associated with fewer antisocial symptoms than in ASPD; otherwise, however, there are few differences between these two conditions. Disorders of this type are associated with premature mortality (often from unnatural causes) and comorbid mood, anxiety, substance use, and other personality disorders, suicidality, and medical illnesses and injuries. In contrast, those with the psychopathic subtype of ASPD often have low levels of anxiety and are particularly charming and ruthless, experiencing little guilt when taking advantage of or harming others. In the 2012–2013 National Epidemiologic Survey on Alcohol and Related Conditions–III study that assessed 36,309 community-dwelling US adults, researchers found the lifetime prevalence of ASPD was 4.3% and of AABS was 20.3% (Goldstein et al., 2016). These conditions were most common among males, Whites, Native Americans, young adults, the unmarried, the poorly educated, those with lower income, and persons living in the Western United States. Severe delinquency, ASPD, and AABS take a huge toll on individuals with these disorders, their family and friends, and society at large.

Our systematic review identified 104 quantitative studies on R/S and delinquent or criminal behaviors published prior to 2010 (Koenig et al., 2012). Of those studies, 79% reported inverse relationships (five at a trend level), whereas only 3% (3 studies) found positive relationships between R/S and higher rates of delinquency/crime. Of the 60 studies with the best methodology, 82% reported inverse relationships and only one study found a positive relationship.

Recent research published since 2010 confirms the results from earlier studies. For example, in a 6-year prospective study, Eisenberg et al. (2011) assessed religious coping (RC) in 686 Italian youth from ages 16–17 to ages 22–23 years to determine the trajectory of change in RC over time using latent class analysis. RC was assessed with a 4-item scale ("I put my trust in God"; "I try to find comfort in my religion"; "I seek God's help"; and "I pray more than usual"). Also assessed were self-rated religiosity and frequency of participation in religious activities. Externalizing behavior (antisocial behaviors), prosocial behaviors, and involvement with deviant peers were also assessed. Results indicated that four latent classes with regard to trajectories of RC over time were identified: high stable (HS = 18.4%), decreasing (D = 31.5%), increasing (I = 18.7%), and low stable (LS = 31.5%). Not surprisingly, participation in religious activities at least twice a month at baseline differed significantly between groups: HS = 46.7%, D = 12.7%, I = 22.7%, and LS = 3.9%. Results indicated that prosocial behaviors were more common among those with high-stable RC. With regard to externalizing behavior (stealing, lying, delinquency, violence, etc.), those in the decreasing trajectory of RC (D) and those in the increasing trajectory (I) of RC (surprisingly) were more likely to engage in these antisocial activities (and both were more likely than those in the high-stable group to do so). Similar findings were reported for involvement with deviant peers. These findings primarily related to boys, not girls (where low level of antisocial behavior was found). Researchers explained that increasing RC among boys with increased externalizing behaviors and involvement with deviant peers was likely due to these boys having difficulty adjusting, prompting them to turn to religion for help in gettingback on track.

Li (2014) analyzed data from a 2-year prospective study of 2,922 youth aged 12–14 years and their parents participating in the National Longitudinal Survey of Youth, examining the relationship between family religiosity and youth crime/delinquency. Delinquency (past year) was assessed during Wave 2 based on questions that asked about running away from home, carrying a handgun, belonging to a gang, destroying property, stealing, property crimes, violence and aggression, selling illegal drugs, and being arrested. Family religiosity at Wave 1 was assessed by a 3-item index that measured frequency of attending religious services by each parent and frequency of family religious activities together. Also assessed were family relationships (interparental conflict and affection for parents), parenting practices (parental monitoring and positive reinforcement), other mediators (family involvement in school activities and school commitment), and behavioral/emotional problems. Control variables included gender, race, physical environment risk, and substance abuse at school. Structural equation modeling was used to analyze the data. Results indicated that family religiosity was inversely related to interparental conflict, positively related to parental monitoring, positively related to affection for parents, inversely related to behavioral/emotional problems, positively related to family involvement in school, positively related to school commitment, and inversely related to delinquency (i.e., family religiosity was positively related to everything good and negatively related to everything bad, including delinquency).

Analyzing data from a US nationally representative sample of 90,202 adolescents (ages 12–17 years) and 93,710 young adults (ages 18–25 years), Salas-Wright, Vaughn, and Maynard (2014a) examined the relationship between religiosity and crime, as well as the buffering effect of religiosity on the relationship between risk propensity and crime. Five years of data were acquired from the National Survey on Drug Use and Health. Criminal behavior was assessed by two questions asking about selling illegal drugs and involvement in theft within the past 12 months. Religiosity was assessed by religious service attendance and private religiosity. Risk propensity was measured by two items assessing enjoyment of risky or dangerous behaviors. Control variables included age, race, and family income. Results indicated that both religious attendance and private religiosity were inversely associated to drug selling in both males and females and in both adolescents and young adults. This was especially true for private religiosity in female adolescents, where private religiosity also buffered the relationship between risk propensity and criminal behavior. Among females, the relationship between risk propensity and criminal behavior was particularly strong in those with low private religiosity. Religiosity was also inversely related to theft in all groups. While public religiosity buffered the effects of risk propensity theft in adolescent boys, private religiosity had no buffering effect in any group. In another publication on the adolescent sample above, Salas-Wright, Vaughn, and Maynard (2014b) reported similar inverse relationships between religious involvement and violence (fighting, group fighting, etc.). This was true in the overall sample, and in all racial, gender, and family income subgroups.

In an 18-month, 3-wave prospective study of 1,354 delinquents aged 14–18 years judged to have committed a serious crime, Barbieri and Craig (2017) examined the effects of Wave 2 religiosity on Wave 3 offending (destroying/damaging property, fire-setting, burglary, shoplifting, trafficking, fraud, vehicle theft, selling drugs, carjacking, etc.). In addition, they examined the moderating effects of religiosity on the relationship between Wave 2 "strain" (youth being victimized themselves by being chased, beaten up, mugged, threatened with harm, raped, attacked, and shot at) and Wave 3 "offending." Religiosity was assessed by a 3-item measure that asked about experiencing God's love and care, degree of personal relationship with God, and help received from religion to deal with problems. Criminal propensity, age, gender, race, prior petitions, exposure to violence, and street time were all controlled for in these analyses. Results indicated that while religiosity predicted less offending in the overall sample and in Whites and Hispanics, it did not do so in Blacks. The authors explained that while Black youth may be more likely to rely on religion to cope, religious coping may not be as effective as in Whites and Hispanics. Religiosity did not buffer the effects of strain on delinquency in the overall sample or in racial subgroups.

With regard to the protective effect of religiosity during childhood on risk of violence during adulthood, Dubow et al. (2016) prospectively followed 372 males in Columbia County (New York) for 22 to 40 years from ages 8 to 30–48 years. The purpose was to examine risk and protective factors at ages 8 and 19 years on the expression of adult violence at ages 30–48 (i.e., choked someone, slapped or kicked someone, punched or beat someone, knifed or shot someone, or threatened to do so). Participants were divided into violent (n = 96) versus nonviolent (n = 276) groups. Parental and youth religious attendance was assessed at ages 8 and 19 years, along with other childhood and adolescent risk and protective factors. Logistic regression analyses revealed that parental religious attendance (but not youth attendance) had a significant protective effect on adulthood violence, reducing the likelihood by 27% (adjusted OR = 0.73, p = 0.02) independent of other risk and protective factors.

In one of the few studies that examined effects of religiosity on crime/delinquency in Muslims, Ozbay (2016) surveyed 619 undergraduate university students, 352 academic and nonacademic staff at a public university, and 498 shop owners in a small city in Turkey. Crime/delinquency was measured by several scales that assessed behaviors such as carrying knives or guns, fighting, assault, cheating, stealing, using drugs, engaging in violence, and so on. Religiosity was assessed by family religiosity, personal religiosity, and a 9-item religious practices scale (in students only). Results in university students indicated that family and student religiosity were significantly and inversely related to deviance/crime. In university staff, having religious symbols in their offices (picture of Rumi, sayings from the Qur'an, religious plants, etc.) was significantly and *positively* associated with greater lifetime deviance and performance of violent acts. No significant relationships were found among shop owners. Regression analyses confirmed the inverse relationships in university students between youth religiosity and current and lifetime deviance/crime (both $p < 0.01$), but relationship between religious office symbols and lifetime deviance/violence in university staff weakened to nonsignificance when gender, occupational position, and belief in fate were controlled for.

Finally, Coid et al. (2016) surveyed a random sample of 3,679 adult men aged 18–34 years in Great Britain, examining risk factors for holding extremist views toward Britain and its involvement in the war in Afghanistan. Included in this study was an analysis of the relationship between psychiatric disorders (including ASPD) and religion/religiosity. Religion was determined as Christian, Hindu, and Muslim, whereas religiosity was measured by frequency of attendance at religious services and frequency of praying. Muslim and Hindu religious affiliations were associated with a lower risk of ASPD (OR = 0.26, 95% CI = 0.15–0.46, and OR = 0.36, 95% CI = 0.14–0.90, respectively). Both, frequency of religious attendance and frequency of prayer, were also related to a lower risk of ASPD (OR = 0.78, 95% CI = 0.69–0.88 and OR = 0.82, 95% CI = 0.75–0.90, respectively, both $p < 0.001$).

Conclusions

There is little doubt that religious involvement is associated with lower rates of delinquency during youth and lower crime/violence during adulthood. Both cross-sectional and prospective studies report similar findings. It has been said that when religion is unable to restrain from the "inside out," then government will have to restrain from the "outside in." Indeed, the review above substantiates this old saying.

SUMMARY AND CONCLUSIONS

A systematic review of quantitative research published prior to the year 2010 and a selective review of more recent high-quality studies on religiosity and negative emotions/behaviors have been presented in this chapter. In the majority of studies, R/S involvement is related to fewer negative emotions, as well as fewer self-destructive and antisocial behaviors.

More specifically, individuals scoring higher on R/S have less depression, lower suicide, less anxiety, less substance abuse, and engage in fewer delinquent and criminal activities. The findings are especially true for depression, alcohol and drug use, and antisocial behaviors. The vast majority of clinical trials that have tested R/S interventions for depression and anxiety have likewise reported benefits that equal or exceed those received from standard treatments or from control conditions. These findings provide an evidence base that may help guide clinicians in their assessment and treatment of clients with these disorders.

References

Babamohammadi, H., Sotodehasl, N., Koenig, H. G., Jahani, C., & Ghorbani, R. (2015). The effect of Qur'an recitation on anxiety in hemodialysis patients: A randomized clinical trial. *Journal of Religion and Health, 54*(5), 1921–1930.

Barbieri, N., & Craig, J. M. (2017). Do the effects of strain and religiosity on criminal coping differ by race and ethnicity? *Crime and Delinquency* (in press).

Bonelli, R. M., & Koenig, HG. (2013). Mental disorders, religion, and spirituality 1990–2010: A systematic evidence-based review. *Journal of Religion and Health, 52*(2), 657–673.

Coid, J. W., Bhui, K., MacManus, D., Kallis, C., Bebbington, P., & Ullrich, S. (2016). Extremism, religion and psychiatric morbidity in a population-based sample of young men. *The British Journal of Psychiatry, 209*(6), 491–497.

Croezen, S., Avendano, M., Burdorf, A., & van Lenthe, F. J. (2015). Social participation and depression in old age: A fixed-effects analysis in 10 European countries. *American Journal of Epidemiology, 182*(2), 168–176.

Currier, J. M., Holland, J. M., & Drescher, K. D. (2015). Spirituality factors in the prediction of outcomes of PTSD treatment for U.S. military veterans. *Journal of Traumatic Stress, 28*(1), 57–64.

Curtin, S. C., Warner, M., & Hedegaard, H. (2016). *Increase in suicide in the United States, 1999–2014: NCHS Data Brief, No. 241*. Hyattsville, MD: National Center for Health Statistics.

Debnam, K., Milam, A. J., Furr-Holden, C. D., & Bradshaw, C. (2016). Substance Use and Misuse. *The role of stress and spirituality in adolescent substance use, 51*(6), 733–741.

DHHS (2016). U.S. Department of Health and Human Services (HHS), Office of the Surgeon General, Facing Addiction in America: The Surgeon General's Report on Alcohol, Drugs, and Health. Washington, DC: HHS (November). Available from https://addiction.surgeongeneral.gov/.

Drabble, L., Trocki, K. F., & Klinger, J. L. (2016). Religiosity is a protective factor for hazardous drinking and drug use among sexual minority and heterosexual women: Findings from the National Alcohol Survey. *Drug and Alcohol Dependence, 161*, 127–134.

Dubow, E. F., Huesmann, L. R., Boxer, P., & Smith, C. (2016). Childhood and adolescent risk and protective factors for violence in adulthood. *Journal of Criminal Justice, 45*, 26–31.

Eisenberg, N., Castellani, V., Panerai, L., Eggum, N. D., Cohen, A. B., Pastorelli, C., & Caprara, G. V. (2011). Trajectories of religious coping from adolescence into early adulthood: Their form and relations to externalizing problems and prosocial behavior. *Journal of Personality, 79*(4), 841–873.

Ellison, C. G., Bradshaw, M., Flannelly, K. J., & Galek, K. C. (2014). Prayer, attachment to God, and symptoms of anxiety-related disorders among U.S. adults. *Sociology of Religion, 75*, 208–233.

Ferrari, A. J., Somerville, A. J., Baxter, A. J., Norman, R., Patten, S. B., Vos, T., & Whiteford, H. A. (2013). Global variation in the prevalence and incidence of major depressive disorder: a systematic review of the epidemiological literature. *Psychological Medicine, 43*(3), 471–481.

Ford, J. A., & Hill, T. D. (2012). Religiosity and adolescent substance use: Evidence from the National Survey on Drug Use and Health. *Substance Use and Misuse, 47*(7), 787–798.

Goldstein, R. B., Chou, S. P., Saha, T. D., Smith, S. M., Jung, J., Zhang, H., Pickering, R. P., Ruan, W. J., Huang, B., & Grant, B. F. (2016). The epidemiology of antisocial behavioral syndromes in adulthood: Results from the National Epidemiologic Survey on Alcohol and Related Conditions-III. *Journal of Clinical Psychiatry, 78*(1), 90–98.

Gomes, F. C., de Andrade, A. G., Izbicki, R., Moreira-Almeida, A., & de Oliveira, L. G. (2013). Religion as a protective factor against drug use among Brazilian university students: A national survey. *Revisa Brasileira de Psiquiatria (official journal of the Brazilian Psychiatric Association), 35*, 29–37.

Grant, B. F., Goldstein, R. B., Saha, T. D., Chou, S. P., Jung, J., Zhang, H., Pickering, R. P., Ruan, W. J., Smith, S. M., Huang, B., & Hasin, D. S. (2015). Epidemiology of DSM-5 alcohol use disorder: Results from the National Epidemiologic Survey on Alcohol and Related Conditions III. *JAMA Psychiatry, 72*(8), 757–766.

Grant, B. F., Saha, T. D., Ruan, W. J., Goldstein, R. B., Chou, S. P., Jung, J., Zhang, H., Smith, S. M., Pickering, R. P., Huang, B., & Hasin, D. S. (2016). Epidemiology of DSM-5 drug use disorder: Results from the National Epidemiologic Survey on Alcohol and Related Conditions–III. *JAMA Psychiatry, 73*(1), 39–47.

Haber, J. R., Grant, J. D., Jacob, T., Koenig, L. B., & Heath, A. (2012). Alcohol milestones, risk factors, and religion/spirituality in young adult women. *Journal of Studies on Alcohol and Drugs, 73*(1), 34–43.

Haug, S., Nunez, C. L., Becker, J., Gmel, G., & Schaub, M. P. (2014). Predictors of onset of cannabis and other drug use in male young adults: Results from a longitudinal study. *BMC Public Health, 12*, 1202.

Hawton, K., & van Heeringen, K. (2009). Suicide. *Lancet, 373*(9672), 1372–1381.

Heikkinen, M., Aro, H., & Lonnqvist, J (2007). Recent life events, social support and suicide. *Acta Psychatrica Scandinavica, 89*(S377), 65–72.

Henriksson, M., Aro, H., Marttunen, M., Heikkinen, M., Isometsa, E., Kuoppalsalri, K., & Lonnquest, J (1993). Mental disorders and comorbidity in suicide. *American Journal of Psychiatry, 150*, 935–940.

Kelly, J. F., Pagano, M. E., Stout, R. L., & Johnson, S. M. (2011). Influence of religiosity on 12-step participation and treatment response among substance-dependent adolescents. *Journal of Studies on Alcohol and Drugs, 72*(6), 1000–1001.

Kessler, R. C., Berglund, P., Demler, O., Jim, R., Kortez, D., Merikangas, K. R., Rush, A. J., Walters, E. E., & Wang, P. S. (2003). The epidemiology of major depressive disorder: Results from the National Comorbidity Survey Replication (NCS-R). *Journal of the American Medical Association, 289*, 3096–3105.

Kessler, R. C., Petukhova, M., Sampson, N. A., Zaslavsky, A. M., & Wittchen, H. U. (2012). Twelve-month and lifetime prevalence and lifetime morbid risk of anxiety and mood disorders in the United States. *International Journal of Methods in Psychiatric Research, 21*(3), 169–184.

King, M., Llewellyn, H., Leurent, B., Owen, F., Leavey, G., & Tookman, A. (2013a). Spiritual beliefs near the end of life: A prospective cohort study of people with cancer receiving palliative care. *Psycho-Oncology, 22*(11), 2505–2512.

King, M., Marston, L., McManus, S., Brugha, T., Metzer, H., & Bebbington, P. (2013b). Religion, spirituality and mental health: Results from a national study of English households. *British Journal of Psychiatry, 202*(1), 68–73.

Kleiman, E. M., & Liu, R. T. (2014). Prospective prediction of suicide in a nationally representative sample: Religious service attendance as a protective factor. *British Journal of Psychiatry, 204*, 262–266.

Koenig, H. G (2016). Association of religious involvement and suicide. *JAMA Psychiatry, 73*(8), 775–776.

Koenig, H. G., George, L. K., Peterson, B. L., & Pieper, C. F. (1997). Depression in medically ill hospitalized older adults: Prevalence, characteristics, and course of symptoms according to six diagnostic schemes. *American Journal of Psychiatry*, *154*, 1376–1383.

Koenig, H. G., McCollough, M. E., & Larson, D. B. (2001). *Handbook of religion and health* (1st ed.). New York, NY: Oxford University Press.

Koenig, H. G., King, D. E., & Carson, V. B. (2012). *Handbook of religion and health* (2nd ed.). New York, NY: Oxford University Press.

Konkoly-Thege, B., Pilling, J., Szekely, A., & Kopp, M. S. (2012). Relationship between religiosity and health: Evidence from a post-communist country. *International Journal of Behavioral Medicine*, *20*(4), 477–486.

Kulis, S., Hodge, D. R., Ayers, S. L., Brown, E. F., & Marsiglia, F. F. (2012). Spirituality and religion: Intertwined protective factors for substance use among urban American Indian youth. *American Journal of Drug and Alcohol Abuse*, *38*, 444–449.

Li, S., Okereke, O. I., Chang, S. C., Kawachi, I., & VanderWeele, T. J. (2016). Religious service attendance and lower depression among women: A prospective cohort study. *Annals of Behavioral Medicine*, *50*(6), 876–884.

Li, S. D. (2014). Familial religiosity, family processes, and juvenile delinquency in a national sample of early adolescents. *Journal of Early Adolescence*, *34*(4), 436–462.

Martin, R. A., Ellingsen, V. J., Tzilos, G. K., & Rohsenow, D. J. (2015). General and religious coping predict drinking outcomes for alcohol dependent adults in treatment. *American Journal on Addictions*, *24*(3), 240–245.

Maselko, J., Hayward, R. D., Hanlon, A., Buka, S., & Meador, K. (2012). Religious services attendance and major depression: A case of reverse causality? *American Journal of Epidemiology*, *175*(6), 576–583.

Meyers, J. L., Brown, Q., Grant, B. F., & Hasin, D. (2017). Religiosity, race/ethnicity, and alcohol use behaviors in the United States. *Psychological Medicine*, *47*(1), 103–114.

Miller, L., Wickramaratne, P., Gameroff, M. J., Sage, M., Tenke, C. E., & Weissman, M. M. (2012). Religiosity and major depression in adults at high risk: A ten-year prospective study. *American Journal of Psychiatry*, *169*(1), 89–94.

Miller, L. R., Bansal, R., Wickramaratne, P., Hao, Z., Tenke, C., Weissman, M. M., & Peterson, B. S. (2014). Neuroanatomical correlates of religiosity and spirituality: A study in adults at high and low familial risk for depression. *JAMA Psychiatry*, *71*(2), 128–135.

Murray, C., & Lopez, A. (1996). *The global burden of disease*. Cambridge, MA: Harvard University Press.

Ozbay, O. (2016). Does Islam deter crime in a secular Islamic country? The case of Turkey. *Contemporary Social Science*, *11*(4), 315–333.

Robins, E., Murphy, G. E., Wilkinson, R. H., Gassner, S., & Kayes, J. (1979). Some clinical considerations in the prevention of suicide based on a study of 134 successful suicides. *American Journal of Public Health*, *49*(7), 888–899.

Rosmarin, D. H., Bigda-Peyton, J. S., Ongur, D., Pargament, K. I., & Bjorgvinsson, T. (2013). Religious coping among psychotic patients: Relevance to suicidality and treatment outcomes. *Psychiatry Research*, *210*(1), 182–187.

Rosmarin, D. H., Pargament, K. I., Pirutinsky, S., & Mahoney, A. (2010). A randomized controlled evaluation of a spiritually integrated treatment for subclinical anxiety in the Jewish community, delivered via the Internet. *Journal of Anxiety Disorders*, *24*(7), 799–808.

Salas-Wright, C. P., Vaughn, M. G., & Maynard, B. R. (2014a). Buffering effects of religiosity on crime testing the invariance hypothesis across gender and developmental period. *Criminal Justice and Behavior*, *41*(6), 673–691.

Salas-Wright, C. P., Vaughn, M. G., & Maynard, B. R. (2014b). Religiosity and violence among adolescents in the United States: Findings from the National Survey on Drug Use and Health 2006–2010. *Journal of Interpersonal Violence*, *29*(7), 1178–1200.

Sharma, V., Marin, D. B., Koenig, H. G., Feder, A., Iacoviello, B. M., Southwick, S. M., & Pietrzak, R. H. (2017). Religion, spirituality, and mental health of U.S. military veterans: Results from the National Health and Resilience in Veterans Study. *Journal of Affective Disorders*, *217*, 197–204.

Shor, E., & Roelfs, D. J. (2013). The longevity effects of religious and nonreligious participation: A meta-analysis and meta-regression. *Journal for the Scientific Study of Religion*, *52*, 120–145.

Smith, T. B., McCullough, M. E., et al. (2003). Religiousness and depression: Evidence for a main effect and the moderating influence of stressful life events. *Psychological Bulletin*, *129*(4), 614–636.

Tsai, J., Sippel, L. M., Mota, N., Southwick, S. M., & Pietrzak, R. H. (2016). Longitudinal course of posttraumatic growth among US Military Veterans: Results from the National Health and Resilience in Veterans Study. *Depression and Anxiety*, *33*(1), 9–18.

VanderWeele, T. J., Li, S., & Kawachi, I. (2017). Religious service attendance and suicide rates. *JAMA Psychiatry*, *74*(2), 197–198.

VanderWeele, T. J., Li, S., Tsai, A. C., & Kawachi, I. (2016). Association between religious service attendance and lower suicide rates among US women. *JAMA Psychiatry*, *73*(8), 845–851.

Vaughn, M. G., Salas-Wright, C. P., DeLisi, M., & Maynard, B. R. (2014). Violence and externalizing behavior among youth in the United States: Is there a severe 5%? *Youth Violence and Juvenile Justice*, *12*(1), 3–21.

Wang, Z., Koenig, H. G., Zhang, Y., Ma, W., & Huang, Y. (2015). Religious involvement and mental disorders in Mainland China. *PLOS One*, *10*(6), (e0128800).

CHAPTER

5

Chronic Mental and Neurocognitive Disorders

This chapter examines the relationship among religion, chronic mental disorders (schizophrenia and bipolar disorder), and major neurocognitive disorder ("dementia" in pre-DSM-5 terminology). The connection between religiosity and chronic mental disorder is a tricky one, because chronic mental disorders are often manifested by religious symptoms (delusions and hallucinations), and yet religion is also often used to cope with the distress caused by psychotic symptoms and associated life stressors. The relationship with major neurocognitive disorder is also not straightforward. Progressive dementia may interfere with a person's ability to experience and express religious beliefs, while religious involvement may also prevent the onset or slow the course of these disorders through psychological, social, behavioral, and physiological mechanisms. All of these perspectives will be considered here.

SCHIZOPHRENIA

Schizophrenia is a chronic mental disorder manifested by delusions and hallucinations (called "positive symptoms") and blunting of affect, apathy, and loss of social interest (called "negative symptoms"). The disorder often develops in young adulthood and persists throughout life: about one-third have a chronic, progressive course with poor outcomes; a small minority (10%–20%) experience steady recovery with good outcomes; and the remainder have a fluctuating course with partial or full remission followed by recurrences. The 12-month prevalence of schizophrenia is estimated to be about 5.1 per 1000 in the United States (Wu, Shi, Birnbaum, Hudson, & Kessler, 2006) and 3.3 per 1000 worldwide (Saha, Chant, Welham, & McGrath, 2005). This means approximately 22 million people have the disorder (Whiteford, Ferrari, Degenhardt, Feigin, & Vos, 2015). The annual global incidence of schizophrenia is between 11 and 70 per 100,000 per

Religion and Mental Health. http://dx.doi.org/10.1016/B978-0-12-811282-3.00005-7

year (Messias, Chen, & Eaton, 2007). The economic burden is enormous, with estimates ranging as high as $102 billion per year in the United States alone (Chong et al., 2016). Those at greater risk for developing schizophrenia have a positive family history (genetic factors), are born in the winter months, have birth complications, parents of older age, a history of meningitis, maternal infection with influenza, rubella, or herpes simplex during pregnancy, are immigrants from Africa or the Caribbean (or their children), use cannabis, and live in urban areas (Messias et al., 2007). Although early environment and childhood rearing were once thought to be influential (e.g., the rejecting and overprotective "schizophrenogenic mother"), this is no longer emphasized (Hartwell, 1996).

Religious explanations for schizophrenia (or chronic psychosis) have also been put forward in the past (although less so today). These explanations have either been positive in nature (conferred special spiritual status on the psychotic person as a healer with visions into the spirit world) or negative in nature (possessed with an evil spirit that required exorcism for cure). The former explanation often led to community support and even admiration and reverence (Polimeni, 2012) whereas the latter explanation often led to persecution for being demon-possessed (and could lead to death from burning at the stake or hanging during the Middle Ages up through the 18th century) (Ferngren, 2014; Zilboorg & Henry, 1941). The largely biological explanations for schizophrenia today as a genetically transmitted brain disease have "laid to rest" many of these parenting and religious explanations (Gejman, Sanders, & Duan, 2010). The possibility that powerful religious experiences may trigger schizophrenia (or at least psychosis), however, continues to be discussed (Linden, Harris, Whitaker, & Healy, 2010), and religious beliefs may certainly influence the types of persons sought for treatment (religious healers vs. mental health professionals) and compliance with drug treatments (Borras et al., 2007).

Religious delusions and hallucinations are frequent in patients with schizophrenia. Delusions are fixed false beliefs held with greater fervor and not modifiable by rational explanation or evidence to the contrary. Hallucinations are visual, auditory, or tactile perceptions in the absence of external stimuli. These perceptions are experienced as "real" by the individual who may not be able to distinguish them from actual sensory perceptions. As noted earlier, these are called "positive" symptoms in schizophrenia. Delusions of a specifically religious nature are known to be present in 11%–47% of patients with schizophrenia, with the lowest prevalence in Japan (Kitamura, Okazaki, & Funinawa, 1998; Tateyama, Asai, & Hashimoto, 1998), the highest prevalence in the United States (Appelbaum, Robbins, & Roth, 1999; Cothran & Harvey, 1986; Miller & McCormack, 2006), and an intermediate prevalence in Europe and the United Kingdom (Siddle, Haddock, & Tarrier, 2002a; Tateyama et al., 1998), which reflects the religiousness of these areas of the world. The prevalence of religious hallucinations ranges from 12% in China to 52% in South Africa (Cook, 2015). The specific religious content of delusions and hallucinations depends on the majority religion of the region (religious context), appears to change over time as the importance of religion in a society changes, and is often related to historical events (Gearing et al., 2011; Krzystanek, Krysta, Klasik, & Krupka-Matuszczyk, 2012; Reed & Clarke, 2014). Religious delusions are particularly persistent when compared to other delusions. This is perhaps due to their often anomalous and grandiose nature. Such delusions are reported to be particularly resistant to treatment (Kilicaslan, Acar, Eksioglu, Kesebir, & Tezcan, 2016). However, persons with religious delusions are not necessarily less engaged in treatment seeking, and may be particularly open to cognitive-behavioral approaches to therapy (Iyassu et al., 2014).

Clinicians have long had trouble distinguishing religious beliefs from psychotic delusions (Pierre, 2001). Religious beliefs probably lie on a continuum from rational and healthy to neurotic to psychotic, with most of the spectrum in the nonpsychotic range in religious societies. At the boundaries of transition between culturally normative and psychotic, however, such distinctions may be difficult to make (Koenig, 2011). Further difficulty is encountered when evaluating religious beliefs on initial exposure to those who are acutely psychotic. Prolonged observation (a perspective that family and members of the person's religious community often have) may be necessary to separate normal, healthy religious beliefs from symptoms of psychopathology. In psychopathology, religious beliefs do not usually conform to religious and cultural "norms," and those who know the person well can usually detect something wrong or unusual about the beliefs. Delusional religious beliefs are often accompanied by other symptoms of illness—positive and negative symptoms—that are more easily recognized as pathological. This is particularly true in schizophrenia, which is manifested by a host of symptoms other than delusions or hallucinations, which lead to progressive dysfunction and psychosocial disability, not a healthy and socially constructive transformation that often follows genuine religious experience.

Early Research

What, then, has objective research demonstrated about the relationship between religiosity and schizophrenia? Religiosity is not always positively associated with religious delusions, and both a healthy form of religiosity and a pathological form may be distinguishable in the same individual. For example, in a small sample of psychotic patients with either mania or schizophrenia, Cothran and Harvey (1986) found a positive correlation between overall religiosity and religious delusions;

however, those with religious delusions had fewer fundamentalist beliefs and were not as involved in a religious community as were either nondelusional patients or normal controls. Likewise, in a study of 295 patients with schizophrenia in Austria, Rudalevičienė, Stompe, Narbekovas, Raškauskienė, and Bunevičius (2008) found that personal religiosity did not predict religious delusions once other factors were taken into account. Studies of nonpsychiatric populations have likewise distinguished religiosity from schizotypal thinking, finding that religious involvement is actually significantly lower among those scoring higher on schizotypal traits (Feldman & Rust, 1989; Maltby & Day, 2002). Again, healthy and pathological religiosity may be difficult to distinguish especially when self-rated scales are used.

Besides being a manifestation of psychosis, higher rates of religiosity among patients with schizophrenia may be due to a turning to religion in order to cope with pathological symptoms. In a study of 406 psychotic patients in the Los Angeles County mental health system, Tepper, Rogers, Coleman, and Malony (2001) found that 80% used religion to cope, similar to findings among a chronically mentally ill patient population in Australia, where 67% of psychiatric patients reported using religion to cope (D'Souza, 2002). If religious involvement helps individuals with preschizophrenia or schizophrenia to cope better with life stress, then it may help to delay the onset and/or reduce exacerbations of the illness (often precipitated by life stress). Thus, religiosity may represent both a risk factor *and* a protective factor in schizophrenia and may or may not adversely affect adherence to treatment in the balance (Gearing et al., 2011).

Our systematic review of the research prior to 2010 examining the relationship between religiosity/spirituality (R/S) and psychotic symptoms identified 44 quantitative studies conducted in nonpsychiatric populations, psychiatric patients, and psychiatric patients with schizophrenia (Koenig, King, & Carson, 2012; Koenig, McCollough, & Larson, 2001). Of those, 32% (14/44) reported fewer psychotic symptoms in those who were more R/S, 25% (11/44) reported more psychotic symptoms, 23% (10/44) found no association, and 20% (9/44) reported mixed results (in the same study, positive associations with some measures of religiosity and negative associations with others). Among 17 studies of nonpsychiatric populations, 35% (6/17) reported fewer psychotic symptoms in those who were more R/S, 12% (2/17) more symptoms, 24% (4/17) no association, and 29% (5/17) reported mixed results. Of the 16 studies in psychiatric patients, 38% (6/16) reported fewer symptoms, 25% (4/16) more symptoms, 25% (4/16) no association, and 13% (2/16) mixed findings. Finally, among the 11 studies in patients with schizophrenia, 18% (2/11) reported fewer psychotic symptoms in highly R/S patients, 45% (5/11) found more psychotic symptoms, 18% (2/11) found no association, and 18% (2/11) reported mixed results (one study with six of seven associations indicating fewer symptoms). While most of the studies above were cross-sectional, making it difficult to determine whether R/S protects against, predisposes to, or exacerbates psychotic symptoms in schizophrenia and other chronic psychoses, we identified five prospective studies and two clinical trials that are now reviewed below in order of year of publication.

In the first prospective study, Verghese et al. (1989) followed 386 outpatients in India aged 15–45 years with schizophrenia over a two-year period. Participants were followed up once every three months using an assessment tool designed specifically for this study along with the Present State Exam. Outcomes at two years were categorized into very favorable, favorable, intermediate, unfavorable, and very unfavorable. Multivariate analyses indicated worse outcomes among those with longer duration of illness, irregular drug compliance, economic difficulties, dangerous behavior, agitation as a first symptom, and those who decreased their frequency of religious activities. Researchers concluded that "the increase in religiosity that was related to better outcome in the present study could be a means of effectively handling the anxiety of the patients" (p. 502).

In a second prospective study conducted in India, Raguram, Venkateswaran, Ramakrishna, and Weiss (2002) described the effects of living in a Hindu temple on the mental health of 31 persons with severe mental disorder (three-quarters with paranoid schizophrenia). The temple, built over the grave of a holy Hindu man, was known to be visited by those with severe mental illness, many of whom reported experiencing spontaneous improvement in symptoms as a result of spending time there. In this single group experimental study, consecutive persons with mental disorder who visited the temple were approached and asked to stay at the temple for a period of 3 months (receiving no other psychiatric treatment). Investigators assessed symptom severity at baseline using the Brief Psychiatric Rating Scale (BPRS), and again after the 3-month stay in the temple. Results indicated an average 20% reduction in BPRS scores during the study period, similar to that experienced by psychotic patients treated with antipsychotic medication. Qualitative follow-up interviews with family caregivers after study completion confirmed a significant improvement in symptoms during the temple stay, consistent with objective findings on the BPRS.

Benda (2002) conducted a 2-year prospective study of a systematically identified sample of 600 homeless Vietnam veterans with a chronic history of substance abuse, 40% of whom had been previously admitted to a psychiatric hospital for comorbid severe psychiatric illness. The purpose of the study was to examine baseline predictors of rehospitalization. Administered initially was a 5-item measure of religiosity (prayer, Bible study, discussion of religion, church attendance, and belief in a supernatural being). During follow-up, nearly three-quarters of the sample (72%) were readmitted to the hospital for substance abuse or severe mental illness. Those scoring high on religiosity at baseline were 50% more likely to not be hospitalized during the 2-year follow-up (HR = 1.50, 95% CI = 1.33–1.68).

In a prospective study of 155 psychotic inpatients with schizophrenia in the United Kingdom (Manchester), Siddle, Haddock, and Tarrier (2004) measured self-rated religiosity at baseline (dichotomized as religious vs. nonreligious) and then again after 4 weeks of treatment when the psychosis had improved. No difference in psychotic symptoms was found between religious and nonreligious patients either at baseline or on follow-up using the Positive and Negative Symptom Scale for Schizophrenia (PANSS). Researchers also found no difference in treatment response between religious and nonreligious patients (even after patients with religious delusions were removed from the sample). They concluded that neither patient religiosity nor the presence of religious delusions affected treatment response, at least in the short term. In an earlier report from the study, Siddle, Haddock, and Tarrier (2002b) examined the effects of 4 weeks of treatment, this time with patient religiosity as the primary outcome assessed by the 27-item Religious Life Inventory (RLI). The RLI is composed of five subscales: Need, Doubt, Models, Change, and Doctrine. As psychotic symptoms decreased on the PANSS, religiosity also decreased with the greatest decrease in the religious Need subscale. Among those with religious delusions, there was no significant change in the total RLI score or any RLI subscale score in response to treatment. The authors concluded that these findings were consistent with religion being used as a coping mechanism, suggesting that the increased religiosity in patients with schizophrenia may be due to their use of religion to cope with symptoms of the disorder.

Miller and McCormack (2006) examined 77 patients with first-episode schizophrenia living in Glen Oaks, New York. Participants were assessed at baseline and 12 months later examining religiosity, religious delusions, and response of religious symptoms to treatment. Nearly half of the sample (47%) had religious delusions at baseline. By the end of follow-up, however, 58% experienced a full remission of religious delusions. Besides being interwoven with delusions, religious beliefs were also involved in resolving existential crises and appeared to help patients to cope by reestablishing their sense of self. As in other studies, the role of religious beliefs in coping with symptoms was emphasized.

Two clinical trials examining the effects of R/S interventions were also reported. The first study examined the effects of a R/S intervention delivered by student nurses to 20 Christian patients with schizophrenia at a state mental hospital over a 10-week period (Carson & Huss, 1979). Participants were nonrandomly assigned to either the intervention group ($n = 10$) or to a control group ($n = 10$). The intervention consisted of weekly prayer and scripture reading that focused on God's love, concern, and the patient's worth to God. Both student nurses and patients were assessed at baseline and after the 10-week intervention, although participants did not complete any standard outcome measures (only qualitative reports of the experience were recorded). At the end of the study, student nurses said they experienced increased sensitivity to others, a strengthening of their religious beliefs, and a greater sense of being hopeful, realistic, and empathetic. Patients in the intervention group (vs. controls) became more verbal and articulate, were better able to act out their anger and frustration, were more willing to express inner feelings (with more appropriate affect), were more likely to express a desire for a more normal life, and were less likely to complain of somatic symptoms. No evidence was found for any harmful effects of the intervention (i.e., worsening psychotic symptoms).

In the second clinical trial, Lindgren and Coursey (1995) administered a spiritual intervention in 28 patients with serious mental illness (two-thirds with schizophrenia). The intervention consisted of four psychoeducational 90-minute group sessions that sought to help patients utilize spiritual beliefs to improve self-esteem. Participants were randomly assigned to one of the three intervention groups (n = 13) or to one of three waitlist control groups (n = 15) (5–6 in each group). After the intervention, those in the control groups were crossed over to receive the intervention. Results indicated significant within group (pre–post) differences in spiritual support that favored the intervention group, but no differences in depression, hopelessness, self-esteem, or purpose in life scores. When intervention and control groups were compared, no differences on any outcome measure was found, although statistical power was very low.

Conclusions

This systematic review of research conducted prior to 2010 indicates that R/S involvement was associated with fewer psychotic symptoms (one-third of studies), more psychotic symptoms (one-quarter of studies), was not associated with psychotics symptoms, or the findings were mixed. Thus, these results based largely on cross-sectional studies suggest that there is no consistent pattern indicating that religiosity is related to more or fewer psychotic symptoms in schizophrenia. The two clinical trials reviewed above indicate that R/S interventions do not appear to harm patients with schizophrenia. Prospective studies suggest that, outside of religious delusions (which appear not to affect treatment response), the increase in religiosity in these patients is likely due to the use of religion to cope with distressing psychotic symptoms (which religion seems to help).

Latest Research

Since 2010, a number of studies have examined the relationship between religiosity and psychotic symptoms in patients with schizophrenia that may help to confirm or refute earlier studies. Described below are a few of these more recent studies.

In a 3-year follow-up of 115 Swiss outpatients with schizophrenia (63% Christian), Mohr et al. (2010) examined the relationship between change in R/S and change in clinical symptoms over time. While 20% of participants increased in their use of religion as a positive resource and 17% decreased, no significant relationship was found between change in religiosity and change in clinical symptoms or psychosocial functioning from baseline to follow-up. However, compared to the 63% of patients in whom R/S did not change (i.e., remained stable), those who changed in either direction expressed less satisfaction with their lives and social activities. In a second report from this sample, Mohr et al. (2011) reported that among those whose R/S at baseline provided a "positive sense of self or a spiritual sense of their illness that helped them accept it and mobilize their religious resources to cope" (true for 83% of the 92 patients who completed the follow-up), severity of symptoms on the PANSS tended to decrease. In contrast, symptoms tended to increase among those whose "religion contributed to a negative sense of self, in terms of despair and suffering or a spiritual sense of the illness including fear, anger, or guilt" (17%), although neither of these changes were statistically significant.

In a small cross-sectional study of 55 patients with schizophrenia in Taiwan, China, Huang, Shang, Shieh, Lin, and Su (2011) examined the relationship among religiosity, religious delusions/hallucinations, and treatment seeking. This is one of the first studies to examine religiosity in patients with schizophrenia living in China. Surprisingly, over 80% were affiliated with a religious tradition (44% Buddhist, 24% Christian, 16% Taoist, or other religions). Researchers categorized patients into those with positive symptoms ($n = 25$), negative symptoms ($n = 23$), and positive symptoms religious type ($n = 7$). Religiosity was assessed with the 8-item Rohrbaugh-Jessor Religiosity Scale. Psychotic symptoms were measured using the PANSS and Global Assessment of Functioning (GAF) Scale. Satisfaction with psychiatric therapy was assessed on a scale from very unsatisfied (1) to very satisfied (5), and preference for treatment by a question that asked if the patient (1) favored a religious intervention only, (2) favored a religious intervention over psychiatric treatment, (3) favored religious and psychiatric treatments equally, (4) favored psychiatric treatment over a religious intervention, or (5) favored psychiatric treatment only. Results indicated no significant difference on GAF or PANSS symptoms between those with or without a religious affiliation. Overall religiosity was positively related to duration of illness, inversely related to GAF score (indicating lower overall functioning), positively related to religious delusions/hallucinations, but was not related to psychotic symptoms on the PANSS (either the total score or subscale scores). Greater religiosity was related to having a preference for a religious intervention over psychiatric therapy, a finding that persisted after controlling for satisfaction with psychiatric therapy and education level.

Rosmarin, Bigda-Peyton, Öngur, Pargament, and Björgvinsson (2013) prospectively followed 47 patients with current or past psychosis who were participating in a day treatment program affiliated with McLean Hospital (Boston). Participants were followed from the time of entry into the program to the time of discharge (average 8 days). Primary diagnoses were schizophrenia, schizoaffective disorder, or mood disorder with psychosis. Nearly half of the sample was Christian and indicated very strong belief in God. General religious involvement and religious coping were assessed at baseline. Psychosis, depression, anxiety, and well-being were assessed at baseline and follow-up (time of discharge). Positive religious coping at baseline predicted significantly greater improvements in depression, anxiety, and psychological well-being during the course of treatment, but was not associated with change in psychotic symptoms.

In the only clinical trial that could be located since our 2010 review, Nikfarjam (2011) randomized 62 Iranian inpatients with schizophrenia to either a spiritual intervention or a control group. Unfortunately, study details were not available in English. However, the intervention involved prayer and readings from the Qur'an, and outcomes were assessed using the Schizophrenia Quality of Life Scale (SQLS). No significant differences between the two groups were present at baseline. SQLS scores improved significantly from baseline to the end of the intervention in the experimental group ($p < 0.04$), while there was no change in the control group. The researcher concluded that "religious and spiritual training" may improve satisfaction with quality of life in Iranian patients with schizophrenia. The integration of religious and spiritual issues into psychotherapy has been reviewed and discussed by Mizock, Millner, and Russinova (2012). They provide steps on how to sensitively address religious delusions and cultural issues in patients with schizophrenia. A more recent review by Maura and de Mamani (2017) also discusses how to address cultural and religious issues in patients with schizophrenia.

Finally, Smolak et al. (2013) reviewed the results of 43 studies examining the perceptions of families and caregivers on the role of religion in the lives of patients with schizophrenia, how it is perceived as a coping behavior, and how it influences treatment engagement and help-seeking. These investigators found that religious themes were associated with better coping, greater treatment engagement, and more help-seeking. Both family members and caregivers preferred to seek care from religious professionals over mental health professionals.

Conclusions

These more recent studies confirm that positive/healthy forms of religious coping are common among patients with schizophrenia and are related to better mental health outcomes in prospective studies (at least in terms of depression, anxiety, and well-being, and possibly psychotic symptoms as well). Religious delusions/hallucinations tend to be more common in those who are religious (although disentangling healthy religious involvement from psychosis may be difficult). Whether or not religious delusions contribute to treatment resistance remains unclear. Religious patients with schizophrenia may prefer to have religious treatments over secular psychiatric treatments, although studies are inconsistent on whether greater religiosity increases or decreases compliance with secular treatments (Amr, El-Mogy, & El-Masry, 2013; Grover, Davuluri, & Chakrabarti, 2014; Mohr, Brandt, Borras, Gilliéron, & Huguelet, 2006). R/S forms of psychotherapy do not appear to be harmful to patients with schizophrenia, and even if R/S is not specifically used in therapy, mental health professionals should consider the R/S beliefs of patients (and family members) when deciding on treatments. Doing so is essential in order to provide culturally sensitive mental health care.

BIPOLAR DISORDER

Bipolar disorder (BPD) is a mood disorder where patients experience manic symptoms alternating with depressive symptoms, and sometimes mixed symptoms of both depression and mania at the same time. Mood disorders exist on a spectrum from (1) unipolar major depressive disorder to (2) bipolar type-II disorder (BP-II) (i.e., major depression with hypomanic episodes) to (3) subthreshold bipolar disorder (SBD) to (4) bipolar type I disorder (BP-I) with classic manic alternating with depressive episodes. The 12-month prevalence rates for bipolar disorders in the United States are 0.6% for BP-I, 0.8% for BP-II, and 1.4% for SBD (Merikangas et al., 2007). Worldwide rates are about one-third to one-half lower than that in the United States: 0.4% for BP-I, 0.3% for BP-II, and 0.8% for SBD (Merikangas et al., 2011). Overall, then, bipolar disorders have a 12-month prevalence rate of 2.8% in the United States and 1.5% worldwide, which makes them approximately 5 times as common as schizophrenia. Furthermore, BP-I causes more disability worldwide than schizophrenia (BP-I is ranked 22nd in terms of disability adjusted life years compared to schizophrenia at 27th) (Murray & Lopez, 1996). BP-I also has the highest suicide rate among all major psychiatric disorders (Goldstein et al., 2012).

In contrast to research on religiosity and schizophrenia, relatively little attention has been paid to religion's connection with BPD, despite the even greater frequency of hyperreligiosity and religious delusions/hallucinations that occur during manic episodes. Carlson and Goodwin (1973) reported early on that manic patients often experienced religious delusions, and Goodwin and Jamison (1990) reported that 39% of manic patients presented with hyperreligiosity. Brewerton (1994) in a study of 50 adult Hawaii State hospital patients with psychosis reported that 9 of 10 patients with bipolar mania had delusions with religious content. Just as these earlier figures, more recent estimates vary widely. Jerrell and Shugart (2004) reported that only 19% of 184 adults with BPD in South Carolina exhibited hyperreligiosity, which was significantly higher than that found in 83 children/adolescents in the sample, where hyperreligiosity was relatively uncommon. Patel, DelBello, and Strakowski (2006) reported that only 13% of children/adolescents who presented with mania had religious delusions, whereas Appelbaum et al. (1999) found that 33% of 73 adult BPD patients had religious delusions. Religious delusions, then, appear to be more common in adults with BPD and are often of a grandiose nature (i.e., belief that one is God, Jesus, the Devil, or a saint). While figures for religious delusions and hyperreligiosity vary widely, religiosity is no doubt often intertwined with psychotic symptoms in BPD.

Early Research

Our systematic review identified eight studies published prior to 2010 that examined the relationship between religiosity and BPD (Koenig et al., 2001, 2012). These are now reviewed in order of year of publication. In the earliest study, Gallemore, Wilson, and Rhoads (1969) examined the religious life of 62 hospitalized patients in North Carolina with pervasive and severe affective disorders (80% depressed, 20% manic, half recovered, half with active symptoms). Patients were compared with 40 controls without affective disorder matched for age, sex, race, and socioeconomic status. Those with affective disorder were more likely than controls to have experienced a salvation or conversion experience (52% vs. 20%) and less likely to have parents who were indifferent or antireligious (15% vs. 35%). Kirov, Kemp, Kirov, and David (1998) found that nearly one-third of 52 patients from the United Kingdom with psychotic illness (29% with BPD) indicated an increase in religiousness after onset of their illness. Investigators explained that this increase in belief reflected the turning to religion in order to cope with symptoms.

As noted earlier, in a survey of 406 outpatients with persistent mental illness (11% with BP-I disorder and 51% with schizophrenia) in the Los Angeles County mental health system, Tepper et al. (2001) found that religious coping was present in 80% of patients. The most common type of religious activity was prayer, followed by attending religious services and worshiping God. Nearly two-thirds (65%) indicated that religion helped them a moderate to large extent in coping with symptoms and 30% indicated that their religious beliefs/activities were "the most important things that kept them going" (p. 662). Participants for whom religion had become more important when their symptoms worsened experienced fewer hospitalizations during the previous year than did those in whom religion became less important. A greater duration of religious coping and greater percentage of overall time devoted to religious coping were also associated with less depression, hostility, and frustration.

Hempel, Meloy, Stern, Ozone, and Gray (2002) interviewed 148 mentally ill prisoners admitted to a forensic hospital in Texas, examining the characteristics of those who "spoke in tongues" (glossolalia) ($n = 18$) comparing them to mentally ill prisoners who did not ($n = 130$). All 18 of those who spoke in tongues (100%) had a diagnosis of either BPD or schizoaffective disorder bipolar type. Half (50%) of those who spoke in tongues said that religion was part of the motivation for their crimes (vs. 16% of those without glossolalia, $p = 0.002$).

Mitchell and Romans (2003) administered the Royal Free Interview to 81 patients with BPD in New Zealand. Most (86%) rated the practice of their religious faith as important (97% of women, 71% of men), and 79% rated their strength of belief as greater than 5 on a scale from 1 to 10 (where 10 signified "very strong"). Approximately one out of five (19%) indicated that they had encountered conflict between advice from spiritual advisors and that given by mental health professionals. Of those, approximately one-third said their spiritual advisors told them they didn't need to take medications anymore. Compared to those with weaker belief, those with stronger belief were significantly less likely to be compliant with medications ($p = 0.01$).

Baetz, Bowen, Jones, and Koru-Sengul (2006) analyzed data from a random national sample of 37,000 Canadians aged 15 or older, identifying 2.4% who had at some time during their lives experienced a manic episode (1.0% within the past 12 months). Frequency of religious attendance and the spiritual values were assessed, and analyses were adjusted for age, sex, education, income, marital status, chronic health conditions, and social support. Religious attendance was associated with a lower likelihood of ever experiencing mania (OR = 0.87, 95% CI = 0.82–0.92, $p < 0.0005$) and experiencing it in the past 12 months (OR = 0.84, 95% CI = 0.76–0.94, $p < 0.0005$). Spiritual values, in contrast, were associated with an increased likelihood of having mania, again both lifetime (OR = 1.21, 95% CI = 1.12–1.32, $p < 0.0005$) and in the past 12 months (OR = 1.28, 95% CI = 1.10–1.45, $p < 0.0005$). The finding for spiritual values, however, may have been influenced by the way the question was assessed and analyzed. Participants were first asked if spiritual values played an important role in life, and then were asked if this was to help find meaning in life, strength in dealing with everyday difficulties, and understanding life's difficulties (with responses combined to form a single spiritual values variable). This variable was then added into a regression model together with religious attendance (when controlling for attendance in cross-sectional studies, measures of R/S coping often become positively related to poorer mental health).

In a mixed-methods study, Michalak, Yatham, Kolesar, and Lam (2006) interviewed 35 bipolar patients from the United States and Canada to identify factors related to quality of life (QOL). Spirituality was one of six themes that emerged from the interviews. One-third of patients discussed (1) their struggle to disentangle "real" forms of spirituality from the hyperreligiosity associated with mania or hypomania, (2) the adverse impact the disorder had on their involvement in religious community, and (3) the increasing importance of faith when they were in the depressed phase of the illness.

Finally, in one of the largest and most detailed studies of religiosity and BPD, Cruz, Pincus, and Welsh (2010) surveyed 334 veterans with BPD seeking outpatient care at a VA medical center in Pittsburgh. Religiosity was measured by the 5-item DUREL, which assesses organizational religious activity (ORA), nonorganizational religious activity (NORA), and intrinsic religiosity (IR). Clinical state was assessed by the 17-item self-report Internal State Scale, which divided participants into four groups: euthymic (currently not ill), mixed (having both depressive and manic symptoms), pure depressed, and pure manic states. Results indicated that ORA, NORA, and IR were all higher among patients in euthymic states and in those with mixed states. Controlling for demographics, anxiety, hazardous drinking, and level of disability in logistic regression models, however, the positive associations between ORA and IR with euthymic and mixed states lost statistical significance. NORA, however, reversed its association such that prayer/meditation/Bible study became less common in euthymic states and remained increased in mixed states. Researchers concluded that individuals with BPD who are in mixed states seek support from private religious activities; however, they could not rule out that an increase in private religious activities was due to underlying pathology such as religious delusions or pathological hyperreligiosity. No evidence, though, indicated religiosity (IR) or religious activity (ORA or NORA) was higher in patients with active mania.

Conclusions

Given the many different findings (all cross-sectional), it is difficult to generalize anything about the role that religiosity plays in BPD from these early studies. However, as in schizophrenia, religious coping appears to be common among patients with BPD and is often used to deal with distressing symptoms. Religious conversion experiences (and "speaking in tongues") also may be more common in those with BPD, religiousness may increase after initial diagnosis, and strength of religious belief may adversely affect medication compliance (especially when advice from clergy conflicts with that from mental health professionals). Hyperreligiosity and religious delusions tend to occur during active phases of illness, and this may interfere with healthier forms of religious expression. Manic or depressive episodes may also adversely affect public religious activity, although private forms of religious or spiritual expression may increase. Many questions, then, remain unresolved on how religious involvement affects BPD and how BPD affects religious involvement.

Recent Research

More recent studies published since 2010 provide further information that may help to provide consistency to the conclusions above. A selective review of the higher quality studies is now provided, again ordered by year of publication.

In a retrospective case-control study, Dervic et al. (2011) examined 200 BPD patients during the depressed phase of illness, comparing social and clinical characteristics between the religiously affiliated (n = 149) and the religiously unaffiliated (n = 51). Participants were from New York and Pennsylvania. Those with a religious affiliation were more likely than those without to have children (41.8% vs. 15.7%, $p = 0.001$), to have a family-oriented social network (66.1% vs. 24.4%, $p < 0.001$), were less likely to have ever made a suicide attempt (63.1% vs. 80.4%, $p = 0.02$), made fewer suicide attempts (1.6 vs. 2.3, $p = 0.03$), were less likely to have a first-degree relative commit suicide (2.8% vs. 14.0%, $p = 0.003$), were older in age at first suicide attempt (24.5 vs. 20.4, $p = 0.047$) and at first manic episode (25.3 vs. 20.3, $p = 0.004$), were older at first hospitalization (29.1 vs. 24.3, $p = 0.03$), less aggressive on Brown-Goodwin Aggression Inventory (20.1 vs. 22.1, $p = 0.049$), abused alcohol and drugs less often (49.7% vs. 74.5%, $p = 0.002$), reported less childhood abuse (44.1% vs. 63.3%, $p = 0.02$), and indicated more frequent moral or religious objections to suicide (11.2 vs. 6.4, $p < 0.001$). Controlling for other variables using logistic regression, researchers found that lower lifetime aggression and higher moral/religious objections to suicide explained the inverse relationship between religious affiliation and suicide attempts.

Azorin et al. (2013) surveyed 424 consecutive patients in France with major depressive disorder, examining bipolar-like symptoms in those who were highly religious (HR, n = 234) compared to those who were low on religiosity (LR, n = 190). Religiosity was determined using the DUREL. Patients with BP-I disorder were excluded from the sample (although others on the bipolar spectrum were included). The Multiple Visual Analog Scale of Bipolarity (MVAS-BP) was used to assess bipolar-like symptoms. Results indicated a higher level of social disinhibition (44.4 vs. 35.0, p = 0.0001) in HR compared to LR patients, but no differences on activation, expansiveness, or anxiety-depression (the other dimensions assessed by the MVAS-BP scale). HR patients were older at age of onset of major depression (33.4 vs. 29.3 years, p = 0.0001), were more likely to be hospitalized for the current episode (44.0% vs. 34.2%, p = 0.0005), and were more likely to have chronic depression (12.4% vs. 3.2%, p = 0.0001). Importantly, HR patients were more likely to have a first episode of major depression with mixed polarity (8.4% vs. 2.7%, p = 0.0001), were more likely to experience hypomanic switches in response to antidepressants (32.3% vs. 14.1%, p = 0.0005), and were more likely to have bipolar disorder in first-degree relatives (4.9% vs. 1.1%, p = 0.0005). HR and LR patients did not, however, differ on total number of mood episodes, rapid cycling, psychotic features, cyclothymic temperament, or frequency of comorbid bipolar diagnoses. While lifetime suicide attempts were higher in HR than LR patients (9.2% vs. 3.7%, p = 0.0005), this finding was for the entire sample (the majority of whom had strictly unipolar major depressive disorder and remember, BP-I patients were excluded). This is one of the few studies showing increased suicide attempts in more religious subjects, perhaps because the study was done in secular France (where high religiosity may serve as a marker of greater distress prompting religious coping). Stepwise logistic regression indicated that the strongest predictors of high religious involvement were having a depressive temperament (vs. cyclothymic, hyperthymic, or irritable), chronic depression, and having a first episode with mixed polarity. Based on these conflicting findings, then, it is difficult to say whether highly religious patients in secular France are more likely than less religious patients to have depression with bipolar-like symptoms.

In a more religious area of the world, Stroppa and Moreira-Almeida (2013) surveyed 168 Brazilian outpatients with bipolar disorder to examine relationships among religiosity, clinical symptoms, and quality of life (QOL). Religiosity was assessed using the DUREL (ORA, NORA, and IR) and the 14-item Brief RCOPE (positive and negative religious coping). QOL was assessed with the WHOQoL BREF; mania by the Young Mania Rating Scale; and depression by the Montgomery-Asberg Depression Rating Scale. Controlling for sociodemographic characteristics, IR (intrinsic religiosity) and PRC (positive religious coping) were associated with lower depressive symptoms (OR = 0.19, 95% CI = 0.06–0.57, and OR = 0.25, 95% CI = 0.09–0.71, respectively). IR was associated with higher scores on all four domains of QOL (physical, psychological, social, and environmental). PRC was also associated with greater psychological and environmental QOL, whereas negative religious coping (NRC) was associated with lower psychological QOL. When 158 of these patients were followed up two years later, Stroppa, Colugnati, Koenig, and Moreira-Almeida (2017) found that greater baseline IR (T1) predicted higher T2 environmental QOL, and greater PRC (T1) predicted higher T2 physical QOL, mental QOL, social QOL, and environmental QOL. In contrast, NRC predicted more manic symptoms, lower mental QOL and worse environmental QOL. This is the *first prospective study* to examine the relationship between religiosity and BPD.

In another cross-sectional study, Grover, Hazari, Aneja, Chakrabarti, Sharma, and Avasthi (2016) surveyed 185 BPD outpatients in India, examining factors related to recovery from the disorder. Standard scales assessing recovery (Recovery Assessment Scale or RAS), internalized stigma, manic and depressive symptoms, and global functioning were administered. Religious involvement was measured using the Brief RCOPE, DUREL, and a 17-item Religiousness Measures Scale. Positive religious coping (PRC) was associated with better overall recovery on the RAS ($r = 0.17$, $p < 0.05$), and private religious activity was related to "goal and success orientation" on the RAS ($r = 0.15$, $p < 0.05$). No other measures of religiosity, however, were associated with either total RAS score or subscale scores. Based on these findings, the authors suggested that clinicians should be sensitive to religious beliefs of Indian BPD patients and encourage use of positive religious coping. In another report from this same sample, Grover, Hazari, Aneja, Chakrabarti, and Avasthi (2016) reported that 38% of patients had either religious or supernatural content to psychopathology, almost half (45%) believed that supernatural forces were part of the cause for their illness (31% indicating "God's will"), 44% contacted supernatural/religious treatment providers before ever seeing a mental health professional, and 70% said their mental health professional had not asked enough questions to understand their religiosity.

Recent reviews of the literature on risk and protective factors in BPD have likewise emphasized (1) the frequent manifestations of religion in psychopathology, (2) the role that healthy/positive religiosity can play in coping with symptoms, QOL, and protection from suicide, and (3) the need for more research in this area (Da Silva Costa et al., 2015; De Fazio et al., 2015).

Conclusions

Recent research confirms that religion is often involved in the content of pathological psychiatric symptoms and that healthy religious beliefs/practices are often used to cope with distressing symptoms of BPD (and may predict certain aspects of recovery). Consequently, clinicians should take a careful spiritual history to better understand the role that religion plays (including identifying prior treatments sought from religious healers). They should also attempt to distinguish whether (1) religion is a manifestation of psychopathology and should be treated or (2) religion is a healthy positive response to psychopathology and should be supported and encouraged.

MAJOR NEUROCOGNITIVE DISORDER (DEMENTIA)

"Major neurocognitive disorder" (MNCD) is the new term in DSM-V for dementia and refers to a progressive chronic brain disorder. Because MNCD has both psychological and neurological characteristics, it is difficult to strictly categorize as either a mental or a neurological disorder. The most common form of MNCD is Alzheimer's disease (AD) (the underlying etiology responsible for about two-thirds of cases), followed by vascular dementia, alcohol dementia, and several other less frequent dementia subtypes. Regardless of underlying etiology, the presentation is often similar: progressive loss of memory and ability to function and care for self, sometimes with agitation and psychosis, leading to severe disability often requiring total care in institutional settings and ultimately leading to death. The time course of the illness from diagnosis to death ranges from 3 to 12 years (Kua et al., 2014).

The worldwide prevalence of dementia (standardized for age) is 5%–7% of persons age 60 years or over, with the highest prevalence in Latin American (9%) and the lowest prevalence in sub-Saharan Africa (2–4%), and a moderate prevalence in the United States (7%) (Prince et al., 2013). The latest estimate in 2010 of the number of persons with dementia worldwide is 36 million; this figure is expected to double every 20 years to 66 million by 2030 and 115 million by 2050. In the United States, the total monetary cost of dementia in the year 2010 ranged from $157 billion to $215 billion (only $11 billion paid by Medicare) (Hurd, Martorell, Delavande, Mullen, & Langa, 2013). MNCD, then, is a serious, common, and expensive disorder, and the prevalence is projected to increase dramatically in the years ahead, potentially bankrupting many countries throughout the world.

Characteristics that increase the risk of developing dementia are older age, genetic factors (APO-E genotype), cardiovascular risk factors (hypertension, diabetes, high serum lipid levels, coronary artery and cerebrovascular disease), gender (female), hormonal factors (estrogen replacement therapy may reduce risk), oxidative and inflammatory stress, head trauma (accidents), education (low), chemical exposure (solvents and heavy metals), depression and psychological stress (McCullagh, Craig, McIlroy, & Passmore, 2001). In a comprehensive review of this topic, Norton, Matthews, Barnes, Yaffe, and Brayne (2014) concluded that seven factors accounted for nearly half (49.4%) of the cases of Alzheimer's disease: diabetes mellitus, midlife hypertension, midlife obesity, physical inactivity, depression, smoking, and low educational attainment.

What is the relationship, then, between dementia and religious involvement, and what might this mean for clinicians caring for patients with this disorder and for family members? There is ample rationale to suspect such a relationship given the association between religiosity and health behaviors (less smoking and alcohol use), lower risk of stroke, hypertension, cardiovascular disease, depression, anxiety, stress, social isolation, and lower stress hormone levels (cortisol and epinephrine) (Koenig et al., 2012). Religion's protective effects with regard to these etiologic factors should lower the risk of cognitive impairment and dementia. On the other hand, older age, lower education, greater obesity, and female gender (positively correlated with both religious involvement and dementia) could confound this relationship. Cognitive impairment and dementia may also adversely affect religious belief (a cognitive process) and religious behavior by reducing the capacity to engage in such activities.

Early Research

Our systematic review of quantitative studies published in 2010 or earlier on the relationship between religious involvement and cognitive impairment/dementia identified 22 studies (Koenig et al., 2001, 2012). All studies examining this relationship were published after the year 2000. Of these 22 studies, 11 (50%) found a positive relationship between R/S and less cognitive impairment or dementia; three (14%) reported an inverse relationship (more impairment among those who were more R/S); six (27%) found no association; and two reported mixed findings (one of which reported less cognitive impairment among the more R/S in four of five analyses). Eight studies were prospective in nature following participants (usually elderly persons) for 1 to 35 years; of those, five (63%) reported that R/S involvement at baseline predicted a significantly slower rate of cognitive decline, one study found a more rapid decline, and one each found no association or mixed findings. Thus, the majority of these earlier studies support the argument that R/S involvement decreases the risk of cognitive decline with age or when dementia is present.

Recent Research

A number of more recent studies published since 2010 have examined the relationship between R/S and cognitive impairment with aging or dementia, several of which are summarized below.

In 64 outpatients with Alzheimer's disease seen at Padova Hospital, Italy, Coin et al. (2010) examined the relationship between religious activity at baseline and changes in cognitive functioning over the next 12 months using the Mini-Mental State Exam (MMSE). Religious activity was assessed with the Behavioral Religiosity Scale, which measures frequency of religious attendance, praying, reading religious literature, and watching or listening to religious programs on TV or radio. Patients were divided into 2 groups based on religious activity: no or low religiosity (LR) and moderate or high religiosity (HR). Besides cognitive functioning, researchers also assessed patients' physical functioning, behavioral disturbances, and stress level. Results indicated that LR patients experienced a marked worsening in their total cognitive and behavioral test scores during the 12-month follow-up. Compared to HR patients, LR patients were almost seven times more likely to experience a 3-point decrease on their MMSE (OR = 6.7, 95% CI = 1.8–24.7). Investigators concluded that higher religiosity predicts a slower rate of cognitive and behavioral decline in Alzheimer's disease (replicating an earlier finding among AD patients in Canada—see Kaufman, Anaki, Binns, & Freedman, 2007).

Zhang (2010) analyzed data on 8,703 participants aged 80–105 years in the Chinese Healthy Longevity Survey, seeking to determine the relationship between religious participation and cognitive functioning. Subjects were asked a single question on how often they participated in any kind of religious activities (1 = every day, 2 = sometimes, and 3 = never); 16% indicated they participated in religious activities at least sometimes, whereas 84% never participated in religious activities. Controlling for other predictors of cognitive functioning (optimism, happiness, exercise and other leisure time activities, physical disability level, age, education, etc.), Zhang found that religious participation was associated with 30% less cognitive impairment in women ($p < 0.01$) and 54% less cognitive impairment in men ($p < 0.01$).

Inzelberg et al. (2013) conducted a door-to-door survey of 778 women aged 65 years or over in Northern Israel, examining midlife leisure activities that might relate to future cognitive impairment. Participants were divided into three groups: 448 normal controls, 92 with Alzheimer's disease, and 238 with mild cognitive impairment (MCI), determined using a set of standard measures (MMSE and Brookdale Cognitive Screening Test) and a clinical evaluation by neurologists. Participants were asked about 15 leisure activities engaged in during midlife (ages 20–60 years). Prayer was measured by asking participants if they prayed during midlife and the number of hours spent in prayer during midlife (these reports were verified by family members). Results indicated that a higher percentage of women with normal cognitive functioning reported praying during midlife (87%) compared to those with MCI (71%) or AD (69%) ($p < 0.0001$). The relationship with prayer could not be assessed in men because 94% engaged in midlife prayer. After controlling for age and education, women engaging in midlife prayer were 45% less likely to experience MCI (OR = 0.55, 95% CI = 0.33–0.94), although they were not at lower risk for AD. Amount of prayer (i.e., hours/month during midlife) was not related to MCI or AD.

In another study from China, Lin et al. (2015) conducted a case-control study involving 280 patients with AD and 138 with vascular dementia (VD) recruited from academic medical centers in northern Taiwan. All participants were over age 60. Cases with dementia were compared to

466 healthy age-matched controls. Standard criteria were used to make the diagnoses of AD and VD. Taoists/Buddhists (55% of cases and 51% of controls) and Christians (9% of cases and 15% of controls) were compared to those without a religious affiliation (36% of cases, 34% of controls; this was the reference category). Also assessed were leisure activities including exercise and entertainment activities. After adjusting analyses for age, gender, and education, Christians were 59% less likely than those with no religious affiliation to have AD (OR = 0.41, 95% CI = 0.23–0.75) and 58% less likely to have VD (OR = 0.42, 95% CI = 0.19–0.94). Controlling for the presence of the apoE4 gene weakened the relationship with VD slightly (OR = 0.43, 95% CI = 0.19–1.00), but did not affect the association with AD (OR = 0.46, 95% CI = 0.26–0.81). The association in AD was particularly strong in women (OR = 0.38, 95% CI = 0.15–0.92) and in those participating in three or more leisure activities per week, especially exercise (OR = 0.33, 95% CI = 0.14–0.77). Researchers concluded that Chinese persons affiliated with Christianity experienced a lower risk of AD, particularly in women and in those who exercised regularly. They hypothesized that this was due to the fact that Christianity encouraged a healthy lifestyle, cognitive stimulating activities, increased social networks, and effective coping behaviors.

A relatively recent independent systematic review of the research on R/S and dementia identified 11 articles (Agli, Bailly, & Ferrand, 2015). In three articles, those who were more religious experienced a reduction or stabilization of their cognitive disorders. In the other eight articles, the authors noted that religious involvement enabled those with dementia to "accept their disease, maintain their relationships, maintain hope, and find meaning in their lives, thereby improving their quality of life" (p. 715). Other more recent studies support a possible protective role for R/S in slowing cognitive decline with increasing age or in dementia (Foong, Hamid, Ibrahim, & Haron, 2017; Simon & Dong, 2016). Recent research also provides evidence for R/S in maintaining the mental and the physical health of family caregivers (Koenig, Nelson, Shaw, Saxena, & Cohen, 2016a; Koenig, Nelson, Shaw, Saxena, & Cohen, 2016b).

Conclusions

Both earlier and more recent research suggests that R/S involvement may delay the onset of cognitive impairment with age in normal adults and may slow the progression of cognitive impairment in dementia. There are plausible explanations for this effect given the relationship between R/S and major risk factors for cognitive decline and dementia, such as smoking, alcohol use, hypertension, other cardiovascular diseases, depression, anxiety, and psychosocial stress. When seeing adults for early cognitive impairment at risk for major neurocognitive disorder, clinicians may decide to support R/S beliefs or activities if a spiritual history indicates that these are important to the patient or family members who care for them.

SUMMARY AND CONCLUSIONS

This chapter reviewed quantitative studies examining the relationship between religious or spiritual involvement and the prevalence and/or clinical course of schizophrenia, bipolar disorder, and major neurocognitive disorder (dementia). On the one hand, psychotic symptoms with religious content are present in one-quarter to one-half of patients with schizophrenia or bipolar disorder, may indicate a particularly protracted course of illness and resistance to treatment, and may interfere with compliance to drug treatments. On the other hand, healthy nonpsychotic religious beliefs and activities may be important for how patients cope with symptoms of chronic mental illness and may have a positive impact on illness course. Religious involvement also appears in the majority of prospective studies to slow the progression of cognitive impairment with age and slow cognitive decline in those with dementia. These are preliminary findings, of course, which future research will need to verify or refute. However, based on what is currently known, clinicians and religious professionals should consider supporting and encouraging healthy religious beliefs and positive forms of religious coping, if patients indicate these are important and helpful.

References

Agli, O., Bailly, N., & Ferrand, C (2015). Spirituality and religion in older adults with dementia: A systematic review. *International Psychogeriatrics*, *27*(5), 715–725.

Amr, M., El-Mogy, A., & El-Masry, R. (2013). Adherence in Egyptian patients with schizophrenia: The role of insight, medication beliefs and spirituality. *Arab Journal of Psychiatry*, *24*, 60–66.

Appelbaum, P. S., Robbins, P. C., & Roth, L. H. (1999). Dimensional approach to delusions: Comparison across types and diagnoses. *American Journal of Psychiatry*, *156*(12), 1938–1943.

Azorin, J. M., Kaladjian, A., Fakra, E., Adida, M., Belzeaux, R., Hantouche, E., & Lancrenon, S. (2013). Religious involvement in major depression: Protective or risky behavior? The relevance of bipolar spectrum. *Journal of Affective Disorders*, *150*(3), 753–759.

Baetz, M., Bowen, R., Jones, G., & Koru-Sengul, T. (2006). How spiritual values and worship attendance relate to psychiatric disorders in the Canadian population. *Canadian Journal of Psychiatry*, *51*(10), 654–661.

Benda, B. B. (2002). Factors associated with rehospitalization among veterans in a substance abuse treatment program. *Psychiatric Services*, *53*(9), 1176–1178.

Borras, L., Mohr, S., Brandt, P. Y., Gilliéron, C., Eytan, A., & Huguelet, P. (2007). Religious beliefs in schizophrenia: Their relevance for adherence to treatment. *Schizophrenia Bulletin*, *33*(5), 1238–1246.

Brewerton, T. D. (1994). Hyperreligiosity in psychotic disorders. *Journal of Nervous and Mental Disease, 182*(5), 302–304.

Carlson, G. A., & Goodwin, F. K. (1973). The stages of mania: A longitudinal analysis of the manic episode. *Archives of General Psychiatry, 28*(2), 221–228.

Carson, V. B., & Huss, K. (1979). Prayer: An effective therapeutic and teaching tool. *Journal of Psychiatric Nursing and Mental Health Services, 17*, 34–37.

Chong, H. Y., Teoh, S. L., Wu, D. B. C., Kotirum, S., Chiou, C. F., & Chaiyakunapruk, N. (2016). Global economic burden of schizophrenia: A systematic review. *Neuropsychiatric Disease and Treatment, 12*, 357.

Coin, A., Perissinotto, M., Najjar, A., Giaradi, E. M., Inelmen, G., Enzi, E. M., & Sergi, G. (2010). Does religiosity protect against cognitive and behavioral decline in Alzheimer's dementia? *Current Alzheimer Research, 7*(5), 445–452.

Cook, C. C. (2015). Religious psychopathology: The prevalence of religious content of delusions and hallucinations in mental disorder. *International Journal of Social Psychiatry, 61*(4), 404–425.

Cothran, M. M., & Harvey, P. D. (1986). Delusional thinking in psychotics: Correlates of religious content. *Psychological Reports, 58*, 191–199.

Cruz, M., Pincus, H. A., & Welsh, D. E. (2010). The relationship between religious involvement and clinical status of patients with bipolar disorder. *Bipolar Disorders, 12*(1), 68–76.

Da Silva Costa, L., Alencar, Á. P., Neto, P. J. N., dos Santos, M. D. S. V., da Silva, C. G. L., Pinheiro, S. D. F. L., Silveira, R. T., Bianco, B. A., Pinheiro, R. F., Jr, de Lima, M. A., Rolim Neto, M. L., & Reis, A. O. A. (2015). Risk factors for suicide in bipolar disorder: A systematicreview. *Journal of Affective Disorders, 170*, 237–254.

De Fazio, P., Gaetano, R., Caroleo, M., Cerminara, G., Giannini, F., Jaén Moreno, M. J., & Segura-García, C. (2015). Religiousness and spirituality in patients with bipolar disorder. *International Journal of Psychiatry in Clinical Practice, 19*(4), 233–237.

Dervic, K., Carballo, J. J., Baca-Garcia, E., Galfalvy, H. C., Mann, J. J., Brent, D. A., & Oquendo, M. A. (2011). Moral or religious objections to suicide may protect against suicidal behavior in bipolar disorder. *Journal of Clinical Psychiatry, 72*(10), 1390.

D'Souza, R. (2002). Do patients expect psychiatrists to be interested in spiritual issues? *Australasian Psychiatry, 10*(1), 44–47.

Feldman, J., & Rust, J. (1989). Religiosity, schizotypal thinking, and schizophrenia. *Psychological Reports, 65*, 587–593.

Ferngren, G. B. (2014). *Medicine and religion: A historical introduction*. Baltimore, MD: Johns Hopkins University Press.

Foong, H. F., Hamid, T. A., Ibrahim, R., & Haron, S. A. (2017). Moderating effect of intrinsic religiosity on the relationship between depression and cognitive function among community-dwelling older adults. *Aging and Mental Health* (E-pub ahead of press).

Gallemore, J. L., Wilson, W. P., & Rhoads, J. M. (1969). The religious life of patients with affective disorders. *Diseases of the Nervous System, 30*, 483–486.

Gearing, R. E., Alonzo, D., Smolak, A., McHugh, K., Harmon, S., & Baldwin, S. (2011). Association of religion with delusions and hallucinations in the context of schizophrenia: Implications for engagement and adherence. *Schizophrenia Research, 126*(1), 150–163.

Gejman, P. V., Sanders, A. R., & Duan, J. (2010). The role of genetics in the etiology of schizophrenia. *Psychiatric Clinics of North America, 33*(1), 35–66.

Goldstein, T. R., Ha, W., Axelson, D. A., Goldstein, B. I., Liao, F., Gill, M. K., & Keller, M. (2012). Predictors of prospectively examined suicide attempts among youth with bipolar disorder. *Archives of General Psychiatry, 69*(11), 1113–1122.

Goodwin, F. K., & Jamison, K. R. (1990). *Manic-Depressive illness*. New York, NY: Oxford University Press.

Grover, S., Davuluri, T., & Chakrabarti, S. (2014). Religion, spirituality, and schizophrenia: A review. *Indian Journal of Psychological Medicine, 36*(2), 119–124.

Grover, S., Hazari, N., Aneja, J., Chakrabarti, S., & Avasthi, A. (2016a). Influence of religion and supernatural beliefs on clinical manifestation and treatment practices in patients with bipolar disorder. *Nordic Journal of Psychiatry*, *70*(6), 442–449.

Grover, S., Hazari, N., Aneja, J., Chakrabarti, S., Sharma, S., & Avasthi, A. (2016b). Recovery and its correlates among patients with bipolar disorder: A study from a tertiary care centre in North India. *International Journal of Social Psychiatry*, *62*(8), 726–736.

Hartwell, C. E. (1996). The schizophrenogenic mother concept in American psychiatry. *Psychiatry*, *59*(3), 274–297.

Hempel, A. G., Meloy, J. R., Stern, R., Ozone, S. J., & Gray, B. T. (2002). Fiery tongues and mystical motivations: Glossolalia in a forensic population is associated with mania and sexual/religious delusions. *Journal of Forensic Science*, *47*(2), 305–312.

Huang, C. L. C., Shang, C. Y., Shieh, M. S., Lin, H. N., & Su, J. C. J. (2011). The interactions between religion, religiosity, religious delusion/hallucination, and treatment-seeking behavior among schizophrenic patients in Taiwan. *Psychiatry Research*, *187*(3), 347–353.

Hurd, M. D., Martorell, P., Delavande, A., Mullen, K. J., & Langa, K. M. (2013). Monetary costs of dementia in the United States. *New England Journal of Medicine*, *368*, 1326–1334.

Inzelberg, R., Afgin, A., Massarwa, M., Schechtman, E., Israeli-Korn, S., Strugastsky, R., Amin, A., Efrat, K., Lindsay, A. F., & Friedland, R. (2013). Prayer at midlife is associated with reduced risk of cognitive decline in Arabic women. *Current Alzheimer Research*, *10*(3), 340–346.

Iyassu, R., Jolley, S., Bebbington, P., Dunn, G., Emsley, R., Freeman, D., & Garety, P. (2014). Psychological characteristics of religious delusions. *Social Psychiatry and Psychiatric Epidemiology*, *49*(7), 1051–1061.

Jerrell, J. M., & Shugart, M. A. (2004). Community-based care for youths with early and very-early onset bipolar I disorder. *Bipolar Disorders*, *6*(4), 299–304.

Kaufman, Y., Anaki, D., Binns, M., & Freedman, M. (2007). Cognitive decline in Alzheimer disease: Impact of spirituality, religiosity, and QOL. *Neurology*, *68*(18), 1509–1514.

Kilicaslan, E. E., Acar, G., Eksioglu, S., Kesebir, S., & Tezcan, E. (2016). The effect of delusion and hallucination types on treatment response in schizophrenia and schizoaffective disorder. *Journal of Psychiatry and Neurological Sciences*, *29*(1), 29–35.

Kim, D. H. (2016). The relationship between activities of daily living and support burden, depressive symptoms in caregivers of dementia: The moderating effect of religiosity—clinical research center for dementia of South Korea (credos) study. *Alzheimer's and Dementia: The Journal of the Alzheimer's Association*, *12*(7), 607.

Kirov, G., Kemp, R., Kirov, K., & David, A. S. (1998). Religious faith after psychotic illness. *Psychopathology*, *31*(5), 234–245.

Kitamura, T., Okazaki, Y., Funinawa, A., et al. (1998). Dimensions of schizophrenic positive symptoms: An exploratory factor analysis. *European Archives of Psychiatry and Clinical Neurosciences*, *248*, 130-135.

Koenig HG (2011). Schizophrenia and other psychotic disorders. In J. Peteet, F. G. Lu, & W. E. Narrow (Eds.), *Religious and spiritual issues in psychiatric diagnosis: A research agenda for DSM-V* (pp. 31–52). Arlington, VA: American Psychiatric Association Press (chapter 2).

Koenig, H. G., King, D. E., & Carson, V. B. (2012). *Handbook of religion and health* (2nd ed.). New York, NY: Oxford University Press.

Koenig, H. G., McCollough, M. E., & Larson, D. B. (2001). *Handbook of religion* (1st ed.). New York, NY: Oxford University Press.

Koenig, H. G., Nelson, B., Shaw, S. F., Saxena, S., & Cohen, H. J. (2016a). Religious involvement and adaptation in female family caregivers. *Journal of the American Geriatrics Society*, *64*(3), 578–583.

Koenig, H. G., Nelson, B., Shaw, S. F., Saxena, S., & Cohen, H. J. (2016b). Religious involvement and telomere length in women family caregivers. *Journal of Nervous and Mental Disease*, *204*(1), 36–42.

Krzystanek, M., Krysta, K., Klasik, A., & Krupka-Matuszczyk, I. (2012). Religious content of hallucinations in paranoid schizophrenia. *Psychiatria Danubina*, *24*, S65–S69.

Kua, E. H., Ho, E., Tan, H. H., Tsoi, C., Thng, C., & Mahendran, R. (2014). The natural history of dementia. *Psychogeriatrics*, *14*(3), 196–201.

Lin, K. P., Chou, Y. C., Chen, J. H., Chen, C. D., Yang, S. Y., Chen, T. F., & Chen, Y. C. (2015). Religious affiliation and the risk of dementia in Taiwanese elderly. *Archives of Gerontology and Geriatrics*, *60*(3), 501–506.

Linden, S. C., Harris, M., Whitaker, C., & Healy, D. (2010). Religion and psychosis: The effects of the Welsh religious revival in 1904–1905. *Psychological Medicine*, *40*(08), 1317–1323.

Lindgren, K. N., & Coursey, R. D. (1995). Spirituality and serious mental illness: A two-part study. *Psychosocial Rehabilitation Journal*, *18*(3), 93–111.

Maltby, J., & Day, L. (2002). Religious experience, religious orientation and schizotypy. *Mental Health, Religion and Culture*, *5*(2), 163–174.

Maura J., & de Mamani, A. W. (2017). Culturally adapted psychosocial interventions for schizophrenia: A review. *Cognitive and Behavioral Practice*. Available from https://doi.org/10. 1016/j. cbpra. 2017. 01. 004. (E-pub ahead of press).

McCullagh, C. D., Craig, D., McIlroy, S. P., & Passmore, A. P. (2001). Risk factors for dementia. *Advances in Psychiatric Treatment*, *7*(1), 24–31.

Merikangas, K. R., Akiskal, H. S., Angst, J., Greenberg, P. E., Hirschfeld, R. M., Petukhova, M., & Kessler, R. C. (2007). Lifetime and 12-month prevalence of bipolar spectrum disorder in the National Comorbidity Survey replication. *Archives of General Psychiatry*, *64*(5), 543–552.

Merikangas, K. R., Jin, R., He, J. P., Kessler, R. C., Lee, S., Sampson, N. A., & Ladea, M. (2011). Prevalence and correlates of bipolar spectrum disorder in the world mental health survey initiative. *Archives of General Psychiatry*, *68*(3), 241–251.

Messias, E. L., Chen, C. Y., & Eaton, W. W. (2007). Epidemiology of schizophrenia: Review of findings and myths. *Psychiatric Clinics of North America*, *30*(3), 323–338.

Michalak, E. E., Yatham, L. N., Kolesar, S., & Lam, R. W. (2006). Bipolar disorder and quality of life: A patient-centered perspective. *Quality of Life Research*, *15*(1), 25–37.

Miller, R., & McCormack, J. (2006). Faith and religious delusions in first episode schizophrenia. *Social Work in Mental Health*, *4*(4), 37–50.

Mitchell, L., & Romans, S. (2003). Spiritual beliefs in bipolar affective disorder: Their relevance for illness management. *Journal of Affective Disorders*, *75*(3), 247–257.

Mizock, L., Millner, U. C., & Russinova, Z. (2012). Spiritual and religious issues in psychotherapy with schizophrenia: Cultural implications and implementation. *Religions*, *3*(1), 82–98.

Mohr, S., Borras, L., Rieben, I., Betrisey, C., Gillieron, C., Brandt, P. Y., & Huguelet, P. (2010). Evolution of spirituality and religiousness in chronic schizophrenia or schizo-affective disorders: A 3-years follow-up study. *Social Psychiatry and Psychiatric Epidemiology*, *45*(11), 1095–1103.

Mohr, S., Brandt, P. Y., Borras, L., Gilliéron, C., & Huguelet, P. (2006). Toward an integration of spirituality and religiousness into the psychosocial dimension of schizophrenia. *American Journal of Psychiatry*, *163*(11), 1952–1959.

Mohr, S., Perroud, N., Gillieron, C., Brandt, P. Y., Rieben, I., Borras, L., & Huguelet, P. (2011). Spirituality and religiousness as predictive factors of outcome in schizophrenia and schizo-affective disorders. *Psychiatry Research*, *186*(2), 177–182.

Murray, C. J., & Lopez, A. D. (1996). Evidence-based health policy: Lessons from the Global Burden of Disease Study. *Science*, *274*(5288), 740–743.

Nikfarjam, M. (2011). The efficacy of religious training (prayer) on the improvement of the schizophrenic patients' quality of life at Sina Psychiatric Hospital (Bakhtiari Province 2011). *Arak Medical University Journal*, *13*(5), 133–138.

Norton, S., Matthews, F. E., Barnes, D. E., Yaffe, K., & Brayne, C. (2014). Potential for primary prevention of Alzheimer's disease: An analysis of population-based data. *Lancet Neurology*, *13*(8), 788–794.
Patel, N. C., DelBello, M. P., & Strakowski, S. M. (2006). Ethnic differences in symptom presentation of youths with bipolar disorder. *Bipolar Disorders*, *8*(1), 95–99.
Pierre, J. M. (2001). Faith or delusion: At the crossroads of religion and psychosis. *Journal of Psychiatric Practice*, *7*(3), 163–172.
Polimeni, J. (2012). *Shamans among us: Schizophrenia, shamanism and the evolutionary origins of religion*. Morrisville, NC: Lulu.
Prince, M., Bryce, R., Albanese, E., Wimo, A., Ribeiro, W., & Ferri, C. P. (2013). The global prevalence of dementia: A systematic review and metaanalysis. *Alzheimer's and Dementia*, *9*(1), 63–75.
Raguram, R., Venkateswaran, A., Ramakrishna, J., & Weiss, M. G. (2002). Traditional community resources for mental health: A report of temple healing from India. *British Medical Journal*, *325*(7354), 38–40.
Reed, P., & Clarke, N. (2014). Effect of religious context on the content of visual hallucinations in individuals high in religiosity. *Psychiatry Research*, *215*(3), 594–598.
Rosmarin, D. H., Bigda-Peyton, J. S., Öngur, D., Pargament, K. I., & Björgvinsson, T. (2013). Religious coping among psychotic patients: Relevance to suicidality and treatment outcomes. *Psychiatry Research*, *210*(1), 182–187.
Rudalevičien , P., Stompe, T., Narbekovas, A., Raškauskien , N., & Bunevičius, R. (2008). Are religious delusions related to religiosity in schizophrenia. *Medicina (Kaunas)*, *44*(7), 529–535.
Saha, S., Chant, D., Welham, J., & McGrath, J. (2005). A systematic review of the prevalence of schizophrenia. *PLoS Medicine*, *2*(5), 141.
Siddle, R., Haddock, G., Tarrier, N., et al. (2002a). Religious delusions in patients admitted to hospital with schizophrenia. *Social Psychiatry and Psychiatric Epidemiology*, *37*(3), 130–138.
Siddle, R., Haddock, G., Tarrier, N., et al. (2002b). The validation of a religiosity measure for individuals with schizophrenia. *Mental Health, Religion and Culture*, *5*(3), 267–284.
Siddle, R., Haddock, G., Tarrier, N., et al. (2004). Religious beliefs and religious delusions: Response to treatment in schizophrenia. *Mental Health, Religion and Culture*, *7*(3), 211–223.
Simon, M., & Dong, X. (2016). The association between filial piety and cognitive impairment: Findings from a community dwelling older Chinese population. *Alzheimer's and Dementia: The Journal of the Alzheimer's Association*, *12*(7), P606–P607.
Smolak, A., Gearing, R. E., Alonzo, D., Baldwin, S., Harmon, S., & McHugh, K. (2013). Social support and religion: Mental health service use and treatment of schizophrenia. *Community Mental Health Journal*, *49*(4), 444–450.
Stroppa, A., Colugnati, F. A. B., Koenig, H. G., & Moreira-Almeida, A. (2017). Religiosity, depression and quality of life in bipolar disorder: A two-year prospective study. *Revista Brasileira de Psiquiatria (Brazilian Journal of Clinical Psychiatry), in press.*
Stroppa, A., & Moreira-Almeida, A. (2013). Religiosity, mood symptoms, and quality of life in bipolar disorder. *Bipolar Disorders*, *15*(4), 385–393.
Tateyama, M., Asai, M., Hashimoto, M., et al. (1998). Transcultural study of schizophrenic delusions: Tokyo versus Vienna versus Tubingen (Germany). *Psychopathology*, *31*(2), 59–66.
Tepper, L., Rogers, S. A., Coleman, E. M., & Malony, H. N. (2001). The prevalence of religious coping among persons with persistent mental illness. *Psychiatric Services*, *52*(5), 660–665.
Verghese, A., John, J. K., Rajkumar, S., Richard, J., Sethi, B. B., & Trivedi F, K. (1989). Factors associated with the course and outcome of schizophrenia in India: Results of a two-year multicentre follow-up study. *British Journal of Psychiatry*, *154*, 499–503.
Whiteford, H. A., Ferrari, A. J., Degenhardt, L., Feigin, V., & Vos, T. (2015). The global burden of mental, neurological and substance use disorders: An analysis from the Global Burden of Disease Study 2010. *PloS One*, *10*(2), e0116820.

Wu, E. Q., Shi, L., Birnbaum, H., Hudson, T., & Kessler, R. (2006). Annual prevalence of diagnosed schizophrenia in the USA: A claims data analysis approach. *Psychological Medicine, 36*(11), 1535–1540.

Zhang W (2010) Religious participation, gender differences, and cognitive impairment among the oldest old. *China Journal of Aging Research* 160294. Available from http://www.ncbi.nlm.nih.gov/pmc/articles/PMC2990098/.

Zilboorg, G., & Henry, G. W. (1941). *A History of Medical Psychology*. New York, NY: WW Norton Co.

CHAPTER

6

Positive Emotions

The previous two chapters focused on religious involvement and psychopathology. This chapter departs from the pathological and focuses on the opposite—the experience of mental health and well-being characteristic of a full, thriving, and flourishing life. Positive emotions often help to neutralize negative emotions and may prevent the onset of emotional disorders (and/or their consequences). The field of Positive Psychology now exists with hundreds of studies documenting the relationship between positive emotions and both mental and physical health (Lopez, Pedrotti, & Snyder, 2014). Here, we focus on the relationship between religious involvement and positive emotions such as psychological well-being (well-being, happiness, and life satisfaction [LS]), hope, optimism, and meaning/purpose in life, summarizing the results of both early and more recent research.

PSYCHOLOGICAL WELL-BEING

William James (1890) said that "how to gain, how to keep, how to recover happiness is in fact for most men at all times the secret motive of all they do" (p. 19). Psychological well-being has been linked to environmental mastery and personal growth with aging; personality traits such as extraversion, conscientiousness, purpose in life and self-acceptance; better relationships with the family; success at work and other life pursuits; and physical health, health behaviors, and biological outcomes such as gene expression (Ryff, 2014). Is religious involvement, then, related to well-being?

Early Research

Our systematic review of quantitative research published prior to 2010 identified 326 studies that examined the association between

Religion and Mental Health. http://dx.doi.org/10.1016/B978-0-12-811282-3.00006-9

religiosity and well-being, happiness, or life satisfaction (Koenig, King, & Carson, 2012; Koenig, McCollough, & Larson, 2001). Of those, 79% (256 studies) reported positive associations, 1% (3 studies) indicated negative associations, and 20% reported mixed findings or no association. Among the 120 highest quality studies (based on sampling method, sample size, research design, and statistical controls), 82% reported positive associations and 1% (one study) reported a negative association. Unfortunately, most of these studies were cross-sectional, making it difficult to say whether greater religiosity increases well-being or whether greater well-being increases religiosity. Nevertheless, there were a number of longitudinal studies in this early research where researchers examined the effect of religious involvement at one point in time to determine if it might predict future well-being (controlling for baseline well-being). In addition, there have been several single group experimental studies and randomized clinical trials (RCTs) that have examined the effects of religious or spiritual (R/S) interventions on well-being. Because of their importance, all 16 prospective studies in this systematic review are summarized briefly below, usually in the order of year of publication.

In describing these studies, the timing of R/S measurement in relationship to the assessment of well-being is carefully specified. In particular, special attention is paid to pointing out whether baseline values of well-being (T1) are controlled for in the model predicting future well-being (T2). Only in this way, can one determine whether R/S actually predicts an increase (or decrease) in psychological well-being over time (the primary purpose of prospective studies in this area).With regard to observational research, only prospective studies are reviewed here given their important contributions toward identifying causal relationships between religiosity and well-being.

Prospective Studies

In one of the first longitudinal studies, Willits and Crider (1988) analyzed data from a 37-year follow-up of 1385 sophomores (Pennsylvania), assessing adolescent and parent religiosity in 1947 (T1), current religiosity in 1984 (T2), and LS in 1984 (T2). Adolescent religious participation (church, Sunday school, and church socials) and mother and father religious attendance were assessed at T1; current religious attendance and religious belief (5-item scale) were measured at T2. LS at T2 was assessed by four items that measured overall LS, community LS, job LS, and marital LS. Bivariate analyses indicated that father's religious attendance at T1 predicted overall LS at T2 ($r = 0.07$, $p < 0.01$); however, after controlling for gender and family income, the association lost significance. Both father's and mother's T1 religious attendance predicted community LS at T2, but again lost significance, when controlling for gender and income. No T1 religious variables predicted T2 marital LS in either bivariate or multivariate analyses. Adolescent religious participation at T1 (but not parent attendance) significantly predicted job satisfaction at T2 in both bivariate and multivariate analyses ($r = 0.06$, $p < 0.05$; $B = 0.14$, $p < 0.05$). However, T1 job satisfaction was not controlled for in those analyses.

In a small study of 44 participants aged 62–89 (Midwestern United States), Graney (1975) assessed religious attendance at baseline (T1) and then again after 4 years (T2). Happiness (assessed by Bradburn's Affect Balance Scale) was measured only at T2. Religious attendance at T2 was strongly associated with happiness at T2 (Kendall tau = 0.33, $p < 0.01$). However, change in religious attendance (T2 minus T1) only weakly predicted happiness at T2 ($p = 0.07$). As T1 happiness was not measured, it could not be controlled in analyses.

Anson, Antonovsky, and Sagy (1990) examined 805 adults age 60 or above in Israel, of whom 639 were reassessed after 12 months. Structural equation modeling was used to assess the effects of a single question "To what extent do you observe the religious rituals?" at baseline (T1) on LS (satisfaction with family, personal relations, standard of living, social activity, and general LS) at follow-up (T2). Controlling for gender and socioeconomic status as exogenous variables, results indicated that T1 religiosity significantly predicted T2 LS ($T = 2.21$, $p = 0.01$) with T1 LS in the model. While T1 religiosity did not significantly affect T2 psychological distress or physical health, both greater T1 psychological distress and poorer T1 physical health did predict an increase in religiosity from T1 to T2 (suggesting a turning to religion to cope with these difficulties). Because T1 religiosity significantly predicted T2 LS with T1 LS in the model, this indicates that baseline religiosity predicted an increase in LS over time.

Kass, Friedman, Leserman, Zuttermeister, and Benson (1991) followed 83 adults (living in the Northeastern United States) participating in a 10-week experimental study involving the relaxation response. Participants were assessed at baseline (T1) and 10 weeks later (T2). Spirituality was assessed with the 11-item Index of Core Spiritual Experiences (INSPIRIT), and life satisfaction and purpose (LSP) by a subscale of the Index of Positive Psychological Attitudes. Controlling for LSP score at T1 and demographic factors, INSPIRIT scores at T1 significantly predicted T2 LSP scores ($B = 0.15$, $p = 0.02$), again indicating that spirituality predicted an increase in life satisfaction and purpose over time.

In an 11-year prospective study of 3 generations of 624 Mexican Americans living in San Antonio, Texas, Levin, Markides, and Ray (1996) assessed the effects of baseline religious attendance (T1) on LS (measured by 13-item Life Satisfaction Index) at follow-up (T2), controlling for LS at T1 along with sociodemographic and health characteristics using a fully recursive 2-wave path model. T1 religious attendance, however, did not predict T2 LS in any of the 3 generations (young, middle age, or old).

Tix and Frazier (1998) assessed 174 renal transplant patients and 123 significant others at 3 months (T1) and 12 months (T2) postrenal transplantation (University of Minnesota Hospital), assessing religious coping with a 10-item scale and LS with the Diener's 5-item Satisfaction with Life Scale at T1 and T2. Controlling for age, gender, income, and marital status, they found that T1 religious coping significantly predicted T2 LS in both patients and significant others ($B = 0.30$ and $B = 0.35$, respectively, both $p < 0.01$). However, when T1 LS was controlled for in these analyses, significant findings were reduced to nonsignificance ($B = 0.11$ and $B = 0.09$, respectively, both $p > 0.05$), indicating that changes in LS were not predicted by religious coping.

In a 30-year prospective study of 181 California adults followed from early adulthood to late adulthood, Wink and Dillon (2003) examined the effects of religiousness during early adulthood (age 30s, T1) and late middle adulthood (age 50s or early 60s, T2) on well-being in late adulthood (age late 60s and 70s, T3), controlling for social service, community service, and a measure of generativity. Religiousness was assessed by importance of institutionalized or tradition-center religious beliefs/practices in life. Well-being was measured by (1) the degree to which the participant had warm satisfying relationships with others and capacity to maintain a sense of affection/intimacy (personal relations) and (2) the degree of "personal growth." Results indicated that religiousness in early adulthood (T1) and late middle adulthood (T2) predicted *personal relations well-being* in late adulthood (T3) (both $B = 0.22$, $p < 0.05$), but not *personal growth well-being* ($B = 0.15$ and $B = 0.11$, both $p > 0.05$); however, well-being in early adulthood (T1) or late middle adulthood (T2) was not controlled for in these analyses.

Brown, Nesse, House, and Utz (2004) assessed 103 widowed persons (Detroit, MI) at baseline (T0) before being widowed and at 6 (T1), 18 (T2), and 48 months (T3) after their loss, examining the effects of increases in religiosity (assessed by importance of R/S beliefs and religious attendance) on well-being (assessed by five items from Bradburn's Affect Balance Scale). Although increases in religiousness from T0 to T1, T2, and T3 was associated with lower grief at T2 and T3, they did not significantly predict later well-being at any point in time except weakly at T1 ($p < 0.10$); again, baseline well-being (T0) was not controlled for in these analyses.

Frame, Uphold, Shehan, and Reid (2005) assessed spiritual coping (6-item scale) and emotional well-being (7-item scale) at baseline (T1) and 12-month follow-up (T2) in 197 HIV-positive men living in the Southeastern United States. Random effects regression was used to examine the effects of T1 spiritual coping on T2 well-being. T1 spiritual coping did not predict T2 well-being after controlling for T1 well-being, CD4 count, race, education, age, marital status, and time.

In a 3-year prospective study of a nationally representative sample of 852 adults above age 65 in the United States (all practicing Christians), Krause (2006) examined the effects of baseline (T1) religious doubts on LS 3 years later (T2). Religious doubts were measured by a 5-item scale that assessed doubts about religious beliefs, doubts about the church's teachings, and doubts about whether prayer makes a difference. LS was assessed by three questions obtained from standard scales. Controlling for T1 LS and demographic factors, T1 religious doubts were not directly related to T2 LS; however, religious doubts interacted with education level such that among those with less than a college education, higher scores on T1 religious doubt predicted a significant decline in T2 LS (an effect that was not present among those with a college education). Stated in reverse, among older adults who are practicing Christians but have less education, greater certainty in belief is likely to result in an increase in well-being over time.

Park (2006) assessed 69 volunteer adults age 55 or older (Cincinnati, OH) at baseline (T1) and 1 month later (T2). Private religiousness, public religiousness, and religious coping assessed at T1 all positively predicted T2 psychological well-being (assessed by growth from most stressful event, growth from current stressor, and fewer depressive symptoms), controlling for T1 measures of well-being. Eight of nine predictions were statistically significant.

Shaw et al. (2007) followed 97 women with breast cancer participating in a computer support group for low-income women living in rural Wisconsin or Detroit, Michigan. Participants were surveyed before they were enrollment in the program (T1) and then again 4 months later (T2). Message transcripts were analyzed using a word counting program to determine the percentage of words related to religious expression during the 4-month follow-up period, which was the primary religious predictor variable. Emotional well-being was assessed at T1 and T2 using a 6-item scale (sad, worried, pessimistic, etc.); functional well-being was measured with a 5-item scale (able to work, enjoy life in the moment, sleep well, enjoy leisure pursuits, etc.). Controlling for T1 well-being measures as well as demographics, religious beliefs, breast cancer concerns, and negative emotions, the analyses revealed that religious expression significantly predicted increases in T2 functional well-being ($B = 0.310$, $p < 0.001$). The effect of religious expression on T2 emotional well-being was in a similar direction but did not reach statistical significance ($B = 0.173$, $p > 0.05$).

In a 12-month prospective study of 408 Australians with multiple sclerosis (MS) and 232 caregivers, Pakenham (2007) assessed R/S belief and spiritual perspective at baseline (T1) and LS at baseline (T1) and follow-up (T2). Presence of R/S belief was measured using a single question (yes vs. no); spiritual perspective was assessed by an 8-item scale (e.g., multiple sclerosis is part of God's plan/will for me; I got multiple sclerosis so I could grow spiritually/in my faith; etc.). LS was measured using Diener's 5-item Satisfaction with Life Scale. After controlling for LS at T1, neither R/S belief nor spiritual perspective at T1 significantly predicted LS at T2.

Petts and Knoester (2007) analyzed data on 890 first-time married couples and their children (ages 5–17) who participated in Wave I (1987–88) and Wave II (1992–94) of the National Survey of Families and Households, a 5-year prospective study of a national probability sample of US adults. Wave I (T1) religious participation was assessed by frequency of parent religious attendance and religious affiliation (particularly religious homogamy, i.e., both parents with same religious affiliation vs. not). Child well-being was assessed at Wave II (T2) by a single question ("Taking all things together, on a scale from 0 to 10, where 0 means really bad and 10 means absolutely perfect, how would you say things are for you these days?"). In regression models that included 19 control and predictor variables (but not T1 child well-being), no measures of parental religious participation or homogamy significantly predicted T2 child well-being.

In a 23-year prospective study of 456 men from the Boston area (Harvard study examining the development of alcoholism across the lifespan), Koenig and Vaillant (2009) examined the effects of religious attendance at age 47 (T1) on subjective well-being (SWB) at age 70 (T2, final $n = 141$ for regression model). SWB was assessed by satisfaction with work, children, friends, marriage, community service, hobbies, and sports on a 2–10 scale for each. "Health" was a composite variable consisting of objective physical health, subjective health, and subjective well-being combined. With only T1 religious attendance in the model, T1 attendance significantly predicted T2 SWB ($B = 0.39$, $p < 0.001$). When "health" at T1 was entered into the model (which included T1 SWB), the effect remained strong ($B = 0.39$, $p < 0.001$). Adding social class, years of education, mood, alcohol abuse/dependence, and smoking (all assessed at T1) to the model, reduced the effect only slightly ($B = 0.28$, $p = 0.001$). Thus, frequent religious attendance at midlife (ages 45–47) predicted a significant increase in subjective well-being by age 70, independent of other predictors and baseline well-being.

Ai et al. (2010) followed 262 patients receiving a coronary artery bypass graft at the University of Michigan from before surgery (T1) to 30 months afterward (T2) examining the effects of T1 religious involvement on T2 well-being (well-being operationalized as low levels of depression and anxiety). Religious involvement was assessed by use of prayer to cope (3-item index), public religiousness, private religiousness, subjective religiousness, religious reverence (4-item measure), and by positive and negative religious coping. Regression analyses controlled for demographics, physical health factors, T1 depression, T1 hope, and both T1 and T2 optimism. Results indicated that use of prayer to cope at T1 was significantly and inversely related to T2 depressive symptoms ($B = -0.24$, $p < 0.01$); however, religious reverence at T1 significantly and positively predicted T2 depression ($B = 0.20$, $p < 0.05$). With regard to predictors of anxiety, T1 subjective religiousness predicted less T2 anxiety ($B = -0.18$, $p < 0.05$) but religious reverence again predicted greater T2 anxiety ($B = 0.18$, $p < 0.05$), after controlling for T1 anxiety and other variables (as for depression above).

In summary, our systematic review identified 16 prospective studies of R/S and well-being. In most of those studies, cross-sectional analyses indicated a strong positive relationship between R/S and well-being. However, in only 8 of 16 studies (50%) did baseline R/S at T1 predict greater future well-being at T2 in multivariate analyses. In 6 of those 8 studies, baseline T1 well-being was controlled for, providing evidence that baseline R/S predicted an increase in well-being over time (6 of the 11 studies overall that controlled for baseline well-being).

When considering results from prospective studies, however, another important research design issue needs to be considered. This issue is the amount of time necessary for the change in the outcome (psychological well-being) to occur. In studies with only a short follow-up period, it is unlikely that much change in well-being will occur from baseline to follow-up, decreasing the power and likelihood of detecting a significant effect of R/S on change in well-being (since little change has occurred). With this in mind, note that all studies in this review that followed participants for more than 10 years reported that R/S significantly predicted increases in well-being over time.

Experimental Studies

There were five single group experimental studies. The first study involved a 2.5-day wellness educational retreat that included spiritual principles to increase spirituality in 72 cardiac rehab patients and partners in Wisconsin; results indicated that increased spirituality during the retreat was associated with increased psychological well-being (Kennedy, Abbott, & Rosenberg, 2002). The second study involved a Hindu-based lifestyle change program that included 200 participants in India; researchers reported an increase in well-being in the vast majority as a result of the program (Mohan, Prasad, & Rao, 2004). The third study involved 236 participants in Arizona who underwent a single session of Johrei healing (a Japanese spiritual practice); results indicated a significant increase in well-being in the group (Reece, Schwartz, Brooks, & Nangle, 2005). The fourth study involved a 3.5-day spiritual care training program engaged in by 63 palliative care professionals in Munich, Germany; results indicated a significant increase in satisfaction with work (Wasner, Longaker, Fegg, & Borasio, 2005). Finally, Bijlani et al. (2005) examined the effects on well-being of an 8-day lifestyle modification program based on Yoga principles; researchers reported a significant increase in SWB among the 33 adult participants in the program (conducted in India). All of these interventions, then, produced a significant increase in well-being based on before and after assessments. However, all involved relatively poor research designs without a control group. Not much, then, can be concluded from these studies.

Randomized Clinical Trials

Finally, our systematic review identified nine RCTs that examined the effects of R/S interventions on psychological well-being compared to controls. Again, these are reviewed in order of year of publication. The first RCT was conducted by Beutler et al. (1988) who randomized 120 hypertensive patients in the Netherlands to spiritual/paranormal healing by laying on of hands (Group 1), healing at a distance by thought projection (Group 2), or a control group (Group 3). Participants in Group 1 and Group 2 received treatments for 20 minutes once per week for 15 weeks. Results indicated improvements in general well-being in Group 1 that significantly exceeded those in either Group 2 or Group 3.

In the second study, Rye and Pargament (2002) randomized 48 Christian female college students in Ohio to either a religious intervention directed at forgiveness toward a former boyfriend or to a secular intervention, finding no difference between the two interventions with regard to increasing existential well-being. Gerard, Smith, and Simpson (2003) examined the effects of a spiritual healing intervention (prayer/meditations that involved a laying on of hands performed by a single healer) in 68 medical patients with restricted neck movements (stiff neck); again, no significant difference in overall well-being was found between intervention and control groups.

Kristeller, Rhodes, Cripe, and Sheets (2005) alternatively assigned 118 cancer patients to either an intervention group where they received a spiritual history from their oncologists or a control group where they did not. Those in the intervention group experienced significantly greater functional well-being than those in the control group 3 weeks after the intervention. Richards, Berrett, Hardman, and Eggett (2006) randomized 122 women with eating disorders to (1) a 60-minute-weekly spiritual renewal group where participants received Judeo–Christian spiritual readings and educational materials emphasizing spiritual identity, grace, forgiveness, repentance, faith, prayer, and meditation, (2) a cognitive therapy group, or (3) an emotional support group. Those in the spirituality group experienced significantly greater increases in existential well-being than those in either the cognitive therapy or the emotional support group. Oman et al. (2006) randomized 58 health professionals to either an intervention where they received eight 2-hour weekly sessions of a Hindu form of meditation called "passage meditation" (Easwaran) or to a wait-list control group. No significant difference was found between intervention and control groups in overall life satisfaction or job satisfaction.

Moritz et al. (2006) randomized 165 adults with emotional distress to (1) an 8-week spiritual home-study program (prayer, meditation, gratitude, and visualizations involving the divine), (2) an 8-week mindfulness meditation-based stress-reduction program (meditation group), or (3) a wait-list control group. Results indicated an increase in vitality (well-being) in the spirituality group exceeding that in the meditation or control groups. Moadel et al. (2007) randomized 128 breast cancer patients in New York City to either a 12-week Yoga intervention program or a wait-list control group. While no difference was found between groups on emotional well-being in the overall sample, secondary analyses conducted in those who did not receive chemotherapy indicated that those in the Yoga group increased significantly in emotional well-being compared to those in the control group.

Finally, Goldstein (2007) randomized 73 adults in Palo Alto, California, to either a group that received a 3-week "cultivating of sacred moments" intervention for 5 minutes/day for 5 days/week (mindfulness breathing and slowing down, followed by shifting attention to a sacred object and being open to what was sacred in the moment) or to a control group that received a writing task for 5 minutes/day for 5 days/week. No significant difference in SWB was found between the two groups at 3 and 6 weeks of follow-up.

In summary, about half of the clinical trials in this systematic review found that a R/S intervention significantly increased psychological well-being above that of wait-listed or active control conditions. The remaining trials found no difference in well-being between groups. No studies reported that secular interventions were superior to R/S interventions in their effects on well-being. These findings, together with the results of a majority of the prospective studies, support the argument that R/S increases psychological well-being.

Recent Research

To what extent does more recent research support these earlier findings? Below is a selective review of high quality studies (cross-sectional, prospective, clinical trials) reported since 2010.

Kashdan and Nezlek (2012) examined the relationship between R/S and psychological well-being using a daily diary in 87 college students (Virginia) conducted over 1239 days. Daily spirituality (a spirituality "state" indicator) was measured with two questions: "Today, the spiritual part of my life was very important to me" and "Today, my personal relationship with a power greater than myself was important to me." In addition, "trait" spirituality was measured by a 22-item spiritual involvement and beliefs scale. Daily measures of psychological well-being were operationalized as self-esteem, meaning in life, and positive affect. The data were analyzed using a series of multilevel models, and used lagged analyses to determine whether R/S predicted future well-being. Results indicated a significant cross-sectional relationship between daily R/S and meaning in life, self-esteem, and positive affect. A positive relationship was also found between present-day R/S and next day's meaning in life, whereas there was no evidence that meaning in life predicted next day's R/S. Finally, among those with higher trait R/S, greater negative affect and lower positive affect on one day predicted greater R/S on the next day. Thus R/S increased well-being, and low well-being increased R/S (at least among those who were more R/S).

Sorensen et al. (2012) examined the prevalence of "Seeking God's Help" in cancer patients and its relationship to LS and quality of life, analyzing cross-sectional data from the third wave of the Nord-Trondelag Health Study of Norway (2006–08). The sample included 2086 cancer patients and 6258 cancer-free controls. "Seeking God's Help" was measured by a single question: "I seek God's help when I need strength and solace." LS was measured by a single question: "Thinking about your life at the moment, would you say that you, by and large, are satisfied with life, or are you mostly dissatisfied?" Among cancer patients, responses to the Seeking God's Help question indicated that 14% said "often", 45% "sometimes," and 41% said "never"; the distribution of responses was almost identical in cancer-free controls. After controlling for gender, age, anxiety, neuroticism, extraversion, daily smoking, exercise, and outlook, Seeking God's Help was unrelated to LS or to quality of life measures. Thus, in this secular northern European country, only 14% of cancer patients said they often sought God's help; conversely, 41% said they never did so. In fact, those who sought God's help were significantly more anxious and had more insomnia (in other bivariate analyses), consistent with the Kashdan and Nezlek study that found increases in R/S immediately following negative psychological states (suggesting a turn to religion to cope with distress).

The findings in Norway appear to be different from those in the United States, even the northeastern part of the United States that tends to be more secular. Harvard researchers conducted a survey of 69 advanced cancer patients receiving palliative radiation therapy at local Boston hospitals (Vallurupalli et al., 2012). Religious involvement, religious coping, and quality of life were assessed using standard scales. Over three-quarters (76%) indicated they used religious beliefs or activities to at least a moderate extent when managing stress, with nearly 20% indicating religion was the most important factor keeping them going. Controlling for physical functioning, both positive religious coping (PRC) and self-rated spirituality were related to greater overall quality of life ($p = 0.01$ and $p < 0.001$, respectively). Nearly 60% also considered it moderately or very important for oncology physicians and nurses to recognize patients' spiritual needs.

These findings are consistent with the hypothesis that religiosity, at least in cross-sectional studies, is more strongly related to quality of life and well-being in countries where the culture (society) supports religious involvement (Gebauer, Sedikides, & Neberich, 2012; Ju, Zhang, You, Alterman, & Li, 2016). This hypothesis is reinforced by the findings of Hayward and Elliott (2014) who analyzed data from five waves of the World Values Survey involving 317,109 individuals from 88 countries. Happiness was assessed with a single question: "Taking all things together, would you say you are: not at all happy, not very happy, quite happy, or very happy?" Three indicators of religiosity were assessed (attendance, importance of God, and subjective religiousness). Also analyzed were country-level norms for each of these religious variables and government restrictions on religious expression. Linear mixed modeling was used to analyze the data. After adjusting analyses for age, gender, income, and country-level gross domestic product (GDP), government restrictions, and country-level religious norms, results indicated that all three religious measures were positively related to greater happiness (all $p < 0.001$). The strongest positive relationships between religiousness and happiness were found in countries with heavy government restrictions on religious freedom, if the country had high religious norms (e.g., Iran, Pakistan, and Ethiopia). In countries with low government restrictions and low religious involvement (like Northern European countries); however, religiousness was related to somewhat lower happiness. In countries with strong government restrictions on freedom of religious expression and low religious norms (Communist countries), greater religiosity was associated with substantially lower happiness.

However, positive cross-sectional relationships between religiosity and well-being have been reported even in nonreligious regions of the world. Consider the findings from a national random sample of 12,643 adults in Hungary (a former communist country) 13 years after the fall of the Iron Curtain (Thege, Pilling, Székely, & Kopp, 2013). In that study, only 8% of men and 16% of women attended religious services regularly, and religion was either not important or only slightly important in 81% of men and 66% of women. After adjusting for age, gender, and education, however, both religious attendance and importance of religion were strongly associated with greater well-being ($p < 0.001$). Furthermore, not all studies from northern Europe find lower well-being among the more religious, as researchers (Kvande, Klöckner, Moksnes, & Espnes, 2015; Kvande, Klöckner, & Nielsen, 2015) have shown in a random sample of adults in Norway. Finally, relationships between religiosity and well-being even in religious areas of the world may not always be positive in certain populations (Meanley, Pingel, & Bauermeister, 2016). Thus, results may vary depending on the particular culture, the history of that culture (especially where the culture is changing), and the particular population group. Again, however, results from cross-sectional studies alone make it difficult to make any conclusions about how social and cultural factors determine when and how religion is used in coping, which may be important in determining the relationship between religiosity and well-being. Besides cross-sectional studies, however, several recent longitudinal studies have examined whether R/S affects future changes in well-being, controlling for baseline well-being or mental health.

In a 3-year prospective study that examined the effects of the September 11th terrorist attacks on the mental and physical health of Americans, McIntosh, Poulin, Silver, and Holman (2011) assessed R/S involvement shortly after the attacks (November/December) to determine whether it would predict changes in mental health over time. Participants were a representative US national sample of 890 adults. Religiosity was assessed by frequency of attendance at religious or spiritual services (RA); intrinsic religiosity (IR) was measured using two IR items from the 9-item Religious Orientation Scale (Gorsuch). Psychological well-being was assessed using Diener's 8-item scale (affection, joy, love, happiness, contentment, caring, pride, and fondness). Age, gender, ethnicity, and household income were controlled for using multilevel regression. After further controlling for pre-9/11 mental health ailments (anxiety and depression at T1), results indicated that RA and IR at T1 both independently predicted increased T2 psychological well-being when assessed 3 years later ($B = 0.12$, $p < 0.001$, and $B = 0.09$, $p < 0.01$, respectively).

Cowlishaw, Niele, Teshuva, Browning, and Kendig (2013) assessed 185 older adults (average age 80) from 2004 to 2008 in the Melbourne Longitudinal Studies on Healthy Aging (conducted in Australia, an increasingly secular country). Cross-lagged panel analysis was used to examine the relationships between spirituality, sense of coherence (SOC), and LS. Spirituality was assessed by Reed's Spiritual Perspective Scale; SOC by Antonovsky's Orientation to Life Scale that measures meaningfulness (four items), manageability (three items), and comprehensibility (five items); and LS was examined by a 5-item scale assessing satisfaction with health, finances, friendships, handling problems, and life in general. After controlling for baseline LS in 2004 (T1), spirituality in 2004 (T1) predicted significantly greater LS in 2008 (T2), but did so indirectly through the "meaningfulness" dimension of SOC. Spirituality was also a predictor of lower LS indirectly through lower scores on the "comprehensibility" dimension of SOC, although this effect was considerably weaker than the positive effect through meaningfulness. Researchers concluded that finding meaning in stressful life events is a key factor in successful aging, and spirituality appears to assist in this process. They had more difficulty explaining the negative relationship between spirituality and comprehensibility, although hypothesized that spiritual explanations of negative life events may evoke views that these are beyond logic or understanding.

Alternatively, belief in a punishing God could promote rumination and psychological distress, especially when adverse events are experienced without relief.

Semplonius, Good, and Willoughby (2015) prospectively followed 1132 Ontario University students (Canada) over a 3-year period, examining whether religious involvement promotes social ties either (1) directly or (2) indirectly through improving self-regulatory skills and ability to regulate emotions during social interactions. University students were assessed soon after beginning their first year (T1) and again during the winter of the next 2 years (T2 and T3). Religious activities at T1–T3 were assessed by frequency of reading religious texts, attending religious services, and involvement in other religious activities. Involvement in nonreligious clubs was assessed by a single item. Emotional regulation (proxy for psychological well-being) at T1–T3 was measured by a standard 6-item scale, and social ties with a 3-item scale. Cross-lagged path analyses (using AMOS) were used to examine relationships between variables assessed at T1–T3. No direct relationship was found between T1 religious activities and T2–T3 social ties. Indirect relationships, however, were present. Greater T1 religious activities predicted less difficulty with emotion regulation at T2–T3 ($B = -0.06$, $p = 0.01$), which in turn predicted more social ties at T2–T3 ($B = -0.09$, $p < 0.001$), resulting in a significant indirect effect of greater T1 religious activities on T2–T3 social ties ($B = 0.007$, $p = 0.004$) via less difficulties with emotional regulation. Importantly, neither less difficulty with emotional regulation nor social ties predicted greater involvement in religious activities over time, suggesting that the direction of effect was from religious activities to greater emotional regulation and social ties.

Hui et al. (2017) from University of Hong Kong conducted a 3-year prospective study of 455 Chinese college students (average age 24 years, 59% women) to examine the effects of Christian conversion on psychological well-being. Six waves of data were collected between 2009/2010 and 2012/2013 during which 46 participants reported being Christian in 2012–13 who had not reported being a Christian on the previous two waves (called "converts"). In addition, 92 participants were selected who were "nonconverts" based on responses on all six-study waves indicating they were not Christian, and 92 were chosen who were continuous Christians indicating they were Christian on all six waves. The three groups were matched on gender, age, education, and household income. Psychological well-being was operationalized as having low levels of depressed mood, anxiety, and stress assessed by the 21-item Depression Anxiety Stress Scale. When examining the predictors of religious conversion, no psychological characteristics (personality, personal values, or psychological symptoms) distinguished converts from nonconverts; in fact, only one characteristic—the belief that there is only one true religion—was predictive of Christian conversion. With regard to the consequences of religious conversion, analyzing the data using mixed-design repeated-measure analysis of variance (ANOVA), all three indicators of poor psychological well-being decreased more during the 3-year follow-up in Christian converts compared to nonconverts or continuous Christians. For depression the interaction term was marginally significant at $F(2,227) = 2.37$, $p = 0.09$, whereas the interaction was significant for anxiety ($F(2,227) = 4.65$, $p < 0.05$) and especially for stress level ($F(2,227) = 8.46$, $p < 0.001$). Researchers concluded that there findings were consistent with others' observation that religious conversion "predicted subsequent improvement in intrapsychic functioning such as LS, self-esteem, and vitality," and that their own findings "may also account for the often-observed difference between religious people and the nonreligious on well-being measures."

Conclusions

Our systematic review of studies published prior to 2010 revealed that the vast majority (mostly cross-sectional) found a positive correlation between religious involvement and psychological well-being; a handful of prospective studies found that R/S predicted future well-being (controlling for baseline well-being); and about half of RCTs reported that a R/S intervention increased well-being over time compared to control groups (with no studies reporting a reduction in well-being). Recent research appears to support these earlier findings, with such relationships stronger in religious countries, weaker (but still often present) in more secular countries, and possibly reversing in certain populations, especially where there are government restrictions on religion and religious norms are low and in certain groups such as lesbian, gay, bisexual, transgender, or questioning (LGBTQ) communities.

Relationships between R/S and other positive emotions (hope, optimism, and purpose/meaning in life) will now be examined briefly, first summarizing results from studies identified in our systematic review published prior to 2010 (Koenig et al., 2001, 2012) and then selectively reviewing studies published more recently.

HOPE

Early Research

Our systematic review identified 40 studies that quantitatively examined the relationship between R/S involvement and hope; of those, 73% (29/40) reported a significant positive relationship. Of the six highest quality studies, three (50%) reported this finding. All studies were cross-sectional except for four (two prospective and two clinical trials), which will now be reviewed. In the first of two prospective studies, Ai, Park, Huang, Rodgers, and Tice (2007) assessed general religiousness (organizational, nonorganizational, and subjective religiosity) in 309 cardiac patients 2 weeks prior to surgery (T1), while assessing hope approximately 2 days prior to surgery (T2). Although T1 general religiousness was significantly but indirectly related to greater T2 hope, only about 10 days had elapsed between measurements making this essentially a cross-sectional study. In the second prospective study, Arnette, Mascaro, Santana, Davis, and Kaslow (2007) followed 74 low-income Black women for 10 weeks, assessing positive religious coping (PRC) and religious well-being (RWB) at baseline (T1) and predicting hopelessness measured at T1 and T2. Although T1 PRC was inversely related to T2 hopelessness ($r = -0.27$, $p < 0.05$), a structural equation model that included both T1 and T2 hopelessness in the model found no association between T1 PRC or T1 RWB and T2 hopelessness.

In the first clinical trial, Rye et al. (2005) randomly assigned 149 divorced persons to a religious forgiveness intervention, a secular forgiveness intervention, or a nontreated control group. Both the religious and the secular interventions increased hope to a similar degree, but there was no difference between the two treatments. In the second clinical trial, Bay, Beckman, Trippi, Gunderman, and Terry (2008) randomized 166 heart patients to receive either a series of chaplain visits or a control group without visits. Patients in the intervention group that received 5 pastoral care visits did not score higher on the Herth Hope Index than did control patients who were not visited.

In summary, while the majority of cross-sectional studies found that R/S and hope were positively correlated, the single prospective study found no association and two RCT's did not find that R/S interventions increased hope above that of a secular intervention or a nontreated control condition (for pastoral care visits).

Recent Research

Since 2010, several cross-sectional studies continue to report a positive correlation between religiosity and hope (Kim et al., 2014; Melo et al., 2016; Unterrainer, Ladenhauf, Moazedi, Wallner-Liebmann, & Fink, 2010). At least one prospective study has also examined the effects of religiosity on change in hope over time. Ciarrochi and Heaven (2012) surveyed 393 11th grade students at baseline (T1) and 1 year later during 12th grade (T2). Religious values (RV) were assessed using a 3-item measure (being saved from sins and at peace with God; being at one with God or the universe; and following religious faith conscientiously). Trait hope was measured using the 6-item Children's Hope

Scale. Both RV and hope were assessed at T1 and T2. RV at T1 was associated with hope both at T1 ($r = 0.25$, $p < 0.01$) and at T2 ($r = 0.12$, $p < 0.05$). Structural equation modeling revealed that T1 RV significantly predicted an increase in T2 hope, with T1 hope controlled for (this was also true for all three RV measures when examined separately). T1 hope, however, did not predict T2 RV ($B = -0.03$, p = ns), suggesting that the direction of effect was from religious beliefs/values to hope, not vice-versa.

OPTIMISM

Early Research

Our systematic review identified 32 studies, of which 81% (26/32) reported a positive relationship between R/S and optimism; of the 11 highest quality studies, 73% (8/11) reported this link. All studies were cross-sectional except three prospective studies and one RCT. In the first prospective study, Ai, Peterson, Bolling, and Koenig (2002) assessed general religiousness, "prayer for coping," and optimism. Religious involvement was assessed at baseline (T1) 2 weeks prior to cardiac surgery, and optimism (Life Orientation Test [LOT]) was measured 1–2 days prior to surgery (T2). Although a positive association was found between prayer for coping and optimism, since only 10 days separated the two evaluations, this was essentially a cross-sectional study (as in their earlier study of hope). In the second study, Krause (2006) examined the effects of religious doubts on optimism and other positive emotions in 728 older adults followed for 3 years. Baseline religious doubt (T1) was significantly and inversely associated with optimism measured at T2, controlling for T1 optimism. In the third study, Ai et al. (2008) analyzed data from the same study published in 2002 above, examining the association between four different types of prayer at T1 on optimism measured at T2 (10 days later); only petitionary prayer (not conversational, meditative or ritual prayer) was significantly associated with optimism. Again, given the short follow-up, these analyses were essentially cross-sectional.

In the only RCT, Boelens, Reeves, Replogle, and Koenig (2009) examined the effects of a prayer intervention using a cross-over design in 63 depressed or anxious patients randomized to either the intervention (6 weekly prayer sessions) or a wait-list control group. Those in the wait-list control group were crossed over to receive the intervention after the initial 6-week treatment period. A significant increase in optimism (LOT) was found from baseline (T1) to follow-up (end of intervention [T2] and 1-month later [T3]) in the prayer group; no change in optimism, however, was found in the wait-list control group at T2. When controls were crossed over and received the intervention, an increase in optimism from the cross-over (T2) to follow-up (end of intervention [T4] and 1-month later [T5]) was replicated.

In summary, in the only true prospective study, Krause (2006) found that religious doubts predicted a decline in optimism in older adults, and in the only RCT, Boelens et al. (2009) found that a prayer intervention increased optimism over time. These findings are consistent with the cross-sectional finding of a positive correlation between R/S and optimism in the vast majority of studies, and are consistent with the hypothesis that R/S leads to an increase in optimism over time.

Recent Research

A number of high quality cross-sectional studies since 2010 have confirmed the positive association between R/S and optimism (Abdel-Khalek & Lester, 2013; Koenig et al., 2014; Lee, Neblett, & Jackson, 2015; Schnall et al., 2012). At least two longitudinal studies since our earlier review have examined the effects of baseline religiosity on future changes in optimism. McFarland (2010) followed a nationally representative sample of 801 Americans age 65 or above participating in the Religion, Aging, and Health survey, examining the effects of religiosity on optimism over time. Religiosity was assessed at Wave 1 (T1) by a 3-item measure of organizational and a 3-item measure of nonorganizational religiosity (ORA and NORA, respectively); optimism was assessed by a 3-item measure administered at Wave 1 (T1) and Wave II (T2). Regression analyses were stratified by gender, and controlled for demographics, self-esteem, health, and functional limitations. In men, high ORA at T1 predicted significantly higher optimism at T2 ($B = 0.317$, $p \leq 0.001$), independent of T1 optimism; no effect was found for high NORA ($B = 0.025$, p = ns) on T2 optimism. In women, high ORA at T1 did not predict T2 optimism ($B = 0.013$, p = ns), whereas a weak trend was present for high NORA at T1 predicting higher T2 optimism ($B = 0.169$, $p \leq 0.10$). Researchers concluded that the organizational aspects of religion are most important for men with regard to increasing optimism in later life, whereas in women, the nonorganizational aspects are more important.

In an RCT that compared the effects of religiously integrated cognitive behavioral therapy (RCBT) to conventional secular CBT (CCBT) in 132 adults with chronic medical illness and major depression, Koenig, Pearce, Nelson, and Daher (2015) examined the effects of baseline religiosity (assessed by a 29-item multidimensional scale) on changes in optimism (assessed by the 10-item LOT-R) during a 24-week follow-up period. Results indicated that baseline religiosity was strongly correlated with baseline optimism ($r = 0.31$, $p < 0.001$) and when included in a mixed effects growth curve model predicting change in optimism, baseline religiosity predicted an increase in optimism during the 24-week follow-up independent of treatment group ($B = 0.07$, $SE = 0.02$, $p < 0.0001$). Furthermore, RCBT tended to increase optimism more than CCBT in the clinical trial, although the effect size was small (group by time interaction $B = -0.75$, $SE = 0.57$, $p = 0.185$, Cohen's $d = 0.23$).

PURPOSE AND MEANING IN LIFE

Early Research

Our systematic review identified 45 studies published prior to 2010, of which 93% (42/45) reported a positive relationship between R/S and purpose/meaning in life (PIL); of the 10 highest quality studies, all 10 did so (100%). These studies were all cross-sectional except for three prospective studies, three single group experimental studies, and one RCT, which will now be summarized. In the first prospective study, Kass et al. (1991) examined the effects of baseline (T1) R/S (measured by the INSPIRIT) on PIL at T1 and 10 weeks later (T2) in 83 adult medical patients in a clinical trial involving the relaxation response (Boston). After controlling for T1 PIL and age, R/S at T1 significantly predicted T2 PIL ($B = 0.15$, $p = 0.02$).

In the second prospective study, Murphy, Johnson, and Lohan (2003) followed 173 parents in the northwestern United States after loss of a child due to a violent death, examining predictors of meaning. Parents were assessed from 4 months (T1) to 60 months postdeath (T2). Religious coping was assessed with a 4-item subscale from Carver's COPE. Finding meaning in the child's death by the 5th year of follow-up (T2) was the primary outcome (achieved by 57% of parents). Assuming that the predictors of finding meaning were assessed at T1 (although this was not explicitly stated), logistic regression analyses ($n = 126$) revealed that only two baseline characteristics were significant: participating in a support group and religious coping ($OR = 1.63$, $p = 0.02$).

Finally, Park, Malone, Suresh, Bliss, and Rosen (2008) prospectively followed 155 patients with congestive heart failure over 6 months (Ohio), examining predictors of meaning in life (assessed using a standard 5-item scale) assessed at baseline (T1) and follow-up (T2). Religious coping was measured using a 2-item subscale of the Brief COPE assessed at T1. With T1 meaning and other types of coping in the regression model, T1 religious coping significantly predicted T2 meaning ($B = 0.18$, $p < 0.05$).

In the first of the three single group experimental studies, Kennedy et al. (2002) followed 72 rehabilitating cardiac patients and spouses who participated in a 2.5-day education retreat (including yoga, meditation, visualization, and prayer). A 3-item measure of R/S beliefs and a single item assessing meaning in life were administered at baseline (T1) and after the retreat (T2). Increase in R/S between T1 and T2 was positively correlated with increase in meaning in life between T1 and T2 ($r = 0.49$, $p < 0.001$). In the second and third experimental studies (both reported in a single publication), Hicks and King (2008) assessed religiosity at baseline (T1) and meaning in life both before (T1) and after (T2) an experimental intervention conducted in University of Missouri college students. In both studies, religious commitment was assessed with Worthington's 10-item scale, and meaning in life was measured with four items from the Purpose in Life Scale (PILS). In the first study, researchers induced either a positive or a neutral mood state in 150 students, finding that induction of positive mood led to higher meaning in life for individuals low in religiosity, but not for individuals high in religiosity. This caused researchers to conclude that religious commitment is a "preferred cue" due to its durability and positive association with meaning in life.

In the second experimental study involving 61 college students, Hicks and King (2008) assessed religiosity at baseline (T1) and meaning in life before (T1) and after (T2) priming students with religious words (heaven, hell, and neutral), finding that religiosity positively predicted meaning in life scores for those primed with the either neutral or positive religious words (i.e., heaven), but not in those primed with negative religious words (i.e., hell), causing researchers to conclude that when reminded of the potential negative implications of religious beliefs, religiosity weakened as a predictor of meaning in life.

Finally, in the only clinical trial, Burns and Smith (1991) examined the effects of a spiritual intervention in the treatment of substance-dependent male patients newly admitted to a 28-day inpatient treatment program at the Gainesville (Florida) Veterans Administration Hospital. A total of 52 patients were alternatively assigned in groups of approximately eight individuals to one of two treatment conditions: a spiritual awareness program ($n = 37$) versus a standard treatment program ($n = 15$). The PIL scale was administered before and after the interventions. The 8-hour spiritual awareness program focused on increasing participants' awareness of spiritual issues by relating spirituality to everyday life experiences involving abusing drugs and/or alcohol, and by emphasizing spirituality as a coping method. Although PIL scores increased significantly from baseline to follow-up in the spirituality group (T1 = 89 to T2 = 96, $p = 0.01$), they also increased in the control group (T1 = 89 to T2 = 96). Thus, PIL in both groups increased to a similar degree.

In summary, the early research indicates that almost all cross-sectional studies find a significant positive relationship between R/S and purpose/meaning in life. Prospective studies likewise indicate that R/S at baseline predicts increases in PIL over time, even after controlling for baseline PIL. Finally, a single nonrandomized clinical trial found a similar increase in PIL after both a R/S and a control intervention.

Recent Research

Cross-sectional studies continue to report a strong and consistent positive correlation between religious involvement and purpose in life (Bamonti, Lombardi, Duberstein, King, & Van Orden, 2016; Francis, Jewell, & Robbins, 2010; Koenig et al., 2014; Wang, Koenig, Ma, & Al Shohaib, 2016). Prospective studies do likewise. In a 1-year prospective study of 386 low income, predominantly Black single mothers assessed pre-Hurricane Katrina/Rita (T1) and approximately 1 year afterwards (T2), Chan, Rhodes, and Pérez (2012) used structural equation modeling to examine the effects of pre-disaster (T1) religiousness on post-disaster optimism/PIL (T2) (assessed with the LOT and Life Engagement Test) and psychological distress (T2) (assessed by Kessler's K6 Scale). Results indicated that T1 religiousness (attendance and self-rated importance) predicted greater T2 optimism/PIL, and T2 optimism/PIL mediated the inverse relationship between T1 religiousness and T2 psychological distress. A second prospective study was reported as part of an RCT that compared the effects of RCBT and CCBT on PIL (assessed using the 20-item PIL scale) in 132 persons with major depression and chronic medical illness. In that study, Daher et al. (2016) found that baseline religiosity (assessed by a 29-item multidimensional scale) was both positively correlated with PIL at baseline ($r = 0.34$, $p < 0.0001$) and predicted an increase in PIL during the 24-week follow-up ($B = 0.23$, SE = 0.05, $p < 0.0001$) independent of treatment group.

SUMMARY AND CONCLUSIONS

Although the vast majority of the research is cross-sectional, most studies report a positive correlation between religious/spiritual involvement and greater psychological well-being, hope, optimism, and purpose/meaning in life. A number of early and more recent prospective studies have also examined the effects of baseline religiosity on change in positive emotions over time, with the majority reporting results that support the cross-sectional findings. Furthermore, a few experimental studies and clinical trials have examined the effects of R/S interventions on positive emotions, with results supporting the findings from observational studies. The evidence base, then, is growing for religion's positive effects on well-being, life satisfaction, happiness, hope, optimism, and purpose/meaning in life, and now exceeds that for studies finding positive effects on negative emotional states and chronic mental disorders. The next chapter examines the underlying psychological, social, and behavioral mechanisms that may help to explain how religious involvement influences mental health.

References

Abdel-Khalek, A., & Lester, D. (2013). Mental health, subjective well-being, and religiosity: Significant associations in Kuwait and USA. *Journal of Muslim Mental Health, 7*(2), 63–76.

Ai, A. L., Ladd, K. L., Peterson, C., Cook, C. A., Shearer, M., & Koenig, H. G. (2010). Long-term adjustment after surviving open heart surgery: The effect of using prayer for coping replicated in a prospective design. *Gerontologist, 50*(6), 798–809.

Ai, A. L., Park, C. L., Huang, B., Rodgers, W., & Tice, T. N. (2007). Psychosocial mediation of religious coping styles: A study of short-term psychological distress following cardiac surgery. *Personality and Social Psychology Bulletin, 33*(6), 867–882.

Ai, A. L., Peterson, C., Bolling, S. F., & Koenig, H. G. (2002). Private prayer and optimism in middle-aged and older patients awaiting cardiac surgery. *Gerontologist, 42*(1), 70–81.

Ai, A. L., Tice, T. N., Huang, B., Rodgers, W., & Bolling, S. F. (2008). Types of prayer, optimism, and well-being of middle-aged and older patients undergoing open-heart surgery. *Mental Health, Religion and Culture, 11*(1), 131–150.

Anson, O., Antonovsky, A., & Sagy, S. (1990). Religiosity and well-being among retirees: A question of causality. *Behavior, Health, and Aging, 1*, 85–97.

Arnette, N. C., Mascaro, N., Santana, M., Davis, S., & Kaslow, N. J. (2007). Enhancing spiritual well-being among suicidal African American female survivors of intimate partner violence. *Journal of Clinical Psychology, 63*(10), 909–924.

Bamonti, P., Lombardi, S., Duberstein, P. R., King, D. A., & Van Orden, K. A. (2016). Spirituality attenuates the association between depression symptom severity and meaning in life. *Aging and Mental Health, 20*(5), 494–499.

Bay, P. S., Beckman, D., Trippi, J., Gunderman, R., & Terry, C. (2008). The effect of pastoral care services on anxiety, depression, hope, religious coping, and religious problem solving styles: A randomized controlled study. *Journal of Religion and Health, 47*(1), 57–69.

Beutler, J. J., Attevelt, J. T., Schouten, S. A., Faber, J. A., Mees, E. J. D., & Geijskes, G. G. (1988). Paranormal healing and hypertension. *British Medical Journal, 296*(6635), 1491–1494.

Bijlani, R. L., Vempati, R. P., Yadav, R. K., Ray, R. B., Gupta, V., Sharma, R., et al. (2005). A brief but comprehensive lifestyle education program based on yoga reduces risk factors for cardiovascular disease and diabetes mellitus. *Journal of Alternative and Complementary Medicine, 11*(2), 267–274.

Boelens, P. A., Reeves, R. R., Replogle, W. H., & Koenig, H. G. (2009). A randomized trial of the effect of prayer on depression and anxiety. *International Journal of Psychiatry in Medicine, 39*, 377–392.

Brown, S. L., Nesse, R. M., House, J. S., & Utz, R. L. (2004). Religion and emotional compensation: Results from a prospective study of widowhood. *Personality and Social Psychology Bulletin, 30*(9), 1165–1174.

Burns, C. M., & Smith, L. L. (1991). Evaluating spiritual well-being among drug and alcohol dependent patients: A pilot study examining the effects of supportive/educative nursing interventions. *Addictions Nursing Network, 3*(3), 89–94.

Chan, C. S., Rhodes, J. E., & Pérez, J. E. (2012). A prospective study of religiousness and psychological distress among female survivors of Hurricanes Katrina and Rita. *American Journal of Community Psychology, 49*(1–2), 168–181.

Ciarrochi, J., & Heaven, P. C. (2012). Religious values and the development of trait hope and self-esteem in adolescents. *Journal for the Scientific Study of Religion, 51*(4), 676–688.

Cowlishaw, S., Niele, S., Teshuva, K., Browning, C., & Kendig, H. (2013). Older adults' spirituality and life satisfaction: A longitudinal test of social support and sense of coherence as mediating mechanisms. *Ageing and Society, 33*(07), 1243–1262.

Daher, N., Koenig, H. G., Pearce, M. J., Nelson, B., Shaw, S. F., Berk, L. S., & King, M. B. (2016). Effects of religious versus conventional cognitive behavioral therapy on purpose in life in clients with major depression and chronic medical illness: A randomized clinical trial. *International Journal of Existential Psychology and Psychotherapy, 6*(1), 16.

Frame, M. W., Uphold, C. R., Shehan, C. L., & Reid, K. J. (2005). Effects of spirituality on health-related quality of life in men with HIV/AIDS: Implications for counseling. *Counseling and Values*, *50*(1), 5–19.

Francis, L. J., Jewell, A., & Robbins, M. (2010). The relationship between religious orientation, personality, and purpose in life among an older Methodist sample. *Mental Health, Religion and Culture*, *13*(7–8), 777–791.

Gebauer, J. E., Sedikides, C., & Neberich, W. (2012). Religiosity, social self-esteem, and psychological adjustment on the cross-cultural specificity of the psychological benefits of religiosity. *Psychological Science*, *23*(2), 158–160.

Gerard, S., Smith, B. H., & Simpson, J. A. (2003). A randomized controlled trial of spiritual healing in restricted neck movement. *Journal of Alternative and Complementary Medicine*, *9*, 467–477.

Goldstein, E. D. (2007). Sacred moments: Implications on well-being and stress. *Journal of Clinical Psychology*, *63*(10), 1001–1019.

Graney, M. J. (1975). Happiness and social participation in aging. *Journal of Gerontology*, *30*, 701–706.

Hayward, R. D., & Elliott, M. (2014). Cross-national analysis of the influence of cultural norms and government restrictions on the relationship between religion and well-being. *Review of Religious Research*, *56*(1), 23–43.

Hicks, J. A., & King, L. A. (2008). Religious commitment and positive mood as information about meaning in life. *Journal of Research in Personality*, *42*(1), 43–57.

Hui, C. H., Cheung, S. H., Lam, J., Lau, E. Y. Y., Yuliawati, L., & Cheung, S. F. (2017). In search of the psychological antecedents and consequences of Christian conversion: A three-year prospective study. *Psychology of Religion and Spirituality*, *9*(2), 220.

James, W. (1890). *The principles of psychology*. New York, NY: Holt.

Ju, C., Zhang, B., You, X., Alterman, V., & Li, Y. (2016). Religiousness, social support and subjective well-being: An exploratory study among adolescents in an Asian atheist country. *International Journal of Psychology*, 1–10.

Kashdan, T. B., & Nezlek, J. B. (2012). Whether, when, and how is spirituality related to well-being? Moving beyond single occasion questionnaires to understanding daily process. *Personality and Social Psychology Bulletin*, *38*(11), 1523–1535.

Kass, J. D., Friedman, R., Leserman, J., Zuttermeister, P. C., & Benson, H. (1991). Health outcomes and a new index of spiritual experience (INSPIRIT). *Journal for the Scientific Study of Religion*, *30*, 203–211.

Kennedy, J. E., Abbott, R. A., & Rosenberg, B. S. (2002). Changes in spirituality and well-being in a retreat program for cardiac patients. *Alternative Therapies in Health and Medicine*, *8*(4), 64–66 68–70, 72–73.

Kim, S. Y., Kim, J. M., Kim, S. W., Kang, H. J., Shin, I. S., Shim, H. J., & Yoon, J. S. (2014). Determinants of a hopeful attitude among family caregivers in a palliative care setting. *General Hospital Psychiatry*, *36*(2), 165–171.

Koenig, H. G., Berk, L. S., Daher, N. S., Pearce, M. J., Bellinger, D. L., Robins, C. J., & King, M. B. (2014). Religious involvement is associated with greater purpose, optimism, generosity and gratitude in persons with major depression and chronic medical illness. *Journal of Psychosomatic Research*, *77*(2), 135–143.

Koenig, H. G., King, D. E., & Carson, V. B. (2012). *Handbook of religion and health* (2nd ed.). New York, NY: Oxford University Press.

Koenig, H. G., McCollough, M. E., & Larson, D. B. (2001). *Handbook of religion health* (1st ed.). New York, NY: Oxford University Press.

Koenig, H. G., Pearce, M. J., Nelson, B., & Daher, N. (2015). Effects of religious versus standard cognitive-behavioral therapy on optimism in persons with major depression and chronic medical illness. *Depression and Anxiety*, *32*(11), 835–842.

Koenig, L. B., & Vaillant, G. E. (2009). A prospective study of church attendance and health over the lifespan. *Health Psychology*, *28*(1), 117–124.

Krause, N. (2006). Religious doubt and psychological well-being: A longitudinal investigation. *Review of Religious Research, 47*, 287–302.

Kristeller, J. L., Rhodes, M., Cripe, L. D., & Sheets, V. (2005). Oncologist Assisted Spiritual Intervention Study (OASIS): Patient acceptability and initial evidence of effects. *International Journal of Psychiatry in Medicine, 35*(4), 329–347.

Kvande, M. N., Klöckner, C. A., Moksnes, U. K., & Espnes, G. A. (2015a). Do optimism and pessimism mediate the relationship between religious coping and existential well-being? Examining mechanisms in a Norwegian population sample. *The International Journal for the Psychology of Religion, 25*(2), 130–151.

Kvande, M. N., Klöckner, C. A., & Nielsen, M. E. (2015b). Church attendance and religious experience: Differential associations to well-being for Norwegian women and men? *SAGE Open, 5*(4), doi: 10.1177/2158244015612876.

Lee, D. B., Neblett, E. W., Jr., & Jackson, V. (2015). The role of optimism and religious involvement in the association between race-related stress and anxiety symptomatology. *Journal of Black Psychology, 41*(3), 221–246.

Levin, J. S., Markides, K. S., & Ray, L. A. (1996). Religious attendance and psychological well-being in Mexican Americans: A panel analysis of three-generations data. *Gerontologist, 36*, 454–463.

Lopez, S. J., Pedrotti, J. T., & Snyder, C. R. (2014). *Positive psychology: The scientific and practical explorations of human strengths* (3rd ed.). Thousand Oaks, CA: Sage Publishing.

McFarland, M. J. (2010). Religion and mental health among older adults: Do the effects of religious involvement vary by gender? *Journals of Gerontology (Series B), 65*(5), 621–630.

McIntosh, D. N., Poulin, M. J., Silver, R. C., & Holman, E. A. (2011). The distinct roles of spirituality and religiosity in physical and mental health after collective trauma: A national longitudinal study of responses to the 9/11 attacks. *Journal of Behavioral Medicine, 34*(6), 497–507.

Meanley, S., Pingel, E. S., & Bauermeister, J. A. (2016). Psychological well-being among religious and spiritual-identified young gay and bisexual men. *Sexuality Research and Social Policy, 13*(1), 35–45.

Melo, G. A. A., Silva, R. A., Silva, M. F. C., Galvão, M. T. G., Silva, V. M., & Caetano, J. Á. (2016). Religiosity and hope in patients with chronic renal failure: Coping strategies. *International Archives of Medicine, 9*(133), 1–9. doi: 10.3823/2004.

Moadel, A. B., Shah, C., Wylie-Rosett, J., Harris, M. S., Patel, S. R., Hall, C. B., et al. (2007). Randomized controlled trial of yoga among a multiethnic sample of breast cancer patients: Effects on quality of life. *Journal of Clinical Oncology, 25*(28), 4387–4395.

Mohan, K., Prasad, S. V., & Rao, P. (2004). Effects of spiritually based lifestyle change programme on well-being. *Journal of Indian Psychology, 22*(1), 6–13.

Moritz, S., Quan, H., Rickhi, B., Liu, M., Angen, M., Vintila, R., et al. (2006). A home study-based spirituality education program decreases emotional distress and increases quality of life – a randomized, controlled trial. *Alternative Therapies in Health and Medicine, 12*(6), 26–35.

Murphy, S. A., Johnson, L. C., & Lohan, J. (2003). Finding meaning in a child's violent death: A five-year prospective analysis of parents' personal narratives and empirical data. *Death Studies, 27*(5), 381–404.

Oman, D., Hedberg, J., & Thoresen, C. E. (2006). Passage meditation reduces perceived stress in health professionals: A randomized, controlled trial. *Journal of consulting and clinical psychology, 74*(4), 714–719.

Pakenham, K. I. (2007). Making sense of multiple sclerosis. *Rehabilitation Psychology, 52*(4), 380–389.

Park, C. L. (2006). Exploring relations among religiousness, meaning, and adjustment to lifetime and current stressful encounters in later life. *Anxiety, Stress, and Coping, 19*(1), 33–45.

Park, C. L., Malone, M. R., Suresh, D. P., Bliss, D., & Rosen, R. I. (2008). Coping, meaning in life, and quality of life in congestive heart failure patients. *Quality of Life Research, 17*(1), 21–26.

Petts, R. J., & Knoester, C. (2007). Parents' religious heterogamy and children's well-being. *Journal for the Scientific Study of Religion*, *46*(3), 373–389.

Reece, K., Schwartz, G. E., Brooks, A. J., & Nangle, G. (2005). Positive well-being changes associated with giving and receiving Johrei healing. *Journal of Alternative and Complementary Medicine*, *11*(3), 455–457.

Richards, P. S., Berrett, M. E., Hardman, R. K., & Eggett, D. L. (2006). Comparative efficacy of spirituality, cognitive, and emotional support groups for treating eating disorder inpatients. *Eating Disorders*, *14*(5), 401–415.

Rye, M. S., & Pargament, K. I. (2002). Forgiveness and romantic relationships in college: Can it heal the wounded heart? *Journal of Clinical Psychology*, *58*(4), 419–441.

Rye, M. S., Pargament, K. I., Pan, W., Yingling, D. W., Shogren, K. A., & Ito, M. (2005). Can group interventions facilitate forgiveness of an ex-spouse? A randomized clinical trial. *Journal of Consulting and Clinical Psychology*, *73*(5), 880–892.

Ryff, C. D. (2014). Psychological well-being revisited: Advances in the science and practice of eudaimonia. *Psychotherapy and Psychosomatics*, *83*(1), 10–28.

Schnall, E., Kalkstein, S., Fitchett, G., Salmoirago-Blotcher, E., Ockene, J., Tindle, H. A., & Wassertheil-Smoller, S. (2012). Psychological and social characteristics associated with religiosity in women's health initiative participants. *Journal of Religion and Health*, *51*(1), 20–31.

Semplonius, T., Good, M., & Willoughby, T. (2015). Religious and non-religious activity engagement as assets in promoting social ties throughout university: The role of emotion regulation. *Journal of Youth and Adolescence*, *44*(8), 1592–1606.

Shaw, B., Han, J. Y., Kim, E., Gustafson, D., Hawkins, R., Cleary, J., et al. (2007). Effects of prayer and religious expression within computer support groups on women with breast cancer. *Psychooncology*, *16*(7), 676–687.

Sorensen, T., Dahl, A. A., Fossa, S. D., Holmen, J., Lien, L., & Danbolt, L. J. (2012). Is 'seeking God's help' associated with life satisfaction and disease-specific quality of life in cancer patients? The Hunt Study. *Archive for the Psychology of Religion*, *34*, 191–213.

Thege, B. K., Pilling, J., Székely, A., & Kopp, M. S. (2013). Relationship between religiosity and health: Evidence from a post-communist country. *International Journal of Behavioral Medicine*, *20*(4), 477–486.

Tix, A. P., & Frazier, P. A. (1998). The use of religious coping during stressful life events: Main effects, moderation, and medication. *Journal of Consulting and Clinical Psychology*, *66*(2), 411–422.

Unterrainer, H. F., Ladenhauf, K. H., Moazedi, M. L., Wallner-Liebmann, S. J., & Fink, A. (2010). Dimensions of religious/spiritual well-being and their relation to personality and psychological well-being. *Personality and Individual Differences*, *49*(3), 192–197.

Vallurupalli, M., Lauderdale, K., Balboni, M., Phelps, A. C., Block, S. D., Ng, A. K., Kachnic, L. A., VanderWeele, T. J., & Balboni, T. A. (2012). The role of spirituality and religious coping in the quality of life of patients with advanced cancer receiving palliative radiation therapy. *Journal of Supportive Oncology*, *10*(2), 81–87.

Wang, Z., Koenig, H. G., Ma, H., & Al Shohaib, S. (2016). Religion, purpose in life, social support, and psychological distress in Chinese University students. *Journal of Religion and Health*, *55*(3), 1055–1064.

Wasner, M., Longaker, C., Fegg, M. J., & Borasio, G. D. (2005). Effects of spiritual care training for palliative care professionals. *Palliative Medicine*, *19*(2), 99–104.

Willits, F. K., & Crider, D. M. (1988). Religion and well-being: Men and women in the middle years. *Review of Religious Research*, *29*, 281–294.

Wink, P., & Dillon, M. (2003). Religiousness, spirituality, and psychosocial functioning in late adulthood: Findings from a longitudinal study. *Psychology and Aging*, *18*(4), 916–924.

CHAPTER

7

Mechanisms

In this chapter, we examine the genetic, biological, psychological, social, environmental, and individual factors that may help explain the relationship between religion and mental health.

Many factors influence mental health over the lifespan, and based on the evidence summarized in earlier chapters religious involvement is likely one of them. It is not, however, the only one. Nor does religion usually affect mental health directly, but rather indirectly through other factors that influence mental health. Thus, any discussion of how religion affects mental health must begin with a discussion of the known determinants of mental health (Compton & Shim, 2015; Healthy People 2020, 2017). Those determinants can be lumped into six major categories: genetic factors, biological factors, psychological factors, social factors, environmental factors, and individual factors (particularly those involving personal choice). A seventh major category also exists that involves interactions between the six basic categories above.

GENETIC FACTORS

Genetic factors are those passed down from parents to children based on the particular DNA makeup of their genes. This involves the transmission of inherited predispositions, tendencies, strengths, and weaknesses from parents (who received genes from their parents, etc., throughout the generational line) that influence mental health. Besides inherited genes, there are random changes in genetic composition resulting from "errors" in genetic transmission that are unpredictable, which may lead to mutations in approximately 1% of transmitted DNA (Pray, 2008). Again, genes account only for predispositions and tendencies with regard to mental health, and seldom (if ever) are deterministic like the transmission of race, sexual orientation, or hair color. Genes can also be turned on and off depending on environmental influences (called epigenetics), which will be discussed further below.

Religion and Mental Health. http://dx.doi.org/10.1016/B978-0-12-811282-3.00007-0

BIOLOGICAL FACTORS

Biological factors that influence mental health are heavily affected by genes, environment, and aging. Cardiovascular disease, cancer, neurological and brain diseases, immune and endocrine functions, and level of chronic inflammation are examples of biological factors that can influence mental health. Levels of central nervous system catecholamines such as serotonin, epinephrine, and dopamine are chemicals in the brain that help to determine mood state and anxiety level along with more serious mental health symptoms such as delusions, hallucinations, and other psychotic symptoms (Schildkraut, 1965; Whybrow, Akiskal, & McKinney, 2012). Brain structure and central nervous system connections (neurocircuitry), intimately connected to mental health, may also be influenced by genetic or environmental factors, affecting vulnerability to depression, bipolar disorder, schizophrenia, delusional disorder, and behavioral disorders such as attention deficit and hyperactivity disorder, conduct disorder, and antisocial tendencies (Price & Drevets, 2010). Biological factors likewise affect the development of alcoholism, drug dependency, and other addictive disorders.

Biological factors include changes that occur as people grow older, including increased susceptibility to diseases such as hearing loss, vision loss, changes in cognitive function, and declines in physical functioning due to changes in muscles, ligaments, and bone. These decrements in physical health with aging may impact mental health by affecting ability to independently function and engage in meaningful activities with others. One of the strongest risk factors for depression in later life is physical disability (Blazer, Burchett, & George, 1991; Cole & Dendukuri, 2003; Turner & Noh, 1988).

PSYCHOLOGICAL FACTORS

Psychological factors that influence mental health include beliefs (worldview), attitudes, motivations, emotional attachments, and coping responses to life stressors. Underlying beliefs, assumptions, and expectations about the world affect mental health by giving rise to emotions in response to life events, which then drive behavior that in turn leads to consequences that further affect mental health. The most common (and most effective) treatment of emotional and behavioral disorders is cognitive-behavioral therapy (CBT), which depends on identifying maladaptive beliefs and assumptions, challenging them, and then replacing them with healthier, more realistic beliefs, assumptions, attitudes, and behaviors (Hofmann, Asnaani, Vonk, Sawyer, & Fang, 2012). For example, something happens and the person has a thought in response to the event.

That thought soon gives rise to an emotion, which may then lead to a behavior that affects the person, their environment, and/or others around them, all leading to either positive or negative effects on mental health.

Psychological attachments to family, friends, and more broadly, to job, position, possessions, goals, etc., also strongly influence mental health. This has given rise to Attachment Theory as one explanation for emotional problems that affect mental health during adulthood (Goldberg, Muir, & Kerr, 2013; Mikulincer & Shaver, 2008). When one is emotionally attached to someone or something, a loss or change in the attachment object creates grief, and the fear of that loss creates anxiety, thus disrupting mental health and ability to function. The psychological stress resulting from disruptions in attachment can influence the developing brain throughout the lifespan, thereby affecting vulnerability to mental health problems (Lupien, McEwen, Gunnar, & Heim, 2009).

Coping responses are mobilized when negative life stressors create unwanted change, loss, and disturb mental health and well-being. Appraisals (or perceptions) of unwanted change strongly influence the impact that stressful life events will have on mental health. For those with adequate coping resources, unwanted life stress is less likely to impact mental health in a negative manner. Coping responses are categorized as healthy and unhealthy depending on the situation (Folkman & Moskowitz, 2004). Lazarus and Folkman's (1987)'s transactional model divides coping responses into emotion-focused and problem-focused behaviors. According to this model, a person appraises the level of threat of a situation and then implements coping strategies that may be of two types: emotion-focused or problem-focused. Emotion-focused coping refers to the behaviors people use to manage the psychological distress itself which include actions such as seeking social support, relaxing, or using mindfulness techniques. Problem-focused coping involves strategies used to address the problem that is causing the distress such as conflict resolution or may involve other efforts to resolve the underlying problem. Some coping responses are considered adaptive (confrontive and optimistic), while others are considered nonadaptive (evasive or fatalistic). Psychological coping responses can influence mental health one way or another depending on whether they are adaptive or not.

SOCIAL FACTORS

The groundwork for mental health is laid immediately after birth with the quality of the nurturing environment. This is often expressed by the match between the temperamental needs of the infant and those of the mother or primary caregiver (Thomas & Chess, 1977). A poor fit between infant and caregiver (e.g., an irritable or demanding infant, and a stressed out, depressed, or distant mother) spells trouble for mental health later on, especially if other nurturing caregivers are not readily available. Without such nurturing the infant will have difficulty developing a basic sense of trust (i.e., trust that their needs will be met). Next, is the quality of caregiving that the toddler or young child receives as early attachments continue to develop (Goldberg et al., 2013). Adverse early life experiences during childhood due to emotional, sexual, or physical abuse by caretakers and/or bullying at school by peers or teachers can also increase vulnerability to emotional problems later on.

Social determinants of mental health beyond early and later childhood include the dynamics within the person's own marital and family life, experiences of discrimination and social exclusion (including indirect influences passed down from parents who were discriminated against or excluded), experiences of stigma from having intellectual disability or neurological brain conditions such as autism, and a lack of social support due to inadequate development of social skills. Included here is the priority that a society places on mental health in terms of resources it allocates for the treatment of mental disorders.

Social support from family and friends has been shown to improve coping with stress and adaptation to trauma and loss (Cohen & Wills, 1985), to lower rates of depression and anxiety (Lin, Dean, & Ensel, 2013), and to predict better physical health more generally (Uchino, 2006). Indeed, social support is the basis for supportive psychotherapy in the treatment of many emotional disorders (Rockland, 1993).

ENVIRONMENTAL FACTORS

Environment plays a huge role in determining mental health, from fertilization of the ovum by the sperm during conception, through the development of the early embryo, through implantation in the uterus, through development and maturation of the fetus in the womb, and the birth of the infant (including any physical trauma that may occur during that process) (Johnson, 2001). The months leading up to birth (middle of second trimester, all of the third trimester) and the first 2 years of life are particularly vulnerable times for infant brain development and growth. By birth, the infant's brain has reached 27% of its eventual adult size, and continues to grow rapidly for the next 2 years, reaching 75% of adult brain size by 18 months and 90% by 4 years of age (De Souza, Fernandes, & Tavares do Carmo, 2011; Dobbing & Sands, 1979; Pinyerd, 1992). If the mother is addicted to alcohol or drugs, is taking teratogenic medications, or does not have adequate nutrition during pregnancy (for mental health reasons, economic reasons, or poor access to prenatal care), these factors can all adversely affect brain development and increase vulnerability to mental health problems later in life.

Other environmental factors influencing mental health during childhood, adolescence, and adulthood include traumatic accidents (self-caused and other perpetrated), natural disasters, inadequate educational opportunities, poor quality of schools, poor access to employment, housing insecurity, neighborhood violence and crime, access to illegal drugs, and lack of available safe spaces (e.g., parks for exercise, recreation). Thus, the biological environment during fetal growth and infancy, psychological and social environment from infancy to adulthood, and the physical environment can all influence mental health in a variety of ways.

INDIVIDUAL FACTORS

The last major category of determinants of mental health is individual factors. Foremost among those factors is "personal choice." The decisions that individuals make influence their psychological, social, and physical environment (and may even indirectly affect their own and their children's genetic makeup through epigenetic effects). The most obvious choices involve decisions concerning (1) relationships with family, friends, co-workers, and those in the broader community; (2) use of time; (3) fulfillment of basic needs (eating, drinking, sleeping, and sex); (4) engagement in pleasurable habits (smoking, alcohol, and drug use); (5) participation in health maintenance activities (exercise, weight control, diet, and seeking timely healthcare); and (6) engagement in mentally healthy activities (volunteering and other prosocial behaviors).

Although the existence of "freedom of choice" and "free will" has long been debated by philosophers (Hart, 1955; Kane, 1998), psychologists (Monroe & Malle, 2010), economists (Sen, 1988), and physical scientists (Pattanaik & Xu, 2000), most agree that people have at least some freedom to make conscious choices and decisions that influence their lives. Freedom of choice gradually increases from infancy onward as the capacity to make conscious independent decisions increases. Young persons are not usually held accountable by the state for their choices while under the care of parents unless there is a clear infraction of the law. When they reach adulthood, however, most societies insist that people (if deemed mentally competent) carry the full weight of responsibility for their choices. The freedom to choose is a precious privilege, but the responsibilities that accompany it are sobering. Society, culture, family, public education, and the legal system shape the moral values that provide a context in which individual choices are made. They must all balance individual freedom with the responsibility of ensuring the collective health and safety of the community.

Today, however, the range of choices is widening. Western society places a high value on autonomy and freedom of expression, which has contributed to the expansion of choices and the loosening of restrictions. Modern progressive views have also led to a redefinition of what is considered moral behavior and action, leading to situational ethics. Greater freedom and more choices, however, are not necessarily conducive to greater well-being and may adversely affect mental health (just as having many restrictions and few choices can adversely affect mental health) (Schwartz, 2000). American psychologist Barry Schwartz (2004) writes about the "paradox of choice," noting that an expanding array of choices often leads to depression and feelings of loneliness. This, he explains, may result from a decrease in the quality of engagement with family, friends, and community (which in the past met personal needs that people increasingly now meet on their own, because of the value placed on independence and autonomy). This may be particularly true for younger generations, who have more and more options to choose from, but less and less moral standards to guide those choices. The default choice for many youth (and adults today) is whatever feels good and maximizes pleasure. Core beliefs and attitudes influence personal choices, and personal choices in turn influence behaviors that over time form habits that affect mental health.

INTERACTIONS BETWEEN CATEGORIES

While these categories of mental health determinants have their own independent effects, they also interact with and influence each other. Genetics directly influences physical health, susceptibility to disease, and the timing of disease expression with aging. Likewise, genes affect personality traits and psychological perceptions that determine how a person reacts to the environment. The environment and how one responds to the environment, in turn, may have influences on genes through epigenetic influences (usually early in life, but possibly also during adulthood). Epigenetics is a new and growing area of research that examines the effects of the environment on gene structure and expression. Nurturing activities during critical periods of development (particularly during infancy) may affect gene structure by the process of methylation, which can increase or dampen later adaptive responses to psychological stressors (see Denhardt, 2017, for a review of this area).

Similarly, physical health influences psychological state, which can affect motivation to maintain physical health and well-being. Physical health also influences personal choices and behaviors that result. Those behaviors lead to habits that influence physical health (drinking, smoking, drug use, etc.) and consequently mental health. Both physical health and psychological factors affect social relationships. Social relationships, in turn, influence physical health both directly through access to caregivers and indirectly through psychoneuroimmunological mechanisms. Social relationships also affect psychological coping by providing social support for adapting to stressful life events.

The environment from conception to late life is the setting in which everything takes place, affecting vulnerability to mental and physical illness, adaptation to stress, and access to healthy social relationships. Educational resources and job opportunities influence later access to healthcare (ability to afford insurance) and to safe living environments (free from crime, drugs, and pollution), as well as to healthy social relationships and resources for coping with life stressors, all of which influence physical health and susceptibility to disease. Freedom from discrimination and stigma facilitate positive psychological attitudes and prosocial behaviors, which in turn affect mental health and well-being.

Personal choices likewise interact with many of these other determinants of mental health. This includes physical health (by affecting decisions regarding engagement in health behaviors); psychological factors (by decisions leading to the development of healthy attitudes and habits); the environment (through decisions to seek healthy social relationships, maintain family ties, complete education, obtain meaningful employment, and avoid drugs, alcohol, and risky sexual activities resulting in out-of-wedlock births that derail education); and may even affect genetic structure and expression (through decisions that affect the environment leading to epigenetic influences). Personal choices have both short-term consequences for the individual and long-term consequences for the individual and the generations that follow. Those long-term effects resulting from personal choice act through the environment that persons create for children and grandchildren, which may affect their genes, brain development, susceptibility to illness, level of social engagement, and the personal choices that progeny will later make themselves (due to role modeling of parents).

Indeed, this complex web of mental health determinants continues to influence generation after generation down through the ages. Unlike genes and biological changes with normal aging, psychological tendencies and traits that are inherited, and many uncontrollable environmental situations, personal decision-making is something that is fully under the control of the individual and has the potential to both enhance mental health and be a powerful force for positive social change.

RELIGION AS A DETERMINANT OF MENTAL HEALTH

Religious involvement affects (and may be affected by) every one of the six determinants of mental health above (Fig. 7.1). These effects accumulate throughout the lifespan, beginning with the genes transmitted from

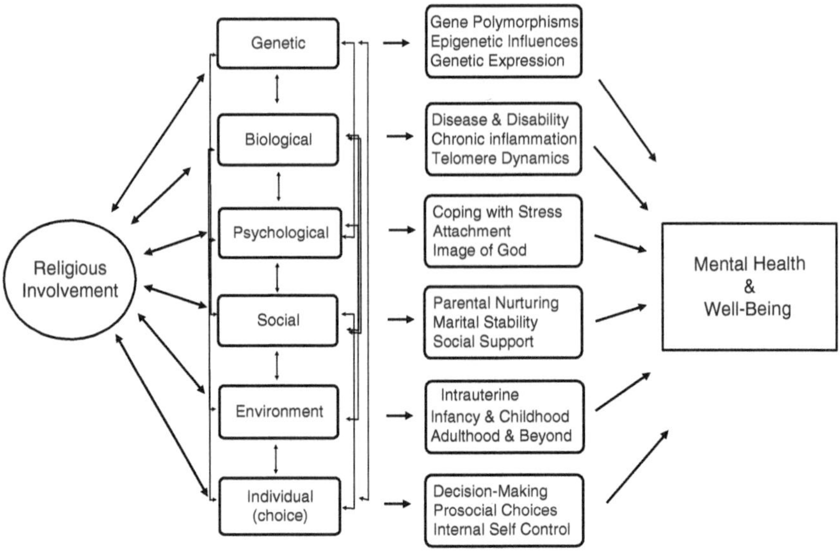

FIGURE 7.1 **Pathways by which religious involvement may affect mental health.**

parents and continuing through intrauterine development (affected by the religiosity of parents and the impact of religiosity on parents' lives), progressing through birth, early childhood, older childhood and adolescence (also affected by religiosity of parents), young adulthood and middle age (as religion affects the development and maintenance of family life and engagement at work), through retirement, late life, and through the terminal stages of life and its end. A lifespan approach, then, is the only way to understand the many ways that religious involvement affects mental health and well-being.

Genetic Factors

Religiosity has been associated with genes that potentially influence mental health and vulnerability to substance abuse, including genotypes of the serotonin transporter (SLCA4), serotonin receptor (HTR1A), monoamine oxidase A (uMAOA-VNTR), alcohol dehydrogenase (ADH), and dopamine (DRD2) genes. Genotypes of the SLCA4 gene (SS/SL) that confer high risk for drug use/abuse and depression have been shown to be less common in highly religious individuals (Dew & Koenig, 2014; Koenig et al., 2015). Genotype may also influence responsiveness to mental health treatments. For example, depressed individuals with the C/C genotype of the HTR1A may be more responsive to religiously integrated CBT than to conventional CBT (Koenig et al., 2015). Religiosity also appears to modify the relationship between high risk ADH gene variants and alcohol use/dependence (with a weaker relationship in those with high religiosity and a much stronger relationship in those with low or absent religiosity) (Chartier et al., 2016). Thus, some of the effects of religious involvement on reducing substance use may in part be explained by genetic factors that protect those who are more religious (also see Vance et al., 2014). How such associations with religious involvement may have come about remains a mystery (although "natural selection" is a possibility).

More recently, Anderson et al. (2017) at Columbia University examined the associations between the importance of religion/spirituality (R/S) and the presence of single nucleotide polymorphisms (SNP) of serotonin (HTR1B, HTR2A), dopamine (DRD2), oxytocin (OXTR), and monoamine vesicular transporter (VMAT1) genes in those at high ($n = 96$) and low familial risk ($n = 96$) for major depressive disorder (MDD) as part of a 30-year longitudinal study. Participants were children (mean age 47.5 years) and grandchildren (mean age 19.3 years) of those with MDD (high risk) and those without MDD (low risk). R/S was assessed with the question: "How important to you is religion or spirituality?" (1 = not important at all; 4 = very important). Results indicated no significant associations with R/S in the high risk (HR) group. However, among those at low familial risk for depression (LR), controlling for age and gender, R/S was related to the minor allele of the serotonin gene (HTR1B SNP rs130058, $B = -0.493$, $p = 0.001$), but also to the major allele of the oxytocin gene (SNP rs2254298, $B = 0.527$, $p = 0.024$), serotonin gene (HTR1B SNP rs11568817, $B = 0.258$, $p = 0.029$), monoamine vesicular transporter gene (SNP rs1390938, $B = 0.268$, $p = 0.033$), and (most importantly) the major allele of the dopamine gene (SNP rs1800497, $B = 0.433$, $p = 0.026$). In the LR group, the minor allele (A) of the dopamine gene (SNP rs1800497) was also related to greater risk of life-time major depression ($B = -1.022$, $p = 0.012$). Among those at LR for depression, then, highly R/S persons were less likely to have the minor allele (A) than the major allele (G) of the dopamine gene. The minor allele (A) is known to exhibit reduced brain dopamine binding and reduced receptor density, thereby increasing risk for mood disorders and other psychopathology (and found to be related to a greater risk of lifetime depression in this sample). Among those at LR for depression, then, those high on R/S may be genetically protected from experiencing depression.

Yet to be explored is the effects of religious involvement over a lifetime on changes in gene activation or expression, particularly as a result of methylation or acetylation of genes during infancy and possibly later in life. Epigenetics, a process that occurs as a result of social and environmental influences in both animals and humans, involves changes above the genome that regulate genetic expression without changing the DNA sequence. There is evidence that a nurturing early environment may affect the methylation process for key genes that control physiological responses to stress (McEwen, 2017; McGowan, Sasaki, & D'Alessio, 2009). This leaves open the possibility that religiosity by encouraging prosocial and nurturing behaviors by parents (i.e., making them more able to meet the infant's needs by improving stress tolerance and/or reducing parental depression, anxiety, or substance use) may affect the methylation process in infants and thereby improving stress responses later in life. There is also the possibility that epigenetic "marks" on the genome acquired during infancy might be altered later in life (Szyf, 2016a, 2016b), thus providing a mechanism by which nurturing religious experiences during adulthood (e.g., a transformative experience of God's unconditional love) may affect genome structure and expression. Furthermore, such genetic alterations may then be transmitted to future generations (as shown in animal models—see Weaver, 2010).

Biological Factors

Religious involvement appears to be related to a number of physiological processes that eventually lead to physical disease (and in some cases mental illness). For example, psychological stress has long been known to increase inflammation in the body (Maes et al., 1998). Chronic inflammation has been associated with a host of physical illnesses such as atherosclerosis (coronary artery disease and stroke), arthritis, Crohn's disease, asthma and other autoimmune disorders, neurodegenerative disorders, diabetes, and obesity, to name just a few (Kotas & Medzhitov, 2015). Furthermore, chronic inflammation may also lead to emotional problems such as MDD, which may in turn also increase inflammation (Slavich & Irwin, 2014). If religious involvement reduces stress and the accompanying inflammation, then religiosity may improve mental health (1) indirectly by reducing disabling physical illnesses due to chronic inflammation and (2) directly by reducing mental disorders that are caused by chronic inflammation. Indeed, religious involvement has been associated with lower levels of inflammatory markers such as C-reactive protein (Ford, Loucks, & Berkman, 2006; King, Mainous, & Pearson, 2002; King, Mainous, Steyer, & Pearson, 2001) and proinflammatory cytokines such as interleukin-6 (Ai et al., 2009; Koenig et al., 1997; Lutgendorf, Russell, Ullrich, Harris, & Wallace, 2004). More recent discussions affirm the mediating role that chronic inflammation may play in the effects of religion on mental and physical health (Hill, Rote, Ellison, & Burdette, 2014). There is also recent research confirming the impact that religious involvement may have on immune and endocrine function (Henry, Ironson, Gonzalez, & Schneiderman, 2014; Ironson, Kremer, & Lucette, 2016; Ironson et al., 2011; Kelsch et al., 2013; Kremer et al., 2014; Van Wagoner et al., 2016).

Indeed, a large and growing research literature indicates less overall medical illness, physical disability, cognitive dysfunction (see Chapter 5), and greater longevity among those who are more religious, which could be explained by psychosocial influences on immunological/inflammatory, endocrine, and cardiovascular systems (Koenig & Cohen, 2002; Koenig, King, & Carson, 2012; Li, Stampfer, Williams, & VanderWeele, 2016; VanderWeele et al., 2017). Brain structure itself may also be modified by religious involvement. As noted in Chapter 4, Miller et al. (2014) found that persons at high risk for depression who indicated that religion or spirituality was very important (vs. only somewhat or not at all important) had thicker cortices in the left and right parietal and occipital regions, the mesial frontal lobe of the right hemisphere, and the cuneus and precuneus lobes of the left hemisphere. Controlling for education actually increased the number of regions with significantly increased cortical thickness. Participants reporting frequent religious attendance also had thicker cortices in the same regions as did those indicating high religious/spiritual importance, although the associations lost statistical significance after adjusting for multiple comparisons. Since the severity of depressive symptoms correlated inversely with cortical thickness in the parietal lobes bilaterally more strongly in the high risk patients than in low risk patients, researchers surmised that thicker cortices in these regions likely protect against depressive symptoms in high risk individuals.

At least three studies have now also demonstrated that religiosity is either directly (Hill, Ellison, Burdette, Taylor, & Friedman, 2016; Koenig, Nelson, Shaw, Saxena, & Cohen, 2016) or indirectly (Hill, Vaghela, Ellison, & Rote, 2017) related to chromosomal telomere length (TL). Telomeres regions are found at the ends of chromosomes and contain noncoding DNA material that helps to prevent the loss of important DNA from chromosome ends during cell division. These telomere regions shorten after each cell replication cycle, and when they shorten to a critical point, the result is genomic instability, end-to-end chromosome fusion, and loss of ability for cell replenishment. The cell goes into senescence and organ degeneration occurs as cells can no longer replicate to maintain homeostasis. Longer telomeres predict a longer lifespan, and shortened TL has been associated with a wide variety of age-related conditions such as cardiovascular disease, diabetes or insulin resistance, dementia, and cancer. Psychosocial stress has been shown in many studies to shorten TL, probably by increasing inflammation which increases the speed of telomere degeneration (Mathur et al., 2016). By improving coping with stress, religious involvement may reduce systemic inflammation, slow the speed of telomere degeneration, decrease age-related diseases, and in this way increase longevity and physical well-being. Given the strong connections between physical health, physical functioning, and emotional disorder, religiosity by reducing physical illness, age-related diseases, and functional disability may have a positive impact on mental health through this pathway.

Psychological Factors

One of the most important ways that religious involvement influences mental health is by its role as a coping resource (see Chapter 3). Religious beliefs and practices are mobilized in response to stressors in order to derive comfort, meaning, control, and social support. Evidence for the benefits derived from religious coping comes from the high proportion of individuals who use religion to cope during stressful times (who report qualitatively that it has been helpful) and quantitative research demonstrating a positive relationship between religious coping responses and various mental health states such as depression, particularly when examined in stressed populations (Smith, McCullough, & Poll, 2003).

A psychological factor related to mental health is the person's priorities in life. There are many competing forces for our attention, time, and financial resources. As noted earlier, if the priorities that a person values most are somehow endangered, then emotional distress is the inevitable result. A primary priority (object of attachment) can be many things. It can be another person—family member, friend, or lover. It can be an ability, skill, job or occupation. It can be a physical health problem (and desire to be free from the health problem). It can be the need to be valued or respected by others. It can be whatever one is desperately trying to avoid. Whenever a person, situation, or possession takes center stage, its loss or change will result in suffering, that is, anxiety, depression, and emotional pain. As noted in Chapter 3, this point is perhaps most clearly made within the Buddhist religious tradition (Koenig, 2017a). Buddhism claims that all things in this world are subject to change and loss, and with attachment to persons, possessions, and goals, comes suffering. The Buddha realized this at the moment of his Enlightenment. At that time he discovered the Four Noble Truths. Those Truths, he believed, held the key to suffering, and more importantly, the way to relieve it. Those four truths are that suffering exists, that suffering arises from attachment to impermanent things, that suffering ceases when attachment ceases, and that freedom from suffering is possible by following the Eightfold Path (e.g., nonattachment, compassion, right living, meditation, mindfulness, etc.).

Monotheistic religious traditions emphasize a similar point, but approach it somewhat differently. Those traditions stress an attachment to the Divine or God (Granqvist, 2014). When the Divine becomes one's primary attachment object (indeed, the First Commandment in Judaism, Christianity, and Islam), then all other priorities become secondary and their loss or change causes less suffering. According to these belief systems, when the

Divine is one's highest priority and most important attachment figure in life, everything else is then relegated to its proper place. The belief is that the connection to the Divine remains intact regardless of what else happens, and if maintained through prayer and acts of devotion, there is no worry ever of its loss (Psalm 139). This helps to neutralize suffering—not eliminate it, but reduce it down to a more proper and manageable size, one that does not dominate, control, or direct one's happiness. Research indicates that when attachment to God is secure, religious involvement is related to better mental health. In contrast, among those in whom the attachment is insecure, religious activity may actually worsen mental health and lead to greater anxiety (Bradshaw, Ellison, & Marcum, 2010; Ellison, Bradshaw, Flannelly, & Galek, 2014).

The benefits derived from religious coping activities such as prayer, meditation, Scripture study, or engagement in the religious community also depend to some extent on a person's image of the Divine (Bradshaw, Ellison, & Flannelly, 2008; Bradshaw et al., 2010). That image likely influences the quality of the relationship to the Divine. In other words, the beliefs that a person has about the characteristics, nature, and intention of God may influence a person's connection with God and the consequences that has for mental health. On the one hand, belief in a powerful and strong but loving God who is caring, merciful, readily available, responsive, and desires the best for the individual—that image of God is likely to have a positive impact on mental health and well-being (Koenig, 2016). Persons who believe that God loves them, has a purpose for their lives, and desires to interact with and help them (like a loving parent) is likely to find in religion a powerful coping resource when adversity strikes, and may also serve to motivate these individuals to love and care for others, who will then be available for support when needed. Surrendering and submitting one's will to such a God (reflected by higher levels of religious commitment), then, while not easy, may nevertheless lead to a fuller and happier life and better mental health, not only for the individual but also for the surrounding community.

On the other hand, belief in a powerful and strong God who is controlling, policing, punishing, unforgiving, and vengeful may have the opposite effect on health and well-being (Exline, Pargament, Grubbs, & Yali, 2014; Gerber, Boals, & Schuettler, 2011; Pargament, Smith, Koenig, & Perez, 1998). Likewise, belief in a distant and unavailable God, or a weak and impotent God, is not likely to have much positive effect on well-being. Similarly, a lack of personal connection to God is not likely to impact mental or physical health, any more so than not believing in God (Bradshaw et al., 2010). Finally, not believing in God at all may be better than believing in an angry, punishing, or merciless God (Ironson et al., 2011; Silton, Flannelly, Galek, & Ellison, 2014). Studies have shown that a negative image of God may lead to the creation of a "punishment orientation" (Exline,

Grubbs, & Homolka, 2015; Krauss & Hood, 2013) and "negative meaning making" that adversely affects mental health (Park, 2013). This has become known as negative religious coping or religious/spiritual struggle. There is a vast and growing literature that connects religious/spiritual struggle with poor mental health and altered physiological functioning, lower resilience and greater impairment (Ano & Vasconcelles, 2005; Weber & Pargament, 2014) (see Chapter 8). Positive religious coping, in contrast, which sees God as a partner in dealing with trauma and stress, has been associated with better mental health in many studies, both cross-sectional and prospective. Positive religious coping may lead to an even stronger relationship with God, one that gives hope and meaning to life during stressful circumstances (Robinson, 2014).

Thus, in monotheistic religions, a person's image of God (one that affects the relationship with God and degree to which God is perceived as a primary attachment figure) may help or hinder a person's use of religion to cope with negative life situations and traumatic events. As noted above, there may also be mental health effects of having a pantheistic view of God as taught in Eastern religions (Hinduism and Buddhism), that is, seeing God as synonymous with everything in the universe (Koenig, 2017a, 2017b). Rather than viewing God as personal, interactive with humans, and distinct from creation, some Eastern religions see God as infused in everything and not separate from humanity. In Hinduism, for example, the true identity of the individual (the *atman*) is seen as a part of God (the *Paratman*), rather than as a separate ego that divides the person from the Divine (and everyone else). The *atman* or "true Self" is distinguished from the false self or ego. The *atman* is part of the *Paratman* just like water molecules in an ocean wave are part of the ocean. This belief too may influence mental health by affecting one's view of life, interpretation of traumatic events, and responses to them.

However, the Eastern faith traditions also vary in terms of how they view God. This depends on the particular beliefs, which include a view of God that is personal. *SaguNa Brahman* refers to the personal characteristics of the Universal Essence or Supreme God (Koenig, 2017b). These personal features stand in contrast to the impersonal or transcendent characteristics of God (*NriguNa Brahman*). In one of the most holy and widely read Hindu scripture, the Bhagavad Gita, the Divine is reincarnated as a human, Lord Krishna. The Gita is about a conversation between Lord Krishna and a warrior, Arjuna. Arjuna is about to go to war, but is conflicted about his role in battle. Here, God (as Lord Krishna) is displayed as a loving and concerned Deity who wants to be involved in the world and wishes to help humans to fulfill their duties and flourish. Similarly, in Buddhism there are Divine compassionate beings called *Bodhisattvas* who listen to the pleas of the faithful and become involved in the world to help humans overcome adverse life situations (Koenig, 2017a; Leighton, 1998).

Of course, Eastern religions may also have fatalistic views involving acceptance of suffering as part of one's "karma," which can affect attitudes toward those who are suffering and also affect help-seeking behaviors when professional assistance is needed. Thus, all major faith traditions have views of God that positively impact mental health (bring comfort and hope), or have beliefs about God that are negative (create guilt and feelings of condemnation) that may worsen mental health and/or adversely affect treatment-seeking behaviors.

Social Factors

Most major religions promote childbearing and emphasize the importance of nurturing children within a stable family environment. Not surprisingly, then, religious involvement is consistently related to greater marital satisfaction, marital stability, and lower child and spouse abuse (although is associated with higher rates of corporeal punishment) (Ellison, 1996; Ellison & Anderson, 2001; Ellison, Trinitapoli, Anderson, & Johnson, 2007; Wolf & Kepple, 2017). Our systematic review found that 86% (68/79) quantitative studies published prior to 2010 reported greater marital satisfaction and stability among those who were more religious (Koenig et al., 2012). In parents who are more religious, lower rates of depression, anxiety, alcohol use/abuse, and drug use/abuse (Chapter 4) and greater well-being and happiness (Chapter 5) ought to influence emotional and physiological health during pregnancy and influence parents' availability to meet the emotional needs of infancy and early childhood, increasing the likelihood of developing basic trust and stable attachments. Reduced rates of delinquency and crime among religious youth and those raised in religious families (see Chapter 4) supports such speculations.

Religion also influences other social determinants of mental health. While it cannot be denied that religion has often contributed to discrimination and stigma, it has also served to buffer against the negative effects on mental health produced by socially alienating processes (Battle & DeFreece, 2014; Butler-Barnes et al., 2016; Corona et al., 2017; Hodge, Zidan, & Husain, 2015; Jeffries, Dodge, & Sandfort, 2008; Ojeda & Pina-Watson, 2013; Porter, Brennan-Ing, Burr, Dugan, & Karpiak, 2017; Szaflarski, 2013). Furthermore, most major world religions strongly emphasize compassion for the sick, care for the intellectually disabled, care for those with emotional or neurological disorders, and often politically advocate for these groups (Koenig, 2005). Finally, based on our systematic review of quantitative research, religiosity is strongly associated with social support in most of the research that has looked at this relationship (82% (61/74) of published studies) (Koenig et al., 2012).

Some researchers, in fact, emphasize that all of the effects of religion on mental and physical health are due to social factors (Shor &

Roelfs, 2013; Stavrova, Fetchenhauer, & Schlösser, 2013). While no doubt social factors are important and a part of the mechanism by which religion affects mental health, it is by no means the only factor—at least according to the latest research. With regard to suicide, for example, data from the Nurses' Health Study analyzed by VanderWeele, Li, Tsai, and Kawachi (2016) from the Harvard School of Public Health found that frequent religious attendance predicted lower rates of suicide. This effect persisted after controlling for a comprehensive list of other forms of social involvement (and was the most powerful protective factor of all social network predictors). This is also true for religious involvement and physical health, which as noted above, influences mental health. For example, when Li et al. (2016) examined predictors of mortality in the Nurses' Health Study, they found that only 23% of the effect of religious attendance on extending longevity could be explained by social factors. Sociologists of religion have likewise found that social factors explain only a relatively small proportion of religion's effect on mental health (Acevedo, Ellison, & Xu, 2014). Thus, while social factors play an important role in the mechanism by which religion affects mental health, there are other factors that likely contribute as well—particularly psychological, behavioral, and environmental ones.

Environmental Factors

Already described is the impact that religious involvement by parents during pregnancy and early childhood may have on shaping a positive environment for physiological and psychological development, including brain development and growth. Again, if alcohol and drug use are less frequent, children more valued (beginning in the womb), emotional problems less common, and emotional well-being and social support greater, then this cannot help but provide an environment in which vulnerability to mental illness might be reduced and resources provided for a flourishing life. For the individual, with less substance use/abuse and its consequences (teenage pregnancy, etc.), there is a greater likelihood that a person will complete their education, obtain a good job, have health insurance that will give them access to timely medical and psychiatric care when needed, have fewer substance-induced automobile accidents, and live in a neighborhood with better quality schools for their children and less neighborhood violence and crime. Furthermore, even when people are victims of natural disasters or accidents from no fault of their own, religion provides a way to cope and adapt to these traumas in healthy ways (vs. turning to drugs or alcohol or other maladaptive behaviors to relieve distress).

In many cases, then, religious involvement may interrupt the complex web of causation that leads to stressful environments and mental health problems. This does not mean that religious involvement always produces better psychological, social, and physical environments (as the situation in the Middle East underscores). Furthermore, the benefits to the environment that religion conveys may not always be obvious. Consider minority communities where poverty, violence, crime, and drug/alcohol use are rampant, and yet religious involvement is widespread. Mississippi, Alabama, Georgia, and other "Bible belt" states have some of the highest rates of mental, physical, and community-wide health and economic problems. Doesn't this mean that religion is actually contributing to the problem? Conclusions of this type are often called the "ecologic fallacy," where inferences about the nature of individuals are made based on groups to which they belong. It is specifically in these areas (poverty-stricken, disadvantaged communities) that the relationship at the individual level between religiosity, mental health and well-being is often the strongest (Stavrova et al., 2013). Indeed, one can only imagine what these underprivileged communities would look like without religious influences that are literally holding them together.

Personal Choice

Religious training during youth and religious involvement during adulthood are important determinants of decisions and choices that people make. Religious values help to guide personal choices that ultimately affect the psychosocial and physical environments in which individuals find themselves. Religious beliefs and teachings emphasize prosocial choices that may affect the mental health of the individual and the flourishing of communities in which she or he lives (of course, this does not apply those who are radicalized, although this group makes up an extremely small percentage of religious persons). Level of community religious involvement is often a strong predictor of "social capital" (after controlling for socioeconomic conditions). Our systematic review of quantitative studies published prior to 2010 identified 14 studies that examined this relationship; close to 80% found a significant association between community religiosity and higher levels of social capital (Koenig et al., 2012).

Some of this effect is the result of greater altruism and volunteering by religious individuals (found in more than 70% (33/47) of studies identified in our systematic review). Also, as noted in Chapter 4, there is growing evidence that religious involvement reduces delinquency during youth and decreases crime during adulthood. An important social function of religion has long been to provide moral standards to guide individual decision-making, thereby serving as a form of "internal" social control that encourages prosocial rather than antisocial choices. With secularization has come the expansion of choices that are considered morally acceptable, and as religious forms of internal control have lessened, "external" controls by the state have become more necessary.

Consider the following effect of secularization in the United States. Crime rates around the world are highest in poverty-stricken and low-income countries. However, according to the "crime index by country" in 2017, the United States was rated relatively high (53rd highest out of 125 countries) (Numbeo, 2017) despite being one of the wealthiest countries in the world (ranked 13th out of 189) (Gregson, 2017) and one of the most free countries in the world (ranked 23rd out of 159 countries) (Vásquez & Porcˇnik, 2016). Illicit drug overdose is now the leading cause of death among those under age 50 in the United States (Scotti, 2017). Among the 15 countries lowest on the crime index (out of 125) were Qatar, Singapore, United Arab Emirates, Saudi Arabia, and Oman (Numbeo, 2017), which are also some of the most religious countries in the world. There are many factors that contribute to crime rates, and it is well-documented that individuals also turn to religion to cope with crime and poverty (Crabtree, 2010).

The point is that a country such as the United States that has many personal freedoms and economic resources, and is arguably becoming more and more secular, has relatively high and increasing drug use and crime rates. Such trends have also been observed at the individual level (Hoskin, Hartley, Ellis, & McMurray, 2017). In a now classic article published in *Psychological Bulletin* (and featured in the New York Times), McCullough and Willoughby (2009) argue that encouraging self-regulation or self-control (with regard to eating, drinking, drug use, sex, greed, etc.) is one of the primary ways that religion affects both mental and physical health.

SUMMARY AND CONCLUSIONS

Those who are more religiously committed and engaged in religious activities (public and private religious practices) may experience better mental health because of a host of genetic, biological, psychological, social, environmental, and individual factors, all interacting with and influencing one another. Genetic factors in religious persons may predispose them to better mental health by having genes that lower vulnerability to substance abuse and other psychopathology. Religious involvement may reduce immune, endocrine, inflammatory, and neurological factors that increase risk of medical illness and functional disability. Given that physical health is one of the strongest predictors of mental health, this represents an important indirect pathway by which religion may affect mental health. Religious factors such as having a positive image of God (loving vs. punishing) and a secure attachment to God (or, in the Buddhist tradition, avoiding attachments of any kind) may improve coping with stress, loss, and change. Religious involvement may positively impact the capacity of parents to be nurturing, thus increasing the stability of a child's early relationships and later social and marital relationships. Religion may also contribute to a more positive environment by affecting brain growth during fetal development (due to religious parents having less psychopathology or substance abuse problems), by affecting childhood and adolescence (due to religious parental and peer influences), and by behaviors (based on moral standards set by religious parents) that will later affect access to education, job opportunities, safe living environments, and health insurance. Finally, religious beliefs may affect individual choices and decisions that affect behaviors and habits that ultimately influence the quality of physical health, social relationships, and environmental circumstances. Thus, across the lifespan, religion has the potential to have an enormous influence on mental health and well-being (even though it may not always do so for everyone). In the next chapter, the "other side" of religious faith will be examined, one that involves religious/spiritual struggles and doubts that may adversely affect mental health.

References

Acevedo, G. A., Ellison, C. G., & Xu, X. (2014). Is it really religion? Comparing the main and stress-buffering effects of religious and secular civic engagement on psychological distress. *Society and Mental Health*, *4*(2), 111–128.

Ai, A. L., Seymour, E. M., Tice, N., Kronfol, Z., Appel, H., & Bolling, S. F. (2009). Spiritual struggle related to plasma interleukin-6 prior to cardiac surgery. *Psychology of Religion and Spirituality*, *1*(2), 112–128.

Anderson, M. R., Miller, L., Wickramaratne, P., Svob, C., Odgerel, Z., Zhao, R., & Weissman, M. M. (2017). Genetic correlates of spirituality/religion and depression: A study in offspring and grandchildren at high and low familial risk for depression. *Spirituality in Clinical Practice*, *4*(1), 43–63.

Ano, G. G., & Vasconcelles, E. B. (2005). Religious coping and psychological adjustment to stress: A meta-analysis. *Journal of Clinical Psychology*, *61*(4), 461–480.

Battle, J., & DeFreece, A. (2014). The impact of community involvement, religion, and spirituality on happiness and health among a National Sample of Black Lesbians. *Women, Gender, and Families of Color*, *2*(1), 1–31.

Blazer, D., Burchett, B., & George, L. K. (1991). The association of age and depression among the elderly: An epidemiologic exploration. *Journal of Gerontology*, *46*(6), M210–M215.

Bradshaw, M., Ellison, C. G., & Flannelly, K. J. (2008). Prayer, God imagery, and symptoms of psychopathology. *Journal for the Scientific Study of Religion*, *47*, 644–659.

Bradshaw, M., Ellison, C. G., & Marcum, J. P. (2010). Attachment to God, images of God, and psychological distress in a nationwide sample of Presbyterians. *International Journal for the Psychology of Religion*, *20*(2), 130–147.

Butler-Barnes, S. T., Martin, P. P., Copeland-Linder, N., Seaton, E. K., Matusko, N., Caldwell, C. H., & Jackson, J. S. (2016). The protective role of religious involvement in African American and Caribbean Black adolescents' experiences of racial discrimination. *Youth and Society*doi: 10.1177/0044118X15626063.

Chartier, K. G., Dick, D. M., Almasy, L., Chan, G., Aliev, F., Schuckit, M. A., & Nurnberger, J., Jr. (2016). Interactions between alcohol metabolism genes and religious involvement in association with maximum drinks and alcohol dependence symptoms. *Journal of Studies on Alcohol and Drugs*, *77*(3), 393–404.

Cohen, S., & Wills, T. A. (1985). Stress, social support, and the buffering hypothesis. *Psychological Bulletin*, *98*(2), 310.

Cole, M. G., & Dendukuri, N. (2003). Risk factors for depression among elderly community subjects: A systematic review and meta-analysis. *American Journal of Psychiatry*, *160*(6), 1147–1156.

Compton, M. T., & Shim, R. S. (Eds.). (2015). *The social determinants of mental health*. Arlington, VA: American Psychiatric Association Publishing.

Corona, R., Rodríguez, V. M., McDonald, S. E., Velazquez, E., Rodríguez, A., & Fuentes, V. E. (2017). Associations between cultural stressors, cultural values, and Latina/o college students' mental health. *Journal of Youth and Adolescence*, *46*(1), 63–77.

Crabtree, S. (2010). Religiosity highest in world's poorest nations. *Gallup Poll*. Retrieved from http://www.gallup.com/poll/142727/religiosity-highest-world-poorest-nations.aspx.

De Souza, A., Fernandes, F., & Tavares do Carmo, M. (2011). Effects of maternal malnutrition and postnatal nutritional rehabilitation on brain fatty acids, learning and memory. *Nutrition Reviews*, *69*, 132–144.

Denhardt, D. (April 27, 2017). Effect of stress on human biology: Epigenetics, adaptation, inheritance and social significance. *Journal of Cellular Physiology*doi: 10.1002/jcp.25837.

Dew, R. E., & Koenig, H. G. (2014). Religious involvement, the serotonin transporter promoter polymorphism, and drug use in young adults. *International Journal of Social Sciences Studies*, *2*(1), 98–104.

Dobbing, J., & Sands, J. (1979). Comparative aspects of the brain growth spurt. *Early Human Development*, *3*, 79–83.

Ellison, C. G. (1996). Conservative protestantism and the corporal punishment of children: Clarifying the issues. *Journal for the Scientific Study of Religion*, *35*(1), 1–16.

Ellison, C. G., & Anderson, K. L. (2001). Religious involvement and domestic violence among US couples. *Journal for the Scientific Study of Religion*, *40*(2), 269–286.

Ellison, C. G., Bradshaw, M., Flannelly, K. J., & Galek, K. C. (2014). Prayer, attachment to God, and symptoms of anxiety-related disorders among U.S. adults. *Sociology of Religion*, *75*, 208–233.

Ellison, C. G., Trinitapoli, J. A., Anderson, K. L., & Johnson, B. R. (2007). Race/ethnicity, religious involvement, and domestic violence. *Violence Against Women*, *13*(11), 1094–1112.

Exline, J. J., Grubbs, J. B., & Homolka, S. J. (2015). Seeing God as cruel or distant: Links with divine struggles involving anger, doubt, and fear of God's disapproval. *International Journal for the Psychology of Religion*, *25*(1), 29–41.

Exline, J. J., Pargament, K. I., Grubbs, J. B., & Yali, A. M. (2014). The Religious and Spiritual Struggles Scale: Development and initial validation. *Psychology of Religion and Spirituality*, *6*(3), 208–222.

Folkman, S., & Moskowitz, J. T. (2004). Coping: Pitfalls and promise. *Annual Review of Psychology*, *55*, 745–774.

Ford, E. S., Loucks, E. B., & Berkman, L. F. (2006). Social integration and concentrations of C-reactive protein among US adults. *Annals of Epidemiology*, *16*(2), 78–84.

Gerber, M. M., Boals, A., & Schuettler, D. (2011). The unique contributions of positive and negative religious coping to posttraumatic growth and PTSD. *Psychology of Religion and Spirituality*, *3*(4), 298–307.

Goldberg, S., Muir, R., & Kerr, J. (2013). *Attachment theory: Social, developmental and clinical perspectives*. New York, NY: Routledge (Taylor & Francis).

Granqvist, P. (2014). Mental health and religion from an attachment viewpoint: Overview with implications for future research. *Mental Health, Religion and Culture*, *17*(8), 777–793.

Gregson, J. (February 13, 2017). Richest countries in the world. *Global Finance* Retrieved from https://www.gfmag.com/global-data/economic-data/richest-countries-in-the-world?page=12.

Hart, H. L. (1955). Are there any natural rights? *The Philosophical Review*, *64*(2), 175–191.

Healthy People 2020 (2017). *Mental health across the life stages*. Retrieved from https://www.healthypeople.gov/2020/leading-health-indicators/2020-lhi-topics/Mental-Health/determinants.

Henry, S. M., Ironson, G., Gonzalez, B., & Schneiderman, N. (2014). Buffers of impact of bereavement or divorce on viral load in HIV: Role of religious coping and social support. *Annals of Behavioral Medicine, 47*(Suppl. 1, D-064), s260.

Hill, T. D., Ellison, C. G., Burdette, A. M., Taylor, J., & Friedman, K. L. (2016). Dimensions of religious involvement and leukocyte telomere length. *Social Science and Medicine, 163,* 168–175.

Hill, T. D., Rote, S. M., Ellison, C. G., & Burdette, A. M. (2014). Religious attendance and biological functioning: A multiple specification approach. *Journal of Aging and Health, 26*(5), 766–785.

Hill, T. D., Vaghela, P., Ellison, C. G., & Rote, S. (2017). Processes linking religious involvement and telomere length. *Biodemography and Social Biology, 63*(2), 167–188.

Hodge, D. R., Zidan, T., & Husain, A. (2015). Modeling the relationships between discrimination, depression, substance use, and spirituality with Muslims in the United States. *Social Work Research, 39*(4), 223–233.

Hofmann, S. G., Asnaani, A., Vonk, I. J., Sawyer, A. T., & Fang, A. (2012). The efficacy of cognitive behavioral therapy: A review of meta-analyses. *Cognitive Therapy and Research, 36*(5), 427–440.

Hoskin, A. W., Hartley, R. D., Ellis, L., & McMurray, H. (2017). Does religiosity explain cross national differences in crime? The case of American versus Malaysian university students. *Journal of Religion and Society, 19,* 1–17.

Ironson, G., Kremer, H., & Lucette, A. (2016). Relationship between spiritual coping and survival in patients with HIV. *Journal of General Internal Medicine, 31*(9), 1068–1076.

Ironson, G., Stuetzle, R., Ironson, D., Balbin, E., Kremer, H., George, A., & Fletcher, M. A. (2011). View of God as benevolent and forgiving or punishing and judgmental predicts HIV disease progression. *Journal of Behavioral Medicine, 34*(6), 414–425.

Jeffries, W. L., Dodge, B., & Sandfort, T. G. M. (2008). Religion and spirituality among bisexual black men in the USA. *Culture, Health and Sexuality, 10*(5), 463–477.

Johnson, M. H. (2001). Functional brain development in humans. *Nature Reviews. Neuroscience, 2*(7), 475–483.

Kane, R. (1998). *The significance of free will.* Oxford University Press.

Kelsch, C. B., Ironson, G., Szeto, A., Kremer, H., Schneiderman, N., & Mendez, A. J. (2013). The relationship of spirituality, benefit finding, and other psychosocial variables to the hormone oxytocin in HIV/AIDS. *Research in the Social Scientific Study of Religion, 24,* 137–162.

King, D. E., Mainous, A. G., 3rd., & Pearson, W. S. (2002). C-reactive protein, diabetes, and attendance at religious services. *Diabetes Care, 25*(7), 1172–1176.

King, D. E., Mainous, A. G., 3rd., Steyer, T. E., & Pearson, W. (2001). The relationship between attendance at religious services and cardiovascular inflammatory markers. *International Journal of Psychiatry in Medicine, 31*(4), 415–425.

Koenig, H. G. (2005). *Faith and mental health: Religious resources for healing.* Templeton Foundation Press.

Koenig, H. G. (2016). *You are my beloved. Really?* Amazon: CreateSpace Publishing Platform.

Koenig, H. G. (2017a). *Buddhism and mental health: Beliefs research and applications.* Amazon: CreateSpace Publishing Platform.

Koenig, H. G. (2017b). *Hinduism and mental health: Beliefs research and applications.* Amazon: CreateSpace Publishing Platform.

Koenig, H. G., & Cohen, H. J. (2002). *The link between religion and health: Psychoneuroimmunology and the faith factor.* New York, NY: Oxford University Press.

Koenig, H. G., Cohen, H. J., George, L. K., Hays, J. C., Larson, D. B., & Blazer, D. G. (1997). Attendance at religious services, interleukin-6, and other biological indicators of immune function in older adults. *International Journal of Psychiatry in Medicine, 27,* 233–250.

Koenig, H. G., Gutiérrez, B., Cervilla, J., Pearce, M. J., Daher, N., Nelson, B., Shaw, S. F., Cohen, H. J., & King, M. B. (2015). Genes, religion, and response to religious vs conventional psychotherapy: A randomized clinical trial in medically ill patients with major depression. *Austin Journal of Psychiatry and Behavioral Sciences, 2*(1), 1036.

Koenig, H. G., King, D. E., & Carson, V. B. (2012). *Handbook of religion and health* (2nd ed.). New York, NY: Oxford University Press.

Koenig, H. G., Nelson, B., Shaw, S. F., Saxena, S., & Cohen, H. J. (2016). Religious involvement and telomere length in women family caregivers. *Journal of Nervous and Mental Disease, 204*(1), 36–42.

Kotas, M. E., & Medzhitov, R. (2015). Homeostasis, inflammation, and disease susceptibility. *Cell, 160*(5), 816–827.

Krauss, S. W., & Hood, R. W., Jr. (2013). *A new approach to religious orientation: The Commitment Reflectivity Circumplex*. Amsterdam, Netherlands: Rodopi.

Kremer, H., Ironson, G., Kaplan, L., Stuetzele, R., Baker, N., & Fletcher, M. A. (2014). Spiritual coping predicts CD4-cell preservation and undetectable viral load over four years. *AIDS Care, 27*(1), 71–79.

Lazarus, R. S., & Folkman, S. (1987). Transactional theory and research on emotions and coping. *European Journal of Personality, 1*, 141–169.

Leighton, T. D. (1998). *Bodhisattva archetypes: Classic Buddhist guides to awakening and their modern expression*. New York, NY: Penguin Arkana pp. 158–205.

Li, S., Stampfer, M. J., Williams, D. R., & VanderWeele, T. J. (2016). Association of religious service attendance with mortality among women. *JAMA Internal Medicine, 176*(6), 777–785.

Lin, N., Dean, A., & Ensel, W. M. (Eds.). (2013). *Social support, life events and depression*. San Diego, CA: Academic Press.

Lupien, S. J., McEwen, B. S., Gunnar, M. R., & Heim, C. (2009). Effects of stress throughout the lifespan on the brain, behaviour and cognition. *Nature Reviews. Neuroscience, 10*(6), 434–445.

Lutgendorf, S. K., Russell, D., Ullrich, P., Harris, T. B., & Wallace, R. (2004). Religious participation, interleukin-6, and mortality in older adults. *Health Psychology, 23*(5), 465–475.

Maes, M., Song, C., Lin, A., De Jongh, R., Van Gastel, A., Kenis, G., & Demedts, P. (1998). The effects of psychological stress on humans: Increased production of pro-inflammatory cytokines and Th1-like response in stress-induced anxiety. *Cytokine, 10*(4), 313–318.

Mathur, M. B., Epel, E., Kind, S., Desai, M., Parks, C. G., Sandler, D. P., & Khazeni, N. (2016). Perceived stress and telomere length: A systematic review, meta-analysis, and methodologic considerations for advancing the field. *Brain, Behavior, and Immunity, 54*, 158–169.

McCullough, M. E., & Willoughby, B. L. (2009). Religion, self-regulation, and self-control: Associations, explanations, and implications. *Psychological Bulletin, 135*(1), 69–93.

McEwen, B. S. (2017). Neurobiological and systemic effects of chronic stress. *Chronic Stress, 1*, 1–11. doi: 10.1177/2470547017692328.

McGowan, P. O., Sasaki, A., D'Alessio, A. C., et al. (2009). Epigenetic regulation of the glucocorticoid receptor in human brain associates with childhood abuse. *Nature Neuroscience, 12*, 241–243.

Mikulincer, M., & Shaver, P. R. (2008). Adult attachment and affect regulation. In J. Cassidy, & P. R. Shaver (Eds.), *Handbook of attachment: Theory, research, and clinical applications* (2nd ed., pp. 503–531). New York, NY: Guilford Press.

Miller, L. R., Bansal, R., Wickramaratne, P., Hao, Z., Tenke, C., Weissman, M. M., & Peterson, B. S. (2014). Neuroanatomical correlates of religiosity and spirituality: A study in adults at high and low familial risk for depression. *JAMA Psychiatry, 71*(2), 128–135.

Monroe, A. E., & Malle, B. F. (2010). From uncaused will to conscious choice: The need to study, not speculate about people's folk concept of free will. *Review of Philosophy and Psychology, 1*(2), 211–224.

Numbeo (2017). Crime index for country 2017. *Numbeo.com*. Retrieved from https://www.numbeo.com/crime/rankings_by_country.jsp.

Ojeda, L., & Pina-Watson, B. (2013). Day laborers' life satisfaction: The role of familismo, spirituality, work, health, and discrimination. *Cultural Diversity and Ethnic Minority Psychology*, *19*(3), 270–278.

Pargament, K. I., Smith, B. W., Koenig, H. G., & Perez, L. (1998). Patterns of positive and negative religious coping with major life stressors. *Journal for the Scientific Study of Religion*, 710–724.

Park, C. L. (2013). The meaning making model: A framework for understanding meaning, spirituality, and stress-related growth in health psychology. *European Health Psychologist*, *15*(2), 40–47.

Pattanaik, P. K., & Xu, Y. (2000). On diversity and freedom of choice. *Mathematical Social Sciences*, *40*(2), 123–130.

Pinyerd, B. J. (1992). Assessment of infant growth. *Journal of Pediatric Health Care*, *6*(5), 302–308.

Porter, K. E., Brennan-Ing, M., Burr, J. A., Dugan, E., & Karpiak, S. E. (2017). Stigma and psychological well-being among older adults with HIV: The impact of spirituality and integrative health approaches. *The Gerontologist*, *57*(2), 219–228.

Pray, L. (2008). DNA replication and causes of mutation. *Nature Education*, *1*(1), 214.

Price, J. L., & Drevets, W. C. (2010). Neurocircuitry of mood disorders. *Neuropsychopharmacology*, *35*(1), 192–216.

Robinson, L. R. (2014). I can do all things: Positive religious coping and its effects on risk reduction. In *142nd American Public Health Association annual meeting and exposition* (November 15–November 19, 2014, New Orleans).

Rockland, L. H. (1993). A review of supportive psychotherapy, 1986–1992. *Psychiatric Services*, *44*(11), 1053–1060.

Schildkraut, J. J. (1965). The catecholamine hypothesis of affective disorders: A review of supporting evidence. *American Journal of Psychiatry*, *122*(5), 509–522.

Schwartz, B. (2000). Self-determination: The tyranny of freedom. *American Psychologist*, *55*(1), 79–88.

Schwartz, B. (2004). *The paradox of choice: Why more is less – how the culture of abundance robs us of satisfaction*. New York: Ecco (Harper Collins).

Scotti, A. (June 5, 2017). Drug overdoses are the leading cause of death among people under 50. *New York Daily News* Retrieved from http://www.nydailynews.com/life-style/drugoverdoses-leading-death-people-50-article-1.3223333.

Sen, A. (1988). Freedom of choice: Concept and content. *European Economic Review*, *32*(2–3), 269–294.

Shor, E., & Roelfs, D. J. (2013). The longevity effects of religious and nonreligious participation: A meta-analysis and meta-regression. *Journal for the Scientific Study of Religion*, *52*, 120–145.

Silton, N. R., Flannelly, K. J., Galek, K., & Ellison, C. G. (2014). Beliefs about God and mental health among American adults. *Journal of Religion and Health*, *53*(5), 1285–1296.

Slavich, G. M., & Irwin, M. R. (2014). From stress to inflammation and major depressive disorder: A social signal transduction theory of depression. *Psychological Bulletin*, *140*(3), 774–815.

Smith, T. B., McCullough, M. E., & Poll, J. (2003). Religiousness and depression: Evidence for a main effect and the moderating influence of stressful life events. *Psychological Bulletin*, *129*(4), 614.

Stavrova, O., Fetchenhauer, D., & Schlösser, T. (2013). Why are religious people happy? The effect of the social norm of religiosity across countries. *Social Science Research*, *42*(1), 90–105.

Szaflarski, M. (2013). Spirituality and religion among HIV-infected individuals. *Current HIV/AIDS Reports*, *10*(4), 324–332.

Szyf, M. (2016a). Maternal care and DNA methylation. In A. Sale (Ed.), *Environmental experience and plasticity of the developing brain*. New York, NY: Wiley Blackwell pp. 99–116.

Szyf, M. (2016b). Nurture alters nature through epigenetic modifications of DNA. In 2016 *American Association for the Advancement of Science annual meeting* (February 11–15, Washington, DC).

Thomas, A., & Chess, S. (1977). *Temperament and development*. New York: Brunner/Mazel.
Turner, R. J., & Noh, S. (1988). Physical disability and depression: A longitudinal analysis. *Journal of Health and Social Behavior*, *29*(1), 23–37.
Uchino, B. N. (2006). Social support and health: A review of physiological processes potentially underlying links to disease outcomes. *Journal of Behavioral Medicine*, *29*(4), 377–387.
Van Wagoner, N., Elopre, L., Westfall, A. O., Mugavero, M. J., Turan, J., & Hook, E. W. (2016). Reported church attendance at the time of entry into HIV Care is associated with viral load suppression at 12 months. *AIDS and Behavior*, *20*(8), 1706–1712.
Vance, T., Maes, H. H., & Kendler, K. S. (2014). A multivariate twin study of the dimensions of religiosity and common psychiatric and substance use disorders. *Journal of Nervous and Mental Disease*, *202*, 360–367.
VanderWeele, T. J., Li, S., Tsai, A. C., & Kawachi, I. (2016). Association between religious service attendance and lower suicide rates among US women. *JAMA Psychiatry*, *73*(8), 845–851.
VanderWeele, T. J., Yu, J., Cozier, Y. C., Wise, L., Argentieri, M. A., Rosenberg, L., & Shields, A. E. (2017). Attendance at religious services, prayer, religious coping, and religious/spiritual identity as predictors of all-cause mortality in the Black Women's Health Study. *American Journal of Epidemiology*, *185*(7), 515–522.
Vásquez, I., & Porcˇnik, T. (2016). *Human freedom index: A global measurement of personal, civil, and economic freedom*. Washington, DC: Cato Institute.
Weaver, I. C. G. (2010). Epigenetic programming of stress responses and trans-generational inheritance through natural variations in maternal care: A role for DNA methylation in experience-dependent (re)programming of defensive responses. In J. D. Clelland (Ed.), *Handbook of neurochemistry and molecular neurobiology: Genomics, proteomics and the nervous system* (pp. 87–112). New York: Springer.
Weber, S. R., & Pargament, K. I. (2014). The role of religion and spirituality in mental health. *Current Opinion in Psychiatry*, *27*(5), 358–363.
Whybrow, P. C., Akiskal, H. S., & McKinney, W. T., Jr. (2012). *Mood disorders: Toward a new psychobiology*. New York, NY: Springer Science & Business Media.
Wolf, J. P., & Kepple, N. J. (2017). Individual-and county-level religious participation, corporal punishment, and physical abuse of children: An exploratory study. *Journal of Interpersonal Violence* [E-pub ahead of press, doi:0886260516674197].

CHAPTER

8

Religious Struggles and Doubt

RELIGIOUS STRUGGLES

Most individuals struggle with and have doubts about their religious faith, but usually not to the point that it adversely affects their faith or causes them to turn completely away from or become hostile toward religion. The recognition of religious struggles dates back to Biblical times with the struggles of Jacob with God (Genesis 32:24-30). Similarly, the "dark night of the soul," as described by the 16th century Carmelite mystic St. John of the Cross, is a well-known experience of the deeply religious (Underhill, 1974). Religious struggles and doubts were not always considered by saints and holy people as something bad, but rather a natural companion to the spiritual life that stimulated spiritual growth and ultimately led to a deeper and closer relationship with God. Almost all the founders of major religions today went through such a struggle. Consider the Buddha and his early strivings toward enlightenment (Gethin, 1998), the struggles of Abraham to believe in "the promise" despite being childless (Genesis 12-22), the initial problems that Moses faced after killing the Egyptian slave master (Exodus 2:11-22), the trials of Arjuna in the Bhagavad Gita (Johnson, 1994), the difficulties faced by the Prophet Mohammed as he sought to establish Islam in a polytheistic society (Armstrong, 2006), not to mention Jesus's suffering and death on the cross (Matthew 27:46: "My God, my God, why hast thou forsaken me?"). Many can identify with the sufferings and strivings of these greater religious leaders.

However, within academic circles, the notion of religious struggles was first described and measured for research purposes by psychologist Ken Pargament. He began writing about religious coping methods involving God's anger and punishment in the mid-1980s (Pargament & Hahn, 1986) and referred to it indirectly in work on self-directing forms of religious coping in the late 1980s (Pargament et al., 1988). Later he addressed negative forms of religious coping under the categories of spiritual "discontent" and "punishing reappraisal" (Pargament, 1997; Pargament et al., 1990, 1992). Pargament began using the term "negative religious coping" in the mid- to late-1990s,

Religion and Mental Health. http://dx.doi.org/10.1016/B978-0-12-811282-3.00008-2

culminating in the publication of the now widely used Brief RCOPE, which includes a 7-item negative religious coping (NRC) subscale (Pargament, Smith, Koenig, & Perez, 1998). Examples of statements that make up the NRC subscale are: "I wondered whether God had abandoned me"; "I felt punished by God for my lack of devotion"; "I questioned God's love for me"; and "I wondered whether my church had abandoned me." Respondents indicate how well the statement applies to them on a 0–3 scale from "not at all" to "a great deal." Hundreds of studies have now used the 7-item NRC subscale in relationship to mental and physical health. It was not until 2001, though, that Pargament used the term "religious struggle" to describe these NRC activities (Pargament, Koenig, Tarakeshwar, & Hahn, 2001). Shorter versions of the NRC subscale have also been used in research, including a 3-item measure published in Fetzer Institute's Brief Multi-dimensional Measurement of Religiousness/Spirituality (Pargament, 1999).

The groundwork on which Pargament developed his religious struggles concept was laid to some extent by C. Daniel Batson in the 1970s and 1980s (Batson, 1976; Batson & Ventis, 1982), which ultimately produced the Quest Scale (Batson & Schoenrade, 1991a, 1991b). The Quest Scale is composed of statements such as "I am constantly questioning my religious beliefs"; "Questions are for more central to my religious experience that our answers"; "For me, doubting is an important part of what it means to be religious"; and "I find religious doubts upsetting." Respondents indicate their agreement on a scale from 1 to 9 (strongly disagree to strongly agree). Compared to Pargament's NRC subscale, however, the Quest Scale has not been used much in research, particularly since the year 2000.

Most recently, psychologist Julie Exline has expanded the concept of religious and spiritual struggles (SS) and strain in her writings (Exline & Rose, 2005; Exline, Yali, & Lobel, 1999; Exline, Yali, & Sanderson, 2000), culminating in the 26-item Religious and Spiritual Struggles Scale (RSSS) developed with Pargament (Exline, Pargament, Grubbs, & Yali, 2014). The RSSS assesses six domains of struggle, including struggles with the Divine (or perceived relationship with God), demonic (demonic forces persecuting or causing negative events), interpersonal (struggles with religious people or institutions), moral (strains involved in following moral or ethical guidelines), doubt (doubts or questions about religious/spiritual beliefs), and ultimate meaning (struggles regarding the meaning and purpose of life). Individuals rate their responses to each item on a scale from 1 (not at all/does not apply) to 5 (a great deal). There is considerable overlap between the NRC subscale of the Brief RCOPE and the RSSS, although the RSSS provides a more detailed examination of spiritual struggles and expands into other areas that the Brief RCOPE does not cover. Ellison and Lee (2010) nicely summarize the types of religious issues that people struggle with into three categories: "(1) divine, or troubled relationships with God; (2) interpersonal, or negative social encounters in religious settings; and (3) intrapsychic, or chronic religious doubting."

RELIGIOUS DOUBT

A common subtype of religious struggle is religious doubt. Sociologist Neal Krause has since the 1990s examined the relationship between religious doubt (RD) and psychological well-being (Krause, Ingersoll-Dayton, Ellison, & Wulff, 1999). However, he has not typically used a standard measure of religious struggle or doubt, instead preferring to ask a set of short questions with strong face validity (e.g., doubts about religious faith due to evil in the world, personal suffering, and feeling that life really has no meaning; doubts about things taught in church; doubts about whether prayer makes a difference; doubts that God is directly involved in daily life; and so forth) (Krause, 2003, 2006; Krause et al., 1999). He and his colleagues have consistently found in both cross-sectional and prospective studies that RD is associated with worse mental health, lower well-being, more depressive symptoms, and worse self-rated health, particularly among those who perform formal roles in church, have negative interactions with other church members, have lower education, and attempt to suppress their RDs rather than work through them (Hayward & Krause, 2014; Krause, 2003, 2006, 2012; Krause & Ellison, 2009; Krause et al., 1999; Krause & Wulff, 2004). He has also found that the deleterious effects of RD on mental health appear to be reduced among those who exhibit altruistic helping behaviors toward strangers (but not toward friends or family members, interestingly) (Krause, 2015). Other researchers have confirmed and extended these observations regarding the negative associations between RD and psychological well-being (Abu-Raiya, Pargament, Krause, & Ironson, 2015; Gauthier, Christopher, Walter, Mourad, & Marek, 2006; Henrie & Patrick, 2014) and have documented a positive effect of anxiety over time on increasing RD (Wilt, Grubbs, Lindberg, Exline, & Pargament, 2017) (i.e., reverse causation).

STRUGGLE IN PANTHEISTIC RELIGIONS

Religious struggles are not limited to members of monotheistic religions. Indeed, consider the struggles of Arjuna in the Bhagavad Gita, and the lessons that those struggles taught him as he was guided through them by Lord Krishna (Johnson, 1994). Likewise, the Buddha sought many different paths, struggling intensely for 6 years (almost drowning at one point from weakness due to starvation) before reaching Enlightenment (Conze, 1959). Eastern religions strongly emphasize the need for novices of the faith to seek guidance from someone such as a guru or teacher who is more mature and advanced along the spiritual path. Indeed, lack of such direction can lead to ego dissolution, depersonalization, dissociation, and confusion (even psychosis in those who are vulnerable) (Kuijpers, Van der Heijden, Tuinier, & Verhoeven, 2007; Vives, Martin, Trebbau, &

Aliño, 2011; Waelde, 2004). The spiritual path in these traditions, as in the monotheistic traditions, is one of struggle. When that struggle toward spiritual growth stops (and one becomes content with the status quo) short of Enlightenment, spiritual leaders emphasize, there is an inevitable backsliding toward a less mature state and perhaps even toward a less healthy mental state.

RELATED ISSUES

Three issues that closely relate to religious struggle and doubt are (1) how one's image of God influences such struggles, (2) whether these struggles really reflect the "dark side" of religion, and (3) how to distinguish healthy from unhealthy struggles/doubts.

Image of God

Considerable attention was paid in the last chapter to one's image of God as a possible mechanism by which religion affects mental health, at least among monotheists. Once a person has resolved her/his doubts about God's existence and concludes that God does exist, how does a person's beliefs about the nature and characteristics of God influence their mental health? Is God viewed as impersonal? Is God viewed as distant and unconcerned? Is God viewed as weak and powerless? Is God viewed as punishing or vindictive, a policeman or prison guard of sorts whose primary objective is to ensure that humans obey laws that limit their freedom and fun? Or, as noted earlier, is God viewed as personal, concerned, loving, forgiving, understanding, merciful, as a friend who is "closer than a brother" (Proverbs 18:24), on the person's side wanting to maximize their joy and fulfillment in life—a creator who knows how humans are put together, both their strengths and weaknesses, and deeply cares. Struggle over how one views God is certainly a type of religious struggle, and is central to many of the questions on scales used to measure religious struggle today (see NRC subscale of Brief RCOPE and Exline's RSSS).

Dark Side of Religion

Do religious struggle and doubt represent the "dark side" of religion, a type of cognitive state that adversely affects mental health? Or perhaps this struggle represents the opposite—a temporary process that ultimately leads to the light? Certainly, the vast majority of studies suggest that those with religious struggle/doubt have worse mental health (see below). Furthermore, studies often report that those with higher levels of RD or struggle tend to be individuals who are less active in their religious faith and often less religiously committed. But, might RD (doubts about the existence of God or the nature of God) be preliminary to something better? Might such doubts represent a state that exists prior to (or perhaps part of) the process of spiritual growth? Might it lead to a resolution of doubts and a movement toward a deeper spiritual and emotional life, one that is more complete and well-rounded? Indeed, any conclusion about whether such doubts represent the dark side of religion or are part of a process of religious growth cannot be made without some type of longitudinal assessment to determine where these doubts lead to. Admittedly, no studies (to this author's knowledge) have yet compared the trajectory of mental health over time between those without religious struggles/doubts, religious doubters, and those without any religious belief at all (e.g., atheists or agnostics).

Healthy vs. Unhealthy Struggles

As suggested above, there may be a type of religious struggle that ultimately leads to growth, to a deeper and more centered faith (or the opposite in some cases, to a settled and contented state of disbelief). There is also a struggle that leads nowhere (a constant state of churning discontent) or worse, to cynicism, pessimism, and self-centeredness, persecuted by and alienated from God, lacking any sense of ultimate purpose or meaning in life. For many, as noted earlier, this likely has something to do with one's image of God and beliefs about the intentions of God. Has there been any research that has examined the long-term course of religious struggle to differentiate between these two types of struggle (healthy vs. unhealthy), so that clinicians and clergy may distinguish one from the other? Indeed, treatments may differ depending on the type of religious struggle. One type might be encouraged and gently guided, whereas the other diagnosed as a pathological state in need of treatment, both pastoral and clinical.

RELIGIOUS STRUGGLES AND MENTAL HEALTH

Much research has examined the connections between religious struggles and mental health. One of the first reviews of research conducted prior to 2003 on the type of religious coping conceptualized by Pargament (including NRC, i.e., religious struggles) was a meta-analysis performed by Ano and Vasconcelles (2005). In that review, 49 studies were identified. Of those, 16 examined the relationship between NRC and positive psychological adjustment, and 22 examined that between NRC and negative psychological adjustment. The cumulative effect size for positive adjustment was 0.02 (95% CI −0.02 to 0.05) and for negative adjustment was

0.22 (95% CI 0.19–0.24). In fact, 21 of the 22 studies examining the association with negative psychological adjustment were in the positive direction (i.e., NRC associated with worse mental health).

Almost all of these studies, however, were cross-sectional. To this author's knowledge, only one prospective study published prior to 2000 examined whether NRC predicted mental health outcomes over time. Pargament et al. (1994) examined the effects of NRC (religious discontent with God, church, or faith) on positive and negative affects (PANAS) and global psychological distress (GHQ) in 215 college students (mean age 20 years). All measures were assessed at baseline (T1, February 20, 1991) and 3 weeks later (T2, March 11, 1991) (both during the Gulf War). At baseline, NRC was positively associated with negative affect in the cross-sectional analysis ($B = 0.27$, $p < 0.001$). After controlling for T1 measures of mental health in longitudinal analyses, however, T1 NRC did not predict T2 positive affect, negative affect, or global psychological distress. Admittedly, 3 weeks was not much time for mental health to change.

Recent research confirms the positive association between religious struggles and poor mental health. Our systematic review conducted from 2000 to 2010 (Koenig, King, & Carson, 2012) identified 60 studies that examined the association between NRC and mental health outcomes (Table 8.1). This review had very little overlap (8%) with the Ano and Vasconcelles (2005) review. Of those 60 studies, 52 were cross-sectional and 8 were prospective. Of the 52 cross-sectional studies, 45 (87%) reported significant negative correlations between NRC and mental health; 5 reported no association; 1 reported mixed results (NRC correlated with positive reframing, but also with self-blame) (Gall, 2003); and 1 reported a significant positive association with mental health. Interestingly, this last study—the only one that found a positive association between NRC and better mental health—was performed in 30 religious clergy (Proffitt, Cann, Calhoun, & Tedeschi, 2007).

In the eight prospective studies, cross-sectional analyses at baseline uniformly indicated negative associations between NRC and mental health. However, of those studies, only four found that baseline NRC predicted a decline in mental health over time (i.e., predicted a decline in T2 mental health outcome when T1 mental health outcome was controlled). Those four studies are now reviewed in order of publication date, to give a sense of how the literature has developed over time. In the first study, a 2-year prospective study involving 268 medically ill hospitalized older adults, Pargament, Koenig, Tarakeshwar, and Hahn (2004) examined the effects of baseline NRC (T1) on quality of life (QOL) and depressive symptoms at 2-year follow-up (T2). Analyses were controlled for baseline (T1) QOL and depression, and further adjusted for age, race, gender, education, and baseline physical health. Baseline T1 NRC did not significantly predict change in either T2 QOL ($B = -0.02$) or T2 depressed

TABLE 8.1 Systematic Review of Studies Examining Negative Religious Coping (Religious Struggles) and Mental Health Between 2000 and 2010

Authors	Population (*n*)	Design	Finding
Ai et al. (2003)	Muslim war refugees (138)	CS	Neg
Ai et al. (2005)	Muslim war refugees (138)	CS	Neg
Ai et al. (2006)	Cardiac surgery patients (335)	CS	NA
Anderson et al. (2005)	Bereaved mothers (57)	CS	NA
Balboni et al. (2007)	Cancer patients (230)	CS	Neg
Belavich et al. (2002)	Surgical waiting room (155)	CS	Neg
Benore et al. (2008)	Children with asthma (87)	CS	Neg
		P	Neg
Bjorck et al. (2007)	Church members (336)	CS	Neg
Bosworth et al. (2003)	Depressed PP (114)	CS	Neg
		P	NA
Bradley et al. (2005)	Suicide attempters (134)	CS	Neg
Burker et al. (2004)	Pulmonary disease (81)	CS	Neg
Cardella et al. (2004)	Parents, child with cancer (166)	CS	Neg
Case et al. (2001)	Psychologists (392)	CS	Neg
Conners et al. (2006)	Substance abuse PP (217)	CS	Neg
Cotton et al. (2006)	HIV/AIDS (450)	CS	Neg
Dumas et al. (2006)	Young parents (149)	CS	Neg
Fallot et al. (2005)	Dual diagnosis PP (663)	CS	Neg
Feder et al. (2008)	Prisoners of war (27)	CS	NA
Fitchett et al. (2004)	Medical patients (238)	CS	Neg
Freiheit et al. (2006)	College students (124)	CS	Neg
Gall (2000)	Breast cancer (32)	CS	Neg
Gall (2003)	Elderly Canadians (75)	CS	Mixed
Gall (2004)	Prostate cancer (34)	CS	Neg
Gall (2006)	Adults abused (101)	CS	Neg
Hebert et al. (2009)	Breast cancer (86)	CS	Neg
		P	NA
Hills et al. (2005)	Hospice/palliative (31)	CS	Neg

(*Continued*)

TABLE 8.1 Systematic Review of Studies Examining Negative Religious Coping (Religious Struggles) and Mental Health Between 2000 and 2010 (*cont.*)

Authors	Population (*n*)	Design	Finding
Keefe et al. (2001)	Rheumatoid arthritis (35)	CS	Neg
Kim K.H. (2006)	Community adults (546)	CS	Neg
Kudel et al. (2006)	HIV/AIDS (443)	CS	Neg
Lewis et al. (2005)	Adults in England (138)	CS	NA
Lonczak et al. (2006)	Prisoners (305)	CS	Neg
Maltby and Day (2003)	Community adults (360)	CS	Neg
Maltby and Day (2004)	Community adults (420)	CS	Neg
McConnell et al. (2006)	Internet survey (1629)	CS	Neg
Miller J.F. et al. (2007)	Rehab patients & spouses (44)	CS	Neg
Pargament et al. (2000)	College students (540)	CS	Neg
Pargament et al. (2001)	Church members (2818)	CS	Neg
Pargament et al. (2004)	Elderly medical patients (268)	CS	Neg
		P	Neg
Pargament et al. (2005)	Community adults (117)	CS	Neg
Pearce et al. (2006)	Caregivers cancer patients (162)	CS	Neg
Phillips et al. (2004)	College students (262)	CS	Neg
Phillips and Stein (2007)	PP schizo/bipolar (48)	CS	Neg
		P	NA
Proffitt et al. (2007)	Clergy (30)	CS	Pos (PTG)
Schanowitz et al. (2006)	Nursing home patients (100)	CS	Neg
Schottenbauer et al. (2006)	Community adults (1076)	CS	Neg
Schwartz et al. (2003)	Church members (2016)	CS	Neg
Shah et al. (2001)	Dementia caregivers (48)	CS	Neg
Sherman et al. (2005)	Multiple myeloma (213)	CS	Neg
Sherman et al. (2009)	Multiple myeloma (94)	CS	Neg
		P	Neg
Smith et al. (2000)	Adults (Midwest flood) (209)	CS	Neg
		P	NA

TABLE 8.1 Systematic Review of Studies Examining Negative Religious Coping (Religious Struggles) and Mental Health Between 2000 and 2010 (*cont.*)

Authors	Population (*n*)	Design	Finding
Szewczyk et al. (2006)	High school students (228)	CS	Neg
Tarakeshwar et al. (2001)	Parents of autistic child (45)	CS	NA
Tarakeshwar et al. (2006)	Advanced cancer (170)	CS	Neg
Trevino et al. (2010)	HIV/AIDS (429)	CS	Neg
		P	Neg
Van Dyke et al. (2009)	Catholic children (76)	CS	Neg
Vandecreek et al. (2004)	Rheumatoid arthritis (181)	CS	Neg
Witvliet et al. (2004)	Veterans, PTSD (213)	CS	Neg
Yi et al. (2006)	Physician house officers (227)	CS	Neg
Zwingmann et al. (2006)	Breast cancer (156)	CS	Neg
Zwingmann et al. (2008)	Breast cancer (167)	CS	Neg

CS, cross-sectional; *NA*, no association; *Neg*, worse mental health; *P*, prospective; *Pos*, better mental health; *PP*, psychiatric patients; *PTG*, posttraumatic growth. Complete reference citations are available in Koenig et al. (2012).

mood (B = 0.02). In subgroup analyses of the nine individual NRC subscales, however, T1 demonic reappraisal predicted a decrease in T2 QOL, and T1 interpersonal religious discontent predicted an increase in T2 depressed mood.

Benore, Pargament, and Pendleton (2008) examined the impact of NRC on the adjustment of 87 children aged 8–17 years admitted to the hospital for an exacerbation of asthma (average age 11.6 years, 55% males, 94% African–Americans, and 80% traditional Christians). Participants were assessed at baseline (T1) with the 34-item Children's Religious Coping Scale that was adapted from the RCOPE, including 14 NRC items. Children also completed scales assessing asthma-related QOL, psychosocial competence, depression, and two anxiety subtypes ("not calm" and "worried") at baseline (T1) and 1-month follow-up (T2) (n = 62). Controlling for age, gender, religious importance, perceived overall health, asthma control, and T1 mental health outcomes, T1 NRC significantly predicted higher T2 anxiety ("not calm" subtype) (B = 0.439, $p \leq 0.01$), an effect that remained significant after controlling for secular coping behaviors. However, T1 NRC did not predict the anxiety subtype "worried," QOL, psychosocial competence, or depression at T2 (once T1 measures were controlled for).

Sherman, Plante, Simonton, Latif, and Anaissie (2009) followed 94 multiple myeloma patients undergoing autologous stem cell transplantation from baseline (pretransplant) (T1) to an average of 10 days posttransplantation (T2) (average total follow-up time = 3.4 months). NRC (measured by the 7-item Brief RCOPE subscale) and other religious measures were assessed at baseline (T1) and examined as the predictors of anxiety, depression, emotional well-being, and other health outcomes at follow-up (T2), controlling for T1 mental health measures. Regression analyses indicated that T1 NRC predicted an increase in T2 anxiety ($B = 0.21$, $p < 0.05$), an increase in T2 depression ($B = 0.26$, $p < 0.01$), a decrease in T2 emotional well-being ($B = 0.22$, $p < 0.05$), and among those who scored high on both positive religious coping (PRC) and NRC, a decrease in physical well-being, all independent of T1 outcomes. Of particular importance in this study, investigators also examined the effects of T1 physical well-being and T1 depression on T2 NRC, controlling for T1 NRC and medical comorbidities; no association was found. Thus while NRC predicted a worsening of mental and physical well-being over time, the reverse was not true.

Finally, Trevino et al. (2010) surveyed 429 patients with HIV/AIDS at baseline (T1) and again 12–18 months later (T2). Administered at T1 were the 14-item Brief RCOPE (including the 7-item NRC subscale), a demographic questionnaire, and measures of QOL, depressive symptoms, and self-esteem (along with scales assessing HIV symptoms, social support, spiritual outcomes, and religious involvement). At baseline, as in the other three prospective studies above, cross-sectional analyses indicated that T1 NRC was associated with poorer mental health (i.e., lower overall T1 QOL and all eight subscales, more HIV symptoms, greater depression, lower social support, and lower self-esteem). In longitudinal analyses, controlling for age, race, gender, education, sexual orientation, years since HIV diagnosis, religious affiliation, PRC, and T1 mental health outcomes, T1 NRC predicted a decrease in overall QOL ($B = -0.13$, $p < 0.05$, especially HIV mastery, $B = -0.12$, $p < 0.05$) and an increase in depressive symptoms ($B = 0.12$, $p < 0.05$). Again, longitudinal analyses indicated that NRC influenced changes in mental health over time.

Conclusions

NRC is almost always correlated with worse mental health on cross-sectional analyses. There is some evidence (50% of studies) that NRC predicts a worsening in mental health outcomes over time (after T1 outcome measures are controlled for). Not all prospective studies (50%), though, find that NRC predicts poor mental health over time. Importantly, does poor mental health predict higher levels of NRC in the future? Only one of those eight studies examined that, and found that depression did not increase NRC over time, controlling for baseline NRC. But that is only one study. The question of causation, then, remains. Do religious doubt/struggles cause worse mental health, or alternatively, does worse mental health (depression, anxiety, and emotional distress) give rise to religious doubt/struggles. Might religious struggles and doubts simply be a symptom of depression or emotional distress? For example, when people are depressed or anxious, they have worries and doubts about many things. Why not have such worries and doubts about religion? This point is a crucial one. If the latter is true, then religious or pastoral care interventions directed at NRC may not be needed; indeed, drugs that improve mental health (antidepressants and antianxiety agents) or secular psychotherapy may be sufficient to improve both mental distress and NRC at the same time (see Kataria et al., 2016).

To what extent has more recent research since 2010 added to this literature base, particularly in terms of identifying the causal direction between religious struggle/doubt and mental health, and in separating healthy from unhealthy religious struggles? As noted earlier, some religious struggles may be healthy and lead to greater spiritual growth. However, it may have more to do with the individual than it is has to do with the particular religious struggle, as Proffitt et al. (2007)'s study of clergy suggests.

RECENT RESEARCH ON RELIGIOUS STRUGGLE/DOUBT

The following is a thorough (though nonsystematic) review of the literature that focuses on prospective studies only, those reported since 2010. The 10 studies thus identified are summarized in the order of year of publication below (again, to give a sense of how the literature has developed over time).

Pirutinsky, Rosmarin, Pargament, and Midlarsky (2011) directly addressed the question of whether NRC accompanies, precedes, or follows depressive symptoms, studying 80 Orthodox Jews using an Internet-based survey. Participants underwent an Internet-based intervention for "worry and stress" during which participants were randomized to receive a spiritually integrated treatment, progressive muscle relaxation, or no treatment. Measures of depression (20-item Center for Epidemiologic Studies-Depression or CES-D) and NRC (4-item negative subscale of the Jewish Religious Coping Scale, i.e., JCOPE) were completed at baseline pretreatment (T1) and at posttreatment 2 weeks later (T2). Structural equation modeling was used to analyze the data. The best-fitting model indicated that NRC predicted future depressive symptoms: T1 NRC significantly predicted T2 depressive symptoms ($B = 0.65$, $p < 0.01$), but T1 depressive symptoms did not predict T2 NRC ($B = 0.02$, p = NS). Researchers concluded that NRC "precedes and perhaps causes depressive symptoms among Orthodox Jews." This is the second study to find that while baseline NRC significantly predicted a worsening of mental health, baseline depressive symptoms (poor mental health) did not predict an increase in NRC over time (see Sherman et al., 2009).

Thuné-Boyle, Stygall, Keshtgar, Davidson, and Newman (2011) enrolled 155 recently diagnosed breast cancer patients in the United Kingdom into a longitudinal study, assessing participants at the time of surgery (T1) and at 3 months (T2) and 12 months (T3) postsurgery, and examining prevalence and change in religious coping strategies over time. NRC was assessed by a 3-item spiritual discontent subscale of the RCOPE (e.g., wondered why punished or abandoned by God; 37% felt this way to some extent after surgery). NRC was highest at T1 and T3, and was lowest at T2 (3 months postsurgery) ($p = 0.0005$). One explanation is that at the time of surgery, patients were most upset about the new diagnosis and more likely to blame God for it. These feelings may partially resolve during the first few months after surgery, when patients are being carefully monitored and looked after by medical staff. By 12 months postsurgery, researchers explained, patients were no longer being as carefully monitored, which may have given rise to feelings of abandonment (which translated over to feelings about God as well). Mental health outcomes, unfortunately, were not examined.

Park, Wortmann, and Edmondson (2011) surveyed 111 patients with severe congestive heart failure (stage III or IV) at baseline (T1) and 3 months later (T2). Religious struggle (NRC) was assessed with the 6-item Religious Strain Scale that assessed anger toward and alienation from God (Exline et al., 2000). Also assessed were measures of adjustment, that is, life satisfaction, depression, and mental/physical health-related quality of life (HRQOL). At baseline, NRC was associated with worse life satisfaction ($r = -0.23$, $p < 0.05$) and greater depression ($r = 0.29$, $p < 0.01$), but was unrelated to HRQOL. Longitudinal analyses revealed that T1 NRC *did not* significantly predict T2 life satisfaction, depression, or HRQOL, after controlling for age, education, number comorbidities, and T1 adjustment variables.

Rosmarin, Bigda-Peyton, Öngur, Pargament, and Björgvinsson (2013) prospectively followed 47 psychiatric patients with current or past psychotic disorders, tracking them from admission (T1) to a day treatment program at McLean Hospital (Harvard) until discharge from that program after an averge 8 days later (T2). The multidisciplinary treatment program included case management, psychopharmacology, psychovocational counseling, psychotherapy, milieu therapy, and group therapy (but did not include any particular treatment targeting NRC). Participants completed measures of religious involvement, suicidality, psychosis, depression, anxiety, and psychological well-being at baseline and discharge. PRC and NRC (Brief RCOPE) were assessed at baseline only. Baseline NRC was again associated with all T1 measures of worse psychopathology and lower levels of psychological well-being. Baseline NRC predicted a *decrease* in depressive symptoms from T1 to T2, controlling for age, race, and T1 depression ($B = 0.41$, $p \leq 0.05$), but did not predict change in other outcomes (psychosis, anxiety, or psychological well-being). When PRC was controlled for in the analysis, the effect of NRC on depressive symptoms was reduced to nonsignificance. However, what is surprising here is that prior to controlling for PRC, T1 NRC predicted an *improvement* in depressive symptoms (and recall that there were no specific treatments directed at NRC during the program). Unfortunately, NRC was not assessed at T2 to determine whether NRC improved as well with nonspecific treatment.

Reynolds, Mrug, Hensler, Guion, and Madan-Swain (2014) examined the longitudinal relationship between religious coping and psychological adjustment among 128 adolescents with cystic fibrosis or juvenile diabetes. Religious coping was measured with the 14-item Brief RCOPE, depressive symptoms by a 12-item subscale of the BASC-2, and adolescent conduct problems by a 14-item scale of the BASC-2. Measures were administered at baseline (T1) and 2 years later (T2). In cross-sectional analyses, NRC as usual was positively correlated with depressive symptoms both at T1 ($r = 0.37$, $p < 0.01$) and T2 ($r = 0.26$, $p < 0.05$), and with conduct problems at T1 ($r = 0.21$, $p < 0.05$) but not T2 ($r = 0.20$, p = NS). Cross-lagged analyses were conducted to determine whether NRC predicted depressive symptoms/conduct problems or whether depressive symptoms/conduct problems predicted NRC. Results indicated that T1 NRC was not a significant predictor of either T2 depressive symptoms or T2 conduct problems, after adjusting for age, gender, ethnicity, diagnosis, annual family income, PRC, and T1 outcomes. T1 conduct problems did not predict T2 NRC with T1 NRC in the model. However, T1 depression did significantly predict changes in NRC from T1 to T2 ($B = 0.33$, $p < 0.01$). Thus, this study suggests that depression influences changes in NRC over time (not vice-versa), in contrast to what earlier studies reported.

In the first mainland European study, Braam et al. (2014) examined the relationship between depression and God's image/religious coping during a 12-year follow-up of 343 Dutch respondents (Longitudinal Aging Study Amsterdam). Participants were initially assessed in 1992/1993 (T1), and then at 3 (T2), 6 (T3), 9 (T4), and 12 (T5, 2005) years later. Depression was measured with the CES-D at all five time points. Feelings about God were assessed using a 34-item Questionnaire on God Image, which has three subscales measuring (1) positive feelings (thankfulness, proximity, trust, security, and love); (2) fear of God (fear of not being good enough, fear of punishment, uncertainty, guilt, and shame); and (3) feeling wronged by God (disappointment, anger, oppression, loneliness, need for more freedom, dissatisfaction, and desolation). A 9-item version of the Brief RCOPE was also administered, which included 4 items assessing NRC. God image and NRC were both assessed only in 2005 (T5). Five trajectories of change in depressive symptoms were created based on the five administrations of the CES-D during the 12-year follow-up: (1) never depressed (CES-D < 16 at all times); (2) past depression, remitted before T4 (2001/2003); (3) depression recently remitted just before 2005; (4) depression persistent (recent and current, 2005); and (5) emergent (new/recurrent depression in 2005). NRC and feeling wronged by God at T5 were both strongly related to persistent depression (trajectory 4) and emergent depression (trajectory 5). Scores on NRC and feeling wronged by God were highest among those with the most severe depression (major depression) and lowest in those who were never depressed (trajectory 1). As there is no information on NRC prior to 2005, it is not possible to determine whether NRC preceded or followed the development of depression; however, it is clear that NRC and feeling wronged by God were most common among those experiencing the most persistent, most recent, and most severe depression.

In the first study to examine the longitudinal effects of NRC on mental health (QOL) in Muslims, Rohani, Abedi, Omranipour, and Langius-Eklöf (2015) surveyed a sample of 162 Iranian women with breast cancer and a matched control group ($n = 210$) at prediagnosis (T1) and 6 months postdiagnosis (T2). QOL (European Organization for Research and Treatment of Cancer QLQ-C30) and religious coping (Brief RCOPE) were assessed at baseline 1–14 days before surgery in the cancer patients and just prior to mammography/breast ultrasound in control patients; all scales were readministered after 6 months by a mailed questionnaire. NRC was infrequent in both breast cancer patients and in controls, and there was no difference in NRC scores between baseline and follow-up in either group. T2 NRC was not associated with T2 QOL in cross-sectional analyses; the effect of T1 NRC on T2 QOL was not examined.

Hayward and Krause (2016) assessed 1084 Christian adults aged 66 or above during an 11-year period, with follow-up assessments ranging in number from 2 to 5 (mean number of assessments = 3.6). A 10-item Religious Coping Scale (5 assessing PRC and 5 assessing NRC) was administered at each study wave. Demographics, health and well-being, and religious factors such as denomination, frequency of religious attendance, religious commitment, and religious doubt (RD) were all measured at baseline only (T1). Growth mixture modeling was used to assess trajectories of change of PRC and NRC. Three trajectory classes were identified for NRC: Class 1, rapidly increasing NRC ($n = 29$); Class 2, slight decrease and relatively stable NRC ($n = 995$); and Class 3, rapidly decreasing NRC ($n = 51$). Logistic regression was used to determine the baseline predictors of each trajectory class compared to each other, controlling for baseline demographics, health, and religious characteristics. Compared to Class 2 (low, stable NRC), those in Class 1 (rapidly increasing NRC) reported higher religious attendance (OR = 1.23, $p = 0.04$) and more RD

(OR = 1.22, $p = 0.001$) at baseline. Compared to Class 2, those in Class 3 (rapidly decreasing NRC) reported more RD (OR = 1.19, $p < 0.01$) and *higher* depressive symptoms (OR = 1.07, $p < 0.05$) at baseline. No baseline characteristics distinguished Class 1 (increasing NRC) from Class 3 (decreasing NRC). RD, then, predicted both rapidly increasing and rapidly decreasing NRC. Authors explained that how persons resolve their RDs might explain the trajectories taken (successful resolution resulting in decreasing NRC, unsuccessful resolution leading to increasing NRC). Higher baseline depression, surprisingly, predicted rapidly decreasing NRC (Class 3) compared to low and stable NRC (Class 2).

Tobin and Slatcher (2016) analyzed data from a 10-year prospective study that examined religious coping, religious participation, and diurnal cortisol profiles in 1470 participants aged 25–74 years participating in the Midlife in the United States Study (MIDUS). Religious participation data (frequency of attendance at religious services and other religious groups) were collected at baseline (T1), whereas religious coping, emotion focused coping, social support, and diurnal cortisol profiles were collected at follow-up only (T2). T2 PRC was assessed with a 4-item scale, and T2 NRC was assessed by a 2-item scale (abandoned by God and feel punished by God). Not surprisingly, T1 religious participation was positively correlated with T2 PRC ($r = 0.53$, $p < 0.001$) and inversely associated with T2 NRC ($r = -0.08$, $p < 0.01$). T1 religious participation was associated with a steeper (healthier) cortisol slope at T2 ($B = -0.002$, $p < 0.05$), an effect that barely lost statistical significance when T2 NRC was controlled for $B = -0.002$, $p = 0.055$; T2 NRC was related to a flatter (less healthy) cortisol slope ($B = 0.005$, $p < 0.001$). Researchers concluded that religious participation at T1 was indirectly related to a healthier cortisol slope at T2 through NRC at T2. All analyses between NRC and cortisol slope (the "mental health" outcome in this study), however, were cross-sectional at T2.

Holt, Roth, Huang, Park, and Clark (2017) followed a national random sample of 565 African–Americans (average age 59) surveyed during three waves of telephone interviews over a 5-year period (T1 = baseline, T2 = 2.5 years, and T3 = 5 years). The 14-item Brief RCOPE was administered at all three follow-ups, as were health behaviors and self-rated health. NRC changed minimally (decreased) over time, and neither religious beliefs nor religious behaviors were associated with change in NRC over time. NRC did not mediate the relationship between religious beliefs and health-related outcomes. Thus, NRC changed little and had little or no influence on health outcomes over 5 years among this largely middle-aged sample of African–Americans. Mental health outcomes were not reported.

Wilt et al. (2017) assessed anxiety symptoms and RD in three separate samples over time during periods that ranged from 2 weeks to 1 year. The first sample, 268 undergraduates, was assessed at baseline (T1) and after 2 weeks (T2); the second sample, 527 adults, was assessed at baseline (T1) and after 1 month (T2); and the third sample, 292 undergraduates, was assessed at baseline (T1) and after 1 year (T2). General anxiety symptoms were measured using the Generalized Anxiety Disorder-7 item (GAD-7) scale and RD by the 4-item Doubt subscale from Exline's RSSS. All three samples received similar measures at baseline (T1) and follow-up (T2). Path analysis was used to assess several models examining the relationship between anxiety and RD over time. Results indicated that for each sample, (1) the measures of anxiety and RD were highly stable across time (little or no change); (2) there was a moderate positive concurrent association between anxiety and RD ($r = 0.20$–0.30); and (3) anxiety at T1 consistently predicted small but significant increases in RD at T2, with T1 RD in the model. In contrast, there was only mixed support for T1 RD predicting T2 anxiety symptoms with T1 anxiety in the model. Authors concluded that anxiety most likely led to an increase in RD, rather than vice versa (i.e., RD causing anxiety to increase).

Finally, Park, Holt, Le, Christie, and Williams (2017) examined the effects of NRC on depressive symptoms, positive affect, negative affect, self-esteem, and meaning in life in a 2.5-year prospective study of a national random sample of approximately 900 African–Americans aged 21 years or older. NRC was assessed with the 7-item subscale of the Brief RCOPE, and mental health outcomes were assessed using standard validated scales. Hierarchical regression analyses indicated that after controlling for demographics, health, and T1 mental health outcomes, T1 NRC predicted greater T2 depressive symptoms ($B = 0.08$, $p < 0.01$), more negative affect ($B = 0.13$, $p < 0.001$), and lower self-esteem ($B = -0.14$, $p < 0.001$). The effects of T1 mental health outcomes on T2 NRC were not examined.

Conclusions

Recent research, then, does not help much in resolving the question of whether religious struggles (NRC) or religious doubt (RD) leads to poor mental health, whether poor mental health leads to greater NRC/RD, or whether NRC/RD is simply a symptom of poor mental health. Of the 12 prospective studies of NRC reviewed above, 7 examined the relationship between NRC and mental health outcomes over time, each reporting somewhat different findings. One study (Pirutinsky et al., 2011) confirmed the earlier finding by Sherman et al. (2009) that T1 NRC predicted an increase in depression from T1 to T2, while T1 depression did not predict an increase in NRC from T1 to T2, suggesting that T1 NRC was affecting depressive symptoms (not vice–versa). Another study (Park et al., 2017) also found that T1 NRC predicted greater T2 depression, negative affect, and lower self-esteem (but did not examine the effect of T1 mental health outcomes on T2 NRC). However, one study found that T1 NRC did not predict an increase in depression or other indicators of mental health over time (Park et al., 2011); one study found that T1 NRC predicted an *improvement* in depressive symptoms in response to nonspecific clinical treatment (Rosmarin et al., 2013); one study reported that T1 depression predicted a *more rapid decline* in NRC over time (Hayward & Krause, 2016); and two studies found that T1 depression/anxiety predicted an *increase* in NRC, while T1 NRC had little effect on depression/anxiety over time (Reynolds et al., 2014; Wilt et al., 2017). Thus, the question of whether NRC leads to worse mental health or whether worse mental health leads to NRC remains unresolved.

HEALTHY VS. UNHEALTHY RELIGIOUS STRUGGLES

Much less research has attempted to distinguish healthy from unhealthy forms of religious struggle. In the only prospective study to do so, Desai and Pargament (2015) examined the predictors of growth and decline among college students with spiritual struggles (SS or NRC) attending a university in the mid-western US. Participants who indicated SS during an online survey (127 out of 332) were reassessed 4–6 weeks later. SS was assessed by single items asking about interpersonal and divine SS, items from the Spiritual Dissatisfaction subscale of the Negative Religious Coping Scale (NRCOPE), and 12 SS items developed by the authors. The threshold for participant qualification was set low (those indicating "a little bit" or more on one or the other item asking about interpersonal and divine SS and endorsement of at least "a little bit" on one of the NRCOPE items). Primary outcomes were (1) secular growth (assessed by Posttraumatic Growth Inventory, PGI); (2) spiritual growth ("Spirituality has become more important to me" with responses ranging from 1 to 7 in terms of agreement); (3) struggle resolution ("I feel that my spiritual struggle has…" become worse, not changed, partially resolved, or completely resolved); and (4) spiritual decline (assessed by a 5-item scale developed by the authors). Baseline predictors included SS characteristics (struggle severity assessed by a 15-item Impact of Event Scale and a single item assessing meaning derived from SS), religious history (5-item religious assimilation scale and an 8-item attachment to God scale), positive religious coping (29-item PRC scale), and support (measures of secular and religious support). Results indicated that *secular growth* was predicted by greater SS severity, greater meaning derived from SS, and greater PRC; *spiritual growth* was predicted by less SS severity, greater meaning, stable attachment to God, greater religious assimilation, and greater PRC; *resolution* was predicted by greater meaning, greater religious assimilation, more religious support, and greater PRC; and *spiritual decline* was predicted by greater SS severity, less meaning, unstable attachment to God, less religious assimilation, less religious support, and less PRC. Researchers concluded that predictors that strengthened the person's religious orienting system were associated with growth, whereas those that weakened it predicted decline; SS severity was related to both growth and decline outcomes.

In a cross-sectional study examining predictors of growth versus decline following SS (NRC), Exline, Hall, Pargament, and Harriott (2016) analyzed data from 454 Christian college students who could recall and describe a specific SS they had experienced in the last few months (moral, divine, doubt, interpersonal, or ultimate meaning). Personal growth, the primary outcome variable, was assessed by spiritual growth (Spiritual Transformation Scale) and post-traumatic growth (PG Inventory). Using structural equation modeling to analyze the data, personal growth was directly related to greater PRC and perceptions that God was initiating helpful action, and was indirectly related to greater religious engagement, viewing God as benevolent, and having a positive relationship to God. Thus, characteristics related to the student's relationship with God were key in predicting whether growth or decline in mental health occurred.

Religious characteristics that buffer the relationship between SS/NRC and psychological distress have also been examined. Abu-Raiya, Pargament, and Krause (2016) analyzed cross-sectional data on 2140 US adults participating in the Landmark Spirituality and Health Survey. SS (NRC) was assessed by a 15-item version of Exline's RSSS. SS was positively related to depressive symptoms and inversely related to happiness. Characteristics that buffered this relationship were greater religious support, religious hope, religious commitment, and life sanctification. The buffering effect of these religious characteristics were especially strong for the SS-happiness relationship, although religious commitment and life sanctification also buffered the SS-depression relationship. Research has also examined other characteristics of those in whom the relationship between NRC and poor psychological outcomes is particularly strong, such as individuals indicating high levels of general experiential avoidance (e.g., "I am afraid of my feelings") or NRC-specific experiential avoidance (e.g., "I avoid putting myself in situations where my spiritual suffering might increase") (Dworsky, Pargament, Wong, & Exline, 2016).

Thus a number of religious and personality characteristics—particularly the presence of positive religious coping, religious support, high religious commitment, positive views of God and God's intentions, and lack of experiential avoidance—appear to be associated with better psychological outcomes in those with religious/spiritual struggles. This research, however, is clearly in its infancy and much more needs to be done, particularly in terms of designing prospective studies longer than 4–6 weeks.

INTERVENTIONS FOR RELIGIOUS/SPIRITUAL STRUGGLE

One way to shed light on the chicken versus egg dilemma is to determine whether religious/spiritual interventions targeted specifically at religious/spiritual struggle (NRC/SS) improve mental health outcomes, or whether general mental health treatments (without a focus on NRC/SS) improve the NRC/SS. A few clinical trials of this nature have been conducted and reported in the literature. Based on a thorough but nonsystematic review of that literature, a total of seven clinical trials were identified over the past 20 years. Four of the identified interventions involved more general spiritual interventions or secular treatments, and three focused specifically on treating NRC.

In the first of the general spiritual interventions, Cole and Pargament (1999) developed a program for cancer patients titled "Re-Creating Your Life: During and after Cancer." This treatment approach integrates spiritual issues and resources as part of the treatment, focusing on existential concerns related to control, identity, relationships, and meaning, which includes some attention to religious/spiritual struggles. This report described the intervention in 10 patients, and while outcome details are not provided, the results were reported as "promising." In a later report by Cole, this intervention (now a manualized treatment called "spiritually focused psychotherapy" or SFT) was examined in a small pilot study involving 16 patients, with 9 self-selected to SFT and 7 to an untreated control group (Cole, 2005). SFT was performed in weekly group therapy format conducted over 6–8 weeks (two groups were held during the trial). Outcomes were physical symptoms, treatment side effects, pain level, depression, and anxiety, all assessed at baseline, the end of treatment, and 2-month follow-up. At baseline, NRC (7-item subscale of Brief RCOPE) was related to greater depression, anxiety, pain frequency and severity, and poorer physical well-being in cross-sectional analyses. Depression and pain severity remained stable over time for those in the SFT group but worsened in the control group. Effects on NRC, though, were not reported.

To the author's knowledge, the first report to examine the effects of a spiritual intervention specifically on NRC was conducted by Oman et al. (2007). These investigators examined the effects of two Buddhist-based meditation and mindfulness spiritual interventions in 44 college students. Participants were randomized to Mindfulness-Based Stress Reduction (MBSR, Kabat-Zinn) (n = 16), Passage Meditation (PM, Eastwaran) (n = 16), or a wait-list control group (n = 15). Switching between groups was allowed and three participants dropped out after randomization. The intervention in the active treatment groups consisted of eight weekly training sessions. Participants were 49% Roman Catholic, and 42% had no religious affiliation. Self-efficacy, life goals, and religious involvement were assessed at baseline, after the intervention, and at 8-week follow-up. Included among measures of religious involvement was a 2-item NRC subscale (punishing God reappraisal and spiritual discontent). Results indicated that participants in each active treatment group demonstrated large, significant reductions in NRC. Compared to the wait-list control group, PM had an effect size (Cohen's d) of −1.16 (p = 0.009) immediately postintervention, which persisted to the 8-week follow-up (d = −0.68,

$p = 0.053$). A similar but weaker effect was found for MBSR ($d = -0.80$, $p = 0.04$, postintervention; $d = -0.67$, $p = 0.07$, 8-week follow-up). Self-efficacy also improved significantly more in the intervention groups compared to the control group. No changes were seen in PRC during the trial. Interestingly, this study showed that nontheistic spiritual meditation, approaches that did not even focus on God or on NRC, nevertheless reduced NRC for up to 8 weeks after the intervention.

The second study to report the effects of a general spiritual intervention that included NRC and indicators of mental health as outcomes was a pastoral care intervention performed by a chaplain. Bay, Beckman, Trippi, Gunderman, and Terry (2008) examined the effects of pastoral care on depression, anxiety, hope, PRC, and NRC assessed by the 14-item Brief RCOPE. Participants were 170 patients receiving coronary artery bypass graft surgery, who were randomized to either the intervention ($n = 85$) or a control group ($n = 85$). The control group did not receive hospital chaplain visits (although both groups could receive visits from parish clergy). The pastoral intervention was delivered by a single chaplain (the lead author) and consisted of one presurgical visit and three postsurgical visits in the hospital, and one visit with family members during the actual surgery. The chaplain listened to the patient's concerns, provided supportive pastoral care, focused on the patient's spiritual needs, discussed their hopes, and encouraged the patient to use religious and psychological resources in planning a positive future (i.e., the intervention, again, did not focus on NRC/SS). Participants were assessed at presurgery and at 1- and 6-month postsurgery. Results indicated that the chaplain intervention had no significant effect on anxiety, depression, or hope, compared to the control group. However, PRC increased during the trial in the intervention group and decreased in the control group ($p = 0.081$); in contrast, NRC decreased during the trial in the intervention group, but increased in the control group ($p = 0.056$). This finding indicated that NRC can change independent of depressive symptoms, anxiety, and hope, suggesting that these are separate constructs (and that NRC may decrease in response to a general spiritual intervention).

In another randomized clinical trial, one that examined the effects of religiously integrated cognitive behavioral therapy (RCBT) versus conventional cognitive behavioral therapy (CCBT) in the treatment of major depression, Pearce and Koenig (2016) compared the effects of these two active interventions on NRC (7-item subscale of the Brief RCOPE) in 132 depressed persons with chronic medical illness. Participants received 10 weekly sessions over 12 weeks, and were assessed at baseline, 12 weeks (posttreatment), and 24 weeks (12 weeks later). RCBT ($n = 65$) included a focus on religious struggles as part of the treatment (1 of the 10 sessions), whereas CCBT ($n = 67$) focused on psychological struggles more generally (also 1 of the 10 sessions). At baseline, the average NRC score was 3.4 (on a 0–21 scale) and progressively decreased over time in both treatment groups (average 2.7 at 12 weeks and 2.5 at 24 weeks, $p = 0.003$) along with a reduction in depressive symptoms (BDI-II). Results indicated no difference in NRC or depressive symptoms between treatment groups at baseline, 12 weeks, or 24 weeks. The mixed effects regression model confirmed no significant difference in the effects of RCBT versus CCBT on NRC during the trial or 12-week follow-up (time by group interaction $B = -0.48$, SE = 0.31, $t = -1.53$, and $p = 0.13$), although this difference approached statistical significance in the per-protocol analysis ($B = -0.59$, SE = 0.35, $t = -1.71$, and $p = 0.09$). However, the effect actually favored the CCBT group. Change in NRC and change in depressive symptoms during the trial were only weakly correlated ($r = 0.19$, $p = 0.069$). These findings suggest that (1) spiritual interventions targeting NRC may not always be superior to standard secular interventions in reducing NRC, and (2) NRC and depressive symptoms appeared to change at trajectories different from one another.

Finally, three clinical trials have now examined the effects of spiritual interventions designed specifically to address NRC. First, Bowland, Edmond, and Fallot (2012) examined the effects of a spiritually focused group intervention that addressed spiritual and psychological struggles in 43 older women survivors of interpersonal trauma (child abuse, sexual assault, or domestic violence). Participants were randomized to the intervention ($n = 21$, conducted in three groups) or a wait-list control group ($n = 22$). The manualized spiritual intervention consisted of eleven 90-minute weekly group sessions, and focused on addressing SS resulting from trauma and developing spiritual coping resources. Post-traumatic stress disorder (PTSD) symptoms, depressive symptoms (two measures), and somatic symptoms were measured using standard scales. Participants were assessed at baseline (T1), after treatment (T2), and 3 months later (T3). Results indicated that compared to the control group, those receiving the intervention experienced significantly greater improvement in mental health outcomes (F (4, 38) = 7.1, $p = 0.0002$), especially depressive symptoms (Hedges' g effect size = 1.35, indicating a large effect). Effects were maintained at the 3-month follow-up (T3). Thus a group spiritual intervention designed to address NRC produced significant and large improvements in mental health outcomes in this group of traumatized older women. Effects of the intervention on NRC (assessed with the 5-item Interpersonal Religious Discontent subscale of the RCOPE) were unfortunately not reported. Lack of an attention control group makes it difficult to determine whether the effect on mental health was due to the content of the intervention or simply to the social interaction that occurred during the eleven 90-minute group meetings.

Next, Dworsky et al. (2013) examined the effects of the "Winding Road" intervention, a spiritually integrated intervention designed to address SS in college students. This 9-week group-based intervention focused on encouraging participants to accept spiritual questions, doubts, and conflicts; facilitating exploration of spiritual/religious struggle; reducing stigma associated with SS; deepening conceptualizations of spirituality and the Divine; facilitating greater integration of spirituality into daily life; and increasing emotional, behavioral, and spiritual flexibility when addressing SS. Participants were undergraduate students experiencing SS recruited from a medium-sized university in Northwest Ohio. Participants ($n = 10$) completed pre- and posttreatment assessments in this single-group experimental study (i.e., there was no control group). NRC was assessed with a 23-item scale modified from the RCOPE. Results based on differences between pretreatment and posttreatment scores indicated a significant reduction in NRC scores from baseline (56.9, SD = 14.5) to end of treatment (46.5, SD = 16.4) ($t = 2.87$, $p < 0.01$). There was also a significant decrease in psychological distress ($p < 0.01$), a significant increase in positive affect ($p < 0.05$), and negative affect tended to decrease as well ($t = 1.82$, $p > 0.05$). This study suggests that a spiritual intervention directed specifically at religious/spiritual struggles can decrease NRC and increase positive emotions. Whether it does so better than secular psychotherapy, social interaction as part of a group, or simply the passage of time, given the lack of a control group, remains unknown.

In the most recent study, Ano, Pargament, Wong, and Pomerleau (2017) developed a manual-based group intervention called the "From Vice to Virtue" program that was directed at a type of spiritual struggle, "moral" struggle. Participants were 50 Christian volunteers who were randomly assigned to the intervention ($n = 25$) or a wait-list control condition ($n = 25$). The intervention consisted of four weekly 90-minute group sessions that focused on the "spiritual struggle of attempting to cultivate virtue and resist vice within the context of religion, falling short as a result of natural human limitations, and persistently being faced with one's imperfections." Outcomes were assessed at baseline, immediately postintervention, and at 4-week follow-up. Religious/spiritual involvement, goal attainment (Kiresuk & Sherman scale, which has vice and virtue subscales), depression and anxiety (DASS-21), and spiritual development (24-item scale by Alter) were assessed using standard scales. Results indicated that by the end of the trial those in the treatment group were significantly more able to cultivate virtues and resist vices compared to those in the control group. No significant differences between treatment and controls groups, however, were found for depressive symptoms/anxiety or spiritual development. Although NRC was not specifically assessed in this study, the attempts to cultivate virtue and resist vices involve a type of spiritual/religious struggle. Again, this study suffers from lack of an attention control group, limiting its conclusions.

Perhaps a more definitive answer to the question of whether NRC results in worse mental health or is simply a result or manifestation of poor mental health might be found in a study that examines the effect of *drugs alone* on NRC. If NRC could be improved by medication alone (just as drugs relieve depressive or anxiety symptoms), then pastoral care or spiritual interventions specifically for NRC may not be needed. In a study that at least peripherally addressed this question, researchers in India examined 66 treatment-naïve patients with a first episode of depressive disorder, assessing depressive symptoms at baseline and after 6 weeks of treatment with the antidepressant escitalopram (Lexapro) (Kataria et al., 2016). A version of the Brief RCOPE was used that included a 5-item NRC subscale (lower scores indicating higher NRC). Depressive symptoms were assessed with the observer-rated 17-item HAM-D. The majority of participants were Hindu (70%). Duration of depression was less than 12 months in 52% of the participants. At baseline, the cross-sectional correlation between depressive symptoms and NRC was $r = -0.35$ ($p = 0.006$). After 6 weeks of antidepressant treatment, improvement in HAM-D scores was negatively correlated with NRC ($r = -0.052$, $p < 0.0001$) (i.e., improvement in depression scores was associated with a reduction in NRC). Those who responded to treatment (>50% reduction in HAM-D) scored lower on NRC ($t = 2.88$, $p = 0.006$) than did those who did not respond. Unclear in the report, however, whether NRC was measured at baseline only or also on follow-up. The findings indicated that NRC (whenever it was measured) was associated with a worse response to drug treatment. This is not exactly the ideal study to answer the chicken versus egg predicament, as the change in NRC from before to after antidepressant treatment was not examined.

Conclusions

Four general spiritual/religious interventions were identified that primarily targeted emotional distress (depression/anxiety/stress), although may have also addressed NRC to some extent. Of those four studies, three significantly reduced emotional distress and three reduced NRC as well. Included here is one study of Buddhist meditation that did not focus on NRC or even God, and yet still significantly reduced NRC and increased self-efficacy. Also included here is a study finding that religious CBT and conventional secular CBT reduced both depressive symptoms and NRC, with CCBT reducing NRC somewhat more so than RCBT that targeted NRC. Of the remaining two studies, one reduced depressive symptoms, but did not examine change in NRC, and one reduced NRC, but did not affect levels of depression, anxiety, or hope. Of the three interventions that specifically targeted NRC, two reduced depression although only one examined changes in NRC (which decreased), and one improved virtues and reduced vices (equivalent to NRC), but had no effect on mental health outcomes (depression or anxiety).

This hodgepodge of findings from intervention studies leaves us in the dark with regard to whether the treatments designed specifically to target

NRC are any more effective in reducing NRC and improving mental health than general spiritual interventions (that do not target NRC or only partly do so) or even secular interventions (psychotherapy or drugs alone). Much, then, remains unknown about whether NRC affects mental health, mental health affects NRC, or NRC is simply a symptom of poor mental health. Not yet adequately explored is whether certain forms of NRC lead to better mental health, while other forms lead to worse mental health over the long term.

SUMMARY AND CONCLUSIONS

In many world religions, religious struggle is part of the normal spiritual path, is expected, and is often required for spiritual growth to occur. Many cross-sectional studies have examined the relationship between religious or spiritual struggle/doubt (NRC) and mental health (nearly 75 such studies published prior to 2010 and at least that many published since), almost all of which report a positive association between NRC and worse mental health. Of 21 prospective studies reviewed here, 12 (5 prior to 2010 and 7 since 2010) appropriately controlled for baseline outcomes when examining the effect of either baseline NRC or poor mental health on future outcomes. Of those 12 studies, 6 found that baseline NRC predicted worse future mental health, 3 found that baseline NRC did not predict mental health or predicted an improvement in mental health, 2 found that baseline poor mental health (anxiety or depression) predicted a worsening of future NRC, and the remaining study found that poor mental health (depression) predicted a more rapid decrease in NRC. Finally, intervention studies specifically targeting NRC appear to reduce NRC and improve mental health outcomes, but it is not clear whether such therapies do that any better than general spiritual interventions or completely secular psychotherapies (or drug therapy alone). So, again, is NRC an etiological factor that adversely affects mental health? Is NRC the result of poor mental health? Or is NRC simply another symptom of depression or general emotional distress? The evidence is mixed. More than likely, NRC affects mental health and mental health affects NRC. We know even less about how to distinguish between forms of religious struggle that lead to spiritual and psychological growth (and perhaps better mental health) from those forms that lead to mental illness and distress that destroys both mental and spiritual health. Future studies are desperately needed to fill both of these knowledge gaps. For possible ways forward, see the discussion by Pargament and Lomax (2013) in the next chapter.

Acknowledgment

A special thanks to Ken Pargament who reviewed this chapter and provided some of the most recent studies summarized here.

References

Abu-Raiya, H., Pargament, K. I., & Krause, N. (2016). Religion as problem, religion as solution: Religious buffers of the links between religious/spiritual struggles and well-being/mental health. *Quality of Life Research*, *25*(5), 1265–1274.

Abu-Raiya, H., Pargament, K. I., Krause, N., & Ironson, G. (2015). Robust links between religious/spiritual struggles, psychological distress, and well-being in a national sample of American adults. *American Journal of Orthopsychiatry*, *85*(6), 565–575.

Ano, G. G., Pargament, K. I., Wong, S., & Pomerleau, J. (2017). From vice to virtue: Evaluating a manual ice intervention for moral spiritual struggles. *Spirituality in Clinical Practice*, *4*(2), 129–144.

Ano, G. G., & Vasconcelles, E. B. (2005). Religious coping and psychological adjustment to stress: A meta-analysis. *Journal of Clinical Psychology*, *61*(4), 461–480.

Armstrong, K. (2006). *Muhammad: A prophet for our time*. New York, NY: HarperCollins Publishers (pp. 53–87).

Batson, C. D. (1976). Religion as prosocial: Agent or double agent? *Journal for the Scientific Study of Religion*, *15*, 29–45.

Batson, C. D., & Schoenrade, P. A. (1991a). Measuring religion as quest: 1) Validity concerns. *Journal for the Scientific Study of Religion*, *30*, 416–429.

Batson, C. D., & Schoenrade, P. A. (1991b). Measuring religion as quest: 2) Reliability concerns. *Journal for the Scientific Study of Religion*, 430–447.

Batson, C. D., & Ventis, W. L. (1982). *The religious experience*. New York, NY: Oxford University Press.

Bay, P. S., Beckman, D., Trippi, J., Gunderman, R., & Terry, C. (2008). The effect of pastoral care services on anxiety, depression, hope, religious coping, and religious problem solving styles: A randomized controlled study. *Journal of Religion and Health*, *47*(1), 57–69.

Benore, E., Pargament, K. I., & Pendleton, S. (2008). An initial examination of religious coping in children with asthma. *International Journal for the Psychology of Religion*, *18*(4), 267–290.

Bowland, S., Edmond, T., & Fallot, R. D. (2012). Evaluation of a spiritually focused intervention with older trauma survivors. *Social Work*, *57*(1), 73–82.

Braam, A. W., Schaap-Jonker, H., van der Horst, M. H., Steunenberg, G., Beekman, A. T., van Tilburg, W., & Deeg, DJ. (2014). Twelve-year history of late-life depression and subsequent feelings to God. *American Journal of Geriatric Psychiatry*, *22*(11), 1272–1281.

Cole, B. S. (2005). Spiritually-focused psychotherapy for people diagnosed with cancer: A pilot outcome study. *Mental Health, Religion and Culture*, *8*(3), 217–226.

Cole, B., & Pargament, K. (1999). Re-creating your life: A spiritual/psychotherapeutic intervention for people diagnosed with cancer. *Psycho-Oncology*, *8*(5), 395–407.

Conze, E., translator (1959). *Buddhist scriptures* (pp. 47–51). London: Penguin.

Desai, K. M., & Pargament, K. I. (2015). Predictors of growth and decline following spiritual struggles. *International Journal for the Psychology of Religion*, *25*(1), 42–56.

Dworsky, C. K. O., Pargament, K. I., Gibbel, M. R., Krumrei, E. J., Faigin, C. A., Haugen, M. R. G., Desai, K. M., Lauricella, S. K., Lynn, Q., & Warner, H. L. (2013). Winding road: Preliminary report for a spiritually integrated intervention addressing college students' spiritual struggles. *Research in the Social Scientific Study of Religion*, *24*, 309–339.

Dworsky, C. K. O., Pargament, K. I., Wong, S., & Exline, J. J. (2016). Suppressing spiritual struggles: The role of experiential avoidance in mental health. *Journal of Contextual Behavioral Science*, *5*(4), 258–265.

Ellison, C. G., & Lee, J. (2010). Spiritual struggles and psychological distress: Is there a dark side of religion? *Social Indicators Research*, *98*(3), 501–517.

Exline, J. J., Hall, T. W., Pargament, K. I., & Harriott, V. A. (2016). Predictors of growth from spiritual struggle among Christian undergraduates: Religious coping and perceptions of helpful action by God are both important. *Journal of Positive Psychology*, *12*(5), 501–508.

Exline, J. J., Pargament, K. I., Grubbs, J. B., & Yali, A. M. (2014). The Religious and Spiritual Struggles Scale: Development and initial validation. *Psychology of Religion and Spirituality*, *6*(3), 208–222.

Exline, J. J., & Rose, E. (2005). Religious and spiritual struggles, Chapter 19. In R. F. Paloutzian, & C. L. Park (Eds.), *Handbook of the psychology of religion and spirituality* (2nd ed., pp. 315–330). New York, NY: Guilford Press.

Exline, J. J., Yali, A. M., & Lobel, M. (1999). When God disappoints: Difficulty forgiving God and its role in negative emotion. *Journal of Health Psychology*, *4*(3), 365–379.

Exline, J. J., Yali, A. M., & Sanderson, W. C. (2000). Guilt, discord, and alienation: The role of religious strain in depression and suicidality. *Journal of Clinical Psychology*, *56*(12), 1481–1496.

Gall, T. L. (2003). The role of religious resources for older adults coping with illness. *The Journal of Pastoral Care and Counseling*, *57*, 211–224.

Gauthier, K. J., Christopher, A. N., Walter, M. I., Mourad, R., & Marek, P. (2006). Religiosity, religious doubt, and the need for cognition: Their interactive relationship with life satisfaction. *Journal of Happiness Studies*, *7*(2), 139–154.

Gethin, R. (1998). *Foundations of Buddhism*. New York, NY: Oxford University Press (pp. 19–22).

Hayward, R. D., & Krause, N. (2014). How religious doubt moderates depression symptoms following older adult bereavement. *Death Studies*, *38*(4), 217–223.

Hayward, R. D., & Krause, N. (2016). Classes of individual growth trajectories of religious coping in older adulthood: Patterns and predictors. *Research on Aging*, *38*(5), 554–579.

Henrie, J., & Patrick, J. H. (2014). Religiousness, religious doubt, and death anxiety. *International Journal of Aging and Human Development*, *78*(3), 203–227.

Holt, C. L., Roth, D. L., Huang, J., Park, C., & Clark, E. M. (2017). Longitudinal effects of religious involvement on religious coping and health behaviors in a national sample of African Americans. *Social Science and Medicine*, *187*, 11–19.

Johnson, W. J. (1994). *The Bhagavad Gita: A new translation (Oxford World Classics)*. Oxford, UK: Oxford University Press (pp. 5–6).

Kataria, L. R., Shah, S. H., Tanna, K. J., Arora, R. S., Shah, N. H., & Chhasatia, A. H. (2016). Religious coping as a predictor of outcome in major depressive disorder. *Indian Journal of Social Psychiatry*, *32*(4), 332–336.

Koenig, H. G., King, D. E., & Carson, V. B. (2012). *Handbook of religion health* (2nd ed.). New York, NY: Oxford University Press.

Krause, N. (2003). A preliminary assessment of race differences in the relationship between religious doubt and depressive symptoms. *Review of Religious Research*, *45*(2), 93–115.

Krause, N. (2006). Religious doubt and psychological well-being: A longitudinal investigation. *Review of Religious Research*, *47*(3), 287–302.

Krause, N. (2012). Religious doubt, financial strain, and depressive symptoms among older Mexican Americans. *Mental Health Religion and Culture*, *15*(4), 335–348.

Krause, N. (2015). Religious doubt, helping others, and psychological well-being. *Journal of Religion and Health*, *54*(2), 745–758.

Krause, N., & Ellison, C. G. (2009). The doubting process: A longitudinal study of the precipitants and consequences of religious doubt in older adults. *Journal for the Scientific Study of Religion*, *48*(2), 293–312.

Krause, N., Ingersoll-Dayton, B., Ellison, C. G., & Wulff, K. M. (1999). Aging, religious doubt, and psychological well-being. *Gerontologist*, *39*(5), 525–533.

Krause, N., & Wulff, K. M. (2004). Religious doubt and health: Exploring the potential dark side of religion. *Sociology of Religion*, *65*(1), 35–56.

Kuijpers, H. J. H., Van der Heijden, F. M. M. A., Tuinier, S., & Verhoeven, W. M. A. (2007). Meditation-induced psychosis. *Psychopathology*, *40*(6), 461–464.

Oman, D., Shapiro, S. L., Thoresen, C. E., Flinders, T., Driskill, J. D., & Plante, T. G. (2007). Learning from spiritual models and meditation: A randomized evaluation of a college course. *Pastoral Psychology*, *55*(4), 473–493.

Pargament, K. I. (1997). New York, NY: Guilford Press (pp. 226–232).

Pargament, K. I. (1999). Religious/spiritual coping. In *Brief Multi-dimensional Measurement of Religiousness/Spirituality* (pp. 43–56 (see pp. 52–53)). Kalamazoo, MI: The Fetzer Institute. Retrieved from https://www.gem-beta.org/public/DownloadMeasure.aspx?mid=1155.

Pargament, K. I., Ensing, D. S., Falgout, K., Olsen, H., Reilly, B., Van Haitsma, K., & Warren, R. (1990). God help me (I): Religious coping efforts as predictors of the outcomes to significant negative life events. *American Journal of Community Psychology, 18*(6), 793–824.

Pargament, K. I., & Hahn, J. (1986). God and the just world: Causal and coping attributions to God in health situations. *Journal for the Scientific Study of Religion, 25*, 193–207.

Pargament, K. I., Ishler, K., Dubow, E., Stanik, P., Rouiller, R., Crowe, P., Cullman, E., Albert, M., & Royster, B. J. (1994). Methods of religious coping with the Gulf War: Cross-sectional and longitudinal analyses. *Journal for the Scientific Study of Religion, 33*, 347–361.

Pargament, K. I., Kennell, J., Hathaway, W., Grevengoed, N., Newman, J., & Jones, W. (1988). Religion and the problem-solving process: Three styles of coping. *Journal for the Scientific Study of Religion, 27*, 90–104.

Pargament, K. I., Koenig, H. G., Tarakeshwar, N., & Hahn, J. (2001). Religious struggle as a predictor of mortality among medically ill elderly patients: A 2-year longitudinal study. *Archives of internal Medicine, 161*(15), 1881–1885.

Pargament, K. I., Koenig, H. G., Tarakeshwar, N., & Hahn, J. (2004). Religious coping methods as predictors of psychological, physical and spiritual outcomes among medically ill elderly patients: A two-year longitudinal study. *Journal of Health Psychology, 9*(6), 713–730.

Pargament, K. I., & Lomax, J. W. (2013). Understanding and addressing religion among people with mental illness. *World Psychiatry, 12*(1), 26–32.

Pargament, K. I., Olsen, H., Reilly, B., Falgout, K., Ensing, D. S., & Van Haitsma, K. (1992). God help me (II): The relationship of religious orientations to religious coping with negative life events. *Journal for the Scientific Study of Religion*, 504–513.

Pargament, K. I., Smith, B. W., Koenig, H. G., & Perez, L. (1998). Patterns of positive and negative religious coping with major life stressors. *Journal for the Scientific Study of Religion, 37*(4), 710–724.

Park, C. L., Holt, C. L., Le, D., Christie, J., & Williams, B. R. (April 27, 2017). Positive and negative religious coping styles as prospective predictors of well-being in African Americans. *Psychology of Religion and Spirituality* doi: 10.1037/rel0000124.

Park, C. L., Wortmann, J. H., & Edmondson, D. (2011). Religious struggle as a predictor of subsequent mental and physical well-being in advanced heart failure patients. *Journal of Behavioral Medicine, 34*(6), 426–436.

Pearce, M. J., & Koenig, H. G. (2016). Spiritual struggles and religious cognitive behavioral therapy: A randomized clinical trial in those with depression and chronic medical illness. *Journal of Psychology and Theology, 44*(1), 3–15.

Pirutinsky, S., Rosmarin, D. H., Pargament, K. I., & Midlarsky, E. (2011). Does negative religious coping accompany, precede, or follow depression among Orthodox Jews? *Journal of Affective Disorders, 132*(3), 401–405.

Proffitt, D., Cann, A., Calhoun, L. G., & Tedeschi, R. G. (2007). Judeo-Christian clergy and personal crisis: Religion, posttraumatic growth and well being. *Journal of Religion and Health, 46*(2), 219–231.

Reynolds, N., Mrug, S., Hensler, M., Guion, K., & Madan-Swain, A. (2014). Spiritual coping and adjustment in adolescents with chronic illness: A 2-year prospective study. *Journal of Pediatric Psychology, 39*(5), 542–551.

Rohani, C., Abedi, H. A., Omranipour, R., & Langius-Eklöf, A. (2015). Health-related quality of life and the predictive role of sense of coherence, spirituality and religious coping in a sample of Iranian women with breast cancer: A prospective study with comparative design. *Health and Quality of Life Outcomes, 13*(1), 1–14 40.

Rosmarin, D. H., Bigda-Peyton, J. S., Öngur, D., Pargament, K. I., & Björgvinsson, T. (2013). Religious coping among psychotic patients: Relevance to suicidality and treatment outcomes. *Psychiatry Research*, *210*(1), 182–187.

Sherman, A. C., Plante, T. G., Simonton, S., Latif, U., & Anaissie, E. J. (2009). Prospective study of religious coping among patients undergoing autologous stem cell transplantation. *Journal of Behavioral Medicine*, *32*(1), 118–128.

Thuné-Boyle, I. C. V., Stygall, J., Keshtgar, M. R. S., Davidson, T. I., & Newman, S. P. (2011). Religious coping strategies in patients diagnosed with breast cancer in the UK. *Psycho-Oncology*, *20*(7), 771–782.

Tobin, E. T., & Slatcher, R. B. (2016). Religious participation predicts diurnal cortisol profiles 10 years later via lower levels of religious struggle. *Health Psychology*, *35*(12), 1356–1363.

Trevino, K. M., Pargament, K. I., Cotton, S., Leonard, A. C., Hahn, J., Caprini-Faigin, C. A., et al. (2010). Religious coping and physiological, psychological, social, and spiritual outcomes in patients with HIV/AIDS: Cross-sectional and longitudinal findings. *AIDS and Behavior*, *14*(2), 379–389.

Underhill, E. (1974). *Mysticism* (12th ed.). New York, NY: New American Library (p. 83).

Vives, S. G., Martin, J. G. A., Trebbau, H., & Aliño, J. L. I. (2011). Meditation and psychosis (P03-31). *European Psychiatry*, *26*, 1200.

Waelde, L. C. (2004). Dissociation and meditation. *Journal of Trauma and Dissociation*, *5*(2), 147–162.

Wilt, J. A., Grubbs, J. B., Lindberg, M. J., Exline, J. J., & Pargament, K. I. (2017). Anxiety predicts increases in struggles with religious/spiritual doubt over two weeks, one month, and one year. *International Journal for the Psychology of Religion*, *27*(1), 26–34.

CHAPTER

9

Questions Answered, Questions That Remain

In this chapter, I discuss what is generally known and accepted about the relationship between religion and mental health (MH), and in particular, what needs to be known, that is, what questions remain unanswered. Given that we are in a relatively early stage in the study of religion and MH (compared to other factors affecting MH), we know very little compared to what needs to be known. There is a vast horizon of unexplored topics and gaps in knowledge that lay ahead. Many aspects of this relationship need further systematic study. As noted in Chapter 7, religion has the potential to affect almost every facet of mental, social, and behavioral health across the lifespan from in utero development through the dying process at the end of life. This research field is an enormous one and there is plenty of room for everybody here for examining almost every conceivable research question. However, given that resources are limited (both time and money to support research), the author's focus here is on research questions that need answering most urgently. First, however, what questions have already been answered?

QUESTIONS ANSWERED

First, we know that religious affiliation, belief, and practice are widespread around the world, even within scientifically advanced countries such as the United States, where a majority of the population indicates that religion is "very important" in their lives (Gallup Poll, 2016). Religion is especially important to members of minority groups and to population groups around the world where the majority are poor and have few material resources (e.g., Africa, South and Central America, India, and Middle Eastern countries). The Gallup Organization, Pew Research Center, and World Values Survey Association have repeatedly demonstrated

Religion and Mental Health. http://dx.doi.org/10.1016/B978-0-12-811282-3.00009-4

this by conducting international surveys of random national samples (Gallup Poll, 2017; Pew Research Center, 2017; World Values Survey, 2017). Admittedly, secularization is occurring in many regions of the world as a result of scientific progress, industrialization, and sometimes government restrictions on religion; despite this, however, the vast majority of the world's population remains religious. According to the Pew Research Center, 84% of the world's population in 2010 (5.8 billion of 6.9 billion) indicated affiliation with a religious group (78% of the US population) (Pew Research Center, 2012). As noted in the Introduction to this book, only about 5% of the world's population say they are convinced atheists (latest available data), and there is even some evidence that the prevalence of atheism is decreasing with time (although formal religious affiliation may be decreasing as well, particularly in the Western world, as indicated by an increasing prevalence of "nones").

Second, we know that religion is often turned to for coping with loss, suffering, and distress—particularly after all other avenues have been exhausted. Religious beliefs give meaning to life events, provide a worldview that allows for prediction and control, and provide support (both human and divine) when adversity strikes. Indeed, prior to the rise of professional MH care systems, it was religious organizations that provided a "de facto" MH system for populations around the world (Koenig, 2005). Housing for the mentally ill and MH care were first provided by religious organizations, which built and staffed the world's first mental hospitals (and prior to that, the mentally ill were often cared for in monasteries by monks). Religious groups continue to serve this role today for many minority populations and those living in rural or poverty-stricken regions that cannot afford MH care (Blank, Mahmood, Fox, & Guterbock, 2002; Fox, Merwin, & Blank, 1995; Larson et al., 1988; Milstein, Manierre, Susman, & Bruce, 2008). As noted earlier, clergy in the United States are at the front line in terms of provision of MH services, delivering nearly as much individual and family counseling as the entire membership of the American Psychological Association (Koenig, 2005, pp. 173–174; Weaver, 1995).

Third, we know that religious involvement at least in cross-sectional analyses is related to better MH, better social health, and better health behaviors in the vast majority of studies. The relationship is strongest for positive emotions (well-being, happiness, meaning, purpose, and hope), social support, and drug and alcohol use, factors known to affect MH (see Chapters 4 and 6). Whether religious involvement actually leads to or causes better MH, greater social support, and better health behaviors is less established (see below).

Fourth, religiously/spiritually integrated structured therapies for MH problems (particularly depression and anxiety) appear to improve outcomes to a similar degree as secular psychotherapies, particularly in clients who are more religious and prefer this approach (see Chapter 11).

Again, though, much more research is needed to substantiate the existing evidence base for religious or spiritually-integrated psychotherapies.

REMAINING QUESTIONS

Although there has been enormous progress over the past 30 years, almost every imaginable question about the relationship between religion and MH needs further study. Presented here are 20 broad questions whose answers could significantly advance knowledge about the relationship between religion and MH. These questions are not ordered in terms of importance (they are all important), but each question has been rated based on how easy it will be to study (E) and how much it will likely cost (C), each on a 1–10 scale from easy/low cost to difficult/high cost.

1. **Causality** (E = 7; C = 7, although cost will be less if existing datasets are used).
   Is the relationship between religiosity and MH a causal one, that is, does religiosity itself affect MH? This is a critical question and the answer will determine where attention should be targeted to improve MH. There is a considerable and growing evidence suggesting that religious involvement leads to or causes better MH. However, this is by no means established beyond reasonable doubt. It is highly likely that causality here is bidirectional in nature and genetic factors may also play a role. While prospective studies indicate that religious attendance prevents the development of depression, there is also evidence that depression may prevent religious attendance (Maselko, Hayward, Hanlon, Buka, & Meador, 2012) and that, as noted in Chapter 4, the relationship is likely bidirectional (Li et al., 2016a). Active involvement in a religious community provides many potential benefits that may help to reduce stress and prevent depression; however, depressed mood no doubt influences the desire for social interactions (due to social withdrawal and loss of interest) as well as the motivation to attend religious services.
   Thus future research needs to analyze data from prospective studies in a way that can tease out the influence that religion has on MH from the influence that MH has on religion. Tyler VanderWeele, Professor of Epidemiology and Biostatistics at the Harvard School of Public Health, has described the kinds of studies and methods of analysis needed to sort out these influences (VanderWeele, 2015; VanderWeele, Jackson, & Li, 2016). VanderWeele et al. (2016) describe a hierarchy of evidence for causality across study designs. That hierarchy will be illustrated here using religious attendance and depression as an example (similar to what VanderWeele does in the article).

Lowest on the hierarchy are cross-sectional data with religious attendance and depression measured simultaneously. The next rung up on the ladder is longitudinal data with religious attendance measured at T1 prior to depression at T2, with the analysis of the relationship controlled for characteristics that may confound it (such as gender, race, and age).

Third, and higher up on the ladder toward explaining causality, is longitudinal data where religious attendance is measured at baseline (T1), depression is assessed at a future time (T2), and baseline confounders are controlled, including baseline T1 depression (this is the way prospective studies of negative religious coping and mental health were described in the last chapter). Fourth, and further up on the ladder, is longitudinal data analyzed as described in the third step above *plus* additional control for religious attendance preceding T1 baseline attendance. This, of course, requires more than two waves of data collection, that is, an assessment of religious attendance at T0 measured several years prior to T1 baseline attendance. The fifth level would involve measuring religious attendance and depression repeatedly over time, controlling for confounders and using marginal structural models or other causal models to analyze the data. The highest level of evidence and top rung on the ladder is a randomized clinical trial (RCT) where participants are randomized to either a group that attended religious services or a group that did not, and the effects on depression then compared (while minimizing noncompliance and dropouts).

Short of an RCT, then, the best method for establishing causality using observational data would be to measure both the exposure (religious characteristic) and outcome (MH status) repeatedly during the follow-up period (at least 2-3 times), using a particular method (marginal structural modeling) to analyze the data.

The closest that anyone has come thus far to the fifth rung on this ladder is Li, Okereke, Chang, Kawachi, and VanderWeele (2016a) using data from the Nurses' Health Study, a longitudinal study of 48,984 US nurses with a follow-up period of 16 years where religious attendance and depression were measured repeatedly every 4 years from 1992 to 2008. The Nurses' Health Study, of course, is a multimillion dollar study designed and carried out by the Harvard School of Public Health with continuous funding from NIH since 1976.

Given the cost and expertise necessary conduct such a study, this might seem beyond the reach of most of us mere mortals trying to contribute to the literature.

Nevertheless, there remain many unanswered questions that investigators can seek to explore that could contribute to the evidence base, particularly in terms of designing studies and analyzing the data at levels two and three in the hierarchy above. Furthermore, religious measures are now being added to ongoing large prospective studies here in the United States and around the world that will in the future allow those with statistical expertise to analyze and report on these data (Shields, 2016–2019).

2. **Religious Struggles** (E = 7; C = 7).
Given the strong and consistent association between NRC and poor MH, research is needed to determine whether NRC is a cause, the result, or a symptom of emotional distress. The analyses described above are capable of sorting out such causal issues, particularly level three or above on the hierarchy. For example, more prospective studies with lagged analyses are needed to compare the effect of T1 NRC on T2 MH outcome (controlling for T1 MH) with the effect of T1 MH on T2 NRC (controlling for T1 NRC). If the effect of T1 NRC on T2 MH is greater than the effect of T1 MH on T2 NRC, then this would support the hypothesis that the influence of NRC on MH is greater than the influence of MH on NRC (as in the Pirutinsky, Rosmarin, Pargament, & Midlarsky, 2011; Sherman, Plante, Simonton, Latif, & Anaissie, 2009, studies described in the last chapter).
Ideally, one would need a 4-arm RCT to fully investigate the causal direction between NRC and poor MH and identify the best treatment. Consider a trial in persons with major depressive disorder with coexistent NRC. The four treatment arms would be (1) drug treatment, (2) secular psychotherapy, (3) general spiritually integrated therapy (SIT) (or pastoral care as an alternative), and (4) SIT that specifically targets NRC. The results of such a study would be very informative. If the improvement in NRC in groups 1 or 2 were similar to (or better than) the other treatment approaches (groups 3 or 4), then there would be no need for any kind of spiritually integrated approach, and one could conclude that NRC is simply a symptom or consequence of depression and will improve with the treatment of depression (having established that the causal direction is from depression to NRC). If NRC improved more in the group receiving general SIT (Group 3) than the groups receiving drugs or secular therapy (Groups 1 or 2), and better or similar to NRC-specific SIT (Group 4), then there would be no need for a therapy that focused on NRC. A broad SIT (or general pastoral care) would be sufficient. Of course, if the NRC-specific SIT did the best (better than groups 1-3), then this would favor a SIT that focused on NRC (and would establish that NRC was causal in affecting depression, assuming that depression improved along with NRC).
Given the difficulty in conducting a 4-arm trial (in terms of cost and management), one might begin with a more modest stepwise approach. First, one might examine the effects of an antidepressant drug on depressive symptoms and NRC (i.e., a single

group experimental study, which would be easy and cost little if piggybacked onto an ongoing drug study). If NRC decreased or resolved as depressive symptoms decreased or resolved, then one could conclude that NRC is simply a symptom of depression and that antidepressant treatment alone is sufficient to treat it without any further specific therapy. If NRC did not decrease or resolve as depression improved (suggesting that NRC is not simply a symptom of depression), then the next step would be to compare the effects of secular psychotherapy targeting depression to a general SIT (or pastoral care) using an RCT design. This would determine whether a spiritually integrated approach might be preferred, or whether standard secular therapy is sufficient. If there was greater improvement in NRC with general SIT than with secular therapy (but NRC did not completely resolve), then the next step would be to compare general SIT with NRC-specific SIT in an RCT. This would determine whether or not a SIT that specifically focuses on NRC is necessary to more completely resolve NRC (and consequently decrease depressive symptoms or other negative MH outcomes).

3. **Religiosity as a Marker for Mental Distress** (E = 2; C = 2). Does greater religiosity in some areas of the world serve as a marker for increased emotional distress, thus confounding its relationship to MH? This gives rise to a methodological question. How does turning to religion as a result of stress, adversity, and suffering affect researchers' attempts to identify a relationship between religiosity and MH? How might this dynamic be taken into account when conducting, analyzing, and interpreting the results of research? This is a major issue, especially when doing research in areas of the world that are not particularly religious (such as the UK, Europe, and the Far East). Research conducted in these regions often report no relationship or worse MH among those who are more religious, with researchers concluding that religion either does not affect MH or adversely affects it. Such a conclusion may not be correct. As indicated earlier, this is like examining depressive symptoms in people who are taking or not taking antidepressants. No doubt, one would find that those who are taking antidepressants are more depressed than those who are not taking these drugs. Would one conclude that the antidepressant was the cause for the depressive symptoms?

   In regions of the world where religion is not supported by the culture, it is likely that the threshold for turning to religion in response to stress is higher, such that religiosity becomes a marker for distress (as noted in Chapter 3). If that is true, then a positive relationship between religiosity and poor MH might be expected, and does not mean that religiosity causes poor MH, but rather that poor MH causes an increase in religiosity (i.e., reverse causation). How might studies be designed to take such dynamics into account?

4. **Better Measures of Religiosity** (E = 6; C = 2).
How does one identify and quantify a deep transformative religious faith that has a robust impact on MH using more objective measures? Currently, all measures rely on subjective self-report. The most commonly used measures consist of 1–10 questions to assess religiosity, which is relatively easy and fast. However, are there better ways of doing so? What about "informant" measures (i.e., asking relatives or friends how religious they perceive the person to be)? How about developing an exciting videogame that could assess a person's religiosity depending on the choices that they make during the game? These methods of assessing religiosity are more time intensive and might be impractical in a large survey. However, they are examples of possible ways by which objectivity could be increased when assessing religiosity, rather than depending entirely on self-report. Even self-report measures, though, might be improved to increase the objectivity of data collection. For example, the 10-item Belief into Action Scale (BIAC) was designed to be more objective by indirectly assessing how religious a person is by asking him or her how much time and resources are spent on religious activity. Unfortunately, the BIAC does not include informant measures or other creative ways verifying what the person says (see Chapter 2 on Measurement).

5. **Effects Across the Lifespan** (E = 3; C = 10).
What is the effect of religious involvement on MH across the lifespan, from in utero and early infancy (religious influences on parents' lives that affect the individual) through adolescence, young adulthood, middle age, and all the way to the end of life? As noted in Chapter 7 on mechanisms, religion may affect MH in many ways and does so throughout a person's life. However, most studies only examine the religious belief and activity at one point in time, or at best, over 10 or 20 years. Few if any studies have taken the lifespan approach—assessing religious belief/activity repeatedly at different points across a person's entire lifetime. The only exception is the Terman studies, which included extremely gifted children (making it difficult to generalize results to a broader population) and did not assess religiosity in detail (or parents' religiosity) (McCullough, Enders, Brion, & Jain, 2005; McCullough, Tsang, & Brion, 2003). The same is true for the Berkeley Guidance and Oakland Growth studies that assessed participants from adolescence to late adulthood (Wink, Ciciolla, Dillon, & Tracy, 2007). Assessing religiosity was not a specific aim of either of these studies, and so was not given much attention. Admittedly, such a study would not be easy to design nor would it be inexpensive to conduct, as it would require more than one generation of researchers. However, anything close to a study of this type would

be informative. As large multi-decade longitudinal studies begin to include religious measures as part of their assessments, multiple assessments of religiousness and MH characteristics may become possible across much of participants' lifetimes. Whether the measures of religiosity included in such studies will be detailed enough to acquire the kind of information needed is another story.

A less-expensive option might be to take a historical approach, retrospectively asking people toward the end of their lives how much exposure they have had to religion. This might involve asking about the importance of religion and frequency of religious activity at different times from childhood to the present (including their parents' religious belief/activity around the time of the person's birth and early childhood). Current and past MH could also be inquired about. "Exposure" is a key concept in epidemiology. As discussed in Chapter 2, public health specialists never simply ask how many cigarettes per day a person currently smokes without asking how many years they have been smoking. This is done to determine pack-years of smoking (lifetime exposure). The same could be done for exposure to religion (and MH) across the lifespan, although this method relies heavily on the participant's memory. Both decline of memory with aging and recall bias could be problems with this approach.

6. **Chronic Mental Illness** (E = 3; C = 3).
Is religious involvement beneficial to persons with severe, chronic mental illness, or does it worsen prognosis (as long claimed by MH professionals who have sought to limit patients' exposure to religion)? A deep divide, along with outright antagonism, developed between psychiatry and religion due to the writings of Jean Charcot (1887) and Sigmund Freud (1907, 1927), one that has been perpetuated by their followers (Rank, 1930) and more recently by contemporary psychologists and psychiatrists (Ellis, 1980; Sloan, 2006; Watters, 1992), and even incorporated into the Diagnostic and Statistical Manual of Mental Disorders (Larson et al., 1993). Some MH professionals have argued that psychoanalysis may replace religion, or lessen the need for it (Moscovici, 1961). Certainly, there have been exceptions among mental health professionals (Jung, Fromm, Bergin, Larson, and others) who have objected to such negative characterizations of religion (e.g., universal obsessional neurosis). Nevertheless, the divide remains deep and very much alive within psychology and psychiatry today. One result has been the tendency by MH researchers to avoid religion. Consequently, very little systematic quantitative research exists on the role that religion plays in schizophrenia, bipolar disorder, chronic depression, severe personality disorders, or other chronic mental disorders, conditions known to be so difficult to treat. The same

applies to mental disorders in children such as attention deficit and hyperactivity disorder (ADHD), where there is less than a handful of studies examining the relationship between religiosity and this disorder, either the religiosity of the child/adolescent or their parents (see Dew, Daniel, & Koenig, 2007, for one of the few studies in this area).

Thus there is tremendous opportunity and need to examine whether religious involvement during childhood or adulthood prevents, improves, or leads to chronic mental disorder, as current research has only scratched the surface. Studies on the long-term effects of religious involvement on the course of schizophrenia, bipolar disorder, borderline personality disorder, antisocial personality disorder, severe melancholic depression, or ADHD are almost completely absent, with only a few exceptions (and these are usually short-term studies—see Chapter 5). Systematic research examining the effects of religion on MH has generally been done by sociologists, not psychiatrists who manage and treat people with such disorders. Thus there is great opportunity for research to be conducted in this area, particularly longitudinal studies that examine religion's effects over time and clinical trials that test the efficacy and safety of religious interventions in those with chronic mental illness (for an example, see Kehoe, 1999). As psychiatrists are often involved in drug studies, this also presents an opportunity to examine the effects of religious involvement on clinical response to drug treatment (see below) *and* to examine the effects of drugs on religious beliefs and experiences. Anecdotal experience suggests that drugs such as serotonin reuptake inhibitors, benzodiazepines, and especially antipsychotics may dampen religious experiences, although no systematic study of such effects has been reported.

7. **Prevention of Substance Abuse** (E = 3; C = 6).
How might religiosity prevent the development of substance use disorders? Given the hundreds of studies that document an inverse relationship between substance use/abuse and religious involvement, particularly among young persons, further attention needs to be paid to when, in whom, and how religious beliefs and commitments might help to prevent the the onset and development of substance use disorders. Alcoholics Anonymous and Narcotics Anonymous, which are based on religious/spiritual principles, have been life-saving for many who have already developed substance abuse problems. However, little research has examined the ways that religions (many with strong teachings that discourage substance use) prevent substance use among the youth and how MH providers and systems may support such efforts.

8. **Instilling Human Virtues** (E = 3; C = 6–9, depending on study design). How does religion effectively instill human virtues that ultimately lead to more complete, full, and flourishing lives? Parents and teachers have long sought to instill human virtues in their children, and governments have attempted to do likewise in adults (by the force of law). All major world religions promote moral and ethical virtues among members, from childhood during early training to adulthood through sermons and special classes. The virtues include gratitude, humility, forgiveness, generosity, altruism, and self-discipline. All of these provide fertile ground for good MH, and their absence often produces the opposite. Indeed, at the end of the spectrum are those with antisocial personality disorders or psychopathy who fill jails and prisons. Studies thus far suggest that greater religiosity is related to higher levels of all the human virtues mentioned (Koenig, King, & Carson, 2012), helping to explain how religiosity may prevent emotional disorder and improve MH. However, as noted earlier, almost all of these studies are cross-sectional, leaving open the possibility that reverse causation is responsible, that is, those without virtues of this type tend to avoid religion, or perhaps these associations are explained by genetic factors. Thus long-term prospective studies beginning in early childhood are needed, as are intervention studies that seek to increase human virtues (as early in life as possible) utilizing religiously integrated treatments.

9. **Influences on Physical Health and Neuropsychiatric Functioning** (E = 6; C = 6).
   Physical health status and neuropsychiatric functioning—factors affecting a person's independence and ability to function—are known to strongly influence MH at all ages. Might religiosity influence physical health and functioning through cognitive, social, and behavioral mechanisms, and in this way influence MH? There is growing evidence suggesting that religious involvement can affect physical health, although the volume of such research is smaller than for religiosity and MH (Koenig et al., 2012). The impact of religiosity on physical health is particularly true for frequency of religious attendance, which has been shown to predict greater longevity, a good overall indicator of the cumulative effects of a behavior on health (Li, Stampfer, Williams, & VanderWeele, 2016b; VanderWeele et al., 2017). However, there is much less evidence for an effect on physical health of other measures of religiosity besides religious attendance. Again, this is likely due to the fact that people often turn to religion (prayer and other private religious activity) as they get sicker and closer to death, a dynamic that may hide or cover up a relationship between these indicators of religious involvement and good physical health. Another reason why it is more difficult to show

a relationship between religiosity and physical health is that MH is more proximal to religiosity than physical health, that is, religiosity must act through psychosocial and behavioral mechanisms to affect physical health, making the connection more difficult to demonstrate. Nevertheless, given that physical health and neuropsychiatric functioning have such a large influence on MH, this is one mechanism that needs further exploration preferably through longitudinal studies. This includes studying the effects of religiosity on:

a. cognitive and physical functioning with increasing age and/or in dementing disorders;
b. cardiovascular functions and disorders (cardiovascular reactivity, blood pressure, hypertension, and coronary artery disease);
c. neurological diseases (stroke, dementia, multiple sclerosis, and Parkinson's disease);
d. cancer (both behavior-related such as lung cancer and stress-related such as breast or colon cancer);
e. autoimmune disorders that may be stress-related (irritable bowel syndrome, inflammatory bowel disease, Crohn's disease, peptic ulcer disease, rheumatoid arthritis, psoriatic arthritis, and asthma)
f. chronic pain conditions (accidental injury, inflammatory, or iatrogenic from medical and surgical procedures); and
g. physiological functions that predispose to physical disease (markers of immune function, neuroendocrine function, and inflammation).

Research is needed on the effects of religiosity on (1) the development of these disorders, (2) the frequency of disease exacerbations and their overall longitudinal course, and (3) associated effects on functioning. In particular, research is needed to identify the relationship between religiosity and chronic physical illness (80% of which is due to lifestyle/behavioral factors potentially influenced by religious involvement). Again, research done thus far has only scratched the surface, even in studies conducted in English-speaking Christian populations. Much less research exists on religiosity and physical health in other world religions.

10. Caregiver Adaptation (E = 3; C = 4–6, depending on design). What effect does religion have on adaptation to the caregiver role? Given improvements in medical care, people are living longer and longer but often with chronic illness. The increase in populations over the age of 65 years, both in the United States and around the world, has challenged the capacity of healthcare systems to care for older adults, especially in institutional settings. Thus, there will be more and more pressure on family members to care for loved ones with chronic mental and neurological illnesses (dementia, in particular). Much research has shown that caring for a severely disabled loved one can adversely affect both mental and physical health. Therefore research examining how religious involvement may help (or hinder) adaptation of caregivers to the daily rigors of the caregiver role will be increasingly needed. Longitudinal studies, in particular, are necessary to determine whether religious involvement can increase the emotional resiliency of caregivers and if so, how it accomplishes that (see Hebert, Dang, & Schulz, 2007, for an example). While further research in Christian-majority populations in the United States is crucial, research is also needed in non-Christian religions and outside the United States, where information on religiosity and caregiver stress is almost nonexistent. How different religious traditions in different cultures deal with the problem of caring for the sick more generally, and for disabled family members in particular, may also be enlightening to those living in more developed countries of the world.

11. **Aspects of Religion (or the Individual)** (E = 3; C = 3). What specific aspects of religion are most beneficial to MH? Are there particular religious teachings that affect beliefs and attitudes that form a person's worldview (cognitive schema) more helpful than others? What about the behaviors that religions encourage (socialization, acts of altruism, participation in healing rituals such as confession, forgiveness, or receiving the Eucharist in Christianity) or behaviors that religions discourage (substance abuse, extramarital sex, criminal activity)? Is the emphasis on behavior more beneficial to MH than the emphasis on religious belief or are both important? Might this depend on the particular religion? For example, Buddhism and Judaism emphasize behavior, whereas Christianity and Islam emphasize belief. These questions should be studied within each major world religion and across religions.

    Rather than the religion, perhaps it is the particular individual, their environment, and life experience that determines whether religious beliefs or practices will help or hinder MH. Very little research has examined the influence of personality on likelihood of becoming religious or whether religiosity modifies the relationship between personality and MH. What little work that has been done suggests that certain personality styles may influence the likelihood of turning to religion or maintaining religious beliefs later in life (McCullough et al., 2003, 2005; Wink et al., 2007) (and perhaps also explains why some persons shy away from religion). Religious involvement may also alter personality through religious conversion, as William James (1902) so articulately described, a phenomenon that may occur even in late adulthood. Research has found that religiosity can cause changes in personality style of older adults in as short a period as 6 years (Koenig, Siegler, Meador, & George, 1990).

These studies, however, are few and far between, and almost no research of this type has been done in non-Christian populations.

12. **Impact on Relationship with God** (E = 2; C = 2).
How does a person's relationship with God influence the connection between religious beliefs/practices and MH? There is at least preliminary research suggesting that an individual's image of God may influence this relationship. A few studies have found that the relationship between prayer and MH depends on a person's attachment to God (see Chapter 7). Such findings make sense from a theological perspective, but much more research is needed to document this. Research is necessary to determine in what circumstances and in what individuals the benefits of religious practice to MH are maximized. Qualitative studies and cross-sectional research may provide some initial insights on this question, but longitudinal studies will eventually be needed to identify causal direction. For the person who is happy and content to begin with, it may be much easier to form a positive relationship with God than for a person who is besought with suffering and difficulties (alternatively, it may be easier because they are so desperate).

13. **Religious Transformation** (E = 2–6; C = 2–7, depending on research design).
Who has not heard of people who say that they have had a religious conversion experience that resulted in a cessation of drinking, drugs, or crime, and the turning around of their lives? Is this true? How often does it occur, in what circumstances does this happen, and in whom does it happen? People with dramatic religion conversion experiences may also just as dramatically fall back into their old habits and self-destructive ways. What distinguishes these individuals? What aspects of religion help individuals after conversion to reach and stay on a healthy path of psychological and spiritual growth? Again, these are questions that may be initially addressed with qualitative studies, and eventually tested in longitudinal studies.

14. **Religious Transmission** (E = 5; C = 7).
How is religion transmitted from one generation to the next? More information is needed about this process. A child who excels in school, completes her/his education, and has strong moral and ethical values is likely to be a successful and productive adult who will contribute to society and transmit these values to their own children. The child who becomes involved in drugs, delinquent activities, or experiences a teenage pregnancy is likely to have her or his education derailed, become involved in an unhealthy peer group, and find himself or herself at high risk for MH problems. If religious involvement helps

youth to avoid alcohol, drugs, cigarettes, pregnancy out of wedlock, failing or dropping out of school, or engaging in delinquent activity, as a large and growingvolume of research is showing, might it not be important for MH professionasl to know what factors enable or facilitate this process? What types of child-rearing practices are most successful in this regard? How important are parental religiosity, adult role models, religious education, approach to religious education (home-based vs. school-based), approach to rule enforcement (lax and flexible vs. strict and consistent), encouraging freedom of choice (vs. providing more limited choices), and changes in child-rearing practices as the child grows older and moves into the teen years? These are important questions that will set the trajectory of a young person's life (and MH) for years to come. Research can help to guide parents and teachers in this regard.

15. **Negative Effects of Religion** (E = 4; C = 3).
Can religion adversely affect MH? How and under what circumstances does this occur? Is it due to the religious teachings themselves (e.g., inducing guilt over failure to meet the high standards of the faith), or is it the misinterpretation of those teachings by vulnerable individuals with MH problems (and/or the possible manipulation of these individuals by others)? If the latter, then all religions may "appear to" adversely affect MH, since the problem is not the particular religion but rather the individual and those who take advantage of him or her. Are there certain religious teachings in each religion that are more easily manipulated or misinterpreted by those with MH issues? For example, certain scriptures in Christianity may lead to the belief that prayer and Bible study are sufficient to resolve all MH problems no matter how severe. This may prevent a person from seeking of professional MH care when needed. Another example is sexual abuse by priests, which likely has more to do with the sick individual and requirements of the priesthood (celibacy, etc.) than to religious teachings that stress exactly the opposite (Matthew 18:6; Mark 9:42; Luke 17:2). An example in Islam is suicide bombers who end their lives believing that they are serving God (manipulated by different terror groups to misinterpret scriptures from the Qur'an). These are just a few examples of how a mentally ill or psychopathic individual may use their religious position or take a scripture out of context and apply it in a way that adversely affects their own MH or that of others. More research is needed to identify scriptures from each religious tradition that may be taken out of context by vulnerable individuals, as well as to determine the MH characteristics of individuals likely to do so. Those characteristics include developmental experiences during childhood and life events during adulthood, both religion-related and non-religion related that may affect such interpretations.

Assuming for the moment that religion (because of certain beliefs or teachings) can itself causes neurosis or other MH problems, what particular aspects of each religion produce such effects? How often does this occur, and in what circumstances? How might clinicians address such problems when prescribed treatments conflict with core beliefs? See Chapter 13 for further discussion of this complex issue.

16. **Mental Health of Atheists** (E = 4; C = 6).
How does the MH and well-being of atheists compare to the MH of those who are religious? This question needs to be studied not only in cross-sectional analyses but also across the lifespan. Questions of this type have been difficult to answer because there are so few atheists in the general population who participate in surveys. This is even true for studies involving large national samples. Nevertheless, with the Internet, research on atheists is much easier to perform. Atheists tend to be male, white, young, well-educated, highly rational, and often have considerable material resources. These are demographic and personality traits that favor good MH. However, little is known about how atheists fare as they age and encounter stresses involved in loss of health and independence that may challenge their rational approach to coping. Little is also known about factors during childhood or adulthood that lead to the rejection of traditional religious belief, particularly in societies where religious beliefs and values are widespread in the culture (as in the United States). For further information on this topic see Zuckerman (2009), Whitley (2010), and Weber, Pargament, Kunik, Lomax, and Stanley (2012).

17. **Genetic and Epigenetic Influences** (E = 3; C = 9).
Does genetic makeup influence the likelihood that a person will become religious, and can religiosity (of the individual or their parents) influence genetic makeup through epigenetic effects? In the chapter on Mechanisms, several studies were summarized that examined the association between genetic polymorphisms and religious involvement. Much more research is needed to determine whether certain gene polymorphisms (or aspects of the genome that regulate gene expression) might either increase or decrease religious involvement, particularly those genes affecting vulnerability to MH problems (e.g., depression, bipolar disorder, and substance abuse/dependence). Furthermore, how might religiosity influence genetic expression? We know that the environment may affect genetic makeup through epigenetic influences, with more nurturing environments during early childhood affecting gene methylation leading to healthier stress responses later in life. Lack of such nurturance produces the opposite (see Chapter 7). If greater

religiosity enables parents to be more nurturing (or more available) during early infancy, this is one way that religion may affect the child's genome. There is also evidence that nurturing experiences during adulthood may affect the methylation process. Thus, if a person is involved in a supportive, nurturing religious community, this may have the potential to affect their genome. What is completely unknown, however, is whether *being* a nurturing person as a result of religiosity or religious conversion might influence the person's own genetic makeup, allowing such changes to be transmitted to future generations. Admittedly, questions like this are highly speculative at this time. However, the technology is now advancing so that researchers will be able to examine such questions at increasingly lower cost.

18. **Interaction with Drug Treatment** (E = 1; C = 1).
Does religiosity interact with drug treatment? Greatly needed, relatively easy to carry out, and inexpensive are studies that examine the interaction between religious involvement and drug treatments, especially if piggybacked onto existing studies. To this author's knowledge, no such study like this has been conducted in the MH area. At least one study, however, has reported that response rates are higher and side-effects lower to chemotherapy in those scoring high on a spirituality measure (Lissoni et al., 2008). How easy it would be to simply add a religious measure to the baseline evaluation in an RCT testing the effectiveness of a new drug treatment (antidepressant, antianxiety, antipsychotic, or mood stabilizer) or other biological therapies such as electroconvulsive therapy. When the time comes to analyze the outcome data, the interaction between religiosity and treatment group could be examined, and comparison of the beneficial effects and side effects made between those with high and low religiosity. This has been done for psychotherapy (Bowen, Baetz, & D'Arcy, 2006), although not yet for drug therapies.

19. **Efficacy of Religiously-Integrated Treatments** (E = 8; C = 8).
Are religiously-integrated treatments as effective as (or more effective than) existing secular treatments? How can MH professionals harness the power of the patient's religious faith in terms of either specific psychotherapies or more general (and simple) clinical interventions. There is growing evidence that religiously/spiritually-integrated psychotherapies are effective for the treatment of depression, anxiety, and substance use disorders. The research shows that such treatments are similar in effectiveness or more effective than secular therapies, especially in highly religious clients. However, this is based on only a few RCTs (Gonçalves, Lucchetti, Menezes, & Vallada, 2015; Koenig et al., 2015; Propst,

Ostrom, Watkins, Dean, & Mashburn, 1992; Rosmarin, Pargament, Pirutinsky, & Mahoney, 2010; see Chapter 11). There is also evidence that relatively simple religious interventions may impact MH outcomes. For example, studies of in-person Christian prayer have been reported to be effective in relieving depression and anxiety in medical settings (Boelens, Reeves, Replogle, & Koenig, 2009, 2012). Likewise, listening to recitation of the Qur'an has been shown to reduce both symptoms of depression (Babamohamadi et al., 2017) and anxiety (Babamohamadi, Sotodehasl, Koenig, Jahani, & Ghorbani, 2015) in Muslim hemodialysis patients compared to controls. These studies provide preliminary evidence supporting the effectiveness of religious interventions, but better-designed studies are clearly needed. "Better designed" means comparing the religious treatment with an active control group receiving similar amounts of social attention (or preferably receiving a proven secular treatment), and by carefully manualizing interventions so that they can be replicated by others.

Intervention studies of this kind are a major research need to help establish a solid evidence base for religiously integrated treatments. Studies are particularly needed to determine their efficacy (compared to secular therapies) in persons known to be highly religious and receptive to such treatments (Blacks, Hispanics, Muslims, conservative Protestants and Catholics, etc.). Even single-group experimental studies will add to the evidence base because they establish feasibility, provide information on effect size, and are relatively easy to carry out and much less costly than a RCT.

20. **Spiritual Integration and Outcomes** (E = 2; C = 2).
What are the effects of integrating spirituality into MH care more generally, such as the usefulness of taking a spiritual history? What are the situations in which prayer with patients is appropriate or inappropriate? Is it ever helpful for a clinician to share their own religious beliefs with patients? These are controversial practices, especially as they apply to MH care (where maintaining boundaries is more important than in medical settings). Such activities with patients require evidence that they are effective and not harmful. How do patients feel about these actions by clinicians? Might they be receptive, distressed, or offended? How does one distinguish those who might be receptive from those who would not (see Chapter 12 for further discussion)? What are the effects on MH outcomes and treatment compliance? How might addressing spiritual issues in practice affect the well-being of MH professionals? While some progress has been made in examining these issues in general medical settings (CSTH, 2017), to this author's knowledge no research has yet addressed these questions in MH care settings.

SUMMARY AND CONCLUSIONS

In this chapter, what is known about the relationship between religion and MH has been summarized and a number of high priority areas for future research have been described. A lot is already known, at least enough to continue to move forward. However, many, many questions remain unanswered. We have barely begun to understand the complex relationship between religious involvement and MH within the various faith traditions. Future research should focus on exploring such questions in mental and emotional disorders that are common and have public health importance (e.g., depression, anxiety, psychotic, and neuropsychiatric disorders). Studies of clinical populations involving outpatients and inpatients in MH settings are desperately needed, given the lack of research in this area due to the historical divide between religious and MH professionals. Studies of the general public are also needed that examine whether religious involvement may help to prevent mental disorder and improve overall quality of life by enhancing positive emotions such as hope, meaning, purpose, and psychological well-being. Of highest priority at this time, although difficult to carry out and often very expensive, are longitudinal studies and RCTs. Presented here is a research agenda that will help to inform and guide further studies in this area, studies that will ultimately increase our knowledge and help both clinicians and clergy to utilize religious resources to relieve emotional distress and increase spiritual and psychological well-being.

References

Babamohamadi, H., Sotodehasl, N., Koenig, H. G., Al-Zaben, F., Jahani, C., & Ghorbani, R. (2017). The effect of Holy Qur'an recitation on depressive symptoms in hemodialysis patients: A randomized clinical trial. *Journal of Religion and Health, 56*(1), 345–354.

Babamohamadi, H., Sotodehasl, N., Koenig, H. G., Jahani, C., & Ghorbani, R. (2015). The effect of Holy Qur'an recitation on anxiety in hemodialysis patients: A randomized clinical trial. *Journal of Religion and Health, 54*(5), 1921–1930.

Blank, M. B., Mahmood, M., Fox, J. C., & Guterbock, T. (2002). Alternative mental health services: The role of the Black church in the South. *American Journal of Public Health, 92*(10), 1668–1672.

Boelens, P. A., Reeves, R. R., Replogle, W. H., & Koenig, H. G. (2009). A randomized trial of the effect of prayer on depression and anxiety. *International Journal of Psychiatry in Medicine, 39*, 377–392.

Boelens, P. A., Reeves, R. R., Replogle, W. H., & Koenig, H. G. (2012). The effect of prayer on depression and anxiety: Maintenance of positive influence one year after prayer intervention. *International Journal of Psychiatry in Medicine, 43*(1), 85–98.

Bowen, R., Baetz, M., & D'Arcy, C. (2006). Self-rated importance of religion predicts one-year outcome of patients with panic disorder. *Depression and Anxiety, 23*(5), 266–273.

Charcot, J. M. (1887). *Les Demoniaques dan l'Art (The Demoniacs in art)*. Paris: Macula 1984.

CSTH. (2017). *Integrating spirituality into patient care*. Durham, NC: Duke University Center for Spirituality, Theology and Health Retrieved from https://spiritualityandhealth.duke.edu/index.php/cme-videos.

Dew, R., Daniel, S. S., & Koenig, H. G. (2007). A pilot study on religiousness/spirituality and ADHD. *International Journal of Adolescent Medicine and Health, 19*(4), 507–510.

Ellis, A. (1980). *Case against religion: A psychotherapists view and the case against religiosity*. Austin, TX: American Atheist Press.

Fox, J., Merwin, E., & Blank, M. (1995). De facto mental health services in the rural south. *Journal of Health Care for the Poor and Underserved, 6*(4), 434–468.

Freud, S. (1907). Obsessive acts and religious practices. In J. Strachey (editor and translator), *Standard edition of the complete psychological works of Sigmund Freud*. London: Hogarth Press, 1962.

Freud, S. (1927). Future of an illusion. In J. Strachey (editor and translator), *Standard edition of the complete psychological works of Sigmund Freud*. London: Hogarth Press, 1962.

Gallup Poll. (2016). *Religion* Retrieved from http://www.gallup.com/poll/1690/religion.aspx.

Gallup Poll. (2017). *Religion* Retrieved from http://www.gallup.com/topic/religion.aspx.

Gonçalves, J. P. B., Lucchetti, G., Menezes, P. R., & Vallada, H. (2015). Religious and spiritual interventions in mental health care: A systematic review and meta-analysis of randomized controlled clinical trials. *Psychological Medicine, 45*(14), 2937–2949.

Hebert, R. S., Dang, Q., & Schulz, R. (2007). Religious beliefs and practices are associated with better mental health in family caregivers of patients with dementia: Findings from the REACH study. *American Journal of Geriatric Psychiatry, 15*(4), 292–300.

James, W. (1902). *The varieties of religious experience*. New York, NY: The New American Library.

Kehoe, N. C. (1999). A therapy group on spiritual issues for patients with chronic mental illness. *Psychiatric Services, 50*(8), 1081–1083.

Koenig, H. G. (2005). *Faith and mental health*. Philadelphia, PA: Templeton Foundation Press.

Koenig, H. G., King, D. E., & Carson, V. B. (2012). *Handbook of religion and health* (2nd ed.). New York, NY: Oxford University Press.

Koenig, H. G., Pearce, M. J., Nelson, B., Shaw, S. F., Robins, C. J., Daher, N., Cohen, H. J., Berk, L. S., Bellinger, D., Pargament, K. I., Rosmarin, D. H., Vasegh, S., Kristeller, J., Juthani, N., Nies, D., & King, M. B. (2015). Religious vs. conventional cognitive-behavioral therapy for major depression in persons with chronic medical illness. *Journal of Nervous and Mental Disease, 203*(4), 243–251.

Koenig, H. G., Siegler, I. C., Meador, K. G., & George, L. K. (1990). Religious coping and personality in later life. *International Journal of Geriatric Psychiatry, 5*, 123–131.

Larson, D. B., Hohmann, A. A., Kessler, L. G., Meador, K. G., Boyd, J. H., & McSherry, E. (1988). The couch and the cloth: The need for linkage. *Psychiatric Services, 39*(10), 1064–1069.

Larson, D. B., Thielman, S. B., Greenwold, M. A., Lyons, J. S., Post, S. G., & Sherrill, K. A. (1993). Religious content in the DSM-III-R glossary of technical terms. *American Journal of Psychiatry, 150*, 1884–1885.

Li, S., Okereke, O. I., Chang, S. C., Kawachi, I., & VanderWeele, T. J. (2016a). Religious service attendance and lower depression among women – a prospective cohort study. *Annals of Behavioral Medicine, 50*(6), 876–884.

Li, S., Stampfer, M. J., Williams, D. R., & VanderWeele, T. J. (2016b). Association of religious service attendance with mortality among women. *JAMA Internal Medicine, 176*(6), 777–785.

Lissoni, P., Messina, G., Parolini, D., Balestra, A., Brivio, F., & Fumagalli, L. (2008). A spiritual approach in the treatment of cancer: Relation between faith score and response to chemotherapy in advanced non-small cell lung cancer patients. *In Vivo: International Institute of Anticancer Research, 22*(5), 577–582.

Maselko, J., Hayward, R. D., Hanlon, A., Buka, S., & Meador, K. (2012). Religious service attendance and major depression: A case of reverse causality? *American Journal of Epidemiology, 175*(6), 576–583.

McCullough, M. E., Enders, C. K., Brion, S. L., & Jain, A. R. (2005). The varieties of religious development in adulthood: A longitudinal investigation of religion and rational choice. *Journal of Personality and Social Psychology, 89*(1), 78–89.

McCullough, M. E., Tsang, J. A., & Brion, S. (2003). Personality traits in adolescence as predictors of religiousness in early adulthood: Findings from the Terman Longitudinal Study. *Personality and Social Psychology Bulletin*, *29*(8), 980–991.

Milstein, G., Manierre, A., Susman, V. L., & Bruce, M. L. (2008). Implementation of a program to improve the continuity of mental health care through Clergy Outreach and Professional Engagement (COPE). *Professional Psychology: Research and Practice*, *39*(2), 218.

Moscovici, S. (1961). *Psychoanalysis: Its Image and its public*. Cambridge, UK: Polity Press (2008 English translation) pp. 135–136.

Pew Research Center. (2012). *The global religious landscape*. Retrieved from http://www.pewforum.org/2012/12/18/global-religious-landscape-exec/.

Pew Research Center. (2017). *Religion and public life*. Retrieved from http://www.pewforum.org/.

Pirutinsky, S., Rosmarin, D. H., Pargament, K. I., & Midlarsky, E. (2011). Does negative religious coping accompany, precede, or follow depression among Orthodox Jews? *Journal of affective disorders*, *132*(3), 401–405.

Propst, L. R., Ostrom, R., Watkins, P., Dean, T., & Mashburn, D. (1992). Comparative efficacy of religious and nonreligious cognitive-behavior therapy for the treatment of clinical depression in religious individuals. *Journal of Consulting and Clinical Psychology*, *60*, 94–103.

Rank, O. (1930). *Psychology and the soul: A study of the origin, conceptual evolution, and nature of the soul*. Baltimore: Johns Hopkins University Press 2003.

Rosmarin, D. H., Pargament, K. I., Pirutinsky, S., & Mahoney, A. (2010). A randomized controlled evaluation of a spiritually integrated treatment for subclinical anxiety in the Jewish community, delivered via the Internet. *Journal of Anxiety Disorders*, *24*(7), 799–808.

Sherman, A. C., Plante, T. G., Simonton, S., Latif, U., & Anaissie, E. J. (2009). Prospective study of religious coping among patients undergoing autologous stem cell transplantation. *Journal of Behavioral Medicine*, *32*(1), 118–128.

Shields, A. (2016–2019). *National spirituality and health consortium*. Retrieved from https://www.templeton.org/grant/national-spirituality-and-health-consortium.

Sloan, R. P. (2006). *Blind faith: The unholy alliance of religion and medicine*. New York, NY: St. Martin's Press.

VanderWeele, T. (2015). *Explanation in causal inference: Methods for mediation and interaction*. New York, NY: Oxford University Press.

VanderWeele, T. J., Jackson, J. W., & Li, S. (2016). Causal inference and longitudinal data: A case study of religion and mental health. *Social Psychiatry and Psychiatric Epidemiology*, *51*(11), 1457–1466.

VanderWeele, T. J., Yu, J., Cozier, Y. C., Wise, L., Argentieri, M. A., Rosenberg, L., & Shields, A. E. (2017). Attendance at religious services, prayer, religious coping, and religious/spiritual identity as predictors of all-cause mortality in the Black Women's Health Study. *American Journal of Epidemiology*, *185*(7), 515–522.

Watters, W. (1992). *Deadly doctrine: Health, illness, and Christian God-talk*. Buffalo, NY: Prometheus Books.

Weaver, A. J. (1995). Has there been a failure to prepare and support Parish-based clergy in their role as front-line community mental health workers? A review. *Journal of Pastoral Care*, *49*, 129–149.

Weber, S. R., Pargament, K. I., Kunik, M. E., Lomax, J. W., & Stanley, M. A. (2012). Psychological distress among religious nonbelievers: A systematic review. *Journal of Religion and Health*, *51*(1), 72–86.

Whitley, R. (2010). Atheism and mental health. *Harvard Review of Psychiatry*, *18*(3), 190–194.

Wink, P., Ciciolla, L., Dillon, M., & Tracy, A. (2007). Religiousness, spiritual seeking, and personality: Findings from a longitudinal study. *Journal of Personality*, *75*(5), 1051–1070.

World Values Survey (2017). Retrieved from http://www.worldvaluessurvey.org/wvs.jsp.

Zuckerman, P. (2009). Atheism, secularity, and well-being: How the findings of social science counter negative stereotypes and assumptions. *Sociology Compass*, *3*(6), 949–971.

PART II

Clinical Applications

CHAPTER

10

General Applications in Clinical Practice

The next four chapters examine clinical applications relevant to mental health professionals (MHPs) and clergy (pastoral counselors, chaplains, and community clergy who counsel members of their congregation). This first chapter focuses on general applications that are relevant to all those seen in therapy or counseling settings. These applications are also relevant when medication is the primary treatment, as clinical interactions are important for the therapeutic relationship that will affect compliance and maximize benefits from both psychological and pharmacological therapy.

First, a word needs to be said about language. In Chapters 1 and 2, the measurement of "religion" was emphasized because of the distinctive nature of the term, whereas the measurement of spirituality was discouraged because of its nebulous and broad definition. When it comes to clinical interactions, however, the term "spirituality" is better language to use. The broad, diffuse, and nebulous nature of spirituality makes it excellent for conducting dialogues in clinical settings. As MHPs are likely to see clients from a wide range of religious and nonreligious backgrounds, it is important to use language that is client-centered. The language of spirituality is perfect because it allows clients to define whatever this term means to them. For many, it will mean religion. In that case, the clinician will talk with the patient about their specific religion. For others, spirituality will have nothing to do with a particular religion and instead be something the client has pieced together from a combination of worldviews. For still others, spirituality will mean something in between religion and a broader definition of the term. Regardless of how the word spirituality is defined by clients (and whatever it means to them), this is the language that should be used. The job of the clinician is to find out what the client's definition is and how it is significant for the

Religion and Mental Health. http://dx.doi.org/10.1016/B978-0-12-811282-3.00010-0

client. To do that, a spiritual history must be taken as part of the initial intake evaluation.

THE SPIRITUAL HISTORY

CASE VIGNETTE #1: UNINVOLVED BAPTIST

Tom is a 34 year old salesman who is being seen for the first time by his therapist John. As part of the social history during the intake evaluation, John asks Tom if he has a religious affiliation. Tom responds, "Yes, I'm Baptist, but not very involved." John follows, "Were you ever more involved than you are now?" Tom says, "Yes, a lot more, until I had a falling out with my pastor. He was concerned that I had asked one of the women in the church to go out for dinner and a movie. I told him I didn't realize she was married. That didn't seem to satisfy him. He had no right to butt into my business. So I decided to leave the church." John then said, "How has that experience affected your religious beliefs?" "Well," says Tom, "I've tried to avoid thinking about religion or God lately. I feel bad about this because my religious beliefs had always been important to me in the past, and gotten me through a lot of tough times." John asks, "Does this have anything to do with why you have come to see me today?" Tom responds, "I guess it could be part of it. Since my car accident and back injury two months ago, I haven't been able to return to work, had to drop out of the social scene, and been pretty depressed over all this. It's been hard to rely on my faith now like in the past. I feel like God has rejected me too."

Of all clinical applications, the spiritual history is the most important one to be discussed here. There is a growing consensus that a spiritual history should be taken on all clients seen in mental health settings. In the United States, a spiritual history is necessary to fulfill the requirements set by the Joint Commission for the Accreditation of Hospital Organizations (JCAHO) when treating both hospitalized inpatients and ambulatory outpatients (JCAHO, 2016). The requirement is that the care provider "respects the patient's cultural and personal values, beliefs, and preferences" (RI.01.01.01, EP6). For clients being seen for alcoholism, substance abuse, and emotional and behavioral disorders, the requirement is more explicit: "respects the patient's religion and spiritual beliefs, values, and preferences" (PC.01.02.11; PC.01.02.13). Assessment and reassessment of those religious and spiritual beliefs, values, and preferences is part of the requirement for both inpatients (PC.01.02.13, PC.02.03.01) and outpatients (PC.01.02.01).

Besides beliefs, values, and preferences, JCAHO emphasizes the need to assess a patient's *cultural* beliefs, values, and preferences and provide care in light of those. The elements of performance under PC.01.02.11 (substance abuse) and PC.01.02.13 (mental health care) stress the assessment of "ethnic and *cultural* factors." JCAHO also requires that as part of the education and training of patients (PC.02.03.01), the hospital must provide an assessment of learning needs in the area of the patient's "*cultural* and religious beliefs." Assessment of the patient's cultural background is necessary to provide "culturally competent care." Psychiatrist Robert Whitley (2012) argues that if MHPs wish to provide culturally competent care, they must assess and address the religious or spiritual needs of patients. This is necessary so that the care plan can be developed in light of those beliefs and needs (especially for ethnic minorities who are more likely to have cultural backgrounds formed by their religious or spiritual beliefs).

The only way for clinicians to show respect for a patient's cultural and personal values, beliefs, and preferences (specifically their religious and spiritual beliefs and values) is if they know about them. As noted above, this is a requirement for accreditation and Medicare/Medicaid reimbursement for inpatient and ambulatory services. More than that, it is good clinical practice. The way to learn about the client's religious and spiritual beliefs, values, and preferences is to take a spiritual history. What kinds of questions might the provider ask as part of the spiritual history? Although opinions vary widely in this regard, an earlier version of the JCAHO requirements (no longer on their website) provided the following guidelines:

> Spiritual assessment should, at a minimum, determine the patient's denomination, beliefs, and what spiritual practices are important to the patient. This information would assist in determining the impact of spirituality, if any, on the care/services being provided and will identify if any further assessment is needed. The standards require organizations to define the content and scope of spiritual and other assessments and the qualifications of the individual(s) performing the assessment.

If during this initial screening spirituality were found to be important to the patient, JCAHO then recommended a series of other questions:

> Does the patient use prayer in their life?
> How does the patient express their spirituality?
> What type of spiritual/religious support does the patient desire?
> What is the name of the patient's clergy, ministers, chaplains, pastor, or rabbi?
> What are the patient's spiritual goals?
> Is there a role of church/synagogue in the patient's life?
> How does [the patient's] faith help the patient cope with illness?

MENTAL HEALTH SPIRITUAL HISTORY

As these recommendations for spiritual assessment apply primarily to patients in healthcare settings, more specific and detailed information is needed from those with mental health problems. To the author's knowledge, there is no standard mental health spiritual history that is commonly used by MHPs. A number of spiritual histories, however, have been suggested (Gomi, Starnino, & Canda, 2014; Hodge, 2013; Huguelet et al., 2011; Koenig, 2013; Mathai & North, 2003; Moreira-Almeida, Koenig, & Lucchetti, 2014). What, then, can be recommended? A general statement to begin such an assessment has been suggested by Mathai and North (2003):

> Many people have strong spiritual or religious beliefs that shape their lives, including their health and experiences with illness. If you're comfortable talking about this topic, would you please share any of your beliefs and practices that you might want me to know about as your clinician.

Table 1 in the *Resources section* of this book provides a list of 15 questions to help guide the mental health spiritual history. When taking the spiritual history, as noted earlier, the clinician should listen carefully to the language or words that the client uses to discuss their spirituality. The practitioner should then use this same language during the spiritual history and during any discussion related to spiritual or religious issues in future sessions. Note that not all of the spiritual history needs to be taken at the first visit, and for more sensitive questions (such as how spiritual or religious beliefs might be contributing to the current illness, or exploration of traumatic experiences with religion or spirituality), it is best to wait until a therapeutic alliance has been firmly established and the client feels safe. Similarly, if clients indicate on the initial evaluation that they are not religious or spiritual, then the clinician should not press on with questions at that time but rather circle back around to this topic later on. At that later time, the MHP should gently explore why the client has not utilized spiritual beliefs to help cope with present or past struggles. In a systematic review of the clinician-administered spiritual history, Best, Butow, and Olver (2016) found that 48%–87% of psychiatrists (median 50%) said they often or always took a spiritual history, which was higher than that reported by nonpsychiatrists (9%–63%, median 34%). In the most comprehensive survey of US physicians to date (n = 1144), 49% of nonpsychiatrists indicated they inquired about patients' religious/spiritual issues, compared to 87% of psychiatrists.

Approach

Religious or spiritual issues are a sensitive topic for many clients. In religious regions of the world such as the United States (or countries in Europe that were historically religious), religious beliefs and teachings form the general moral or ethical climate and values of the society. Religious or spiritual topics may evoke feelings about what is good or bad, right or wrong, thereby deeply impacting self-esteem. Many have had traumatic experiences with religion (or spirituality), which may make it difficult for them to talk about these issues. Therefore the clinician must approach this topic slowly and with caution, being sensitive and supportive to responses given, proceeding in a gentle and kind manner. The attitude of the clinician should be one of a humble learner who is relying on clients to teach him or her about their religious or spiritual experiences and how these have impacted their lives and current illness. There is no room for judgment (or implied judgment). There is no room for criticism (or implied criticism). There is no room for argument or disagreement with the client's beliefs, at least initially. There may come a time when beliefs need to be challenged, but not early on. Throughout the spiritual history, the clinician's goal is to convince the client that he or she is on their side, wanting to learn more about the client's experiences with regard to religion/spirituality, both good and bad, so that the clinician can help the client live a fuller and happier life. The spiritual history should also be taken in a way to avoid making nonreligious/nonspiritual clients feel like they should be something they are not. Asking these questions in a straight forward and neutral manner, explaining that this is an important area for some but not all clients, should help minimize the risk of leaving such impressions.

Receptiveness of Mental Health Professionals

How receptive are MHPs to taking a spiritual history and discussing these issues with clients? In a study of outpatients with schizophrenia in Switzerland, Huguelet et al. (2011) found that of the eight psychiatrists involved in their randomized clinical trial, none felt that a spiritual assessment was contraindicated for any patient involved in the study. An earlier study of 230 psychiatrists in the United Kingdom, Neeleman and King (1993) found that 73% of psychiatrists reported no religious affiliation, 81% of men and 41% of women did not believe in God, 42% indicated that religiousness can lead to mental illness, and 58% never made referrals to clergy. However, 92% believed that religion and mental illness were connected and that religious issues should be addressed in treatment (and presumably, assessed).

More recently in a survey of 895 accredited psychotherapists in Germany, Hofmann and Walach (2011) found that 22% said clients mentioned spirituality or religion during the course of therapy and 67% said that clinically relevant questions related to religion or spirituality should be given more attention during the training of MHPs. Investigators did not, however, ask about therapists' attitudes or practices regarding the spiritual history. In a study conducted over the Internet in the United States, Rosmarin, Pirutinsky, Green, and McKay (2013) surveyed 262 members of the Association for Behavioral and Cognitive Therapies (ABCT), finding that 19% never or rarely assessed clients' religiosity or spirituality, whereas 31% sometimes, 31% often, and 20% always did so. With regard to comfort level, 64% indicated they were mostly or very comfortable addressing religious or spiritual issues in treatment. Of course, these were therapists who responded to an Internet survey among the 4835 members of ABCT who received such a request (i.e., only 5% of potential respondents), that is, those with sufficient interest in the topic to take the 5 minutes to respond. Thus these results are likely a best-case scenario.

Client Receptiveness to Spiritual History

What about patients? How receptive are clients toward clinicians taking a spiritual history? Most clients (75%–80%) appear to be receptive to providers taking a spiritual history (Kelly, 1995; Rose, Westefeld, & Ansley, 2001; Stanley et al., 2011). In one of the few studies examining receptiveness to the spiritual history in mental health settings, Mathai and North (2003) surveyed a random sample of 70 parents of children and adolescents receiving treatment at a community mental health center in Australia, finding that 74% felt their spiritual beliefs were relevant to the child's current mental health problem. In Switzerland, Huguelet et al. (2011) conducted a randomized clinical trial involving spiritual assessment of outpatients with schizophrenia (40 receiving the spiritual assessment; 38 receiving traditional assessment). They found that "spiritual assessment was well tolerated by the patients, and none of them spontaneously expressed concerns to their psychiatrists." More than a quarter of the participants in both intervention (26%) and control groups (30%) indicated at baseline that they strongly (i.e., "a lot or totally") wished to discuss religion and spirituality with their psychiatrist. Among those who received the spiritual assessment, only 3% missed appointments during a 3-month follow-up period compared to 26% of those in the control group not receiving the spiritual history. In a survey of 164 group therapy clients seen at university and college counseling centers across the United States, Post and Wade (2014) asked clients about the appropriateness of discussing religion or spirituality during group therapy. Most indicated that it was appropriate for therapists to bring up the topic of spirituality (84%) or religion (76%) in the group, particularly when issues involved spiritual struggles (84%).

Research has also examined patient receptiveness in medical settings. In a qualitative meta-synthesis of 11 studies, Hodge and Horvath (2011) found when assessing patients' spiritual needs, six themes predominated: (1) meaning, purpose, and hope, (2) relationship with God, (3) spiritual practices, (4) religious obligations, (5) interpersonal connections with clergy and members of their faith community, and (6) spiritual needs around interactions with professional staff. These authors concluded that religion/spirituality was clearly a subject on many clients' minds and needed clinical attention. A study of 118 oncology outpatients in the mid-western US indicated that when clinicians took a brief 5–7 minutes spiritual history, it was well-received in most cases and almost immediately had positively affects on patients' mood and functional well-being (within 3 weeks of the assessment), significantly strengthening the physician–patient relationship (Kristeller, Rhodes, Cripe, & Sheets, 2005). In that study, 85% of physicians felt quite or very comfortable with the inquiry and 76% of patients said it was somewhat or very useful. Likewise, in a 12-month intervention conducted in 432 physicians and mid-level providers caring for general medical outpatients, over 80% of clinicians reported that patients indicated acceptance of or appreciation for the spiritual history (vs. puzzlement, indifference, or resistance) (Koenig, Perno, Erkanli, & Hamilton, 2017). Thus it appears that in both mental health care and medical settings, the vast majority of patients are open to discussing religious or spiritual issues as part of their treatment.

Overcoming Resistance

The clinician should initially prepare the client for the spiritual history by explaining the need for it, that is, to provide a more complete understanding of the client's beliefs and experiences so that treatment can be provided in light of them. The spiritual history should not be forced on unwilling clients. However, if the spiritual history is not taken or cut short, the MHP at some point will need to acquire this information to determine whether there are religious or spiritual issues influencing mental health. If the clinician initially runs into resistance, then it is appropriate to back off but not avoid the topic indefinitely. As noted earlier, once a firm therapeutic alliance has been established and the client feels comfortable and safe in the relationship, the clinician may gently return to the subject. This is particularly important as the client's reluctance may be due to traumatic experiences the client is trying to avoid or shut out from consciousness. If that is the case, then it is essential such experiences be gradually uncovered and cognitively "processed" (as any traumatic experience would need to be). If, however, the client is simply not religious/spiritual and never has been, the subject may be dropped and no further attention paid to it. However, the clinician may ask if the client has ever had negative or stressful experiences *as a result of* their not being particularly religious or spiritual (i.e., pressure from friends or family to become religious). Again, this must be a neutral conversation that is intended purely for information gathering and not guilt inducing. Again, being clear and up front with the client about the reasons for this line of inquiry will be helpful.

CONFLICTS BETWEEN BELIEF AND TREATMENT

CASE VIGNETTE #2: ANXIOUS FUNDAMENTALIST

Mary is a 54 year old Caucasian female who has been referred by her primary care physician to a psychiatrist for the treatment of panic attacks. Mary is awakened at night out of a dead sleep with severe feelings of panic that last about five minutes and then gradually taper off, leaving her upset and unable to go back to sleep. This is disrupting her sleep, is causing feels of fatigue during the day, and is affecting her productivity at work. Mary is about to lose her job and is now desperately seeking relief. She arranges a visit to see a psychiatrist. Mary is a devoutly religious person who regularly attends a local Pentecostal church, from which she receives a great deal of support. During the spiritual history, the psychiatrist learns that Mary has been to many healing services at her church, including once when she underwent an exorcism. None of this was helpful, and she had begun to question her faith. Nevertheless, she continues attending church services twice weekly because of the support that she receives there. The psychiatrist recommends a course of the antidepressant paroxetine (Paxil), along with low dose clonazepam (Klonopin), the standard drug protocol for panic disorder symptoms. Mary looks uncomfortable when she hears the recommendation, and responds to the psychiatrist, "I'm not sure if the people in my church would support that. They believe that prayer, memorizing scriptures, and laying on of hands by elders should be enough to resolve my problem. I don't know, though, we've tried all that and I'm still having these attacks. She asks the psychiatrist what she should do. The psychiatrist gently suggests that Mary take the medication, not tell the members of her church about it, and continue to attend church services that include healing prayer. He says, "Could it be that God wants to heal you through a combination of these methods? Do you think he might have sent you here to see me for that reason?" Mary replied, "Maybe so. I'd like to think and pray about that."

If the spiritual history indicates the client has religious or spiritual beliefs that may conflict with treatment, whether the treatment is pharmacological or psychotherapeutic in nature, then this must be explored in detail until the clinician understands the client's perspective and the client feels understood. This provides an opportunity to strengthen the therapeutic alliance. Treatment should be delayed until agreement is arrived at, otherwise noncompliance will likely result. The clinician should also inquire about any resistance that the client's family, friends, or faith community may have to the recommended treatments. If family members and/

or a valued religious community are not supportive, then it is unlikely that the client will stick to and complete the treatment. Many of the more conservative or fundamentalist religious communities continue to have reservations about medications and secular psychotherapies, due to attitudes in the mental health care field that have belittled and undervalued religion. The clinician must get these resistances out into the open, and work through them with the client (and if the client consents, with family members, influential friends, and even the client's clergy if necessary). One options is to conduct cotherapy with a pastoral counselor or clergy in the client's faith tradition.

SPIRITUAL ACTIVITIES WITH CLIENTS

Besides taking a spiritual history, what other spiritual activities are appropriate as part of general mental health care? As noted above, there is general acceptance among health professionals that taking a spiritual history is appropriate and necessary. However, doing anything beyond that is more controversial. Such activities might involve supporting the client's religious beliefs, utilizing the clients' beliefs in therapy, praying with clients, or sharing providers' own religious beliefs with clients. It is difficult for a clinician to get into trouble by simply asking questions and listening, but more active engagement in spiritual practices with patients carries some degree of risk. To this author's knowledge, little systematic research has examined the prevalence of such activities between providers and clients or clients' receptiveness *in mental health settings*. It is clear, however, that spiritual activities clinicians decide to engage in with clients must be guided by the spiritual history.

Supporting Clients' Beliefs

Least controversial is verbally and nonverbally supporting clients' spiritual beliefs and practices that they find comfort in and are already engaged in. Of course, if religious/spiritual beliefs are obviously pathological, then the clinician should remain neutral and inquisitive, seeking to learn more without supporting or challenging. Again, little information exists on how often clinicians support clients' religious/spiritual beliefs or the results of doing so. In our study of 520 physicians and mid-level practitioners working within a faith-based health system (clinicians treating general medical outpatients), we found that 88% of providers indicated that health professionals should sometimes or often encourage patients to become more active in their own religious faith for health reasons (Koenig, Perno, & Hamilton, 2017). Similarly, in a national random sample of 1144 US physicians, Curlin et al. (2007) found that 73% of nonpsychiatrists indicated they often or always encouraged patients in their own religious/spiritual beliefs and practices, compared to 83% of psychiatrists who said they did so.

Utilizing Beliefs in Therapy

Utilizing patients' religious/spiritual beliefs in therapy does not always have to involve conducting a religiously or spiritually integrated therapy. Simply providing support for these beliefs and practices can help to reinforce them and thereby enhance their effectiveness. Furthermore, religious beliefs/practices can be utilized to alter cognitions and behaviors that might be contributing to mental health problems. To do so, the clinician must first be familiar with the client's religious/spiritual belief system. Resources exist to inform MHPs about religious belief systems with which they may be unfamiliar (see religion-specific treatments below). Second, the spiritual history should indicate that the religious/spiritual beliefs of the client are not obviously pathological or contributing to the mental condition. Such a determination may require multiple assessments over time. Thus early on in therapy, it is best to remain neutral, inquisitive, and generally supportive without actually attempting to utilize clients' religious/spiritual resources to alter beliefs or attitudes.

Prayer With Clients

Praying with clients is controversial even in medical settings (Dagi, 1995; Post, Puchalski, & Larson, 2000), where there are fewer boundary issues than in mental health settings. This is particularly true when *the clinician* initiates the prayer, which raises the possibility of coercion (as it is difficult for clients to refuse since they may wish to please the clinician). Less vulnerable patients may sometimes react negatively to such attempts, adversely affecting the therapeutic relationship.

CASE VIGNETTE #3: TRAUMATIZED MOM

William is treating Melanie, a 36-year old woman, for grief following the loss of her husband and son from a tragic private plane crash. This is their second session of cognitive-behavioral therapy (CBT). William, a clinical psychologist, took a brief spiritual history during the initial evaluation, although noted some resistance from Melanie and so cut the spiritual history short. While Melanie was raised in a religious home, she was not particularly religious or spiritual at this time. Her parents had forced her to attend religious services during her teen years. When she got out of the home to attend college, she stopped going to religious services and began pursuing a purely secular lifestyle, including a good deal of partying. She'd been married eight years with two children (a son and daughter) when the plane crash occurred about three months ago. She was now having trouble making sense of why this happened, was not sleeping well, and was irritable and short with her 6-year old daughter. For that reason, she had sought counseling at a local public mental health clinic, where she was assigned to William. On this second session, she was particularly distraught. Doing CBT with Melanie was difficult in her present state of mind. At the end of the session, as she was crying, William (a deeply religious man) asked: "I can see you are having a hard time. Would you like me to pray with you about this?" Melanie frowned, stopped crying, and responded, "What has God got to do with this? He wasn't there to help my husband and son when their plane went down." William responded gently, "I think a prayer would help." Melanie responded angrily, "Then you pray" and got up and left the office. She later contacted the clinic to complain about William.

Where did William go wrong? He took a brief spiritual history on the initial evaluation, which was good. However, he didn't pick up—despite initial signals—on Melanie's anger at God over what had happened. His gentle approach is to be commended. However, sufficient time in therapy had not occurred for a firm therapeutic relationship to develop. His suggestion regarding suggestion regarding prayer caught Melanie off guard. She didn't expect this in a public health clinic, and it set off her anger, given her distraught and irritable state. William clearly took a risk by initiating the request to pray, allowing his own religious beliefs into the treatment setting. Some would argue that he violated a therapeutic boundary, proceeding to initiate prayer rather than allowing the patient to request prayer if desired. He also displayed poor judgment, proceeding without full knowledge of the client's religious state. His timing was clearly off in proposing this "intervention" before Melanie had worked through her anger at God. Prayer, when clinician-initiated, can be a powerful intervention that produces deep healing if done within the context of a strong, long-term therapeutic relationship with a client known to be religious; otherwise, it should be utilized cautiously, if at all.

Even when client-initiated, prayer may be controversial in mental health settings where some clients have boundary issues that an intimate activity such as prayer might cross. Clients have been known to develop romantic fantasies over clinicians after engaging in prayer with them, later reporting that they regretted ever having done so. While more likely to occur in borderline patients or those with severe personality disorders, clinicians should be aware of this possibility. With these warnings in mind, as noted above, a well-timed prayer with a religious client may provide tremendous comfort and cement the therapeutic alliance. Curlin et al. (2007) found that 20% of nonpsychiatrists sometimes, often, or always prayed with patients, compared to 6% of psychiatrists (only 1% often or always did so). Furthermore, 70% of nonpsychiatrists said that it was either never appropriate to pray with patients (16%) or only if the patient asks (54%); among psychiatrists, 68% said it was either never appropriate to pray with patients (34%) or only if the patient asks (34%). In our study of 540 outpatient medical providers affiliated with a faith-based health system, 94% said that it was sometimes or often appropriate for a health professional to pray with a patient if the patient asks, and 47% of these clinicians sometimes or often prayed with patients (Koenig, Perno, & Hamilton, 2017).

Sensible guidelines for praying with clients, when clients initiate the request, are provided by psychologist Michelle Pearce and oncologist Delia Chiaramonte (2017).

Sharing Beliefs

Clients may on occasion inquire about the religious/spiritual beliefs of the MHP, sometimes quite innocently and sometimes in an effort to proselytize the clinician or otherwise derail the therapy. This can be uncomfortable to providers, and is one reason why some MHPs refuse to take a spiritual history or otherwise engage with clients on this topic. Fear of client inquiry, however, should not stop the clinician from exploring this important area. Learning how to respond to clients when this happens is what is important. Most of the time such inquiries are innocent, and a simple honest response from the clinician is often sufficient. If the clinician is reluctant to provide such information, this is perfectly within their right. However, there are diplomatic ways of keeping one's own spiritual beliefs private. A time-tested method is to ask the client why this information is important to him or her, redirecting the conversation to the client's issues. Another response is to reassure the client that their religious or spiritual beliefs will always be respected and valued by the clinician, who will do her or his best to understand them.

The other side of "sharing beliefs" is when the clinician *initiates* the sharing of his or her own beliefs to convince the client of the truth of those beliefs. This is called proselytizing. Clinicians are always trying to share their knowledge based on scientific research with clients as part of the therapy process, and may occasionally share personal experiences with clients. However, proselytizing in a mental health care setting is never appropriate, and given the power differential between client and therapist, this practice is likely to be a violation of patient rights. It is surprising, though, how many clinicians share their own religious beliefs with clients. Curlin et al. (2007) found that 41% of nonpsychiatrists said they respectfully shared their own religious ideas and experiences with patients, compared to 26% of psychiatrists. We found that 91% of outpatient medical providers in a faith-based health system said that it was appropriate for a health professional to share their own religious beliefs with patients *if the patient asks* (Koenig, Perno, & Hamilton, 2017).

BOUNDARIES

CASE VIGNETTE #4: THE EVANGELIST

Sheila was seeing Marla, a social worker, for counseling over an eating disorder that she was struggling with. Sheila, age 22, was a devout Catholic and particularly distressed about her binging habits, followed by the need to purge in order to keep her body weight down. She knew that this behavior was not right and felt very guilty about it. She had repeatedly gone to confession and performed penance, without relief, causing her to seek help from outside the church. Marla, her therapist, was an evangelical Protestant Christian. She took a thorough and detailed spiritual history on initial evaluation, and was well aware of the importance of Sheila's religious beliefs in her life. On the third session, after a therapeutic relationship had developed, Marla asked Sheila "Do you know Jesus? Have you ever been saved?" Sheila responded that she frequently prayed to God, said the rosary at least once a week, and had a crucifix of Jesus above her bed. Marla persisted, "But do you know Jesus as your personal Lord and savior?" Sheila, looking uncomfortable, replied, "I'm not sure what you mean by that?" Marla responded, "Well, your Catholic beliefs and practices may be part of the problem here. You can never be assured eternal salvation unless you are saved. Would you like to say the prayer of salvation with me? Please repeat after me..."

As noted earlier, it is important to maintain boundaries between provider and client. This is done to protect both the client and the therapist, given the sensitive issues that need to be addressed in those who are emotionally vulnerable. Forcing a spiritual history on a reluctant client, then, is inappropriate because it does not respect the client's boundaries. Initiating prayer with patients is likewise usually not appropriate (which 99% of psychiatrists would agree with, according to Curlin et al., 2007), unless it is clear that the client is religious and might appreciate such a request. Likewise, sharing personal religious beliefs and experiences with clients, particularly if not asked, comes close to violating long-established boundaries in the mental health field. It is never appropriate, for example, to ask a client, "Do you know Jesus?" or "Have you been saved." The only exception in this regard are Christian counselors who advertise that they do Bible-based counseling, where clients themselves choose this approach.

While the boundary violation in the case vignette above is obvious, there are more subtle ways that MHPs may impose their own belief systems on unsuspecting clients. For example, a provider who is atheist or agnostic may impose her/his beliefs on a religious client, subtly discouraging the person's attempts to use their faith to cope with problems. Likewise, the indiscriminate prescription and encouragement of mindfulness meditation without full disclosure that this is a practice derived from Buddhist philosophy is also inappropriate, yet increasingly done within the mental health field (e.g., mindful meditation for anxiety, mindfulness-based stress reduction, mindfulness-based cognitive therapy, and so forth). While mindfulness techniques are often described as a secular practice, this is not necessarily true and is particularly inappropriate when there are other approaches within the client's own faith tradition that may be equally as effective (e.g., contemplative Christian practices, see Chapter 11).

PATHOLOGICAL RELIGIOSITY/SPIRITUALITY

CASE VIGNETTE #5: THE CONVERT

Jim, age 20, is brought into the clinic by his mother, Connie. Jim reluctantly gives consent to allow his mother to be with him during the evaluation. Dr. Jones (a psychiatrist) asks Jim what the problem is. Jim says there is no problem, except maybe his mother. Connie says that Jim recently had a "conversion experience," has become increasingly religious, and has now joined a new church that he attends several times per week. She says he tells her that he has been hearing God's voice speaking to him (not an audible voice, but through his thoughts), and believes that he is being "called" into the ministry. The other day she came into his room and found him speaking to himself in rapid, unintelligible words, like a different language. When she interrupted him, Jim told her that he was "speaking in tongues." Connie says that this is just one example of how Jim has been acting strangely since going to this new church. She says that he frequently stops to give money to homeless people on street corners, and gives a significant percentage of his income (close to 10%) to that church. Connie admits she is herself religious, but is a "solid" Episcopalian and much of this seems like nonsense to her. She tells the psychiatrist, "I'm afraid that Jim is developing a psychotic disorder like his older brother Phil has. Phil is taking medication for it under the direction of a psychiatrist and this has helped him. What do you think, doctor?" Dr. Jones conducts a careful psychiatric history, including a spiritual history, but does not detect any "other" psychotic symptoms. Although very religious and a bit excited as he talks about his new faith, Jim's thought processes are coherent and goal directed, and other than perhaps his religious beliefs, has no other delusions. While Jim reports that God is speaking to him, he denies hearing voices in his head. Dr. Jones acknowledges to Connie that Jim is certainly very religious, but is not sure if this represents a psychotic disorder. He suggests she bring him back for evaluation in one month for follow-up, and does not prescribe any medication at this time.

Sometimes it can be difficult to determine whether the relatively sudden onset of intense religious beliefs is normative for a person's particular social or religious group, or represents symptoms of early psychosis. Further follow-up reveals that Jim continues to be very religious but does not demonstrate psychotic symptoms or other indicators of mental illness. He appears to be quite integrated into the social group at his new church and has made several close friendships there. Dr. Jones tells Connie that he doesn't think Jim has a psychotic disorder and does not need medication. However, he'd like to check on Jim in 3–4 months to see how things are going. Jim's presentation here is challenging; in other cases, it may be much easier to differentiate "healthy" from "sick" religion (James, 1902).

CASE VIGNETTE #6: MANIC JACK

Jack, a 24 year old engineer, is brought in by his wife to see a psychiatrist due to "strange behavior." Jack greets the psychiatrist and says that he would definitely like his wife to be with them during this evaluation. He is hoping the psychiatrist will help him to convince her about the truth of his claims. The wife tells the psychiatrist that Jack has not been sleeping much at night, has been very busy in various projects around the house "preparing," and tells her that he believes he is a prophet sent by God to save the world. She notes that they both sometimes get "high" on marijuana, but that Jack seems to stay high a lot longer than she does and talks incessantly about his new found religious beliefs. He insists that like Noah, God has told him that the world will soon experience a disaster, and that he has been chosen to warn humanity. On psychiatric evaluation, Jack admits to racing thoughts that keep him up at night, and on occasion hearing God's audible voice instructing him on preparations he must make. A spiritual history reveals that Jack is not part of any religious group nor attends religious services. Jack indicates that he reads the Bible about three hours per day before leaving for work in the morning. He admits that his supervisor has complained about his work lately, but that as a prophet, he has more important things to do. On psychiatric history, Jack admits that his mother and uncle had some kind of psychiatric problem that required admission to the hospital. After further evaluation, the psychiatrist concludes that Jack is experiencing a manic episode and shares this with Jack and his wife. Appearing quite surprised (and a bit angry), Jack vehemently denies that he has a problem and tells the psychiatrist that they must leave now so he can continue his preparations.

We know that religious delusions are common among those with schizophrenia, bipolar disorder, and other psychotic illnesses. As noted in Chapter 5, an early study of 41 patients with schizophrenia or mania admitted to the New York State Psychiatric Hospital found that 13 had religious delusions (Cothran & Harvey, 1986). Among patients with a diagnosis of schizophrenia, 39% of patients had delusions with religious content; among those with mania, 22% had such delusions. Although patients with religious delusions were more religious overall, they were less likely to report fundamentalist beliefs and were less involved in a religious community compared to nondelusional patients or normal controls. Researchers also noted that the religiosity of patients with religious delusions was "different" than that expressed by nonpsychotic patients or normal controls.

In a study conducted in North Manchester, United Kingdom, Siddle, Haddock, Tarrier, and Faragher (2002) found that 24% of 193 inpatients with schizophrenia had religious delusions. Those with religious delusions had more severe psychotic symptoms, especially hallucinations and bizarre delusions. They also had worse overall functioning and were taking more antipsychotic medication than patients with other types of delusions. Interestingly, no correlation was found between psychotic symptoms and degree of religiosity at baseline. However, religiosity increased or decreased over time depending on the severity of psychotic symptoms. Furthermore, as psychotic symptoms diminished with treatment, so did religiosity (although it is unclear to what extent antipsychotic drug treatment itself affected the ability to have religious experiences, see Chapter 9).

The particular content of religious delusions is often derived from the dominant religion of the culture to which the person belongs. For example, in a small study of four Chinese patients with schizophrenia in Hong Kong, Yip (2003) reported that the content of delusions and hallucinations reflected Chinese religious beliefs involving Buddhist gods, Taoist gods, historical heroic gods, and ancestor worship. The same is true for those from Western countries who have delusions with primarily Christian content and those from Middle Eastern countries whose delusions focus on the Prophet Mohammad or on Jinn (spirits or angels).

Interestingly, religious delusions may vary in frequency depending on the particular theology. In a study of 133 Christian patients with psychosis admitted to the inpatient psychiatric unit at the University of Cincinnati Medical Center, Getz, Fleck, and Strakowski (2001) found that religious delusions were nearly four times more common in Protestants than in Catholics (OR = 3.8, 95% CI 1.3–11.1, $p < 0.02$) and were associated with more frequent religious practice ($r = 0.27$, $p < 0.01$). Severity of delusions, however, did not vary across religious groups. Finally, in a study of 116 consecutive inpatients diagnosed with schizophrenia or schizoaffective disorder in Istanbul, Turkey (a Muslim country), researchers examined the effects of delusion type on treatment response (Kilicaslan, Acar, Eksioglu, Kesebir, & Tezcan, 2016). Those with religious delusions (25%) had significantly longer hospital stays on average than those without (25.6 days vs. 21.9 days, $p = 0.01$).

Thus religious delusions may track along with other psychotic symptoms in terms of severity, and when present, may portend a slower response to treatment, although further research is clearly needed.

A variety of clues may assist MHPs in distinguishing religious beliefs that are pathological from those that are culturally, socially, and religiously normative. Pierre (2001) provides several suggestions that may help to separate out religious delusions and hallucinations from legitimate religious experiences. His first point, interestingly, is that delusional subcultures can exist. In that case, even though the client's religious beliefs appear normative for the group, this does not necessarily mean that beliefs are non-delusional. Second, Pierre notes that religious delusions may result from lesions in the temporal lobe (from stroke or tumor) and must be ruled out by electroencephalogram or imaging techniques (CT scan or MRI). Third, it may be helpful to seek input from religious professionals familiar with the patient's religious beliefs. Typically, members of the faith community have little difficulty distinguishing persons with religious beliefs that are "strange" from those with beliefs considered normal for the group (unless, of course, the patient is a member of a delusional subculture). Finally, for religious delusions to be pathological, Pierre notes that they must impact the patient's social or occupational functioning. If the person's functioning is not at all impaired, then the religious belief cannot be pathological (as the term "pathological" requires that a condition causes impairment of psychological, social, occupational, or recreational functioning). Besides the four points emphasized by Pierre above, there are other ways to distinguish pathological religiosity, the most important being that religious delusions seldom appear without any other psychotic symptoms (an isolated religious delusion is possible, but rare). In such cases, then, a careful psychiatric evaluation along with informant interviews can usually identify other indicators of psychosis.

ENGAGEMENT OF FAMILY

The primary obligation of the therapist or counselor is to their client. No information can be released about the client to family members or anyone else without his or her explicit (often written) permission. However, it is almost always helpful to include family members in the evaluation and/or the treatment when this is possible and the client gives consent. Having a secondary source of information is valuable, both in terms of the mental health history more generally and the spiritual history in particular (helping to sort out whether religious beliefs are normative or pathological, although there are some exceptions, as in Case #5 above). Information about the family's religious history and experiences will be important in determining the impact of religion on the person's life and whether religious beliefs/practices can be utilized as resources. If the client does not have family members or does not agree to allow them to be present in the therapy, then the MHP (or counseling clergy) will have to rely on the client's self-report. If this is the case, then the therapist (as noted above) will need to ask the client about the family's religiosity and the degree to which close family members might support or oppose the treatment (especially if the family is very religious). While this also applies to clients and family members who are Christian, it may be particularly relevant for Muslims, Hindus, and East Asians (given the importance and influence of the family in these traditions and cultures).

RELIGION-SPECIFIC TREATMENTS

This leads to a consideration of specific clinical applications in clients who are members of different religious groups. For more a comprehensive discussion of these applications, the reader is referred to the author's religion and mental health book series (see citations below).

Catholic Christianity

Therapists should be aware of the important role that the Church and the Sacraments play in the lives of clients who are practicing Catholics (Koenig, 2017a). Also be aware that Catholicism already has a way of addressing emotional problems, the sacrament of Confession and the acts of Penance that follow it. Therefore Catholics should be asked about this practice and to what extent it has been helpful (or unhelpful) in the past. The sacrament of Holy Communion is also widely revered by Catholics as a healing ritual, so the frequency of this practice should also be inquired about. Although guilt in Catholicism is often overstated (there is very little objective evidence that Catholics suffer guilt more than anybody else), the Catholic faith is a conservative form of Christianity that has high moral standards that may be easily breached by devout believers. However, the sacrament of confession is there to address the distress that may result from human frailty, where the priest may offer advice and assign activities to help resolve the guilt. Failure for confession to do so, however, may indicate psychopathology that requires more than pastoral counsel or absolution.

Protestant Christianity

Protestant Christianity is likely to be the most common faith tradition of clients whom therapists see in the United States and English-speaking countries throughout the world (Koenig, 2017b). There are many Protestant denominations (reported to be in the thousands), and so the first question in the spiritual history ought to be about the client's specific denomination (both current and denomination they were raised in). Protestant denominations vary in their level of conservativeness, from those with progressive or liberal beliefs to those with conservative or fundamentalist beliefs. Many Protestants (particularly those on the conservative end of the spectrum) emphasize adult conversion experiences, so these should also be asked about. If the client reports having had such an experience, the therapist will want to know if it was sudden or gradual (and what the precipitating factors were). The therapist will want to know how the client interprets the Bible, as either literal or inspired word of God, or as simply figurative or allegorical. Protestants, in general, place more value on the Bible than Catholics who, as noted above, are more likely to emphasize church traditions and sacraments. We have developed a Bible-based religiously integrated form of cognitive behavioral therapy for depression/anxiety that Protestant Christians may be particularly receptive to (CSTH, 2014; Pearce, 2016; Pearce et al., 2015).

Judaism

First, the therapist will want to determine whether the Jewish client is a religious Jew or a secular/cultural Jew (Koenig, 2017c). If the client is a religious Jew, then the clinician should determine what branch of Judaism the person affiliates with (reform/traditional, conservative/religious, or Orthodox/Ultra-Orthodox). For those who are secular, the spiritual history may be relatively short unless religious issues come up during therapy. For religious clients, the therapist will want to know what religious beliefs/practices are particularly important in life, and if the person is actively involved in a Jewish religious community, how supportive members and clergy have been. Since some research suggests that symptoms of depression or obsessive–compulsive disorder are more common among Jews, particularly Orthodox Jews, the MHP will want to screen for emotional problems of this sort. The therapist should be cautious, though, as Orthodox Jews have many rituals that are considered normative. Participation in the Jewish community is often a healing experience itself, and the therapist can seldom go wrong in supporting such involvement. A Jewish version of religiously integrated cognitive behavioral therapy for depression (as with the Christian version) is also readily available and without cost, together with therapist and client workbooks and a brief training video (CSTH, 2014).

Islam

Given the widespread "Islamaphobia" in the world today and the multiple levels of stigma that Muslims must often deal with (Zakaria,

Moffic, & Peteet, 2018), especially Muslims in the Western world, the first goal of the therapist is to provide an open and safe place where clients can freely talk about their religious faith, how important it is to them, and whether they feel good or bad about their religion. There is considerable evidence that anxiety problems are more common among the Muslims, particularly those without a strong religious faith, so therapists should be alert for such symptoms (Koenig & Al Shohaib, 2017). The Qur'an is the sacred and holy religious book of Islam, and is viewed by Muslims with the same reverence that Christians hold for Jesus. To Muslims, the Qur'an is the "Word of God" and is often used when dealing with stress or emotional problems. Reciting certain verses from the Qur'an can be enormously comforting to devout Muslims who are facing difficult times, and therapists should consider utilizing the Qur'an during treatment for that purpose (Koenig & Al Shohaib, 2014, 2017). Again, we have developed a religiously integrated treatment for the depression in Muslims that relies heavily on verses from the Qur'an (CSTH, 2014).

Hinduism

While Hindus may appear to worship "many gods," most believe in one Supreme God who manifests himself in many different forms (Koenig, 2017d). Hindus often revere those different forms, similar to how Catholics revere Mary and different Catholic saints. Hindus are also very accepting and welcoming of those from other religious faiths. Hinduism is often described by Hindus as "a way of life," since it is integrated into all aspects of life. As a result, the religious beliefs and rituals of actively practicing Hindus will often have an influence on mental health (and when psychopathology is present, will likely be interwoven with it). One thing that MHPs need to know about Hindus is the importance of family and community. While Westerners tend to value their independence and self-sufficiency, Hindus rely heavily on relationships within the family and the community (as part of their South Asian culture). Thus the clinician should determine whether the religious or spiritual beliefs of Hindu clients are similar to those of their family of origin, and if not, determine the circumstances that led to a change in faith. If religious beliefs are similar to those of family, then the MHP should be aware that any change made during therapy if not supported by family will have a low likelihood of persistence. Hindus, like Protestants, vary widely in their beliefs and so careful identification of the specific beliefs of the individual client is necessary. We have developed a religiously integrated form of Hindu CBT for depression that is heavily based on the Bhagavad Gita, one of the most sacred of Hindu spiritual texts (CSTH, 2014).

Buddhism

As in Hinduism, out of which Buddhism arose, Buddhist beliefs vary widely requiring that the MHP take a careful spiritual history to identify what those beliefs are (Koenig, 2017e). When becoming a Buddhist today, the person must state publicly that they "take refuge" in the Buddha, the Dhamma (the law or sayings of the Buddha), and the Sangha (Buddhist community). The Buddha provided a role model for Buddhists today, and has described a pathway to what the Buddha believed was the answer to human suffering (and therefore very relevant to mental health). As noted in Chapter 7, at the moment of Enlightenment, the Buddha realized the Four Noble Truths and the Eightfold Path leading to Nirvana and the end of all suffering. The last two steps on the Eightfold Path involve "right mindfulness" and "right concentration." Both of these are forms of meditation, and today's mindfulness-based practices that MHPs prescribe for many clients with emotional problems are derived directly from these last two steps in the Path. Thus therapists should consider encouraging these forms of meditation for relief of stress, anxiety, and depression in Buddhist clients, as they are based on the Buddha's original teachings.

If the client is not an active participant in their Buddhist faith tradition, then the therapist should determine whether the client's family of origin was religious and whether the client's current lack of religious interest has recently changed. As in other faith traditions, if the client has little interest in Buddhism and was raised in a family that was not particularly religious, then further inquiry may be limited; however, being raised within a far Eastern culture may give rise to issues that could influence the client's mental health and therefore should be explored. As noted earlier, the family is very important in Asian cultures, and when possible, should be involved as much as possible (with the client's permission) in the evaluation and/or treatment. Our version of Buddhist CBT for depression (CSTH, 2014) is based heavily on Dhammapada, perhaps the most sacred and well-known of Buddhist scriptures.

WHEN TO REFER

CASE VIGNETTE #7: DEPRESSED ORTHODOX JEW

Sarah, a 58 year old divorced Jewish woman, is being seen by a psychiatrist for the treatment of depression and is receiving psychotherapy by another provider. This is the fifth session with her therapist, Steve. Progress has been slow, despite CBT and several trials of antidepressants prescribed by her psychiatrist. During therapy sessions, she often talks about the importance of her Jewish faith, rituals, and holidays. During therapy, Sarah frequently mentions to her therapist that he just doesn't understand or appreciate the importance of her religious faith or the rituals she engages in. Steve has taken a careful spiritual history and discovered that some of her beliefs and practices seem a bit strange (for example, prolonged religious fasts, accompanied by significant weight loss and anorexia). With her permission (written), Steve contacts her rabbi and asks him if he would be willing to see Sarah for religious counseling, mentioning some his concerns. Her rabbi agrees and an appointment is set up.

CASE VIGNETTE #8: ANXIOUS MUSLIM

Imam Ahmed has been counseling Mohammed, a 49 year old businessman and member of his mosque, who is suffering from severe anxiety. He has met with him at least a half-dozen times now. Ahmed has suggested several passages from the Qur'an to help relieve his anxiety, and has encouraged Mohammed to memorize, recite those passages, and meditate on them. He has also provided practical counsel to help guide Mohammed in responding to day-to-day life events. Despite this, Mohammed seems to worry about everything, focusing on his fear that on Judgement Day he will not be worthy of Paradise. He fears that his earlier lifestyle and many sins will outweigh the good deeds that he has done recently. Mohammed reports that he is beginning to wake up at night with panic attacks. Ahmed suggests that Mohammed see a psychiatrist (whom Ahmed knows and respects), and asks permission from Mohammed to speak with the psychiatrist. Mohammed agrees to make the appointment, and indicates that he would like Imam Ahmed to speak with the psychiatrist.

When should MHPs refer clients to pastoral care counselors, religious counselors, chaplains, or other clergy for counseling? Similarly, when should clergy refer a member of their congregation to a MHP and what kind of MHP? Each of the above case vignettes illustrates when referral is appropriate and necessary, and serves as a starting point for the recommendations below.

Referral to Clergy

When should a MHP refer a client to clergy for counseling? Who are appropriate clergy to refer to and what do they do? The timing of referral or decision to conduct co-therapy with clergy will depend on many factors. Such an action is usually necessary when religious issues are important to the client, interwoven into psychopathology, and the MHP feels uncomfortable in his or her knowledge of the client's faith tradition. This is especially important if there is a potential for conflict between the treatment (psychotherapy or medication) and the client's religious beliefs. The MHP has several options: (1) invite (with permission) the clergy to attend a session with the client, (2) refer the client for a single consultation with the clergy alone, (3) refer the client to clergy for multiple sessions (i.e., co-therapy), or if psychopathology is not severe, (4) completely transfer care of the client to clergy for ongoing counseling. The option the MHP chooses will depend on the severity of the client's condition, their relationship with the client, the complexity of religious issues, and the availability of clergy with counseling experience. Different types of clergy, along with their training and experience with counseling, are the following:

- *Pastoral Counselor*—A pastoral counselor is an ordained clergy and licensed mental health professional (with training at the master's or doctorate level) who provides pastoral care. Pastoral counselors not only usually specialize in a particular faith tradition, but often also provide counseling from a wide range of other religious perspectives.
- *Chaplain*—Chaplains have similar training as pastoral counselors. They are usually ordained clergy with a master's degree and additional training in clinical pastoral education that focuses on providing religious counsel and support to those with health problems. Chaplains, unlike pastoral counselors, are usually not licensed by the state, and so cannot provide "therapy" but rather only religious support and counsel. Although not licensed professional counselors, chaplains may be board certified by their national professional organization (Association of Professional Chaplains, American Association of Catholic Chaplains, etc.).
- *Religious Counselors*—These may be Christian counselors, Jewish counselors, or counselors from other faith traditions who are licensed professionals who provide therapy specifically to members of that tradition. They will often rely on counseling based on their holy scriptures. The American Association of Christian Counselors, for example, has a membership of nearly 50,000 worldwide (approximately half the size of the membership of the American Psychological Association and one-third *more* members than the American Psychiatric Association).
- *Community Clergy*—As noted earlier, community clergy (over 350,000 in the United States alone) provide an enormous amount of individual and marital counseling, equivalent to that provided by the entire membership of the American Psychological Association (Weaver, 1995; Koenig, 2005, pp. 173–174). Clergy may or may not have specific training in counseling, but many have extensive practical experience in doing so.

Referral to Mental Health Professional

When should community clergy, religious counselors, chaplains, or pastoral counselors refer a person to a MHP? Who are the different kinds of MHPs and what do they do? The timing of referral, as with referral to clergy, is especially important as certain emotional or psychotic disorders may increase risk of self-harm or harm to others. Many cases have appeared in the media of people who while receiving counseling from clergy have committed suicide or killed family members because they were not referred in a timely manner for medical treatment or hospitalization. Admittedly, most people with mild to moderate emotional or relationship problems will receive great benefit from counsel with their local clergy. However, there does come a time when referral to a specialized MHP becomes necessary. The time to refer is when clergy feel that the client is not responding to pastoral care, is worsening, has deep psychological problems, or there is evidence of suicidal thoughts, or loss of desire for living. Referral is also necessary when the client displays irrational or psychotic symptoms of any kind such as delusions, hallucinations, or loss of contact with reality. Most of the time, this will involve referral to see a psychiatrist who can prescribe medication or other biological treatments. These biological treatments may be lifesaving for the client, a family member, or others in the community. Furthermore, there are secular and religiously integrated psychotherapies that can get at dysfunctional cognitions and assumptions, deep underlying psychological conflicts, repressed emotions, and traumatic experiences that support and pastoral counseling may not be able to address. It is important, however, to know something about the particular MHP to whom a congregant or client is being referred, as the MHP's worldview is important and will affect to what extent the client's religious beliefs will be respected and honored (Peteet et al., 2016). Thus getting to know the MHP, either through personal encounters or through contact with members of the congregation who are familiar with the MHP, is often necessary. Who are the health professionals that clergy might refer to and what do they do?

- *General Medical Physician*—Any physician can prescribe medication to treat anxiety or depression (and even psychotic symptoms, though medical practitioners rarely do that). Nevertheless, this health professional is not specifically trained to deal with emotional or psychiatric problems and may not be skilled in prescribing medications for this purpose. If a client refuses to see a MHP, though, she or he may agree to see their medical doctor. The medical doctor may be able to convince the client to see a specialized MHP.
- *Psychiatrist*—A psychiatrist is a medical doctor who can prescribe medication or provide biological therapies such as electroconvulsive treatment, transcranial magnetic stimulation, and

other biological therapies for severe mental disorders. They can also admit a client to the hospital if their safety or the safety of others is in danger. Some psychiatrists also provide individual counseling.

- *Psychologist*—A psychologist is a doctor (PhD or PsyD) and licensed professional who can provide specialized psychotherapy for complex emotional or psychological issues. That therapy may be religiously integrated or secular in nature (usually secular).
- *Mental Health Counselor*—These are licensed professional therapists with a master's degree or doctorate in counseling who can provide various types of supportive counseling or administer specialized therapy to individuals or groups. Of course, this includes pastoral counselors and other licensed religious counselors such as Christian counselors.
- *Social Worker*—These are master's degree level licensed professional therapists who can provide various types of supportive counseling or administer specialized types of other therapy often focused on relationships within the family.

Thus, mental health professionals and clergy must work together, and for religious clients with mental health problems, both are often required.

SUMMARY AND CONCLUSIONS

The first and most important clinical application is taking a detailed spiritual history on every client seen by a mental health professional (or member of the congregation counseled by clergy). The spiritual history will provide the necessary background that will allow the therapist or religious counselor to address religious/spiritual issues in a sensitive, informed, and effective manner. Surveys indicate that the majority of mental health professionals now agree on the need for a spiritual history. Less agreed on, however, is the extent to which mental health professionals should perform spiritual interventions or become engaged in spiritual activities with clients. Least controversial among these is supporting the client's own religious or spiritual beliefs/behaviors already being used to cope with stressors. Support of these beliefs and practices, if healthy, will boost their ability to help clients make sense of and adjust to difficult life situations and traumatic experiences. More controversial are praying with clients (especially if the clinician initiates the prayer) and sharing the clinician's own religious beliefs with clients. These practices, while powerful if done with appropriate timing and in the right client, may also be viewed as coercive or proselytizing, which has no place in the professional therapeutic relationship. Providers of mental health care will need to distinguish religious/spiritual beliefs from psychotic delusions or other manifestations of psychopathology. Guidelines have been provided on how to accomplish this, particularly the involvement of family members (or sometimes clergy) as additional informants. Religion-specific treatments are briefly reviewed and resources provided for further information. Finally, working with or referral to clergy is recommended when religious issues are complex and interwoven with psychopathology, and referral to mental health professionals is encouraged when psychological issues are severe and complex. Cooperation between mental health professionals and clergy is essential to provide the best possible care to those struggling with mental health problems. In the United States, the Substance Abuse and Mental Health Services Administration has recommended that spiritual activities be included in mental illness recovery centers throughout the country. Yamada et al. (2014) describe how this is now being done in Los Angeles County, which serves as a model of how mental health and religious professionals can work together.

References

Best, M., Butow, P., & Olver, I. (2016). Doctors discussing religion and spirituality: A systematic literature review. *Palliative Medicine*, *30*, 327–337.

Cothran, M. M., & Harvey, P. D. (1986). Delusional thinking in psychotics: Correlates of religious content. *Psychological Reports*, *58*, 191–199.

CSTH. (2014). *Religiously-Integrated Cognitive Behavioral Therapy (RCBT) manuals and workbooks (including training video)*. Durham, NC: Duke University Center for Spirituality, Theology and Health Retrieved from http://www.spiritualityandhealth.duke.edu/index.php/religious-cbt-study/therapy-manuals.

Curlin, F. A., Lawrence, R. E., Odell, S., Chin, M. H., Lantos, J. D., Koenig, H. G., & Meador, K. G. (2007). Religion, spirituality, and medicine: Psychiatrists' and other physicians' differing observations, interpretations, and clinical approaches. *American Journal of Psychiatry*, *164*(12), 1825–1831.

Dagi, T. F. (1995). Prayer, piety, and professional propriety: Limits on religious expression in hospitals. *Journal of Clinical Ethics*, *6*, 274–279.

Getz, G. E., Fleck, D. E., & Strakowski, S. M. (2001). Frequency and severity of religious delusions in Christian patients with psychosis. *Psychiatry Research*, *103*(1), 87–91.

Gomi, S., Starnino, V. R., & Canda, E. R. (2014). Spiritual assessment in mental health recovery. *Community Mental Health Journal*, *50*(4), 447–453.

Hodge, D. R. (2013). Implicit spiritual assessment: An alternative approach for assessing client spirituality. *Social Work*, *58*(3), 223–230.

Hodge, D. R., & Horvath, V. E. (2011). Spiritual needs in health care settings: A qualitative meta-synthesis of clients' perspectives. *Social Work*, *56*(4), 306–316.

Hofmann, L., & Walach, H. (2011). Spirituality and religiosity in psychotherapy – a representative survey among German psychotherapists. *Psychotherapy Research*, *21*(2), 179–192.

Huguelet, P., Mohr, S., Betrisey, C., Borras, L., Gillieron, C., Marie, A. M., et al. (2011). A randomized trial of spiritual assessment of outpatients with schizophrenia: Patients' and clinicians' experience. *Psychiatric Services*, *62*, 79–86.

James, W. (1902). *Varieties of Religious Experience: A Study in Human Nature*. London, UK: Routledge (Centenary edition, 2002).

JCAHO. (January 1, 2016). Joint Commission for the Accreditation of Hospital Organizations Requirements. In *The Joint Commission, E-dition®*. Oak Brook, IL: Joint Commission Resources (Hospital and Ambulatory Versions).

Kelly, E. W., Jr. (1995). Spirituality and religion in counselor education: A national survey. *Counselor Education and Supervision, 33*, 227–237.

Kilicaslan, E. E., Acar, G., Eksioglu, S., Kesebir, S., & Tezcan, E. (2016). The effect of delusion and hallucination types on treatment response in schizophrenia and schizoaffective disorder. *Dusunen Adam, 29*(1), 29–35.

Koenig, H. G. (2005). *Faith and Mental Health*. Philadelphia, PA: Templeton Foundation Press.

Koenig, H. G. (2013). *Spirituality in patient care*. Philadelphia, PA: Templeton Foundation Press.

Koenig, H. G. (2017a). *Catholic Christianity and mental health: Beliefs research and applications*. Amazon: CreateSpace Publishing Platform.

Koenig, H. G. (2017b). *Protestant Christianity and mental health: Beliefs research and applications*. Amazon: CreateSpace Publishing Platform.

Koenig, H. G. (2017c). *Judaism and mental health: Beliefs research and applications*. Amazon: CreateSpace Publishing Platform.

Koenig, H. G. (2017d). *Hinduism and mental health: Beliefs research and applications*. Amazon: CreateSpace Publishing Platform.

Koenig, H. G. (2017e). *Buddhism and mental health: Beliefs research and applications*. Amazon: CreateSpace Publishing Platform.

Koenig, H. G., & Al Shohaib, S. (2014). *Health and well-Being in Islamic societies: Background, research, and applications*. New York, NY: Springer International.

Koenig, H. G., & Al Shohaib, S. (2017). *Islam and mental health: Beliefs research and applications*. Amazon: CreateSpace Publishing Platform.

Koenig, H. G., Perno, K., Erkanli, A., & Hamilton, T. (2017a). Effects of a 12-month educational intervention on clinicians' attitudes/practices regarding the screening spiritual history. *Southern Medical Journal, 110*(6), 412–418.

Koenig, H. G., Perno, K., & Hamilton, T. (2017b). Integrating spirituality into outpatient practice in the Adventist Health System. *Southern Medical Journal, 110*(1), 1–7.

Kristeller, J. L., Rhodes, M., Cripe, L. D., & Sheets, V. (2005). Oncologist Assisted Spiritual Intervention Study (OASIS): Patient acceptability and initial evidence of effects. *International Journal of Psychiatry in Medicine, 35*(4), 329–347.

Mathai, J., & North, A. (2003). Spiritual history of parents of children attending a child and adolescent mental health service. *Australasian Psychiatry, 11*(2), 172–174.

Moreira-Almeida, A., Koenig, H. G., & Lucchetti, G. (2014). Clinical implications of spirituality to mental health: Review of evidence and practical guidelines. *Revista Brasileira de Psiquiatria, 36*(2), 176–182.

Neeleman, J., & King, M. B. (1993). Psychiatrists' religious attitudes in relation to their clinical practice: A survey of 231 psychiatrists. *Acta Psychiatrica Scandinavia, 88*, 420–424.

Pearce, M. J. (2016). *Cognitive behavioral therapy for Christians with depression: A practical tool-based primer*. Conshohocken, PA: Templeton Foundation Press.

Pearce, M. J., & Chiaramonte, D. (2017). When a patient asks you to pray: What's a provider to do? *International Journal of Palliative Nursing, 23*(7), 108–109.

Pearce, M. J., Koenig, H. G., Robins, C. J., Nelson, B., Shaw, S. F., Cohen, H. J., & King, M. B. (2015). Religiously integrated cognitive behavioral therapy: A new method of treatment for major depression in patients with chronic medical illness. *Psychotherapy, 52*(1), 56–66.

Peteet, J. R., Rodriguez, V. B., Herschkopf, M. D., McCarthy, A., Betts, J., Romo, S., & Murphy, J. M. (2016). Does a therapist's world view matter? *Journal of Religion and Health, 55*, 1097–1106.

Pierre, J. M. (2001). Faith or delusion: At the crossroads of religion and psychosis. *Journal of Psychiatric Practice, 7*(3), 163–172.

Post, S. G., Puchalski, C. M., & Larson, D. B. (2000). Physicians and patient spirituality: Professional boundaries, competency, and ethics. *Annals of Internal Medicine, 132*(7), 578–583.

Post, B. C., & Wade, N. G. (2014). Client perspectives about religion and spirituality in group counseling. *The Counseling Psychologist, 42*(5), 601–627.

Rose, E. M., Westefeld, J. S., & Ansley, T. N. (2001). Spiritual issues in counseling: Clients beliefs and preferences. *Journal of Counseling Psychology*, *48*, 61–71.

Rosmarin, D. H., Pirutinsky, S., Green, D., & McKay, D. (2013). Attitudes toward spirituality/religion among members of the Association for Behavioral and Cognitive Therapies. *Professional Psychology: Research and Practice*, *44*(6), 424–433.

Siddle, R., Haddock, G., Tarrier, N., & Faragher, E. (2002). The validation of a religiosity measure for individuals with schizophrenia. *Mental Health, Religion and Culture*, *5*(3), 267–284.

Stanley, M. A., Bush, A. L., Camp, M. E., Jameson, J. P., Phillips, L. L., Barber, C. R., Zeno, D., Lomax, J. W., & Cully, J. A. (2011). Older adults' preferences for religion/spirituality in treatment of anxiety and depression. *Aging and Mental Health*, *15*(3), 334–343.

Weaver, A. J. (1995). Has there been a failure to prepare and support Parish-based clergy in their role as front-line community mental health workers? A review. *Journal of Pastoral Care*, *49*, 129–149.

Whitley, R. (2012). Religious competence as cultural competence. *Transcultural Psychiatry*, *49*(2), 245–260.

Yamada, A. M., Subica, A. M., Kim, M. A., Nguyen, K. V., Lim, C. S., & Mancuso, L. L. (2014). State of spirituality-infused mental health services in Los Angeles County wellness and client-run centers. *Administration and Policy in Mental Health and Mental Health Services Research*, *41*(6), 835–844.

Yip, K. (2003). Traditional Chinese religious beliefs and superstitions in delusions and hallucinations of Chinese schizophrenic patients. *International Journal of Social Psychiatry*, *49*(2), 97–111.

Zakaria, A., Moffic, S., & Peteet, J. R. (2018). *Islamophobia, Islam and psychiatry: Recognition, prevention, and treatment*. New York, NY: Springer.

CHAPTER

11

Evidence-Based Religious Interventions

"Evidence-based" means that there is objective evidence from randomized clinical trials (and to a lesser degree, from single-group experimental studies) demonstrating the efficacy of an intervention. Perhaps the most important clinical intervention by mental health professionals, often not recognized as an intervention per se, is taking the spiritual history. Simply asking questions about clients' religious or spiritual (R/S) beliefs and experiences may signal to the client that this topic is worthy of the therapist's attention and time to discuss, which may help to either affirm R/S's value in coping or bring R/S experiences to the surface so they can be processed more fully. Whatever the causal mechanisms, there is evidence that the spiritual history by itself may impact a person's mental health. For example, as noted in the last chapter, when oncology outpatients were randomly (alternatively) assigned to either a brief spiritual history by an oncologist or a control group, Kristeller, Rhodes, Cripe, and Sheets (2005) found that depressive symptoms and functional well-being both significantly increased among those receiving the spiritual history (compared to controls) when assessed three weeks later. Further research is needed on the impact of the *mental health spiritual history*, which to this author's knowledge has not yet been systematically studied. Before examining the evidence base for religious interventions, a description of the various approaches is necessary.

APPROACHES

Religious interventions for mental health problems include two basic types: (1) interventions that use religious beliefs/practices alone to affect mental health and (2) religious psychotherapies. Religious interventions of the first type include prayer with clients, religious discussions and guidance, various forms of Western or Eastern meditation, recitation

Religion and Mental Health. http://dx.doi.org/10.1016/B978-0-12-811282-3.00011-2

of sacred scriptures, and other religious practices. Religious interventions of the second type (religious psychotherapies) involve specific therapies that integrate a client's R/S beliefs into standard counseling or psychotherapy (i.e., secular techniques with an established evidence base). There is clearly some overlap between these two types of religious interventions, although that overlap is poorly defined. Approaches to the second type of religious intervention that involve religious/spiritual care, counseling, and psychotherapy can be divided into at least five types: (1) standard secular psychotherapy in religious clients that respects and supports their beliefs (basic care), (2) pastoral care and counseling, (3) religious counseling, (4) spiritually-integrated psychotherapy, and (5) religiously-integrated psychotherapy. All of these are differentiated from general "spiritual care" that might be provided to medical patients by non-chaplain healthcare professionals such as nurses or physicians (Koenig, 2013).

Secular Psychotherapy With Religious Clients

It is debatable whether this form of therapy should even be included as a type of religious psychotherapy. However, to be comprehensive, psychotherapy that touches on religious issues begins with standard secular psychotherapy in situations where religious issues are likely to come up, particularly when treating highly religious clients. The focus of therapy, here, is on cognitive, behavioral, interpersonal, or psychodynamic factors that cause mental health problems, not religion or spirituality. With religious patients, however, their beliefs are likely to affect and be affected by these treatments. Ignoring religious beliefs when conducting secular psychotherapy is simply not possible as religious patients are likely to repeatedly bring up these issues during therapy. The therapist may want to support healthy religious beliefs and challenge unhealthy ones. As indicated in Chapter 10, this must be done in a respectful manner that honors the beliefs that clients hold sacred. Proceeding in this manner is simply consistent with good clinical practice (GCP).

Pastoral Care

As noted in Chapter 10, this type of mental health treatment is provided by chaplains in hospitals (after receiving clinical pastoral education or CPE training) or by community clergy when counseling members of their congregation. "Spiritual directors" might also be included in this category. The latter are individuals who provide spiritual guidance, friendship, or companionship, a practice that arose out of the Catholic Church but has now expanded to other Christian denominations, Judaism, and Buddhism. Spiritual directors typically have a master's degree and have had formal training and supervision of some type. Pastoral care and spiritual direction are considered a form of "precounseling" that might take place prior to seeking care from a professional licensed counselor (below) (Montgomery, 2010).

Religious Counseling

In contrast to secular psychotherapy and pastoral care, religious counseling focuses on providing support and guidance utilizing the specific religious beliefs and practices of clients. As noted in Chapter 10, examples include Christian counseling or other types of religious and pastoral counseling. Christian counseling relies on methods rooted in traditional Christian practices, Biblical scriptures, and Bible study (Collins, 1988; Crabb, 1977; Tan, 1991; Tan, 2011a). Christian counselors are usually licensed professional counselors with a master's degree in mental health counseling or social work and additional special training in techniques that use Christian beliefs in the healing process. Techniques include prayer, teaching biblical concepts, emphasis on forgiveness, confrontation over sinful behaviors, use of guided religious imagery, religious meditation, claiming or praying for divine healing, deliverance or exorcism from the demonic, and more general therapeutic methods such as building a therapeutic alliance, intentional listening, solution-oriented therapy, person-centered therapy, and transactional therapy, all within a framework of Biblical teachings and Christian values.

With 50,000 members worldwide, the American Association of Christian Counselors (as noted in Chapter 10) is growing rapidly and is now nearly half the size of the American Psychological Association (AACC, 2017; APA, 2015). Besides Christian counseling, there are other forms of religious counseling including Jewish counseling (Friedman & Yehuda, 2016), Muslim or Islamic counseling (Rassoo, 2015), Buddhist counseling and psychotherapy (Ennenbach, 2015), and Hindu pastoral counseling and therapy (Udipi, 2015). The goals of each of these forms of religious counseling are to affirm religious beliefs that are helpful, correct erroneous beliefs, increase healthy interpersonal relationships, and help clients realize that they are persons of worth.

Pastoral counselors (as distinct from chaplains and community clergy who provide pastoral care) are licensed professional counselors who provide pastoral counseling from a variety of religious and spiritual perspectives, whatever the client requests. These individuals typically have master's or doctorate degrees in counseling, similar to other counselors, and also may have expertise in religiously/spiritually integrated psychotherapies.

Spiritually-Integrated Psychotherapy

According to psychologist Ken Pargament, "A spiritually-integrated psychotherapy is just that, integrated. It weaves greater sensitivity and explicit attention to the spiritual dimension into the process of psychotherapy. Spirituality can be interwoven into virtually any psychotherapeutic tradition—psychodynamic, cognitive-behavioral, family systems, humanistic, and existential" (Pargament, Murray-Swank, & Tarakeshwar, 2005, p. 161). Spiritually-integrated psychotherapy (SIP) is an approach to psychotherapy that integrates the spiritual dimension of a client's life into the therapy, where "spiritual" is defined as whatever is sacred to the person, where sacred involves that which touches on a person's "most profound of beliefs, practices, emotions, and relationships" (Pargament et al., 2005, p. 162). The sacred will often involve religion and God, but not always. The theoretical basis and practical framework for SIP has been laid out by Pargament in *Spiritually Integrated Psychotherapy: Understanding and Addressing the Sacred* (Pargament, 2011). However, there has been relative limited research examining the evidence for this type of therapy (see below).

Religiously-Integrated Psychotherapy

This approach to psychotherapy is necessarily religion-specific, as there is no general religiously integrated psychotherapy that addresses mental health problems in persons from all different religious faiths. Given the many different religions in the world, however, some limit needs to be placed on the number of specific religions that psychotherapy can be tailored to address. As most of the world's population is affiliated with one of the five major world religions of Christianity, Islam, Hinduism, Buddhism, and Judaism, one might limit religiously-integrated therapies to those faith traditions. However, in all forms of religiously integrated psychotherapy, the first session is spent identifying the specific religious beliefs of the client and the language used to express those beliefs, and then that language is used throughout the therapy (following a client-centered approach). Religious psychotherapies use an existing evidence-based secular psychotherapy framework and integrate the client's religious beliefs and practices into therapy (based on the sacred scriptures or teachings of the client's religion). For example, in conducting religiously- integrated cognitive behavioral therapy for depression in Christians (see below), scriptures from the Bible are used to challenge dysfunctional cognitions and underlying assumptions that are maintaining the depression, replacing them with healthy religious-based beliefs and behaviors that build self-esteem and promote positive social interactions (Pearce et al., 2015; Pearce, 2016).

The above discussion provides a breakdown of the types of religious or spiritual treatments that might be provided (see Sperry, 2016 for more information about these various approaches). What, then, is the evidence base that justifies the use of religious practices alone to benefit mental health or the integration of religious/spiritual beliefs and practices into psychotherapy?

THE EVIDENCE BASE

Studies on religious interventions have typically examined *efficacy*, i.e., whether an intervention produces benefit under ideal circumstances set up when conducting a clinical trial. Much less information is known about the *effectiveness* of religious intervention, i.e., whether they produce benefit under "real world" conditions in clinical settings, although there are now efforts underway to provide such data (Richards & Judd, 2017). The evidence base is now examined for each of the two types of religious interventions discussed earlier: (1) simple religious interventions targeting mental health outcomes and (2) religious psychotherapies.

Religious Interventions

Summarized below are examples of religious interventions whose efficacy in treating mental health problems has been examined in clinical trials, including meditation (mindfulness, transcendental, centering prayer, and other Christian forms), standard prayer (praying, listening to prayer, or being prayed for), watching a religious/spiritual video, listening to scripture recitation, ingesting Talbinah, and religious support/guidance. Individual studies are summarized here, most published since 2010 and many conducted in Muslim countries. Given the large number of studies examining Eastern forms of meditation or yoga, only meta-analyses of those studies are reported here.

In discussing the results of meta-analyses and individual clinical trials, it is important to understand the meaning of an "effect size" (ES). An ES is a quantitative measure of the clinical significance of the difference in the effect of an intervention compared to a controls without the intervention (or to those receiving another intervention). ESs can be expressed as a Pearson correlation (r), Cohen's d (d), Hedge's g (g), or several other ways. When expressed as a Pearson correlation (r), an ES of 0.10 is considered small, 0.30 moderate, and 0.50 or higher large. When expressed as a Cohen's d or Hedge's g, an ES of 0.20 is considered small, 0.50 moderate, and 0.80 or higher large. The ES is sometimes presented in positive numbers and sometimes in negative numbers, but it is the absolute value of the ES that is the difference in the treatment effect.

Meditation

Systematic reviews and meta-analyses of clinical trials have examined the efficacy of Buddhist-based mindfulness meditation (MM). With regard to standard MM, Eberth and Sedlmeier (2012) reported an effect size (r) of 0.27 averaged across all studies and mental health outcomes, measured by "the correlation between group membership—meditation vs. control group—and dependent variable," based on 39 studies. In other words, MM was found to have an overall moderate effect in terms of clinical significance. A meta-analysis of "mindfulness-based therapies" (MBT) that include MM as a central component was conducted by Khoury et al. (2013) for a wide range of mental health outcomes. They reported ESs (in this case, Hedge's g[1]) that ranged from $g = 0.55$ for pre–post comparisons (72 studies), to $g = 0.53$ for wait list control comparisons (67 studies), and to $g = 0.35$ for active treatment control comparisons (68 studies). In other words, the clinical effect of MBT was found to be small to moderate in size. Among studies comparing MBT to active treatment controls, Hedge's g was 0.22 when controls were other psychological treatments (35 studies). No difference ($g = -0.07$ in 9 studies) was found when comparing MBT to traditional CBT or behavioral therapies, and little or no difference ($g = 0.13$ in 3 studies) was found when comparing MBT to pharmacological treatments. A second more detailed review of 47 clinical trials examining MBT reported post-test ESs for improving anxiety of 0.38 (Cohen's d) at 8 weeks (95% CI = 0.12–0.64) and 0.22 at 3–6 months (95% CI = 0.02–0.43); for improving depression, ESs were 0.30 at 8 weeks (95% CI = 0.00–0.59) and 0.23 at 3–6 months (95% CI = 0.05–0.42); again, only modest evidence was found that MBT was better than any active treatment (drugs, exercise, and behavioral therapies) (Goyal et al., 2014).

There have also been meta-analyses of clinical trials examining transcendental meditation (TM) from the Hindu tradition. For example, Orme-Johnson and Barnes (2014) examined the effects of TM on trait anxiety, finding an average ES (Cohen's d) of −0.50 (95% CI = −0.70 to −0.30) when compared to an active alternative control treatment (10 studies), and −0.62 (95% CI = −0.82 to −0.43) when compared to treatment as usual (16 studies), especially in those with higher levels of anxiety. In other words, TM had a moderate to large effect size, depending on the quality of the control group to which it was compared. Cabral, Meyer, and Ames (2011) conducted a meta-analysis of yoga-based therapies for major psychiatric disorders, identifying 10 studies ($n = 343$) with a pooled ES of −3.25 (95% CI = −5.36 to −1.14, $p = 0.002$). Yoga therapies included Hatha yoga, Iyengar yoga, Sudarshan Kriya yoga, and several other integrated or alternative forms of yoga and meditation, and 8 of the 10 studies focused on depression or anxiety. However, in describing the studies, authors were often not clear on what the control groups received, other than that it was not a yoga-based therapy (which means that controls may have received usual care or no treatment, which would explain the very large average ES).

In contrast, few studies have examined the efficacy of Western forms of meditation such as contemplative prayer (Finney & Malony, 2001),

[1]Hedge's g is similar to Cohen's d, but Hedge's g is usually preferred with small sample sizes.

mindfulness meditation from a Christian perspective (Tan, 2011b), or centering prayer (Knabb, 2012). However, at least two clinical trials involving a Christian adaptation of mindfulness meditation (Ford, 2016) and a Christian devotional meditation (Kim, 2014) have reported promising results when compared to active control groups (standard MM or progressive relaxation, respectively). As noted in Chapter 9, this is a huge research gap that needs filling given that Buddhist-based MM is now regularly prescribed for Christian, Muslim, and Jewish clients, without offering alternative approaches to meditation from their own faith traditions (which does not follow the good clinical practice of client-center treatment).

Prayer

Several studies have examined the effects of in-person prayer on mental health outcomes in medical or surgical patients, particularly those with depression or anxiety. For example, Boelens, Reeves, Replogle, and Koenig (2009) randomized 63 primary care medical patients with depression and anxiety symptoms to either six weeks of in-person Christian prayer conducted by a single lay prayer minister or to a wait listed "treatment as usual" control group. The first prayer session was 90 minutes, and the remaining five sessions were 60 minutes each. A history was taken as part of the first session to identify the particular areas for which the participant needed prayer. There was no psychotherapy involved, and direct person-to-person prayer was the only intervention. During the prayer sessions, the prayer minister prayed and was often joined by the participant in praying. Prayers consisted of different forms such as prayer to release hurts, prayer for blessings on those who had offended them, and so forth. Results after six weeks indicated a significant reduction in both depression and anxiety, along with increases in daily spiritual experiences and optimism ($p < 0.01$ compared to controls). These effects were maintained at 1 month following the last prayer session and at 12 months as well (Boelens, Reeves, Replogle, & Koenig, 2012). Those in the wait list control group showed no change prior to being crossed over.

Dehghani Kh, Dehghani, Zarezadeh, and Bs (2012) examined the efficacy of Muslim prayer on anxiety level assessed by Spielberger's State-Trait Anxiety Inventory among mothers in Iran who had a child hospitalized with cancer. Sixty women (mean age 36 years) were randomized to either a prayer group or a "treatment as usual" control group. Women in the intervention group were taught to pray three times a day for 10 minutes each (at the time of Azan preferably and in the hospital mosque), read the Qur'an, remember God by Zikr, attend the hospital mosque, and listen to the Qur'an being recited using a mobile device. Anxiety did not differ between intervention and control groups at baseline. After three weeks, results indicated a significant difference in anxiety scores between intervention and control groups (p = 0.001). Anxiety decreased significantly in the prayer group (within-group change p = 0.001), while there was no change in controls.

Beiranvand, Noaparast, Eslamizade, and Saeedikia (2014) examined the effects of listening to recited Muslim prayer on pain severity in Iranian women following C-section. Investigators randomized 160 Muslim women who had recently undergone C-section with mild pain (visual analogue scale pain level 1–3 out of 10) to either 20 minutes of listening to a recited prayer meditation (headphones on) (n = 80) or to a control group (headphones off). The prayer was "Ya man esmoho davaa va zekroho shafa, Allahomma salle ala mohammad va ale mohammad" (no English interpretation provided). Pain intensity was assessed before, during, and 30 minutes, 60 minutes, 3 hours, and 6 hours after listening to prayer meditation. Results indicated no difference in pain level between the two groups prior to, during, or 30 and 60 minutes after the prayer meditation. However, at 3 hours and 6 hours, pain was significantly better in the prayer meditation group compared to controls (p = 0.003); in addition, there was less postoperative nausea and vomiting ($p < 0.001$) and greater relaxation ($p < 0.001$) among those in the prayer group.

Jafari et al. (2013) examined the effects of a 6-session prayer intervention for improving quality of life (QOL) among women in Iran undergoing radiation therapy for breast cancer. Participants (n = 65) were randomized to either the intervention or a control group that received routine management and educational programs (treatment as usual). Participants in the spiritual intervention received usual care plus the spiritual intervention, which consisted of relaxation and meditation, placing their situation under God's control, imagining God's presence with them, communicating with God, focusing on their relationship with God (and relationship with others), and praying to God for help (prayer therapy). QOL (assessed by the widely used EORTC QLQ-C30) was evaluated before and after six weeks of the spiritual therapy. Overall QOL increased from 44.4 to 68.6 in the intervention group ($p < 0.01$), while there was no significant change in the control group. Pre–post differences at the 6-week follow-up indicated a large ES for the intervention group (d = 2.02, 95% CI = 1.44–2.61) and little or no change in the control group (d = 0.07, 95% CI = −0.42 to 0.56).

Viewing Spiritual Video

McCauley, Haaz, Tarpley, Koenig, and Bartlett (2011) at Johns Hopkins and Duke Universities randomized older medical patients (mean age 66 years) to either watching a half-hour video (n = 45) or to an attention control group (n = 40). Those in the intervention group viewed during the next 4 weeks a video titled "Plans to Prosper: A Patient Guide to Faith and Health," which featured brief discussions of spirituality and health by a panel of physician researchers. In addition, patients completed a workbook. The video focused on five themes: trusting that a Higher Being had a plan and purpose for life events; cleaning house (getting rid of destructive habits); giving thanks to God (appreciating life's blessings); helping others (finding faith-based purpose in life); and asking for help (social and spiritual support from their faith community). Those in the control group watched an educational video focused on reducing cardiac risk factors. Neither intervention required additional clinician time. Over a 5- to 8-week period, energy level increased significantly in the intervention group that watched the spiritual video (pre–post difference $p = 0.02$), while there was no change in the education control group. There was also a trend toward decreased health distress in the group watching the spiritual video ($p = 0.09$). No significant differences were found with regard to pain level, mood, health perceptions, illness intrusiveness, or self-efficacy. Investigators concluded that simply watching a 28-minute video and filling out a workbook resulted in a significant increase in energy among patients with chronic illness.

Qur'an Recitation

As noted in earlier chapters, at least two randomized clinical trials have examined the effects of listening to the Qur'an being recited on anxiety and depression levels in Iranian patients receiving hemodialysis (Babamohamadi et al., 2017; Babamohamadi, Sotodehasl, Koenig, Jahani, & Ghorbani, 2015). In both of these studies, participants were randomized to either an untreated control group or a group that listened to Surah Ya Sin, the 36th surah of the Qur'an, which was recited by a Shateri reader (this surah is considered the "heart" of the Qur'an by many theologians in Iran). Those in the intervention group listened to these verses three times a week for 1 month using MP3 players with headphones, each time for 20 minutes total (5 minutes before dialysis and continued until 15 minutes after the start of dialysis). ESs for between-group differences were large ($d = 1.03$ for anxiety symptoms and $d = 0.85$ for depressive symptoms). For a further explanation of why listening to Qur'an recitation might benefit mental health, see Mahjoob, Nejati, Hosseini, and Bakhshani (2016).

Talbinah Intervention

Badrasawi, Shahar, Manaf, and Haron (2013) examined the effects of ingesting Talbinah on depressive symptoms in 30 depressed older adults in Malaysia. Talbinah is barley syrup cooked with milk and sweetened by honey. In Islam, according to a Hadith by Al-Bukhari, "Aisha [the wife of the Prophet Mohammad] used to recommend At-Talbina for the sick and for such a person as grieved over a dead person. She used to say, "I heard Allah's Apostle saying, 'At-Talbina gives rest to the heart of the patient and makes it active and relieves some of his sorrow and grief'." Participants were 21 men and 9 women institutionalized at a long-term care facility (average age 67 years) with Geriatric Depression Scale (GDS-R-12) scores of 3 or higher. They were randomized to the intervention group (initially $n = 18$) or an untreated control group (initially $n = 18$), with 6 dropouts. Those in the intervention group were given one serving of Talbinah on a daily basis in addition to their regular diet for three weeks. After the 3-week period, participants in the intervention group were withdrawn from Talbinah feedings and underwent a one-week washout, after which those in the control group were given three weeks of Talbinah (crossover trial). Depression, anxiety, stress, and mood measures (standard scales) were assessed at baseline and 3, 4, and 7 weeks of follow-up. Results indicated a significant decrease (pre–post) in the intervention group on depressive symptoms, stress, total mood disturbance, anxiety, tension, dejection, anger/hostility, fatigue, and confusion/bewilderment symptoms. No significant changes (pre–post) were found in the control group (all outcome measures were self-administered).

Religious Interventions in Surgery Patients

Hosseini, Salehi, Khoshknab, Rokofian, and Davidson (2013) randomized 66 Iranian patients undergoing coronary artery bypass graft surgery to either a preoperative religious intervention or a control group receiving usual care. The intervention consisted of five 45–60 minute spiritual/religious sessions (delivered to groups of 5–7 participants each) on five consecutive days during the week prior to surgery. The intervention, which was entirely religious, focused on verses from the Qur'an and Hadith, trusting and relying on Allah, focusing on the blessings of Allah, remembering Allah and reading the Qur'an, and making supplication to Allah (Du'aa). The control group received routine nursing care, including routine perioperative care involving physical care and emotional reassurance. The ethics committee at the hospital, however, required that the control group also receive "some spiritual care" prior to surgery and receive a "condensed version" of the intervention postoperatively. The primary outcome was anxiety measured by the Hamilton Anxiety Scale (HAS), which was administered at baseline and 2 hours prior to surgery. There were no differences in anxiety level or any other sociodemographic or health characteristics at baseline between intervention and control groups. Pre–post measures of anxiety revealed a decline of anxiety in the intervention group (31.9 to 19.5 on the HAS, $p < 0.001$) compared to a significant increase in anxiety in the control group 31.0 to 43.3, $p < 0.001$). As there were no significant between-group differences at baseline, a simple T-test was used to compare postintervention anxiety levels between groups, which indicated a significant difference (19.5 vs. 43.3, $p < 0.001$).

In another study conducted in Iran, Nasiri, Fayazi, Ghaderi, Naseri, and Adarvishi (2014) examined the effects of reciting the phrases Allahu Akbar ("God is the greatest"), Alhamdulilah ("all praise and thanks to God"), and Subhan Allah ("glorious is God") on pain level during the three days following CABG surgery. Researchers reported significant differences between intervention and control groups on all three days ($p < 0.01$). Controls received no intervention, and pain level was assessed blind to treatment group.

Admittedly, many of these studies were of poor quality, comparing effects of religious interventions to control groups without treatment or receiving usual care, and in several studies only reporting within-group pre–post differences (rather than between-group differences). Researcher allegiance is also likely an issue in several of these studies. Nevertheless, the large ESs reported from these simple religious interventions are noteworthy.

Religious Psychotherapy

Treatments that include or integrate the client's religious beliefs into standard secular forms of psychotherapy exist primarily for depression, anxiety, and PTSD. There is also at least anecdotal evidence that spiritual-based group therapies may be beneficial in psychotic patients (Kehoe, 1998; Subica & Yamada, 2017). There have been at least six systematic reviews or meta-analyses published thus far examining the efficacy of religious or spiritual psychotherapies or counseling (Anderson et al., 2015; Gonçalves, Lucchetti, Menezes, & Vallada, 2015; McCullough, 1999; Post & Wade, 2009; Smith, Bartz, & Scott Richards, 2007; Worthington, Hook, Davis, & McDaniel, 2011).

In a meta-analytic review of "religion-accommodative counseling" (RAC), Michael McCullough (1999) identified five studies (a total of 111 clients) that compared standard counseling techniques with RAC. Results indicated no evidence that RAC was more or less efficacious than standard approaches (ES $d = 0.18$, 95% CI = −0.20 to 0.56). McCullough concluded that the implementation of RAC was a matter of patient preference rather than improved efficacy. Smith et al. (2007) conducted a meta-analysis of 31 intervention studies (a total of 1845 clients) that involved "religious and spiritual adaptations to psychotherapy," finding an average ES that was considerably more robust than McCullough had reported ($d = 0.56$, 95% CI = 0.43–0.70), which indicated a moderate to strong effect. However, these investigators included studies with untreated control groups, quasi-experimental designs, and single-group experimental studies (pre–post designs). The largest effects were found in clients being seen for mental health problems (6 studies, $d = 0.75$), single-group experimental studies (7 studies, $d = 0.78$), trials that examined well-being as the outcome (4 studies, $d = 0.96$), and group therapy (22 studies, $d = 0.58$). The most efficacious interventions were those teaching spiritual concepts (14 studies, $d = 0.69$), those *not* using religious imagery or meditation ($d = 0.65$), and those using religious bibliotherapy (9 studies, $d = 0.61$).

Post and Wade (2009) reviewed research in three areas: (1) the religion/spirituality (R/S) of therapists, (2) the feelings of clients about discussing R/S issues in therapy, and (3) R/S interventions. With regard to the first area (4 studies), they concluded that (a) psychologists are much less R/S than clients; (b) students receive minimal training in R/S interventions; (c) R/S problems often emerge gradually during the course of therapy; and (d) the further a religious belief is from mainstream Christianity, the higher the rating of psychopathology (studies were primarily in Christians). Concerning the second area of client preference (7 studies), researchers found that (a) highly conservative Christians are significantly more likely to expect their secular counselor to use religious interventions; (b) 20% of clients indicate significant distress related to R/S concerns; (c) R/S discussions are most helpful when client-initiated; (d) most effective interventions involve those referencing scripture, teaching spiritual concepts, encouraging forgiveness, prompting involvement in religious community, and assessing client spirituality; (e) most religious clients report that despite initial expectations, help from secular therapists is positive; (f) a majority (63%) indicate that discussing religious concerns in therapy is appropriate and many (55%) want to do so in their therapy; and (g) clients expect the therapist to bring up the subject of prayer, especially those for whom prayer is important. With regard to efficacy of R/S interventions, the authors mainly cited the reviews of McCullough (1999) and Smith et al. (2007), and describe a few studies published since 2005, including one of their own that found that congruence between client's and therapist's religious commitment is a key factor in both the strength of the therapeutic alliance and the benefits of the R/S intervention (Wade, Worthington, & Vogel, 2007).

In perhaps the most comprehensive review to date, Worthington et al. (2011) conducted a meta-analysis of 51 samples from 46 studies ($n = 3290$) examining the efficacy of religious accommodative and nonreligious spiritual (R/S) therapies. These interventions were compared to a control condition, alternative treatment, or a subset of studies using a "dismantling design" (R/S and alternative treatment had same theoretical orientation and duration of treatment). Overall, when compared to no treatment controls, the ESs of R/S therapies were moderate for psychological ($d = 0.45$) and spiritual ($d = 0.51$) posttest outcomes. When compared to alternative treatments, results indicated a small ES for psychological outcomes (posttest d = 0.26) and somewhat larger effect for spiritual outcomes (*d* = 0.41); follow-up outcomes were somewhat smaller (*d* = 0.25 for psychological and *d* = 0.32 for spiritual). The ES for R/S treatments compared to alternative treatments with the same theoretical orientation and duration of treatment was small (posttest *d* = 0.13, i.e., no practical or statistical difference) for psychological outcomes and somewhat larger for spiritual outcomes (*d* = 0.33), with beneficial effects maintained at follow-up. Researchers also noted that there was evidence that R/S treatments were more effective in highly R/S clients than in those who were less R/S, citing the Wade et al. (2007) study noted above. Moderator analyses indicated that the efficacy of religious accommodative therapies was similar to those of nonreligious spiritual interventions.

More recently, Gonçalves et al. (2015) conducted a systematic review and meta-analysis of religious and spiritual interventions (RSI) conducted between 2005 and 2013. This review was limited to randomized clinical trials of RSI considered to be "'messages to health' framed by themes of spiritual relevance." Those could involve taking care of the body, discussions of moral or ethical values, or meditation (i.e., inclusion criteria were not very clear, partly due to language problems in this Brazilian review). A total of 23 studies were thus identified, focusing on depressive symptoms ($n = 15$), anxiety symptoms ($n = 14$), PTSD ($n = 5$), alcohol or drug use/abuse ($n = 2$), and social function ($n = 1$). The ES (standard mean difference) was −0.43 (95% CI = −0.61 to −0.25, $p < 0.001$) for anxiety symptoms (meditation and psychotherapy), but was only −0.11 (95% CI = −0.25 to 0.03, $p = 0.12$) for depressive symptoms.

Anderson et al. (2015) conducted a systematic review and meta-analysis of randomized controlled trials of faith-based adaptations of "bona fide psychological therapies for depression or anxiety," identifying 16 such studies up through January 2014 (i.e., studies published between 1984 and 2013). All studies used cognitive or cognitive behavioral models that were faith-adapted (F-CBT). Effect sizes (Hedge's g) were reported by outcome and study type. Study types were Christian CBT, spiritual CBT,[2] and Muslim CBT. For depression where F-CBT was compared to untreated controls (wait list, placebo, or treatment as usual), the average post-test ES for Christian CBT (2 studies, $n = 44$) was $g = -1.40$ (95% CI = −2.09 to −0.70, $p < 0.0001$); for spiritual CBT (2 studies, $n = 96$), ES was $g = -0.48$ (95% = −0.88 to −0.07, $p < 0.02$); and for Muslim CBT (2 studies, $n = 164$), ES was $g = -0.30$, 95% CI = −0.60 to 0.01, $p = 0.06$). For depression where

[2] "Spiritual CBT" is described as using value assessments based on religious/spiritual views; encouraging participation in religious activities; reframing situations using religious ideas of acceptance; and using spiritual strategies to try to cope with and overcome negative cognitions.

F-CBT was compared to standard CBT, the average posttest ES for Christian CBT (4 studies, $n = 124$) was $g = -0.59$, 95% CI = −0.95 to −0.23); for spiritual CBT (1 study, $n = 43$), ES was $g = -0.55$ (95% CI = −1.17 to 0.06); and for Muslim CBT (1 study, $n = 32$), ES was g = −0.31 (95% CI = −1.01 to 0.39). Three studies (2 for spiritual and 1 for Muslim) examined follow-up ESs (4 weeks to 12 weeks posttest); in both spiritual CBT studies, ES decreased to nonsignificance, whereas in the Muslim CBT study ($n = 31$), ES remained robust ($g = -2.75$, 95% CI = −3.76 to −1.73).

In the Anderson et al. (2015) review, predefined study criteria for studies examining anxiety outcomes were not met, so meta-analysis was not performed. However, when compared to control conditions, the posttest ES for Christian CBT (1 study, $n = 43$) was $g = -0.79$ (95% CI = −1.42 to −0.17); for Muslim CBT (3 studies, n's from 62 to 165), ESs ranged from $g = -1.02$ (95% CI = −1.55 to −0.49) to +0.14 (95% CI = −0.16 to 0.45); for Jewish CBT (1 study, $n = 83$), ES was $g = -0.40$ (95% CI = −0.84 to 0.04); and for Taoist CBT (1 study, $n = 87$), ES was $g = -0.87$ (95% CI = −1.31 to −0.43). One Muslim CBT study compared to standard CBT ($n = 46$) reported a strong posttest ES ($g = -1.58$, 95% CI = −2.25 to −0.91). Two studies examined follow-up effect sizes at 6–12 weeks, with the Jewish CBT study ($n = 73$) reporting a persistent effect ($g = -0.99$, 95% CI = −1.50 to −0.48), but in the Muslim CBT study ($n = 62$) the effect diminished to nonsignificance ($g = -0.27$, 95% CI = −0.77 to 0.23).

The authors concluded that while faith-adapted CBT outperformed both control conditions and standard CBT for the treatment of depression (with broadly similar results for anxiety), studies were at risk for various biases, particularly researcher or therapist allegiance (i.e., the principle investigator or therapists were biased toward or favored one treatment over another; in reality, this is a problem in all randomized clinical trials of psychological interventions).

Recent Studies

A number of recent studies have examined the efficacy of religiously or spiritually-integrated psychotherapies for the treatment of depression and anxiety disorders, or have proposed such treatments for further study. These are now described.

Spiritually-Integrated Psychotherapy

Koszycki, Bilodeau, Raab-Mayo, and Bradwejn (2014) examined the efficacy of a multifaith spiritual intervention for generalized anxiety disorder (GAD, assessed by Hamilton Anxiety Rating Scale) compared to supportive therapy (control) in a small randomized clinical trial involving 23 participants (11 = intervention, 12 = control condition). The intervention, taking a Buddhist approach, consisted of 12 individual sessions that provided a rationale for the spiritual approach, utilized the power of forgiveness, encouraged mindfulness, sought to awaken a spiritual vision, recognized the sacred in all things, encouraged relinquishment of attachments, cultivated spiritual practices, focused on ethical living, cultivated generosity and service to others, and sought wisdom in nature, silence, and solitude. Results indicated significant between-group differences in reducing anxiety symptoms (posttest $d = 1.50$, 95% CI = 0.70–2.58) and worry ($d = 0.90$, 95% CI = 0.05–1.80), improving overall severity of distress ($d = 1.64$, 95% CI = 0.70–2.58), and increasing tolerance for uncertainty ($d = 1.04$, 95% CI = 0.17–1.92). Three-month follow-up indicated that the intervention group experienced significantly lower anxiety symptoms compared to the control group on the Hamilton scale ($d = 0.98$, 95% CI = 0.11–1.84), on the Beck Anxiety Inventory ($d = 1.18$, 95% CI = 0.29–2.07), and on overall severity of symptoms ($d = 0.86$, 95 CI = 0.003–1.71).

Ebrahimi, Neshatdoost, Mousavi, Asadollahi, and Nasiri (2013) and Ebrahimi, Nasiri-Dehsorkhi, and Mousavi (2015) examined the effects of a spiritually-integrated psychotherapy (SIP), standard CBT, and medication therapy in 62 Iranian adults aged 20 to 65 years with dysthymic disorder. Participants were randomized to medical-treatment only ($n = 15$), CBT ($n = 16$), SIP ($n = 16$), and a wait list control group ($n = 15$). The intervention involved presenting a religious viewpoint for explaining the development of depression, and then utilizing cognitive, behavioral, and emotional spiritual strategies with religious content to change thinking, behavior, and mood, based on Islamic teachings. Eight 45-minute weekly sessions were conducted. Standard medical treatment for dysthymia was instituted in the medication-only group. The CBT group received eight 45-minute weekly sessions of CBT (similar to the treatment received by the SIP group). The primary outcome was dysfunctional attitudes (Dysfunctional Attitudes Scale) and depressive symptoms (Beck Depression Inventory) assessed at baseline, 1 month, 2 months (post-test), and 3 months later. Results indicated that SIP improved depressive symptoms more than did medication ($p < 0.05$), but was not significantly different from CBT. SIP was also significantly more efficacious in reducing dysfunctional attitudes compared to both the medication-only and the CBT groups (both $p < 0.05$). Researchers concluded that psychotherapy enriched by religious teachings was efficacious in treating depressive symptoms and altering dysfunctional attitudes in dysthymic disorder.

Other individual and group-based spiritually-integrated psychotherapies have shown promise in improving QOL in breast cancer patients, improving images of God in healthy adults, and increasing QOL and spiritual well-being in patients with eating disorder when examined using qualitative methods, but have not been subject to quantitative analysis in a randomized clinical trial (Lea, Richards, Sanders, McBride, & Allen, 2015; Olson et al., 2016; Rettger et al., 2015).

Religiously-Integrated Cognitive Behavioral Therapy

Koenig et al. (2015) examined the effects of religiously-integrated cognitive behavioral therapy (RCBT) compared to conventional secular CBT (CCBT) for depression in clients with chronic medical illness. In this multisite clinical trial, 132 participants with major depressive disorder were randomized to ten 50-minute sessions over 12 weeks of either RCBT ($n = 65$) or CCBT ($n = 67$) and followed up at 4, 8, 12, and 24 weeks from baseline. Depressive symptoms over time were assessed using the Beck Depression Inventory-II (BDI-II). Five versions of RCBT (Christian, Jewish, Muslim, Buddhist, and Hindu) were developed and manualized by experts in these faith traditions. Eight master's level licensed therapists delivered the intervention by telephone (given that participants were chronically ill and would have had difficulty coming into a therapist's office). RCBT was a manual-based intervention using a conventional CBT manual as a template. The primary difference between RCBT and CCBT was that religious rationales were used to challenge dysfunctional cognitions/underlying assumptions and to change behavior (based on the religious scriptures of each faith tradition). Both treatments were broadly spiritual in nature, and included an emphasis on social engagement, purpose and meaning in life, forgiveness, gratitude, and altruism. RCBT included prayer and meditation from the client's faith tradition; therefore, to make these two treatments as similar as possible, mindfulness-based meditation was included in the CCBT intervention (Table 11.1 summarizes the RCBT intervention).

Results at the 12-week primary endpoint indicated that both RCBT and CCBT reduced depressive symptoms from baseline to follow-up ($d = 3.02$ for RCBT and $d = 2.39$ for CCBT)[3] such that over half of participants went into full remission by the 24-week follow-up. No significant difference was found in treatment effect between RCBT and CCBT (group by time interaction $B = 0.54$, SE = 0.64, $t = 0.85$, p = 0.40, Cohen's $d = 0.12$, slightly favoring RCBT). Client religiosity interacted with treatment group such that those who were more religious at baseline were more likely to respond to RCBT than to CCBT ($B = -0.10$, SE = 0.05, $t = -1.99$, p = 0.048). Highly religious clients receiving RCBT were also somewhat more likely to comply with treatment compared to those who were less religious (85.7% vs. 65.9%, p = 0.10). While not powered as a noninferiority trial, this study suggests that RCBT is as effective as CCBT in treating depressed patients with chronic medical illness, particularly among those who are more religious.

We have developed and made available versions of RCBT for Christian, Jewish, Muslim, Buddhist, and Hindu clients (CSTH, 2014). Likewise, other investigators have developed religiously-integrated psychotherapy for Muslim (Abu Raiya & Pargament, 2010) and Jewish clients (Milevsky & Eisenberg, 2012).

[3] Again, a Cohen's $d > 0.80$ indicates a large effect.

TABLE 11.1 Religiously-Integrated Cognitive Behavioral Therapy by Session

Session 1: Assessment and introduction to RCBT; conduct generalized assessment (religious and nonreligious) and introduce therapy model
Session 2: Behavioral activation (walking by faith); review homework assignments, finalize religious assessment, and explain mastery/pleasure worksheets to increase pleasant events
Session 3: Identifying unhelpful thoughts (battlefield of the mind); introduce cognitive processing and discuss alternative ways of responding to negative automatic thoughts, beliefs, and expectations in light of the client's personal value system and goals
Session 4: Challenging unhelpful thoughts (bringing all thoughts captive); reinforce cognitive processing, emphasize discovering alternative beliefs and generating behavioral experiments
Session 5: Dealing with loss of health, functional independence, identity, relationships, and emphasizing the use of religious resources to understand and make sense of those losses
Session 6: Coping with spiritual struggles; review homework using spiritual strategies to combat loss; discuss spiritual struggles, introduce the concepts of gratitude and altruism
Session 7: Gratitude, particularly religious gratitude; give exercises to practice gratitude
Session 8: Altruism and generosity; review gratitude exercises; introduce the notion of expressing religious gratitude by practicing altruism
Session 9: Stress-related and spiritual growth; "look for the positives" through a series of benefit-finding exercises
Session 10: Hope and relapse prevention; review the client's experience with benefit finding exercises and how they affected their beliefs, feelings, and behavior; introduce topic of hope as a general way of being that results from using religious cognitive and behavioral strategies; discuss how to maintain gains in therapy through involvement in faith community (receiving and giving support)

Source: Ciarrocchi, J. W., Schechter, D., Pearce, M. J., & Koenig, H. G. (2014). *Religious cognitive behavioral therapy (Christian version): 10-session treatment manual for depression in clients with chronic physical illness.* Durham, North Carolina: Duke University Center for Spirituality, Theology and Health (complete manual and workbooks available from http://www.spiritualityandhealth.duke.edu/index.php/religious-cbt-study/therapy-manuals).

Spiritually-Integrated Cognitive Processing Therapy

On the horizon is a new religious psychotherapy called religiously/spiritually-integrated cognitive processing therapy (SICPT) for moral injury in PTSD (Table 11.2). Given the role that moral injury (MI) may play in blocking treatment response in PTSD, a religious/spiritual approach to addressing MI would seem logical and obvious. Indeed, all major religions have had to deal with MI resulting from war. This has been

TABLE 11.2 Spiritually-Integrated Cognitive Processing Therapy (SICPT) for Moral Injury in the Setting of PTSD (Session by Session)

Session 1: Introduce moral injury (MI) topic, rationale, and goals for SICPT; provide "stuck points" handout; briefly review trauma; overview treatment sessions; assign impact statement (IS)
Session 2: Meaning of the event and spirituality; have client read IS; discuss meaning of IS; discuss client's spirituality; identify connection between events, thoughts, and feelings; assign ABC sheets
Session 3: Spiritual resources and MI; review ABC worksheets; discuss spiritual resources (including spiritual community); introduce kind attention/compassion for inner conflict; begin to address spiritual/religious struggles if these are present
Session 4: Values, kind attention, and compassion; review ABC worksheets; set intention for kind attention/compassion; introduce spiritual distress/grief; introduce spiritually challenging questions worksheet
Session 5: Challenging questions and spiritual distress; review spiritually challenging questions worksheet; review spiritual distress/grief, and lament; discuss guilt; introduce ritual confession/acknowledgment
Session 6: Confession ritual and problematic thinking; review problem thinking worksheet and spiritual ritual of confession; introduce stages of self/others/God's forgiveness
Session 7: Forgiveness I and challenging beliefs; review challenging beliefs and forgiveness worksheets; introduce REACH forgiveness steps; introduce trust for self/others/God
Session 8: Forgiveness II and trust; address forgiveness/trust stuck points; discuss judgment; review REACH worksheets; introduce making amends; introduce esteem for self/others/God
Session 9: Esteem and making amends; review making amends/esteem-related stuck points; review verbal blessing worksheet; introduce power/control issues related to self/others/God
Session 10: Power, control, and spiritual discrepancies; discuss power/control and self-blame; introduce intimacy issues related to self/others/God; introduce spiritual partnerships
Session 11: Intimacy and spiritual partnerships; discuss reactions to intimacy/spiritual community; introduce safety; introduce posttraumatic growth and spiritual growth
Session 12: Safety and posttraumatic/spiritual growth; identify safety issues, assumptions, remaining stuck points; have client read initial impact statement again; review treatment and client's progress

Source: Pearce, M. J., Haynes, K. N., Currier, J. M., & Koenig, H. G. (2017). *Spiritually-integrated cognitive processing therapy.* Durham, NC: Duke University Center for Spirituality, Theology and Health. Appendix to Resick et al. (2014). *Cognitive processing therapy: Veteran/Military version—Therapist's manual.* Washington, DC: Veterans Administration.

true for thousands of years, and rituals for addressing these issues have been developed. Secular CPT is now the standard psychological therapy for treating PTSD, and SICPT utilizes a CPT framework to integrate clients' religious/spiritual resources into the treatment. We believe that this approach will substantially increase the effectiveness of CPT in the treatment of MI, PTSD, and associated comorbidities (depression, anxiety, relationship problems, etc.). Plans are now in place to pilot test this intervention in a single-group experimental study, and following that, a small randomized clinical trial comparing SICPT to CPT and pastoral care (the 3rd arm provided by chaplains). These studies are preliminary to a large clinical trial planned for the future. A spiritually integrated version will be tested along with versions specific to the religious beliefs of clients (Koenig et al., 2017).

SPECIFIC TECHNIQUES

Although the procedures for conducting some religious/spiritual interventions have been briefly described above, further details and practical suggestions on how to integrate client's religious beliefs/practices into both individual and group therapies have been provided by psychologists long active in this field (Pargament, 2011; Pearce et al., 2015; Pearce, 2016; Post & Wade, 2009; Rosmarin, Pargament, Pirutinsky, & Mahoney, 2010; Shabtai, Pirutinsky, & Rosmarin, 2016; Tan, 2016; Wade, Post, Cornish, Vogel, & Runyon-Weaver, 2014; Worthington & Aten, 2009).

SUMMARY AND CONCLUSIONS

Religious interventions for mental health problems can be categorized into two groups: relatively simple religious practices (pastoral care and advice, religious support, prayer, meditation, scripture study, reciting scriptures, etc.) and religious psychotherapy (pastoral counseling, religious counseling, and religious or spiritually integrated psychotherapies, i.e., treatments typically conducted by licensed therapists). Admittedly, there is considerable overlap between these religious interventions, but their distinction is important because of the training and licensing required. The core of this chapter focuses on reviewing the research evidence base (randomized clinical trials) for religious interventions in both categories described above. This includes recent studies examining the efficacy of religiously/spiritually integrated psychotherapies, and future studies planned in this area. Religious interventions, in general, have a moderate effect size in the treatment of depression, anxiety, and other emotional disorders, although when compared with other active treatments, effect sizes for the difference between religious/spiritual and nonreligious/spiritual treatments tend to be small. There is evidence that the benefits of religious interventions are particularly strong in religious clients, and weaker in those who are not religious. Identifying clients who are most appropriate for religious psychotherapies like those described above is the next task and will be covered in Chapter 12.

References

AACC (2017). American Association of Christian Counselors: Membership. Available from http://www.aacc.net/members/benefits/.

Abu Raiya, H., & Pargament, K. I. (2010). Religiously integrated psychotherapy with Muslim clients: From research to practice. *Professional Psychology: Research and Practice*, *41*(2), 181–188.

Anderson, N., Heywood-Everett, S., Siddiqi, N., Wright, J., Meredith, J., & McMillan, D. (2015). Faith-adapted psychological therapies for depression and anxiety: Systematic review and meta-analysis. *Journal of Affective Disorders*, *176*, 183–196.

APA (2015). American Psychological Association membership statistics. Available from http://www.apa.org/about/apa/archives/membership.aspx.

Babamohamadi, H., Sotodehasl, N., Koenig, H. G., Al Zaben, F., Jahani, C., & Ghorbani, R. (2017). The effect of Holy Qur'an recitation on depressive symptoms in hemodialysis patients: A randomized clinical trial. *Journal of Religion and Health*, *56*(1), 345–354.

Babamohamadi, H., Sotodehasl, N., Koenig, H. G., Jahani, C., & Ghorbani, R. (2015). The effect of Qur'an recitation on anxiety in hemodialysis patients: A randomized clinical trial. *Journal of Religion and Health*, *54*(5), 1921–1930.

Badrasawi, M. M., Shahar, S., Manaf, Z. A., & Haron, H. (2013). Effect of Talbinah food consumption on depressive symptoms among elderly individuals in long term care facilities, randomized clinical trial. *Clinical Interventions in Aging*, *8*, 279–285.

Beiranvand, S., Noaparast, M., Eslamizade, N., & Saeedikia, S. (2014). The effects of religion and spirituality on post-operative pain, hemodynamic functioning and anxiety after cesarean section. *Acta Medica Iranica*, *52*(12), 909–915.

Boelens, P. A., Reeves, R. R., Replogle, W. H., & Koenig, H. G. (2009). A randomized trial of the effect of prayer on depression and anxiety. *International Journal of Psychiatry in Medicine*, *39*, 377–392.

Boelens, P. A., Reeves, R. R., Replogle, W. H., & Koenig, H. G. (2012). The effect of prayer on depression and anxiety: Maintenance of positive influence one year after prayer intervention. *International Journal of Psychiatry and Medicine*, *43*(1), 85–98.

Cabral, P., Meyer, H. B., & Ames, D. (2011). Effectiveness of yoga therapy as a complementary treatment for major psychiatric disorders: A meta-analysis. *Primary Care Companion for CNS Disorders*, *13*(4), (PCC.10r01068. http://doi.org/10.4088/PCC.10r01068).

Collins, G. R. (1988). *Christian counseling: A comprehensive guide*. Nashville, TN: Word Publishers (Thomas Nelson).

Crabb, L. J. (1977). *Effective biblical counseling*. Grand Rapids, MI: Zondervan.

CSTH. (2014). *Religiously-integrated cognitive behavioral therapy (RCBT) manuals and workbooks (including training video)*. Durham, NC: Duke University Center for Spirituality, Theology and Health (Available from http://www.spiritualityandhealth.duke.edu/index.php/religious-cbt-study/therapy-manuals).

Dehghani Kh, M. S., Dehghani, H. M. S., Zarezadeh, A. B. S., & Bs, N. Z. (2012). The effect of prayer on level of anxiety in mothers of children with cancer. *Iran Journal of Pediatric Hematology and Oncology*, *2*(2), 78–83.

Eberth, J., & Sedlmeier, P. (2012). The effects of mindfulness meditation: A meta-analysis. *Mindfulness*, *3*(3), 174–189.

Ebrahimi, A., Nasiri-Dehsorkhi, H., & Mousavi, S. G. (2015). Effectiveness of spiritually augmented psychotherapy on dysfunctional attitudes in patients with dysthymic disorder. *International Journal of Body, Mind and Culture*, *2*(1), 34–40.

Ebrahimi, A., Neshatdoost, H. T., Mousavi, S. G., Asadollahi, G. A., & Nasiri, H. (2013). Controlled randomized clinical trial of spirituality integrated psychotherapy, cognitive-behavioral therapy and medication intervention on depressive symptoms and dysfunctional attitudes in patients with dysthymic disorder. *Advanced Biomedical Research*, *2*, 53–67.

Ennenbach, M. (2015). *Buddhist psychotherapy: A guideline for positive changes*. Twin Lakes, WI: Lotus Press.

Finney, J. R., & Malony, H. N. (2001). An empirical study of contemplative prayer as an adjunct to psychotherapy. In L. J. Francis, & J. Astley (Eds.), *Psychological perspectives on prayer: A reader* (pp. 359–367). Herefordshire, UK: Gracewing.

Ford, K. M. (2016). *The impact of a Christian adaptation to mindfulness training on stress, religious coping and God attachment: A randomized trial*. Lynchburg, VA: Liberty University.

Friedman, M., & Yehuda, R. (2016). *The art of Jewish pastoral counseling*. Abingdon, UK: Routledge.

Gonçalves, J. P. B., Lucchetti, G., Menezes, P. R., & Vallada, H. (2015). Religious and spiritual interventions in mental health care: A systematic review and meta-analysis of randomized controlled clinical trials. *Psychological Medicine*, *45*(14), 2937–2949.

Goyal, M., Singh, S., Sibinga, E. M., Gould, N. F., Rowland-Seymour, A., Sharma, R., & Ranasinghe, P. D. (2014). Meditation programs for psychological stress and well-being: A systematic review and meta-analysis. *JAMA Internal Medicine*, *174*(3), 357–368.

Hosseini, M., Salehi, A., Khoshknab, M. F., Rokofian, A., & Davidson, P. M. (2013). The effect of a preoperative spiritual/religious intervention on anxiety in Shia Muslim patients undergoing coronary artery bypass graft surgery: A randomized controlled trial. *Journal of Holistic Nursing*, *31*(3), 164–172.

Jafari, N., Zamani, A., Farajzadegan, Z., Bahrami, F., Emami, H., & Doghmani, A. (2013). The effect of spiritual therapy for improving the quality of life of women with breast cancer: A randomized controlled trial. *Psychology, Health and Medicine*, *18*(1), 56–69.

Kehoe, N. C. (1998). Religious-issues group therapy. *New Directions for Mental Health Services*, *80*, 40–55.

Khoury, B., Lecomte, T., Fortin, G., Masse, M., Therien, P., Bouchard, V., & Hofmann, S. G. (2013). Mindfulness-based therapy: A comprehensive meta-analysis. *Clinical Psychology Review*, *33*(6), 763–771.

Kim, J. (2014). *The efficacy of Christian devotional meditation on stress, anxiety, depression, and spiritual health with Korean adults in the United States: A randomized comparative study*. Lynchburg, VA: Liberty University.

Knabb, J. J. (2012). Centering prayer as an alternative to mindfulness-based cognitive therapy for depression relapse. *Journal of Religion and Health*, *51*, 908–924.

Koenig, H. G. (2013). *Spirituality in patient care* (3rd ed.). Conshohocken, PA: Templeton Foundation Press.

Koenig, H. G., Boucher, N. A., Oliver, R. J. P., Youssef, N., Mooney, S. R., Currier, J. M., & Pearce, M. (2017). Rationale for spiritually oriented cognitive processing therapy for moral injury in active duty military and veterans with posttraumatic stress disorder. *Journal of Nervous and Mental Disease*, *205*(2), 147–153.

Koenig, H. G., Pearce, M. J., Nelson, B., Shaw, S. F., Robins, C. J., Daher, N., Cohen, H. J., Berk, L. S., Belinger, D., Pargament, K. I., Rosmarin, D. H., Vasegh, S., Kristeller, J., Juthani, N., Nies, D., & King, M. B. (2015). Religious vs. conventional cognitive-behavioral therapy for major depression in persons with chronic medical illness. *Journal of Nervous and Mental Disease, 203*(4), 243–251.

Koszycki, D., Bilodeau, C., Raab-Mayo, K., & Bradwejn, J. (2014). A multifaith spiritually based intervention versus supportive therapy for generalized anxiety disorder: A pilot randomized controlled trial. *Journal of Clinical Psychology, 70*(6), 489–509.

Kristeller, J. L., Rhodes, M., Cripe, L. D., & Sheets, V. (2005). Oncologist Assisted Spiritual Intervention Study (OASIS): Patient acceptability and initial evidence of effects. *International Journal of Psychiatry in Medicine, 35*(4), 329–347.

Lea, T., Richards, P. S., Sanders, P. W., McBride, J. A., & Allen, G. E. (2015). Spiritual pathways to healing and recovery: An intensive single-N study of an eating disorder patient. *Spirituality in Clinical Practice, 2*(3), 191–201.

Mahjoob, M., Nejati, J., Hosseini, A., & Bakhshani, N. M. (2016). The effect of Holy Quran voice on mental health. *Journal of Religion and Health, 55*(1), 38–42.

McCauley, J., Haaz, S., Tarpley, M. J., Koenig, H. G., & Bartlett, S. J. (2011). A randomized controlled trial to assess effectiveness of a spiritually-based intervention to help chronically ill adults. *International Journal of Psychiatry in Medicine, 41*(1), 91–105.

McCullough, M. E. (1999). Research on religion-accommodative counseling: Review and meta-analysis. *Journal of Counseling Psychology, 46*, 92–98.

Milevsky, A., & Eisenberg, M. (2012). Spiritually oriented treatment with Jewish clients: Meditative prayer and religious texts. *Professional Psychology: Research and Practice, 43*(4), 336.

Montgomery, D. (2010). *Pastoral counseling and coaching*. Monticello, California: Compass Works.

Nasiri, M., Fayazi, S., Ghaderi, M., Naseri, M., & Adarvishi, S (2014). The effect of reciting the word "Allah" on pain severity after coronary artery bypass graft surgery: A randomized clinical trial study in Iran. *Anesthesiology and Pain Medicine, 4*(5), e23149.

Olson, T., Tisdale, T. C., Davis, E. B., Park, E. A., Nam, J., Moriarty, G. L., & Hays, L. W. (2016). God image narrative therapy: A mixed-methods investigation of a controlled group-based spiritual intervention. *Spirituality in Clinical Practice, 3*(2), 77–91.

Orme-Johnson, D. W., & Barnes, V. A. (2014). Effects of the transcendental meditation technique on trait anxiety: A meta-analysis of randomized controlled trials. *The Journal of Alternative and Complementary Medicine, 20*(5), 330–341.

Pargament, K. I. (2011). *Spiritually integrated psychotherapy: Understanding and addressing the sacred*. New York, NY: Guilford Press.

Pargament, K. I., Murray-Swank, N. A., & Tarakeshwar, N. (2005). An empirically-based rationale for a spiritually-integrated psychotherapy. *Mental Health, Religion and Culture, 8*(3), 155–165.

Pearce, M. J. (2016). *Cognitive behavioral therapy for Christians with depression: A practical tool-based primer*. Conshohocken, PA: Templeton Foundation Press.

Pearce, M. J., Koenig, H. G., Robins, C. J., Nelson, B., Shaw, S. F., Cohen, H. J., & King, M. B. (2015). Religiously integrated cognitive behavioral therapy: A new method of treatment for major depression in patients with chronic medical illness. *Psychotherapy, 52*(1), 56–66.

Post, B. C., & Wade, N. G. (2009). Religion and spirituality in psychotherapy: A practice-friendly review of research. *Journal of Clinical Psychology, 65*(2), 131–146.

Rassoo, G. H. (2015). *Islamic counselling: An introduction to theory and practice*. Abingdon, UK: Routledge.

Rettger, J., Wall, K., Corwin, D., Davidson, A. N., Lukoff, D., & Koopman, C. (2015). In psycho-spiritual integrative therapy for women with primary breast cancer, what factors account for the benefits? Insights from a multiple case analysis. *Healthcare, 3*(2), 263–283.

Richards, S. P., & Judd, D. (2017). *Enhancing practice-based evidence for spiritually integrated psychotherapies: An interdisciplinary big data project*. Provo, UT: Brigham Young University (supported by a grant from the John Templeton Foundation. Available from http://bridgesconsortium.com/).

Rosmarin, D. H., Pargament, K. I., Pirutinsky, S., & Mahoney, A. (2010). A randomized controlled evaluation of a spiritually integrated treatment for subclinical anxiety in the Jewish community, delivered via the Internet. *Journal of Anxiety Disorders*, *24*(7), 799–808.

Shabtai, D. G., Pirutinsky, S., & Rosmarin, D. H. (2016). Integrating Judaism into cognitive behavioral therapy. In M. Ben-Avie, Y. Ives, & K. Loewenthal (Eds.), *Applied Jewish Values in Social Sciences and Psychology* (pp. 133–149). New York, NY: Springer International Publishing (ch 6).

Smith, T. B., Bartz, J., & Scott Richards, P. (2007). Outcomes of religious and spiritual adaptations to psychotherapy: A meta-analytic review. *Psychotherapy Research*, *17*(6), 643–655.

Sperry, L. (2016). Varieties of religious and spiritual treatment: Spirituality oriented psychotherapy and beyond. *Spirituality in Clinical Practice*, *3*(1), 1–4.

Subica, A. M., & Yamada, A. -M. (2017). Development of a spirituality infused cognitive behavioral intervention for individuals with serious mental illnesses. *Psychiatric Rehabilitation Journal* (Advance online publication. http://dx.doi.org/10.1037/prj0000102).

Tan, S. Y. (1991). Religious values and interventions in lay Christian counseling. *Journal of Psychology and Christianity*, *10*(2), 173–182.

Tan, S. Y. (2011a). *Counseling and psychotherapy: A Christian perspective.* Grand Rapids, MI: Baker Academic.

Tan, S. Y. (2011b). Mindfulness and acceptance-based cognitive behavioral therapies: Empirical evidence and clinical applications from a Christian perspective. *Journal of Psychology and Christianity*, *30*(3), 243–250.

Tan, S. Y. (2016). *ACT for clergy and pastoral counselors: Using acceptance and commitment therapy to bridge psychological and spiritual care*. Oakland, CA: New Harbinger Publications.

Udipi, S. (2015). Hindu approaches to pastoral counseling. In E. A. Maynard, & J. L. Snodgrass (Eds.), *Understanding pastoral counseling* (pp. 291–302). New York, NY: Springer.

Wade, N. G., Post, B. C., Cornish, M. A., Vogel, D. L., & Runyon-Weaver, D. (2014). Religion and spirituality in group psychotherapy: Clinical application and case example. *Spirituality in Clinical Practice*, *1*(2), 133–144.

Wade, N. G., Worthington, E. L., & Vogel, D. L. (2007). Effectiveness of religiously tailored interventions in Christian therapy. *Psychotherapy Research*, *17*, 91–105.

Worthington, E. L., & Aten, J. D. (2009). Psychotherapy with religious and spiritual clients: An introduction. *Journal of Clinical Psychology*, *65*(2), 123–130.

Worthington, E. L., Hook, J. N., Davis, D. E., & McDaniel, M. A. (2011). Religion and spirituality. *Journal of Clinical Psychology*, *67*(2), 204–214.

CHAPTER

12

Identifying the Religious Psychotherapy Client

The focus of this chapter is on identifying the client for whom religious psychotherapy (RPT) might be indicated. RPT is not indicated for all clients, and all clients are not particularly interested in receiving it. Thus, the therapist must decide on who this form of treatment is likely to have the best results in. The first and most important consideration is what the client wants. In all cases, RPT must be client centered, that is, the therapy must focus on the client's religious or spiritual beliefs and the language that the client uses to express them. The second consideration, related to the first, is that therapists who choose to conduct RPT must receive training and probably supervision (either formally or informally) on how to administer the therapy. Both of these issues are now briefly addressed before examining the characteristics of the ideal candidate for RPT.

CLIENT INTEREST

How do clients feel about therapists utilizing clients' religious beliefs and practices in the therapeutic process? When surveyed, many clients (up to 75%–80%) express interest in and receptivity to the integration of religious or spiritual beliefs into psychotherapy (Kelly, 1995; Rose, Westefeld, & Ansley, 2001; Stanley et al., 2011). There is even considerable interest in doing so among psychiatric inpatients with severe mental illness. For example, Rosmarin, Forester, Shassian, Webb, and Bjorgvinsson (2015) at Harvard-affiliated McLean Psychiatric Hospital in Belmont, Massachusetts, surveyed 253 acutely hospitalized psychiatric patients to assess their interest in spiritually oriented psychotherapy. The most common psychiatric condition was a mood disorder (82%) or anxiety disorder (55%); 37% were considered high risk for suicide; and 55% had been previously

Religion and Mental Health. http://dx.doi.org/10.1016/B978-0-12-811282-3.00012-4

hospitalized for psychiatric reasons. Religious affiliations were 22% Catholic, 20% Protestant, 7% Jewish, 5% Buddhist, 7% other, and 40% none. The primary question was "To what extent would you like to include your spirituality in your mental health treatment?" Responses were 23% not at all, 19% slightly, 21% fairly, 20% moderately, and 17% very much. Thus, more than half (58%) indicated at least fair or greater interest, and only about a quarter (23%) were definitely opposed. Interest in spiritual integration was particularly strong in those with major depressive disorder and in those who were more religious/spiritual. However, even among the 40% with no religious affiliation, more than one-third (37%) said they were at least fairly interested in having their spiritual beliefs integrated into therapy and nearly 10% indicated they were very interested. Note that this study took place in a secular academic psychiatric hospital located in the northeast United States, one of the least religious areas of the country.

Thus, there appears to be considerable interest on the client's side. The question now is whether therapists have the training to competently integrate religious or spiritual beliefs of clients into psychotherapy. Administering this type of therapy is not easily done, so mental health professionals and religious professionals who do therapy must be trained to provide RPT. This is necessary in order to meet competency standards that are now being established (Plante, 2007; Vieten et al., 2013; Sperry, 2016).

THERAPIST TRAINING

All educational programs in counseling are required as part of accreditation by the Counsel for Accreditation of Counseling and Related Educational Programs (CACREP) to assess students on competencies related to addressing clients' spiritual and religious domains in clinical practice (CACREP, 2001; CACREP, 2009). Likewise, the Ethical Principles of Psychologists and Code of Conduct in Principle E, Respect for People's Rights and Dignity, states that "Psychologists are aware of and respect cultural, individual and role differences, including those based on … religion … and consider these factors when working with members of such groups" (American Psychological Association, 2010, p. 3). Furthermore, in Standard 3.01, Unfair Discrimination, it states "In their work-related activities, psychologists do not engage in unfair discrimination based on … religion … or any basis proscribed by law" (p. 6). Therefore, at a minimum, psychologists need to consider and respect the religious or spiritual beliefs of clients when providing psychotherapy. The degree to which programs in counseling and psychology actually train therapists on how to do that and how to integrate religion/spirituality into psychotherapy, however, varies widely. One study of members of the Association for Behavioral and Cognitive Therapies (ABCT) found that 71% reported little to no previous clinical training in this area (Rosmarin, Green, Pirutinsky, & McKay, 2013). More recent reports from the United Kingdom report similar lack of training (Jafari, 2016).

A number of programs now exist where specific training on how to include religion or spirituality into counseling/psychotherapy may be obtained. However, there are surprisingly few programs that focus on spiritually- or religiously-integrated psychotherapy, per se. Several colleges and universities offer masters and doctorate degrees in pastoral counseling and Christian counseling (e.g., Liberty University, Grand Canyon University, and Ohio Christian University) (Pastoral Counseling, 2017). Fuller Theological Seminary (2017) also has a school of psychology that provides both masters and doctorate degrees (PhD and PsyD) that include training on how to integrate religion/spirituality into psychotherapy.[1] The Spirituality Mind Body Institute (SMBI) in the department of psychology at Columbia University in New York City offers "a Master's degree in Clinical Psychology and Education with a concentration in Spirituality and Mind Body Practice" (SMBI, 2017). Also, the Spiritual Care Association has a curriculum and courses specifically for chaplains, social workers, clergy, and seminarians to prepare them to address clients' spiritual needs (a slightly different issue) (SCA, 2017).

Wilfrid Laurier University in Waterloo, Ontario (Canada) has a Spiritual Care and Psychotherapy program that awards a graduate diploma that qualifies a practitioner for a license as a mental health professional and for governmental reimbursement (WLU, 2017). To this author's knowledge, there are no such programs in the United States, although some MSW (Masters in Social Work) programs provide training in this area (contact Holly Oxhandler at Baylor University's Garland School of Social Work for more information about those programs).

There are also a number of books and articles that describe how to integrate religion or spirituality into counseling and psychotherapy (Cashwell & Young, 2011; Pargament, 2011; Johnson, 2013; Aten, O'Grady, & Worthington, 2013; Walker, Courtois, & Aten, 2015; Pearce et al., 2015; Pearce, 2016). In fact, there is an entire American Psychological Association journal devoted to integrating spirituality into clinical practice (*Spirituality in Clinical Practice*, which published its inaugural issue in August 2013). Finally, Duke University's Center for Spirituality, Theology, and Health has a short introductory training video on how to provide religiously-integrated cognitive behavioral therapy (RCBT) for depression, which together with manuals and workbooks (freely available on the website), will help mental health and religious professionals conduct this therapy (CSTH, 2016).

[1]Established in 1965, Fuller is the first seminary-based psychology program to receive accreditation from the American Psychological Association.

Holly Oxhandler and Danielle Parrish have developed and validated a 40-item Religious/Spiritually- Integrated Practice Assessment Scale designed to assess clinicians' self-efficacy, attitudes, behaviors, and perceived feasibility with regard to the assessment and integration of clients' religious/spiritual beliefs in clinical practice, and has now been tested in clinical social workers, psychologists, nurses, counselors, and marriage and family therapists (Oxhandler & Parrish, 2016; Oxhandler, 2017). This instrument's 13-item self-efficacy subscale assesses the degree to which a clinician feels competent in integrating clients' religiosity/spirituality into their clinical practice, and may serve as a measure of self-rated competency in this regard. Measures of this type could someday be used to establish competencies required for conducting spiritually or religiously-integrated therapy.

Len Sperry (2016) describes the difference between having basic competencies in terms of providing religious/spiritually sensitive care (that includes incorporating religion/spirituality into the treatment process, such as taking a spiritual history or addressing spiritual concerns brought up by clients) and possessing specialized competencies related to integrating religion or spirituality into psychotherapy. With regard to the first set of competencies, he notes that the ethnical codes of many of the mental health professions now require clinicians to be sensitive to clients' religious/spiritual concerns (as noted above). The competencies required for basic care at this level are different from those required for therapists who wish to provide religious or spiritual oriented psychotherapy, which Sperry emphasizes requires specialized training. This recommendation is consistent with how the research evidence base described in Chapter 11 was presented (i.e., divided into religious interventions and religious psychotherapy).

ASSESSMENT

Deciding on whether or not a client might be a candidate for religious counseling or psychotherapy begins with the spiritual history. As indicated earlier (Chapter 10), taking a spiritual history is the most important of all clinical applications based on the research and good clinical practice (GCP). A spiritual history is needed for all clients prior to beginning psychotherapy or mental health treatment of any kind (including drug therapy). Before competent, client-centered therapy can be conducted, the personal beliefs and values of clients must be known, including something about their religious beliefs and cultural background.

Clues from the spiritual history will provide the necessary information that will allow the therapist to determine whether a client is or is not a candidate for RPT, that is, the integration of a person's religious or spiritual beliefs and practices into psychotherapy. Below are five case vignettes that illustrate clients who may or may not qualify as candidates.

CASE VIGNETTE #1: SAD HOUSEWIFE

Mohammad (psychotherapist) is seeing Faten, a 42-year-old married housewife, for the first time for the treatment of depression following the death of her 16-year-old son and separation from her husband. She and her husband came to the United States about 20-years-ago from Iraq after the war there. After taking a thorough psychological, social, and spiritual history, Mohammad learns that Faten is religious although has many questions about why God has allowed these things to happen in her life. She says that she accepts these events as God's will, but she still cannot make any sense of them and has wondered how she can continue to live with these painful feelings. The antidepressant that her psychiatrist prescribed is helping some, but not enough. She is restless, sad, has lost interest in things, and is losing weight (despite her small frame). Mohammad learns that she is a Sunni Muslim, and that prior to the loss of her son, Faten regularly performed the five obligatory daily prayers, recited the shahada and verses from the Qur'an, gave zakat (donations to the poor), and attended her local mosque. Since her son's death, and especially since her divorce, she has been much less regular in these activities and feels very guilty about this. In the past, her faith had brought comfort and guidance to her when dealing with difficult circumstances, such as the death of her mother and brother during the war (and the discrimination she faced as a Sunni Muslim in a largely Shiite country). Mohammad asks Faten if she would like to address some of these questions about why God has allowed these losses in her life. She says that she has spoken with her Imam about this, but that has not helped. She asks how discussing these religious issues further might help her. Mohammad gently and nonjudgmentally explains that sometimes religious questions like this can interfere with recovery from terrible traumas like she has experienced, and she may feel better once she has worked through them. Faten agrees that she would like to try this, as long as they go slow. Mohammad assures her that they will only go at a pace that she feels comfortable with.

Is Faten a candidate for RPT? Yes, although given initial reluctance, Mohammad will need to proceed cautiously and if progress is not readily made, may need to switch back to purely secular therapy.

CASE VIGNETTE #2: BUDDHIST SEEKER

Alexander is a 28-year-old unmarried unemployed man who has come to a local counseling center because of anxiety and substance abuse (heavy alcohol and cocaine use). He is assigned to Sophia, a therapist trained in cognitive-behavioral methods used for treating clients with substance abuse problems.

During the intake evaluation, Sophia asks about Alexander's religious background. He says that he is not particularly religious, although converted to Buddhism a few years ago, has read some books on the subject, and occasionally goes to the local Buddhist temple, where he has made a few friends. On further questioning about his early religious experiences, Alexander notes that he was raised in a very strict conservative Christian home by religious parents who forced him to attend services and participate in youth group activities. When he reached the age of 18, they kicked him out of the house because he had dropped out of school, was not working, and they caught him smoking marijuana in the backyard. Of course, he stopped all religious activity at that time and remains very angry at his parents, who he feels deserted him. However, over the past few years he has felt something missing from his life and has decided to give Buddhism a try. He read a book about the Buddha's life, and believes that the peace that the Buddha found is what he is looking for. However, the only times he feels any peace now is after a heavy episode of drinking, when he doesn't feel much of anything. He believes, though, that there is more to life than what he is experiencing. Sophia presents the treatment plan to Alexander, which includes a course of CBT directed at helping him curb his substance abuse problems and relaxation exercises to help with his anxiety. She wonders, in light of his spiritual history, whether he would like a Buddhist approach to therapy that might utilize some of the Buddha's teachings and meditation practices. Alexander agrees that he would like this very much.

Is Alexander a candidate for RPT: Yes, he is eager to do so. The question is whether Sophia is competent to provide Buddhist CBT.

CASE VIGNETTE #3: AGNOSTIC COLLEGE STUDENT

Sharon is a 23-year-old college student who recently attempted suicide after her boyfriend broke up with her. Besides seeing a psychiatrist for medical treatment after hospitalization, she is assigned to the college counseling center for therapy. Matthew, a psychologist at the center, is seeing Sharon, will be providing her treatment, and is conducting the intake evaluation. During the spiritual history Sharon reveals that she is not religious. "What about spiritual?" asks Matthew. Sharon responds, "I don't know what you mean by spiritual, but probably not that either." Sharon explains that while she did undergo bat mitzvah in her early teens, she grew up in a secular Jewish home. Her parents never attended synagogue and seldom observed the Jewish holy days. She's not even sure if she believes in God, and volunteers that she thinks religion is the cause for many terrible things that people do in the world. In fact, she used to get into arguments about this with her boyfriend, who was quite religious. She wonders whether this was one reason why he broke up with her. Matthew explains to Sharon that the treatment plan will involve a course of CBT that will help reduce her ruminating thoughts about her boyfriend and get her involved in activities that she previously enjoyed.

Is Sharon a candidate for RPT? No, she is not religious or spiritual and has no desire to engage this subject area.

CASE VIGNETTE #4: GUILTY VETERAN

Jason is a 36-year-old unemployed Army veteran recently discharged from the Service after serving three tours in Afghanistan. He initially joined the Army at the age of 22, and was a member of the U.S. Special Forces for 12 years during which he participated in many covert operations. During one of those operations, his company was ambushed by Taliban forces. He was slightly injured and captured, but witnessed several of his close teammates tortured, killed, and their bodies mutilated. These experiences filled him with pain and rage. Jason spent 2 weeks as a Taliban prisoner until he was rescued by American forces and returned to base. After a month of rest and counseling, he returned to duty. During a mission several months later, while alone on patrol, Jason encountered an Afghan man along the road in a remote mountain area. Assuming he was Taliban, Jason shot and killed him, and then mutilated his body as he had seen the Taliban do to his dear teammates. Afterward, he was overwhelmed with guilt (the man was unarmed), hid the body, and didn't mention any of this to his comrades once he returned to base. Nevertheless, he began to have nightmares and flashbacks that affected his sleep and concentration, impairing his ability to function on his job. His commanding officers noticed the change in his condition, and arranged for him to return to the United States. His condition, though, did not improve when he returned home. After receiving some brief counseling, he was discharged from the service. Jason could not share any of these experiences with his wife, and had withdrawn from her. They were on the verge of divorce. He continued to have nightmares and was easily startled by his young children, who always seemed to be getting on his nerves. As a last ditch effort to save the marriage and family, his wife forced him to seek professional help, which he reluctantly agreed to.

Phillip, a psychologist at the local Veterans Administration (VA) mental health clinic, completed the initial evaluation on Jason, taking a detailed psychological, social, and spiritual history. It was clear that Jason was suffering from Post-Traumatic Stress Disorder (PTSD). Although Jason had a hard time answering the questions during the spiritual history, he told Phillip that he was an only child raised in a Catholic home. His mother was very religious, often prayed with him as a child, and took him to Sunday school and church every week. He later attended a Catholic High School, and continued to go regularly to church after he graduated and periodically after joining the Army. But now, Jason admitted, he was struggling with his religious beliefs. Where was God when his company was ambushed and friends killed? He had prayed every day for their safety. Then look what happened. It was clear that Jason was in turmoil over his religious beliefs, and Philip sensed that there was a lot more going on here than what Jason was telling. Phillip gently revealed to Jason that he had PTSD and recommended a course of cognitive processing therapy, a standard psychotherapy for PTSD at the VA. In addition, Phillip asked Jason if he would be interested in addressing some of the religious questions he was having. Jason paused for a moment before answering, and then agreed. He told Phillip that he wasn't sure how that would help, but religion had always been a comfort to him in the past, although now it was no help. Jason admitted that all of this was debilitating him and destroying his family, so he was willing to try anything.

Is Jason a candidate for RPT? Yes, probably religiously-integrated cognitive processing therapy, but not until he can talk about the Afghan he had killed and work through the religious struggles related to what he did (although that could be part of the RPT).

CASE VIGNETTE #5: RELIGIOUS CLIENT

Wilma is a 61-year-old florist shop owner who comes to a hospital outpatient clinic requesting help for severe panic attacks. Wilma is single, never married, and has no children. As part of her initial evaluation, Bill her psychiatrist takes a thorough social history that includes a spiritual history. She reports that religion is very important in her life and that she attends an evangelical nondenominational church, which she is very involved in and is her primary source of friends and social support. Bill tells Wilma that she has panic disorder, and suggests a course of medication and counseling. He asks Wilma if she has any religious beliefs that might influence either of these. Wilma says that she really doesn't want to take any medication, as she doesn't think her church would approve of that. However, she is willing to do "talk therapy" with someone like a Christian counselor, if the person will respect her religious beliefs and use those beliefs to help with her panic attacks. Bill informs her that the medication will work much quicker than talk therapy, but that there is a counselor in the clinic who is skilled at treating clients with anxiety disorders. He informs her that the counselor does Christian counseling for those who prefer this approach. Would she like him to give the counselor a call and set up an appointment? Wilma readily agrees and thanks Bill for understanding. As she is leaving, Wilma asks Bill if he is Christian. Bill smiles, and responds that he is Christian and religiously prescribes medication for people with panic disorder.

Is Wilma a candidate for RPT? Yes, either Christian counseling or a religiously-integrated psychotherapy from a Christian perspective.

RELIGIOUS PSYCHOTHERAPY INDICATIONS

Below are characteristics of those who would be most receptive to and benefit from RPT (presented below in order of importance):

- clients who request RPT
- clients who are deeply religious, whether or not RPT is requested
- clients whose religious beliefs/practices have been helpful in the past when coping with difficult life circumstances
- clients who use religious words and language during initial or follow-up therapy sessions
- clients with characteristics[2] that indicate likely receptivity to RPT; for example, clients from Africa or the Middle East, where religion is deeply engrained in values and culture (Ebrahimi, Neshatdoost, Mousavi, Asadollahi, & Nasiri, 2013)
- clients who have a history of being deeply religious, but something has changed
- clients in whom religious issues are intertwined with psychopathology, and need to be addressed as part of the treatment
- clients without underlying serious psychopathology who have experienced significant losses or are facing severe situational stressors (and are at least somewhat religious)

RELIGIOUS PSYCHOTHERAPY CONTRAINDICATIONS

In this author's opinion, there are no absolute contraindications to religious interventions. However, there are several relative contraindications, where RPT is best avoided or at least delayed until later on in the therapy:

- clients who, after the options are presented, prefer standard secular psychotherapy
- clients who indicate they not religious or spiritual, especially if they have never been
- clients who complain that religion was forced on them during childhood, against their wishes
- clients who display resistance to questions during the initial spiritual history

[2]Women, older adults, ethnic minorities, and those with less education and few resources tend to be more religious, and therefore more receptive to RPT.

- clients who are actively having religious or spiritual struggles (again, these struggles could be addressed in RPT, but early on in therapy before utilizing religion as a potential resource)
- clients with a history of significant religious trauma, physical or sexual abuse (however, those with religious trauma will need this to be addressed and RPT may be helpful)
- clients with deep psychopathology, in need of expert psychodynamic therapy
- psychopath or highly manipulative clients forced into therapy by the courts
- actively suicidal or homicidal clients (who need immediate hospitalization)
- clients with active psychotic symptoms (who need hospitalization and medication)
- child/adolescents under age 18 whose parents do not give explicit permission for RPT

With clients who are having religious struggles or those who have experienced trauma or abuse, as noted above, the treatment must first focus on helping the person work through these issues before attempting to utilize religious resources in therapy. This includes those with a history of nonclergy sexual abuse in childhood (Kerlin & Sosin, 2016) and LGBTQ clients who may feel marginalized, excluded or rejected by their religious communities (Robertson & Avent, 2016). In all of these cases, clients will not be able to fully tap into religious resources until the religious struggle or trauma is dealt with. Beware that Muslim clients may not readily admit to religious struggles, given a strong emphasis on God's will in Islam and rules about challenging authority. Careful and persistent questioning, though, in a safe and nonjudgmental atmosphere may help the Muslim client express and process such feelings, feelings that are perfectly natural especially after severe trauma.

RELIGIOUS PSYCHOTHERAPY INDICATION UNCLEAR

There are some situations in which RPT may or may not be indicated, depending on the particular client and the particular therapist. An example is when a therapist's religious background is very different from that of the client. Can a devout Christian therapist provide client-centered RPT to a devout Muslim (who does not believe Jesus is God or died on the Cross) or to a devout Buddhist (who may not believe in God at all)? A similar situation arises when a devout Orthodox Jewish therapist seeks to provide RPT to a deeply religious conservative Christian client. The therapist will have to set aside his or her own religious beliefs and engage the client within that client's belief system (which may conflict with the religious beliefs of the therapist). Some therapists are able to do this, but others are not.

In some circumstances, however, RPT may be even more efficacious if the belief systems of therapist and client differ. For example, Propst, Ostrom, Watkins, Dean, and Mashburn (1992) found that when religious cognitive behavioral therapy (RCBT) was administered by nonreligious therapists to Christian religious clients, the therapy was more efficacious than when administered by religious therapists. The reasons for this were not entirely clear in that report. Perhaps nonreligious therapists were more careful and precise when conducting RCBT since they were less familiar with it, or may have been more objective and less judgmental in their application. This finding, though, is yet to be replicated and there is some evidence that moderate similarity in values between therapist and patient is linked to better outcomes (Kelly & Strupp, 1992). Nevertheless, a recent systematic review of this topic concluded that therapist religion/spirituality (R/S) and client–therapist R/S similarity were not consistently related to treatment outcomes (Cummings, Ivan, Carson, Stanley, & Pargament, 2014).

Another situation where the appropriateness of RPT may be less clear is when the therapist is conflicted about their own beliefs or a client's religious beliefs and this causes intrapsychic conflict in the therapist. Such a situation may create countertransference responses that interfere with the successful implementation of RPT (Spero, 1981; Spero, 2010). Likewise, in cases where the client has borderline features (i.e., has serious boundary issues that result in unstable, stormy relationships), caution may be needed if the therapist decides to proceed with RPT. This is particularly true when the therapist is very religious and the client is only marginally so (or vice-versa). At one point, the client may seek the therapist's favor by adopting the therapist's religious views; at another point, the client may resist and reject the therapist's views (as part of the love–hate relationship dynamic that borderline clients are known for).

GROUP VS. INDIVIDUAL RPT

Some clients may find that addressing their religious or spiritual issues within a group setting is less threatening, particularly those suffering from some type of religious trauma, experiencing religious or spiritual struggles, dealing with moral injury from severe trauma (rape, experiences during wartime, etc.), or struggling with addictive disorders. Unfortunately, little has been written about how to truly integrate R/S into group therapy. More information is available on how to address R/S issues if they naturally come up during group therapy. For example, Wade, Post, Cornish, Vogel, and Runyon-Weaver (2014) discuss issues that arise when clients bring up R/S issues during nonthematic group therapy, including (1) how to decide when (and when not) to address R/S when it comes up; (2) how to manage conflicts over R/S issues between group members if these arise; and (3) how to effectively process R/S issues during a group session. They do not, however, discuss how to design and carry out group therapy interventions specifically designed to integrate R/S into the therapy.

Peripherally related to RPT are peer-led support groups such as Alcoholics Anonymous or Narcotics Anonymous that are spiritually based and have had tremendous success in helping clients remain abstinent (Humphreys, Blodgett, & Wagner, 2014; Kelly, 2017). Breitbart (2002) also describes a "meaning-centered" form of group therapy that addresses existential and spiritual concerns that arise in palliative care settings. Participating in such groups may enable clients to progress to a point that they are able to engage in individual one-on-one RPT.

An example of a group intervention with the purpose of integrating R/S into the treatment is Building Spiritual Strength (BSS), an 8-session interfaith manualized group intervention for trauma survivors (Harris et al., 2011; Harris & Minnesota Veterans Administration Hospital, 2015). Both civilian and military versions of BSS have been developed, although the intervention has thus far been tested primarily in traumatized war veterans. BSS addresses spiritual distress associated with trauma and seeks to enhance religious meaning, while minimizing stigma by using faith communities as the treatment setting. The intervention focuses on assisting traumatized individuals to recognize and resolve spiritual concerns that may be contributing to their distress, while maintaining and enhancing areas of healthy spiritual functioning. Such groups are typically led by a psychologist (licensed mental health professional), but can also be led by a chaplain. The choice of group vs. individual RPT will depend on the client's preference, and the availability of therapists trained in these modalities (Jacques, 1998).

INFORMED CONSENT

Before proceeding with a religious intervention, especially RPT, informed consent should be obtained from the client. This means explaining exactly what the therapy will involve and why it is indicated for the client's problem. This may seem obvious, but some therapists may not take the time beforehand to thoroughly discuss this particular approach to therapy. Clients should also be informed that RPT will be done at the client's pace, and that RPT can be stopped at any time and a more secular approach taken if desired. The client must always be made to feel that he or she is in the driver's seat when discussing R/S issues, particularly when integrating those beliefs into therapy.

SUMMARY AND CONCLUSIONS

RPT can be a powerful and effective treatment when conducted in the "right client," at the "right time," by the "right therapist." When conducted in the wrong client or at the wrong time by a therapist who is not adequately trained, RPT may at best have little effect or at worst cause further trauma. This chapter examines the receptiveness of clients to integrating spiritual or religious beliefs into therapy, emphasizes the need for training to competently perform RPT, and presents a number of clinical cases. A description is provided of clients or situations in which the implementation of RPT is indicated, contraindicated (relatively), or unclear. Finally, group RPT is discussed and the need for informed consent is emphasized. With these guidelines (and cautions), mental health and religious professionals will be more successful when applying this form of treatment.

References

American Psychological Association (2010). *Ethical principles of psychologists and code of conduct*. Available from www.apa.org/ethics.

Aten, J., O'Grady, K., & Worthington, E., Jr. (Eds.). (2013). *The psychology of religion and spirituality for clinicians: Using research in your practice*. New York, NY: Routledge (Taylor & Francis).

Breitbart, W. (2002). Spirituality and meaning in supportive care: spirituality-and meaning-centered group psychotherapy interventions in advanced cancer. *Supportive Care in Cancer, 10*(4), 272–280.

CACREP (2001). *Counsel for accreditation of counseling and related educational programs: CACREP, 2001 standards*. Alexandria, VA: CACREP. Available from: http://www.cacrep.org/2001standards.html.

CACREP (2009). *Counsel for accreditation of counseling and related educational programs: CACREP 2009 standards*. Alexandria, VA: CACREP. Available from: http://www.cacrep.org/doc/2009standardswithcover.pdf.

Cashwell, C. S., & Young, J. (2011). *Integrating spirituality and religion into counseling: a guide to competent practice* (2nd ed.). Alexandria, VA: American Counseling Association.

CSTH. (2016). Religious CBT training video: religiously-integrated cognitive behavioral therapy. *Theology and Health*. Durham, NC: Duke University Center for Spirituality Available from: https://spiritualityandhealth.duke.edu/index.php/religious-cbt-study/training-video.

Cummings, J. P., Ivan, M. C., Carson, C. S., Stanley, M. A., & Pargament, K. I. (2014). A systematic review of relations between psychotherapist religiousness/spirituality and therapy-related variables. *Spirituality in Clinical Practice, 1*(2), 116–132.

Ebrahimi, A., Neshatdoost, H. T., Mousavi, S. G., Asadollahi, G. A., & Nasiri, H. (2013). Controlled randomized clinical trial of spirituality integrated psychotherapy, cognitive-behavioral therapy and medication intervention on depressive symptoms and dysfunctional attitudes in patients with dysthymic disorder. *Advanced Biomedical Research, 2*, 53 Available from: http://doi.org/10.4103/2277-9175.114201.

Fuller Theological Seminary (2017). *Fuller theological seminary school of psychology*. Retrieved from http://fuller.edu/school-of-psychology/.

Harris, J. I., Erbes, C. R., Engdahl, B. E., Thuras, P., Murray-Swank, N., Grace, D., Ogden, H., Olson, R. H., Winskowski, A. M., Bacon, R., Malec, C., Campion, K., & Le, T. (2011). The effectiveness of a trauma focused spiritually integrated intervention for veterans exposed to trauma. *Journal of Clinical Psychology*, *67*(4), 425–438.

Harris J. I., & Minnesota Veterans Administration Hospital (2015). *Building spiritual strength: a faith-based intervention designed to address moral injury*. Available from: https://www.bms.com/about-us/responsibility/bristol-myers-squibb-foundation/our-focus-areas/veterans-mental-health-and-well-being/minnesota-veterans-medical-research-and-education-foundation.html.

Humphreys, K., Blodgett, J. C., & Wagner, T. H. (2014). Estimating the efficacy of alcoholics anonymous without self-selection bias: an instrumental variables re-analysis of randomized clinical trials. *Alcoholism: Clinical and Experimental Research*, *38*(11), 2688–2694.

Jacques, J. R. (1998). Working with spiritual and religious themes in group therapy. *International Journal of Group Psychotherapy*, *48*(1), 69–83.

Jafari, S. (2016). Religion and spirituality within counselling/clinical psychology training programmes: a systematic review. *British Journal of Guidance and Counselling*, *44*(3), 257–267.

Johnson, R. (2013). *Spirituality in counseling and psychotherapy: An integrative approach that empowers clients*. Hoboken, NJ: John Wiley.

Kelly, E. W., Jr. (1995). Spirituality and religion in counselor education: a national survey. *Counselor Education and Supervision*, *33*, 227–237.

Kelly, J. F. (2017). Is alcoholics anonymous religious, spiritual, neither? Findings from 25 years of mechanisms of behavior change research. *Addiction*, *112*(6), 929–936.

Kelly, T. A., & Strupp, H. H. (1992). Patient and therapist values in psychotherapy: perceived changes, assimilation, similarity, and outcome. *Journal of Consulting and Clinical Psychology*, *60*(1), 34–40.

Kerlin, A. M., & Sosin, L. S. (2016). Recovery from childhood sexual abuse: a spiritually integrated qualitative exploration of 10 women's journeys. *Journal of Spirituality in Mental Health*, *19*, 189–209.

Oxhandler, H. K. (2017). Revalidating the religious/spiritually integrated practice assessment scale with five helping professions. *Research on Social Work Practice*. E-pub ahead of press http://dx.doi.org/10.1177/1049731516669592.

Oxhandler, H. K., & Parrish, D. E. (2016). The development and validation of the religious/spiritually integrated practice assessment scale. *Research on Social Work Practice*, *26*(3), 295–307.

Pargament, K. I. (2011). *Spiritually integrated psychotherapy: Understanding and addressing the sacred*. New York, NY: Guilford Press.

Pastoral Counseling (2017). *Pastoral Counseling.org. becoming a Christian psychotherapist*. Available from: http://www.pastoralcounseling.org/specialization/christian-psychotherapy.

Pearce, M. J. (2016). *Cognitive behavioral therapy for christians with depression: a practical tool-based primer*. Conshohocken, PA: Templeton Foundation Press.

Pearce, M. J., Koenig, H. G., Robins, C. J., Nelson, B., Shaw, S. F., Cohen, H. J., & King, M. B. (2015). Religiously integrated cognitive behavioral therapy: a new method of treatment for major depression in patients with chronic medical illness. *Psychotherapy*, *52*(1), 56–66.

Plante, T. G. (2007). Integrating spirituality and psychotherapy: ethical issues and principles to consider. *Journal of Clinical Psychology*, *63*(9), 891–902.

Propst, L. R., Ostrom, R., Watkins, P., Dean, T., & Mashburn, D. (1992). Comparative efficacy of religious and nonreligious cognitive-behavioral therapy for the treatment of clinical depression in religious individuals. *Journal of Consulting and Clinical Psychology*, *60*(1), 94–103.

Robertson, D. L., & Avent, J. R. (2016). African American counselors-in-training, the Black Church, and lesbian-, gay-, and bisexual-affirmative counseling: considerations for counselor education programs. *Counseling and Values*, *61*(2), 223–238.

Rose, E. M., Westefeld, J. S., & Ansley, T. N. (2001). Spiritual issues in counseling: clients beliefs and preferences. *Journal of Counseling Psychology*, *48*, 61–71.

Rosmarin, D. H., Forester, B. P., Shassian, D. M., Webb, C. A., & Bjorgvinsson, T. (2015). Interest in spiritually integrated psychotherapy among acute psychiatric patients. *Journal of Consulting and Clinical Psychology*, *83*(6), 1149–1153.

Rosmarin, D. H., Green, D., Pirutinsky, S., & McKay, D. (2013). Attitudes toward spirituality/religion among members of the association for behavioral and cognitive therapies. *Professional Psychology: Research and Practice*, *44*(6), 424–433.

SCA (2017). *Spiritual care association learning center*. Available from: from https://spiritualcareassociation.org/learning-center.html.

SMBI (2017). *Spirituality Mind Body Institute (SMBI) intensive master's program*. Columbia University. Available from: http://www.tc.columbia.edu/counseling-and-clinical-psychology/smbi/sub-sections/new-york-city-smbi/.

Spero, M. H. (1981). Countertransference in religious therapists of religious patients. *American Journal of Psychotherapy*, *35*, 565–575.

Spero, M. H. (2010). Gods of the horizon: the therapist's and the patient's religious representations and the inevitability of countertransference. In P. J. Verhagen, H. M. Van Praag, J. J. Lopez-Ibor, J. Cox, & D. Moussaoui (Eds.), *Religion and psychiatry: Beyond boundaries* (pp. 447–478). New York, NY: Wiley Publishing.

Sperry, L. (2016). Spiritually sensitive clinical practice: differentiating basic from specialized competencies. *Spirituality in Clinical Practice*, *3*(2), 73–76.

Stanley, M. A., Bush, A. L., Camp, M. E., Jameson, J. P., Phillips, L. L., Barber, C. R., Zeno, D., Lomax, J. W., & Cully, J. A. (2011). Older adults' preferences for religion/spirituality in treatment of anxiety and depression. *Aging and Mental Health*, *15*(3), 334–343.

Vieten, C., Scammell, S., Pilato, R., Ammondson, I., Pargament, K. I., & Lukoff, D. (2013). Spiritual and religious competencies for psychologists. *Psychology of Religion and Spirituality*, *5*(3), 129–144.

Wade, N. G., Post, B. C., Cornish, M. A., Vogel, D. L., & Runyon-Weaver, D. (2014). Religion and spirituality in group psychotherapy: clinical application and case example. *Spirituality in Clinical Practice*, *1*(2), 133–144.

Walker, D. F., Courtois, C. A., & Aten, J. D. (2015). *Spiritually oriented psychotherapy for trauma*. Washington, DC: American Psychological Association.

WLU (2017). *Wilfrid Laurier University: spiritual care and psychotherapy (graduate diploma)*. Available from: https://www.wlu.ca/programs/seminary/diplomas/spiritual-care-and-psychotherapy-diploma/index.html.

CHAPTER

13

When Religion is the Problem

Most world religions that have persisted for hundreds or thousands of years promote theologies that are healthy and generally adaptive. Those that do otherwise often do not last over time or across generations, but rather die out and lose followers quickly after the death of their founders. The latter types of religious movements often isolate followers from the general society (maintaining them in closed communities) so that they can indoctrinate members to their exclusivist beliefs that feed on the poor self-esteem and loneliness of the psychologically vulnerable (Horton & Williamson, 1998). These unfortunates are often searching for a cause that gives meaning to life and connects them to others with common beliefs and values, even if those beliefs and values harm themselves and others, worsening mental, social, and sometimes physical health.

Although most of this book has emphasized that religious faith may prevent both emotional distress and psychiatric illness, and help individuals to heal from it, sometimes the problem really seems to be religion. The present author will argue here that in most if not all cases, it is the personality of the individual, their mental condition, or the person's interpretation of religious teachings—not religion itself—that is the problem. This is not an isolated opinion (Wentz, 1993). When a sick person adopts a religion that may initially provide comfort, she or he may be at risk for developing rigid or aberrant religious beliefs that lead to even greater inflexibility and literal interpretation, leading to a downward vicious cycle of worsening mental health. An example of a group that preys on such individuals is the Islamic State of Iraq and the Levant (ISIS or ISIL) with its mission to create a caliphate in the Middle East and worldwide domination (there are plenty of Christian examples as well, several of which will be mentioned below).

In the case of ISIS, a small fundamentalist militant jihadist version of Islam (salafi-tafirii) has been utilized by Islamic extremists to indoctrinate often mentally unstable individuals, immature young persons and even children, to advance their agenda (Neo et al., 2016). The result has

Religion and Mental Health. http://dx.doi.org/10.1016/B978-0-12-811282-3.00013-6

been suicide bombers killing hundreds, the planting of explosive devices in nightclubs and sports stadiums, the use of trucks to run over of civilians in crowded places, the mass slaughter of innocent women and children during war, and the promotion of terror. This is not Islam. This is a distorted, misunderstanding of a religion that, as explicitly stated in the Qur'an, promotes care for the poor, peaceful coexistence with other religions, and a deep love for a merciful and forgiving God, a religion that affirms many Jewish and Christian teachings. Individuals leading terrorist groups like ISIS often have no mental illness other than a deep hatred and anger toward the West (and other Muslims). They justify their actions by cherry-picking verses from the Qur'an and applying them completely out of context to the present day to promote their cause and attract converts who have minimal understanding or knowledge of the Qur'an. After leaving (or being rescued from) groups like ISIS, followers (sometimes children) are often both mentally and spiritually traumatized such that they require deprogramming in order to live a peaceful coexistence with others, as mainstream Islam teaches (Langone, 1995; Al-Alil, 2017).

Christianity, too, can be manipulated to serve the goals of those hungry for power and greedy for wealth, who pursue goals that are the opposite of what this religion teaches (Enroth, 1992). Again, scriptures taken out of context are used to attract naive converts to their cause and justify their manipulation, take advantage of these individuals' talents and strip them of their hard earned resources. Examples are unscrupulous televangelists and faith healers who, charismatic and charming, use a conservative Christian theology to convince faithful followers to turn over their wealth and hope. Examples that come to mind are Jimmy and Tammy Fae Baker, Jim Jones, David Koresh, and other cult leaders who are accountable only to themselves and their thirst for attention and power (Goodall, 2005). Likewise, Christian leaders who preach a "Prosperity Gospel" promise that giving money to their causes and following their teachings will lead to health, wealth and success, give false hope to emotionally unstable often poverty-stricken individuals who are desperate for meaning, material possessions, and happiness (Hunt, 2000; Phiri & Maxwell, 2007). These false prophets leave in their wake disheartened victims whose faith has been shattered, never to trust Christian leaders again, even those who teach and model a solid Bible-based message that emphasizes humility, love for others, self-discipline, sacrifice for the needy, forgiveness, mercy, and true hope and healing that result from surrender to God.

In this brief chapter, I will examine the following three questions: (1) how does one identify a person who is using religion in a way that gives rise to or maintains mental illness?; (2) how does a mental health or religious professional help such individuals?; and (3) is religion always helpful for all people, or are there exceptions?

NEUROTIC USE OF RELIGION

Religious delusions or hallucinations, which are clearly symptoms of psychotic illness and not a consequence of religion, have already been discussed elsewhere (Chapters 5 and 10) so these will not be addressed further except for briefly at the end of this chapter. Here, the focus will be on the unhealthy use of religion, beginning with four case vignettes that illustrate persons who are using religion in a neurotic fashion (Cases #1 and #2), those who are vulnerable to those who manipulate others in the name of religion (Case #3), and the rigid, inflexible application of religious teachings that may cause significant interpersonal conflict and mental distress (Case #4).

CASE VIGNETTE #1

Chuck is a 68-year-old married man who retired from his law practice about 3 years ago. Ten years ago he was diagnosed with a late-onset bipolar disorder after a manic episode followed by a severe depression and attempted suicide, which ended him up in the hospital. For the previous decade, he had experienced "high" periods of increased energy, increased productivity, decreased need for sleep, and increased religious activity, alternating with periods of depression. Chuck was now seeing a psychiatrist who had him stabilized on lithium, an antidepressant, and low doses of antipsychotic medication. He had been free of bipolar symptoms for the past 5 years, and was enjoying his retirement. Chuck was also a very religious man (even when he was not manic). Chuck attended a local Pentecostal church twice a week and got up at 3:00 a.m. to read the Bible until 7:00 a.m. when he had breakfast at a local McDonalds with friends from his church. He also frequently listened to audiotapes of evangelists preaching on supernatural healing. On a recent visit to his psychiatrist, Chuck brought up the topic of supernatural healing and told the psychiatrist that he wanted to come off his medications. The psychiatrist, who respected Chuck's religious beliefs and was convinced those beliefs had help keep him stable over the past few years, listened carefully and then asked him what had led up to this decision. Chuck said that the Holy Spirit had spoken to him (in his mind, not an audible voice) and told him that if he had enough faith, he would stop the medication and be healed. He wanted to try that. The psychiatrist acknowledged the power of faith to heal, but questioned whether stopping his medications was a good idea given that he had been doing so well over the past 5 years on the medication. Chuck was determined, though, and wanted off the medication. Therefore, the psychiatrist suggested that he bring in his wife and pastor on the next visit, and he would discuss the matter further with Chuck at that time. The plan was for him to continue his medication until then. Chuck agreed somewhat reluctantly to this proposal.

During the next visit, the psychiatrist (with permission from Chuck) explained what Chuck had proposed and described the likely consequences to his wife and pastor including the recurrence of a manic episode and possibly a severe depression like the one that led to his hospitalization 10 years ago. Chuck's wife said she thought it was a bad idea, and Chuck's pastor confirmed that. The pastor, who was a quite reasonable fellow, told him that perhaps God had healed him through the medication *and* through his devout religious practices, and encouraged him to stay on the medicine. His psychiatrist readily affirmed what Chuck's wife and pastor had said. Chuck, however, would have none of it. He wanted to stop his medication because he believed that if he did so he would be supernaturally healed. Chuck agreed, however, to follow the psychiatrist's advice on how to best come off the medication, including a slow taper beginning with his antidepressant, then low-dose antipsychotic, and then finally a very slow taper of his lithium until he was drug free. Visits were increased from every 3 months to every 2 weeks during the taper. Everyone agreed to give this a try but under close monitoring. Things were going well until he tapered off the antipsychotic, when he suddenly went into a severe episode of depression. His wife called the psychiatrist and told him that Chuck needed to be seen *now*, so his psychiatrist met him in the hospital emergency room. Chuck looked nothing like the well-dressed, well-kept, articulate, and energetic person whom he had seen barely 2 weeks ago. Chuck now was almost unrecognizable with unkept, wild-looking hair, a food-stained shirt, and overall disheveled appearance, resembling a homeless person more than a retired lawyer. The psychiatrist quickly admitted him to the hospital and restarted him on his medications. After 10 days in the hospital, his depression began to improve and by 2 weeks he was discharged back home. A few weeks later he was seen by his psychiatrist in the clinic, appearing his usual jovial, lawyerly like self. The psychiatrist asked him what he had learned from this experience. Chuck said that he had misinterpreted what the Holy Spirit had told him about the timing of his medication discontinuation.

Chuck's bipolar disorder remained stable for the next 2 years. During which time his wife died and he changed churches, now attending a nondenominational evangelical church across town from his earlier Pentecostal church. During a follow-up visit, Chuck gave his psychiatrist an audiotape from a well-known faith healer. He told the psychiatrist that the timing was now right, and he was ready to go off the medication again. The psychiatrist attempted to reason with him, emphasizing that he had a biological illness like diabetes, and just as diabetics required insulin, he needed the psychiatric medications or would become sick again. Coming off his medication would almost certainly result in another episode of depression or mania, the psychiatrist explained. Chuck said he was willing to take the risk, and insisted on tapering his medication again with or without his psychiatrist's help.

CASE VIGNETTE #2

Barry is a 33-year-old handsome, intelligent, and extroverted individual with a history of emotional abuse and neglect as a child. The trauma he experienced during childhood has affected his ability to form stable attachments with others, and created an insatiable need for control and power. He is unconsciously seeking assurance that he will never experience the type of helplessness he felt as a child. Barry has learned a set of skills that have enabled him to take advantage of psychologically vulnerable but well-meaning individuals to meet his own neurotic needs. He experiences little guilt or shame when others are hurt as a result of his actions. Barry quickly though strategically discardes people once he has no further need for them. Not only does he have no qualms about manipulating or using others, he actually enjoys it because it gives him a feeling of power over these individuals. He also likes taking risks for the thrill of it, and actually has a very high threshold for experiencing anxiety and other negative emotions. He justifies his every action and externalizes blame to the other person. It is never his fault, so there is no need for corrective action. Given his charm, wit, and interpersonal talents, Barry is the kind of person who easily convinces others to follow him.

Barry has learned that religion is a powerful tool that he can use to manipulate others, gain attention and even wealth. Barry is calm and calculating, surprisingly able to delay gratification in order to achieve his goal. As he is so friendly, outgoing, and charismatic, others are naturally drawn to him. This has allowed him to attract quite a following in his local nondenominational church, because of his novel and exciting ideas. Starting out as a youth leader, his exciting ideas eventually ended him up in the pulpit. Since he began preaching, the church has grown rapidly in size and in resources. In fact, the church now even has a television and radio ministry that has greatly increased revenues even further. If Barry should ever go to a mental health professional, which is unlikely unless he is forced to do so, his diagnosis would likely be antisocial or psychopathic personality disorder. However, his leadership position, growing wealth, and influence over others have allowed him to successfully reach his goals and prevent exposure of the real underlying psychological motives for what he does.

CASE VIGNETTE #3

Dorothy is a 43-year-old divorced female with adult children who have left the home and now live in distant cities. She lives alone and supports herself from the income she receives as a secretary at a local car dealership. Since her divorce 4 years ago, Dorothy has lived a pretty boring and lonely life. She has always been somewhat introverted, shy, and dependent on others for praise and appreciation to maintain her self-esteem. Her divorce was devastating and left her depressed and dysfunctional for years afterward. Dorothy is a religious person and church has always been a place where she has made relationships, although her depression has caused her to cut back on attending services and she has lost many relationships that she had when she and her husband attended together. She has felt embarrassed about the divorce, something that has made it more and more difficult for her to attend church as a single person. Dorothy has recently heard from a friend at work about a church with an exciting new preacher. Her friend, who attends this church, has invited her to come along with her to one of the services. She notices when driving to the new church that she enters through some large metal gates. When she arrives at the church, everyone is friendly and welcoming, and she immediately feels at home. The sermon is also riveting as the excitement of the preacher is contagious. She decides that she will go again to this church next Sunday. In fact, two women from the church call on her during the week and ask her to go out to lunch with them, which she readily agrees to.

After attending a few services, she learns that many of the attendees live in the immediate area surrounding the church within those large gates that she drives through when she attends church services. There is a small one-bedroom house now available. Although it seems very expensive, the church treasurer assures her that they will provide her with a loan. She is encouraged to sell her home, put a down payment on the new house, and move into the community. After several months of attending services, she decides to do so. Indeed, services are held several times per week on Sundays, Wednesdays, Friday nights, and sometimes Saturdays. It will be easier for her to attend all the services if she actually lives there. For several months after moving into her new house, Dorothy continues to enjoy attending services and living in this community. However, she has noticed that the leadership—particularly the young preacher whom she has come to know personally—frequently asks for donations and pledges for various church activities. It is clear from the sermons that "true believers" give a minimum of 20% of their gross annual income to the church, relying on God to meet *all* their needs. She also notices that the interest on the loan that she took out from the church to buy her home in the community is pretty high (also 20%). Trying to please the leadership, who always praise her for her faithfulness in giving, she is turning over much of her monthly check from her job over to the church and has now even had to withdraw money from her savings and retirement account to keep up.

The women who were initially so friendly have turned their attention to new members, and stopped including Dorothy in their activities. When she first moved into the community, those women encouraged her to cut herself off from family and friendships outside of the church, because unbelievers could have a negative influence on her spiritual life. Dorothy has begun to feel lonely again and is now cut off from family and old friends. The continuous pressure during sermons to give more and more to the church has caused her to attend fewer and fewer services, which has not gone unnoticed by the leadership. After a while, she starts to think about leaving the church and the community, but is unable to do so because she no longer has any savings left. She has been told by the leadership that she will owe a large sum of money to the church due to the interest that has accumulated on the loan for her house (but they will forgo immediate collection if she remains there).

CASE VIGNETTE #4

Sally, age 61, is from a very close family. She, her brothers, and their parents have had many happy times together on holidays and during vacations. However, one thing separates them. Sally is very religious, attends a different church than the one she was raised in, and her parents, particularly her father, believe differently than she does. This has given rise to numerous heated "discussions." Sally has always been a "nervous" person and worries about everything. Her new faith has been an enormous comfort to her over the years in calming her anxiety. Sally currently attends a nondenominational evangelical Christian church, which she is very involved in. For years, she has spoken to her parents and siblings about their need for salvation, something that her Protestant church strongly emphasizes. Eventually, as a result of Sally's prompting, her mother "came to Christ" and now attends Sally's church with her. Her father, who is Catholic and satisfied with his own faith, has been resistant and somewhat perturbed that his wife no longer attends church services with him. He now gets irritated and upset every time Sally brings up the subject of religion. Over the past 3 years, he has become seriously ill and is now dying. Sally loves her daddy very much, and she has been helping to care for him at home. But this has been hard on her and her dad. She feels desperate about her father's religious condition, and believes (as her church teaches) that he will spend eternity in hell (and she will be separated from him forever) unless he verbally confesses his sins and claims Jesus Christ as his Lord and Savior. As he becomes sicker, she becomes more and more desperate. She repeatedly approaches him about this and begs him to accept the Lord. This upsets her father, who feels that he is religious enough, has been a faithful Catholic all his life, attending church regularly and receiving the Sacraments. He recently received the Sacrament of the Sick from his priest. For Sally, however, this is not enough. He must say the prayer of salvation to be saved. If he dies before that, he will go to hell. Other family members observe how these desperate pleas are affecting her father, Sally, and the relationship between the two, and they have spoken to her about this. However, Sally cannot be convinced otherwise. When her father finally dies (without giving his life to the Lord, despite Sally's insistence), she goes into a deep depression. Sally has sought counseling in her church, but this has not been helpful, and she now decides to see a mental health professional.

The above case vignettes illustrate four types of individuals where religion may be used in aberrant or neurotic ways that are not healthy for either the person or those around him or her. All of these individuals have mental health problems of one sort or another that is driving their behavior. The first case is that of a person who uses religious teachings to serve his own psychological needs, refusing input from others and insisting that religious beliefs on healing justify his potentially harmful decision to stop his medication. Then there is the individual in Case #2 who requires the attention and resources of others to fill a neurotic need for power and control in order to feel less helpless. Third is the psychologically and socially vulnerable individual, someone that people like the man in Case #2 often take advantage of. Fourth, is the genuinely religious individual who holds rigidly onto beliefs that create stress and conflict with other family members, exemplifying what may happen when a person chooses another religion (or religious denomination) different from the religion of their family. These four cases provide clues on how to identify four types of clients who manipulate, abuse, or misinterpret religion, or those who are abused by religion (or their religious leaders). Below are recommendations for treating each of these individuals.

TREATMENT RECOMMENDATIONS

With clients like Case #1, it is easy for the clinician to become frustrated. The underlying motivation for medication discontinuation is not religion, but rather the dislike of the medication, its effects (reducing his manic or hypomanic highs), and/or acknowledging that he has a disease that requires lifelong treatment (bipolar disorder). One response would be for the clinician to challenge the client's manipulation of religion, pointing out what his real motives are. A second response to mentally competent clients is to threaten to no longer manage their illness unless they comply with the treatment (i.e., abandon them). Both of these responses are natural and perfectly understandable, but not effective. The most sensible course of action would be to work with the client, his or her family, and support system (often a religious community), hoping that when others realize the situation they will pressure the client to comply. If the client insists on coming off the medication against medical advice and despite coaxing by family and clergy, the clinician should initiate a gradual, slow taper of each medication, starting with the least important medication, with careful monitoring by family members and the religious community as the client may not have the insight to recognize early signs of worsening illness. Even more challenging is when clients live alone and have no family members or no reliable members of a faith community to monitor them. In that case, clinic visits may be needed on a weekly basis. As noted above, it is easy to reject and abandon such clients; however, agreeing to work with them despite their poor choices will help to strengthen the therapeutic alliance, which will increase the likelihood of future compliance (and the chance that clients will contact the clinician early on when relapse occurs). The goal is to demonstrate to the client that the clinician is on the client's side, truly wants their best, and will work with the client if the client will work with them.

Individuals like the manipulative charismatic leader illustrated in Case #2 are unlikely to seek help from mental health or religious professionals because they don't recognize the need for help, particularly when successfully achieving their goals. Those with antisocial or psychopathic personality traits will ordinarily only seek assistance when forced to do so, for example, by a court of law after their activities have been discovered. This category of individuals like Case #2 includes clergy who physically or sexually abuse minors, as in the recent Catholic Church priest scandals. Note that not all religious leaders in such positions are psychopaths. There may be instances where talented religious leaders will start out with a genuine desire to serve God and help others, but then become derailed by power, success, money, or by uncontrolled sexual urges. When they are caught, they may sincerely repent and even seek help on their own. Often help is sought in religious settings, but they may also seek treatment from mental health professionals. Lengthy psychotherapy may be necessary to uncover and make conscious psychological needs that are causing these individuals to act as they do (often traumatic early life experiences, including abuse). Ideally, such treatment should be conducted by counselors with specific training and experience dealing with these matters, often located in specialized centers.

The third type of client as in Case #3 is genuinely religious but psychologically vulnerable to manipulation by others. This includes those who become involved in cults and groups like ISIS. As noted earlier, an extreme case is the suicide bomber who has been indoctrinated with false religious teachings and manipulated by group leaders to end his or her life by killing others. This individual often sincerely believes she or he is serving God. As noted in the Case, individuals of this type tend to be dependent, need external validation, and may internalize (blame themselves); alternatively, or in addition, they may have repressed rage causing them to reject society and join counter-culture groups that give them a sense of purpose and meaning. Such persons may have a low threshold for depression or anxiety, and be more likely to seek help from either religious or mental health professionals, but only after separation from the group they are involved in. Initially, deprogramming is necessary, and then supportive and possibly psychodynamic psychotherapy may be needed to process issues underlying their psychological vulnerability to manipulation by others. Since initial symptoms of distress may interfere with clients' ability to engage in psychotherapy, medication may be needed in order to lessen paralyzing symptoms. Religiously integrated therapies or pastoral counseling may be helpful to address prior religious traumas that are adversely affecting the client's religious faith and ability to participate in a healthy religious community.

The fourth type of individual is one who is generally mentally stable and genuinely religious, where their religious faith has provided great comfort when coping with life problems. Then a situation arises where their beliefs, particularly if rigid, create distress and conflict with others. In this case, the therapist may not be able to rely on the person's religious community or clergy to help alter the beliefs that are causing distress or to encourage flexibility in adherence to religious teachings. The situation is even more complex if the person has converted to a different religious tradition from the one in which he or she was raised. The same issue as in Case #4 arises when someone who has been raised Muslim converts to Christianity, or someone raised Orthodox Jewish converts to Buddhism. Family members may completely disown such individuals. Even for those within the same religion, different beliefs may cause serious stress and strain on relationships (Exline, Yali, & Sanderson, 2000; Exline, 2002). For persons like the woman in Case #4, a religiously integrated form of cognitive behavioral therapy may help to loosen rigidly held beliefs that are causing distress. For example, emphasizing certain conservative Christian beliefs such as God's love and mercy, over God's unforgiving judgment, may provide some wiggle room to relieve distress from certainty that a loved one is forever damned. In this case, having a respected clergy person from the person's faith tradition support the treatment will help enormously, although such a person may or may not be willing to do so. If the rigidity of religious beliefs cannot be loosened, then treatment with medication may be necessary to relieve symptoms (although this will leave the person vulnerable to future distress over similar situations).

In all four cases above, a detailed spiritual history spanning the client's entire life (from early childhood to the present) is needed to better understand how religious beliefs have become interwoven with psychopathology. This includes inquiry about what the client knows about the mental health of their parents or early caregivers, along with information about those persons' specific religious beliefs. The therapist should also recognize that a client's neurotic use of religion could be serving an important intrapsychic function, one that may be enabling the person to remain mentally intact and able to function in daily life. Thus, patience and skill will be needed to gradually help the person replace their dysfunctional use of religion with healthy uses that serve the same purpose. Again, given the complexity of these issues, mental health professionals should consult with or do cotherapy with a religious professional who has formal mental health training or extensive counseling experience, if one is available and the client is willing.

OTHER PROBLEMS FROM RELIGION

Religion may be problematic in other instances where underlying mental health issues are not as prominent. Two examples are provided here. First, religious activities may dominate a person's life so that they interfere with responsibilities to family or work. Second, some religions may be truly promoting beliefs or practices that are mentally or physically harmful to self or others. These will now be discussed briefly.

Neglected Responsibilities to Others

Religious leaders caught up in their ministries (not unlike leaders in business, industry, healthcare, etc.) may spend large amounts of time and energy on their work, neglecting responsibilities to spouse or children (Richmond, Rayburn, & Rogers, 1985). Instead of taking time to meet the needs of family members—needs that only they can fulfill—these individuals take on all-consuming projects that prevent them from carrying out these other responsibilities. The result may be family disharmony, divorce, delinquency, and other problems that immediately affect the mental health of family members and ultimately the mental health and functioning of the religious leader. Success, productivity, and acquiring fame and fortune, may easily lure some deeply religious individuals to sacrifice their own principles to achieve these ends (under the guise of religious service). Balancing religious activities with those at home is no doubt a fine art, but a necessary one to ensure the mental health of all concerned (Blanton, 1992; Morris & Blanton, 1994).

Religious leaders are not alone here. Religious volunteers from the congregation may likewise spend inordinate amounts of time in religious activities at church, synagogue, mosque or temple, neglecting the needs of family members or responsibilities at work. While well-intentioned, such engrossment in the religious community may interfere with family life and/or result in job loss affecting their ability to support themselves and others. While religious involvement may be associated with better mental health and social functioning, engagement to an extreme degree may have the opposite effect.

Pathological Religion

As noted earlier, few if any religions that persist over time are harmful and produce mental pathology. Claiming that any religion is harmful because one disagrees with its tenants is fraught with potential bias and error, underscoring the need for caution when making such judgments. However, one cannot deny that offshoots from established mainstream religious groups have occurred throughout history promoting beliefs or practices that a reasonable person today might consider problematic. These include religious groups that encourage the handling of snakes or other deadly creatures to prove one's faith; the performance of rituals that involve placing a hurtful "spell" on others; the killing, harming, mistreatment, or exclusion of others for religious reasons; violent attempts to exorcise demons from someone with a mental illness; use of drugs during religious ceremonies that may increase risk of addiction; or belief in divine healing leading to refusal to take a child with a curable illness to a medical doctor, or failure to vaccinate children against infectious diseases that cause serious illness during youth or adulthood or affect pregnancy and fetal brain development. These are just a few examples of where religion has gone awry.

IS RELIGION FOR EVERYBODY?

The final question addressed here is whether religion is for everybody. Are religious beliefs and practices simply not helpful, or even worse, potentially harmful for some individuals? Alternatively, might certain types of religion be good for some but not for others? For example, a religion that emphasizes the need for believers to pray or worship God regularly several times daily for most individuals may enhance their relationship with God, provide direction for daily decisions, and enable them to cope better with life stressors. However, this religion may not be so good for someone with obsessive-compulsive disorder, who repeatedly and obsessively prays as part of their illness (Freud, 1907). Such a person may be viewed in this particular religious community as an exemplary member, encouraged and praised for their faithfulness. In such cases, religious beliefs and support systems might actually reinforce a pathological behavior. Difficulty functioning in other areas of life, though, is likely to give away such an individual as someone suffering from an illness, rather than a person of devout religious faith. In other cases, this might not be so clear.

What about the person with an early psychosis who attends a charismatic Christian church that endorses speaking in tongues, prophesy, and hearing God's voice? Might psychotic symptoms be encouraged or reinforced, rather than recognized for what they are, evidence of mental illness? As noted in Chapters 5 and 10, while clergy or members of the congregation are often able to detect something strange about the individual, borderline cases might not be so clear. Such individuals may be viewed as particularly saintly or possessing a special gift (as in some primitive cultures). Could this reinforce or worsen their psychosis? Research suggests that while intense religious experiences may precipitate a reactive psychosis, they rarely lead to chronic psychotic disorders (Linden, Harris, Whitaker, & Healy, 2010). Furthermore, studies suggest that individuals with psychotic disorders like schizophrenia may have *better outcomes* in less developed or industrialized countries (Jablensky et al., 1992; Padma, 2014) where it is more likely they will be accepted and integrated into the social group as someone special (as a shaman, for example) (Kauffman, 2016). Whether acceptance, support, or encouragement of biologically driven psychotic symptoms improves or worsens them (i.e., a kind of "kindling" effect as seen with repeated mood episodes) is not known, although research is beginning to examine such questions (Luhrmann, Padmavati, Tharoor, & Osei, 2015).

HEALTHY RELIGION

What, then, are the characteristics of a healthy religion? As noted earlier, what one person considers "healthy" another person might consider "sick," so the qualities provided here should be taken with some reservation. Furthermore, claiming a religion is healthy and claiming a religion is "true" are two different things (i.e., a religion may be sick and true, or healthy and false). Nevertheless, from a mental health viewpoint, many would agree that a healthy religion is one that fosters a deep connection with and surrender to the transcendent that **over the long-term** leads to:

1. *Greater peace, purpose, hope, and meaning for the individual* that maximizes their true potential, develops their talents, and improves their functioning, and
2. *Greater love and care for others and self* in a way that (1) promotes stronger, closer, healthier relationships within families; (2) enhances relationships within the broader community (locally, regionally, and globally); (3) prioritizes the meeting of others' physical, psychological, social, and spiritual needs (especially those of persons who are most vulnerable); (4) stimulates the development of families and communities that are inclusive, flexible, allow for different religious and political views, and show respect for and honor every member; and (5) encourages and supports self-discipline and pursuit of a healthy lifestyle.

Each of the major world religions accomplishes these goals to some degree, and also fails to achieve these ends on occasion. Whether one religion does so better than another is subject to debate, and the subject is not an easy one to objectively study given many complex cultural, historical, and social influences. Nevertheless, a religion that encourages the traits above in members ought to be one that mental health professionals can support.

SUMMARY AND CONCLUSIONS

This chapter has examined cases where mental health problems may cause the distorted use or abuse of religious teachings, where religion may be manipulated in ways that take advantage of the emotionally vulnerable, and where religion itself may adversely affect mental health. These cases do not represent the majority of religious individuals or religions, as this book amply documents from the research reviewed here, despite what critics may claim (Dawkins, 2006; Hitchens, 2007; Harris, 2004). Nevertheless, there are times when religion may be the problem. Examples are given to illustrate the neurotic use of religion that will help providers identify such individuals, and recommendations for treatment are provided. Also examined here are extreme levels of religious involvement that may lead to the neglect of responsibilities to others. Whether religion is something for everybody or whether certain types of religion are unhealthy for certain types of people is also discussed. Religious beliefs and practices that may adversely affect mental, social, or physical health are described. Finally, presented here are the characteristics of what might be considered a "healthy" religion, at least from a mental health perspective. While religion may be a powerful source of good mental health for many, this chapter raises the question of whether religion is bad for some, or whether some individuals are bad for religion.

References

Al-Alil, H. (2017). *Educated in terror: Deprogramming the children ISIS taught to kill*. New York, NY: NBC News [July 6. Retrieved from http://www.nbcnews.com/storyline/isis-uncovered/deprogramming-children-isis-n780081].

Blanton, P. W. (1992). Stress in clergy families: managing work and family demands. *Family Perspective*, *26*(3), 315–330.

Dawkins, R. (2006). *The god delusion*. Boston, MA: Houghton Mifflin Harcourt.

Enroth, R. M. (1992). *Churches that abuse*. Grand Rapids, MI: Zondervan.

Exline, J. J. (2002). Stumbling blocks on the religious road: fractured relationships, nagging vices, and the inner struggle to believe. *Psychological Inquiry*, *13*, 182–189.

Exline, J. J., Yali, A. M., & Sanderson, W. C. (2000). Guilt, discord, and alienation: the role of religious strain in depression and suicidality. *Journal of Clinical Psychology*, *56*(12), 1481–1496.

Freud, S. (1907). Obsessive acts and religious practices. In J. Strachey (Ed.), *Standard edition of the complete psychological works of sigmund freud*. London: Hogarth Press [translator 1962].

Goodall, W. (2005). *Why great men fall*. Green Forest, AR: New Leaf Press.

Harris, S. (2004). *The end of faith: religion, terror, and the future of reason*. New York, NY: W.W. Norton & Company.

Hitchens, C. (2007). *God is not great: how religion poisons everything*. New York, NY: Twelve Books.

Horton, A. L., & Williamson, J. A. (1998). *Abuse and religion: When praying isn't enough*. Lanham, MD: Lexington Books (Rowman & Littlefield Publishers).

Hunt, S. (2000). Dramatising the 'Health and Wealth Gospel': belief and practice of a neo-pentecostal 'Faith' ministry. *Journal of Beliefs and Values*, *21*(1), 73–86.

Jablensky, A., Sartorius, N., Ernberg, G., Anker, M., Korten, A., Cooper, J. E., & Bertelsen, A. (1992). Schizophrenia: manifestations, incidence and course in different cultures. A World Health Organization ten-country study. *Psychological Medicine Monograph Supplement, 20,* 1–97.

Kauffman, P. R. (2016). Might hallucinations have social utility? A proposal for scientific study. *Journal of Nervous and Mental Disease, 204*(9), 702–712.

Langone, M. D. (Ed.). (1995). *Recovery from cults: help for victims of psychological and spiritual abuse.* New York, NY: WW Norton & Company.

Linden, S. C., Harris, M., Whitaker, C., & Healy, D. (2010). Religion and psychosis: the effects of the Welsh religious revival in 1904–1905. *Psychological Medicine, 40*(8), 1317–1323.

Luhrmann, T. M., Padmavati, R., Tharoor, H., & Osei, A. (2015). Hearing voices in different cultures: a social kindling hypothesis. *Topics in Cognitive Science, 7*(4), 646–663.

Morris, M. L., & Blanton, P. W. (1994). The influence of work-related stressors on clergy husbands and their wives. *Family Relations, 43,* 189–195.

Neo, L. S., Shi, P., Dillon, L., Tan, J., Wang, Y., & Gomes, D. (2016). Why is ISIS so psychologically attractive? In M. Khader, L. S. Neo, G. Ong, E. Tan, & J. Chin (Eds.), *Countering violent extremism and radicalisation in the digital era* (pp. 149–167). Hershey, PA: IGI Global [Chapter 8].

Padma, T. V. (2014). The outcomes paradox: schizophrenia patients in developing countries seem to fare better than their Western counterparts. Researchers are keen to find out why. *Nature, 508,* S14–S15.

Phiri, I., & Maxwell, J. (2007). *Gospel riches: Africa's rapid embrace of prosperity Pentecostalism provokes concern—and hope (cover story in Health and Wealth in Africa: how the prosperity gospel is taking the continent by storm).* United States: Christianity Today [July 6. Retrieved from http://www.christianitytoday.com/ct/2007/july/12.22.html].

Richmond, L. J., Rayburn, C., & Rogers, L. (1985). Clergymen, clergywomen, and their spouses: stress in professional religious families. *Journal of Career Development, 12*(1), 81–86.

Wentz, R. E. (1993). *Why people do bad things in the name of religion.* Macon, GA: Mercer University Press.

CHAPTER

14

Conclusions and Recommendations

This final chapter summarizes (1) what is known from systematic research about the relationship between religion and mental health, (2) recommendations for future research, (3) suggestions on how to apply what is currently known to the treatment of clients (religious and nonreligious) and (4) advice on what not to do. First is a brief review of the research findings.

THE RESEARCH FINDINGS

The research presented here on the relationship between religion and mental health is based on quantitative measurement, and therefore requires precise and unambiguous definitions of the constructs being assessed. Therefore, Chapter 1 took great pains to define religion and distinguished it from spirituality, noting that religion is a distinct concept that is easily measured, whereas spirituality has become a nebulous and poorly defined term that is of little practical use when conducting research (because of overlapping definitions with mental health). However, the reason for spirituality's lack of utility in research is also its greatest strength when conducting assessments and discussing these issues in clinical practice. The way that spirituality is used today in clinical settings should allow clients themselves to define what this term means to them. Next measures of religiosity were examined and discussed, highlighting those most commonly used in research. Special attention was paid to a new comprehensive measure of religiosity, the Belief into Action Scale (BIAC), which is included in the Resources section of this book, along with other instruments that can ordinarily be used without charge or permission.

Observational and experimental studies were then summarized that have examined the use of religion in coping and the relationship between religious

Religion and Mental Health. http://dx.doi.org/10.1016/B978-0-12-811282-3.00014-8

involvement and negative emotions (depression, anxiety, substance abuse, antisocial behaviors, etc.), chronic mental disorders (schizophrenia, bipolar disorder, dementia), and states characterized by positive emotions (well-being, happiness, optimism, meaning and purpose, etc.). With regard to religious coping, it was determined that religious beliefs and practices are commonly used throughout the world to make sense of and adapt to unwanted change and difficult life circumstances. Such coping behaviors are often associated with better mental health, although in highly secular areas of the world, this may not be the case. In fact, religious coping behaviors have been associated with worse mental health in areas of the world where religion is out of favor or discouraged within the society. In those regions, however, the direction of causation is usually from poor mental health to religion (rather than vice versa) as people seek help from religion only as a last resort in their distress. When that occurs, religiosity often becomes a marker of distress that may disguise any benefits that it may have for mental health. There are also situations even in religious areas of the world, however, where personal behaviors may conflict with strongly held religious beliefs (i.e., high moral standards that may be difficult to live up to) and in this way increase psychological distress.

With regard to negative emotional states and antisocial behaviors, the majority of studies published prior to the year 2010 indicate that religiosity is related to less depression in two-thirds of studies, and less suicidal thoughts and behaviors in 75% of studies, less anxiety in nearly 50% of studies, less substance abuse, delinquency and crime in over 80% of studies. Likewise, more recent research since 2010 generally confirms these findings while using better designs and more sophisticated statistical methods. The question of reverse causation remains an issue, particularly among cross-sectional studies that make up the bulk of this research. On the one hand, anxiety and distress may increase religious coping behaviors such as prayer, producing positive cross-sectional associations with such religious activities. On the other hand, religion may also increase anxiety in some circumstances and thereby serve to motivate change in behavior. Indeed, religion is sometimes described as "comforting the afflicted and afflicting the comforted." Similarly, recent longitudinal studies using state-of-the-art statistical analyses (marginal structural models) suggest that while religious involvement can often prevent the development of emotional disorders such as depression, depression itself may prevent religious activities such as religious attendance resulting in an inverse cross-sectional relationship with depressive symptoms. Religious beliefs and behaviors, then, are often changing and affecting mental health, which is in turn changing and affecting religious beliefs and behaviors, creating a complex dynamic that affects the findings reported in observational studies particularly cross-sectional ones. Nevertheless, the majority of randomized clinical trials also indicate that religious interventions decrease depression and reduce anxiety, not increase them, which has implications for the interpretation of results from observational studies.

Concerning chronic mental conditions such as schizophrenia and bipolar disorder, it was long feared by mental health professionals that religious involvement would worsen symptoms and interfere with treatment. This impression has been influenced by the presence of religious delusions and hallucinations in approximately one-quarter to one-third of persons with psychotic disorders. Furthermore, socially and culturally sanctioned religious beliefs may be difficult to distinguish in equivocal cases from psychotic symptoms. Religious beliefs and behaviors among those with psychoses are often bizarre and usually associated with other symptoms of mental disorder that help to distinguish them from "normal" expressions of religion. Numerous longitudinal studies also suggest that religious involvement may help to improve overall prognosis by reducing psychosocial stress that often precipitates psychotic episodes in those with chronic mental disorder. Furthermore, clinical trials indicate that religious interventions do not appear to harm or exacerbate symptoms in those with chronic mental disorders such as schizophrenia. Much less is known, however, about the relationship between religious involvement, bipolar disorder and other acute psychoses, particularly in the setting of sudden religious conversion experiences that may be accompanied by temporary psychotic symptoms.

Researchers have also examined the relationship between religious involvement and major neurocognitive disorders such as dementia. There is now growing evidence that frequent religious attendance and private religious activity may help to delay cognitive impairment with increasing age and reduce the decline in memory seen in Alzheimer's disease and other dementing disorders. Of eight longitudinal studies identified in our systematic review of research prior to 2010, five reported this finding. Several more recent studies since 2010 have now confirmed these observations. Rational explanations exist that help make sense of such findings. High stress levels and depression are known to cause physiological changes (increases in cortisol and proinflammatory cytokines, for example) that adversely affect brain regions responsible for memory (hippocampus). If religious involvement helps to reduce stress, anxiety and depression, then it may help to prevent the physiological changes that lead to memory decline. Of course, there is also the possibility that cognitive decline may adversely affect religious involvement, again raising the possibility of reverse causation.

Research examining the relationship between religious involvement and positive emotions is even more consistent than that reported for negative emotions. Systematic review of research prior to 2010 found that nearly 80% of studies examining relationships with well-being, happiness, and life satisfaction reported significant positive associations. Recent studies since 2010 overwhelmingly confirm these findings. Although most of that research is cross-sectional, a number of longitudinal studies have been conducted that control for baseline measures of positive emotion, suggesting that religiosity increases positive emotions over time. Similarly, religious involvement is associated with greater hope (over 70% of studies), greater optimism (over 80%), and greater purpose and meaning in life (over 90%), although again most studies have been cross-sectional. Nevertheless, there have been a few single group experimental studies and randomized clinical trials that indicate the direction of causation is likely from religiosity to greater well-being and more positive emotions.

This relatively consistent finding in both early and more recent research that religious involvement is related to better mental health makes rational sense. Chapter 7 described a model that details this logic. The underlying mechanisms include a complex array of factors that are potentially influenced by religion, including genetic, biological, psychological, social, environmental, and individual level factors. These factors likely have influences beginning with brain development in utero (based on maternal stress levels and substance use behaviors), developmental experiences during early childhood and teen years, and later extending into adulthood and later life (by affecting cognitive and behavioral responses to stress). Unfortunately, few studies have assessed the effects of both parental and individual religious involvement on mental health across the lifespan from early stages of fetal development to the end of life, so it is difficult to determine the overall impact that religion may have on mental health. The findings reported thus far, then, may be only the tip of the iceberg.

In contrast to these findings (although actually consistent with them), negative religious coping behaviors and religious doubt (i.e., religious/spiritual struggles or RSS) have been almost uniformly related to worse mental health. Systematic reviews indicate that this is the case in 87%–95% of studies. The big question here is whether RSS are leading to or causing depression, anxiety, and other emotional disorders, or whether RSS simply represents symptoms of emotional disorder/distress. There is evidence for both of these hypotheses. Intervention studies that specifically target RSS both reduce RSS and improve mental health outcomes. However, it is unclear whether such therapies do so any better than general spiritual interventions or completely secular psychotherapies (or even drug treatment alone). Finally, almost nothing is known about how to distinguish the various types of RSS, some of which may lead to spiritual and psychological growth and others that may lead to persistent mental illness that can destroy the person.

RESEARCH NEEDED

Although much has been learned from the thousands of quantitative studies conducted over the past century, the research published thus far has only scratched the surface in terms of understanding the relationship between religion and mental health. The questions that need answering and research that needs to be done represent a vast horizon of possibilities. Some of that research will be expensive, difficult to carry out, and time consuming. Other important studies will be relatively inexpensive and require little extra time and work. Regardless, the payoff in terms of improving public health could be huge. Randomized clinical trials that involve developing and testing of religious interventions are the highest priority at present, since they have the potential to determine causal relationships and identify effective treatments for mental disorder. Unfortunately, these are the most expensive and complex types of studies, especially if done well. If not done well, however, such trials can be misleading and incorrectly discourage the use of truly effective interventions. A second priority is longitudinal studies that assess religious involvement and mental health outcomes repeatedly over long periods of time, allowing for the use of statistical methods that can help sort out issues related to direction of effect and reverse causation. Given that such studies need to be conducted over decades in order to allow for sufficient time for religious beliefs/behaviors to impact mental health and for sufficient change in mental health to occur, they are also likely to be expensive and require teams of investigators from one or more generation to complete. However, there are others options. For example, it takes little additional expense and time to piggyback religious measures onto large longitudinal studies that are being funded for other purposes. Similarly, adding such measures to short-term drug studies may also provide important information on how religiosity affects drug response and how drugs affect religiosity.

Chapter 9 provides details on the types of studies that are needed, including an assessment of relative ease and cost. These include studies that (1) contribute to our understanding of the causal relationship between religion and mental health; (2) investigate whether religious struggles cause or are symptoms of emotional disorder; (3) determine if religiosity is a marker of mental distress in secular areas of the world; (4) identify better and more objective measures of religiosity; (5) examine the effects of religious involvement over the lifespan; (6) explore the role that religion plays in the development and course of chronic mental disorders; (7) test religious interventions that help prevent the development of substance abuse habits during youth; (8) identify religious strategies for instilling human virtues; (9) examine influences of religion on physical health and neuropsychiatric functioning (given effects of physical health on mental health); (10) consider religion's role in family caregiver adaptation (given a world population that is rapidly aging); (11) determine specific aspects of religion that positively affect mental health; (12) examine the effects of a close relationship with God or positive image of God on the relationship between religiosity and mental health; (13) explore the impact of religious transformation and conversion experiences on mental health; (14) determine how religious beliefs and values are best transmitted from generation to generation; (15) examine those aspects of religion that negatively affect mental health; (16) investigate the mental health of atheists across the lifespan; (17) probe the epigenetic influences that religion may have on mental health (and role of genetics in religious predispositions); (18) explore how religion interacts with drug treatments (affects response to drug treatment and is affected by it, as noted above); (19) test the effectiveness of religiously integrated treatments on common mental disorders (depression, anxiety, PTSD); and (20) examine how integrating spiritual and religious beliefs into mental health care affects mental health outcomes. The possibilities for research in this field are literally endless.

RECOMMENDATIONS FOR PRACTICE

Although much more needs to be learned, much is already known and the clinical applications of that knowledge to mental health care are many. The recommendations below are divided into general applications relevant to all clients whether religious or not, and more specific applications that are especially relevant to those who are religious.

General Applications

These include taking a spiritual history, respecting and acknowledging the potential value of religious/spiritual beliefs, supporting the religious beliefs/behaviors of clients (while also supporting the absence of such beliefs in those who are not religious), providing a safe and neutral place for discussing religious beliefs/practices, and in some circumstances, utilizing the religious beliefs of clients to achieve treatment goals.

Taking a Spiritual History

There is almost uniform agreement that taking a detailed and thorough spiritual history is essential for providing competent mental health care that respects the personal beliefs and values of clients. The spiritual history should be conducted in a way that avoids making clients feel guilty because they are not religious or spiritual enough. Similarly, the spiritual history should not make the devoutly religious person feel that their beliefs are irrational or somehow inferior to humanistic or secular beliefs. The therapist is obligated to create a safe and neutral environment in which clients feel free to express their religious views, both positive and negative, without judgment.

Supporting Clients' Beliefs

If the initial spiritual history and early client sessions reveal religious beliefs/activities that are generally positive, helpful in coping, and not overtly pathological, then therapists should consider supporting beliefs both verbally and nonverbally. This is particularly true for involvement in religious community and other prosocial religious activities.

Challenging Clients' Beliefs

If after a thorough assessment *and* the development of a solid therapeutic alliance, it is determined that a client's religious beliefs are contributing to emotional/psychological problems or blocking recovery, then the therapist may need to challenge those beliefs. This must be done with great caution and sensitivity, and probably only after consultation with religious experts in the client's faith tradition. Socratic questioning is probably the best approach to take, asking questions in a way that makes the client feel the therapist is trying to understand his or her sacred beliefs (not dispute them). Furthermore, before dismantling a client's beliefs—even when pathological—therapists should be aware that those beliefs may have a purpose in terms of holding their psychic life together. This means proceeding slowly and providing alternative healthy beliefs from the client's faith tradition that may serve the same function.

Utilizing Beliefs

The devoutly religious client may have religious beliefs that can be utilized to support changes in attitude or behavior. Utilizing beliefs for this purpose stops short of truly integrating religious resources into therapy (as in religiously integrated approaches described below). Instead, utilizing beliefs for this purpose comprises only a small proportion of the overall therapy and is situation specific. For example, if the client's religious belief system emphasizes mercy and forgiveness, then this might be capitalized on to help with excessive feelings of resentment or guilt. Likewise, if a Muslim believes strongly in God's will, then this may be used to help deal with losses and change that are not under the client's control. This may provide hope that something good may result from the loss, since God's is good and God's will is ultimately good and will result in good for the client if the loss is accepted and borne with courage.

Specific Applications

These applications are appropriate for religious clients and may involve either "simple" religious interventions (prescribing religious activities, praying with clients) or integrating religious/spiritual beliefs into standard psychotherapeutic techniques.

"Prescribing" Religious Activities

For the anxious Jewish or Christian client, the therapist may recommend reading something from their sacred scriptures that could generate peace and comfort, such as the 23rd Psalm. The Muslim client might be encouraged to recite certain verses from the Qur'an, such as the 1st or 36th surah, or listen to these verses being recited by a trained reader of the Qur'an. For depressed Protestant Christians, the therapist might recommend the self-help book, "Telling Yourself the Truth," which takes a Bible-based cognitive-behavioral approach toward depression and anxiety (Backus & Chapian, 2000). A more aggressive approach might be to prescribe an activity such as attending religious services. This would be done only if the activity was important to clients in the past but was stopped due to symptoms from mental disorder (social withdrawal, loss of energy or interest), situational factors (lack of transportation), or conflicts within their religious community (problems with other members of the congregation or clergy). For active Catholic clients, the therapist might encourage participation in the Sacraments or involvement in community service or volunteer work in order to enhance self-esteem or improve self-worth. Such prescriptions are probably safest and most appropriately done by religious professionals, whereas mental health professionals will have to proceed more cautiously. This could be done by gently "testing the waters" first to see how receptive the client might be to a particular religious practice before prescribing it, always keeping recommendations client-centered and avoiding any sense of coercion.

Prayer With Clients

A well-timed prayer with a religious client who is overwhelmed with situational stressors can be very powerful and effective in at least temporarily relieving symptoms. In contrast, a poorly timed prayer with the wrong client can be disastrous, viewed as coercive by clients or family members, and result in a successful lawsuit against the practitioner. Prayer in public mental health care settings can be tricky business, and should not be done routinely. Prayer with clients is seldom indicated unless the client requests the prayer, and even then, mental health professionals should explore the underlying motive for requesting prayer. An exception to this rule is the religious counseling setting, where the client comes in specifically for treatment that includes prayer (Christian counseling, for example).

Religiously-Integrated Psychotherapy

This is where the therapist integrates the client's religious beliefs/practices into a standard psychotherapeutic technique (such as cognitive behavioral therapy, cognitive processing therapy, rational emotive therapy, etc.) in order to achieve treatment goals. The first step is to carefully identify healthy religious beliefs and practices and determine the language the client uses to express them. Those beliefs (expressed in the client's language) are then used in CBT, for example, to support change and challenge dysfunctional attitudes, erroneous assumptions, and maladaptive behaviors that are responsible for distress and dysfunction. This is an evidence-based treatment that usually requires specialized training in order to competently administer.

The Do Nots

There are many "do nots" that help to frame religious interventions in clinical settings when treating emotionally frail clients with complex mental health issues. These "boundaries" include the following (some of which are obvious and state previously, but need reinforcing):

- Do not proceed without first taking a detailed and thorough spiritual history
- Do not proselytize or attempt to change religious beliefs that are not clearly dysfunctional
- Do not provide religious advice (unless therapist is a religious professional in the client's faith tradition)
- Do not morally judge clients based on their failure to follow the tenants of their faith tradition; instead provide a safe, open, and unconditionally accepting atmosphere where these issues can be objectively discussed
- Do not challenge what appears to be dysfunctional religious beliefs/practices until a therapeutic relationship has been firmly established and consultation obtained with a respected religious professional in the client's faith tradition
- Do not initiate prayer (usually)
- Do not pray with a client even if requested until after briefly exploring the underlying motive for the request and asking what the client wants prayer for
- Do not attempt religiously/spiritually integrated therapy until after some training has been obtained in this method
- Do not proceed with religiously/spiritually integrated therapy until explicit permission has been obtained from the client
- Do not proceed if the client appears resistant to discuss or utilize religious beliefs in therapy; instead, slow down, step back and later (perhaps a future session) gently explore the reason for the resistance
- Do not attempt religious interventions in clients who are clearly not religious

FINAL CONCLUSIONS

Religious beliefs and practices for thousands of years have served to maintain mental health and well-being and promote interpersonal relationships among humans. No doubt religion has sadly not always served a constructive purpose. Religions are composed of people, and people are fallible, so there is no reason to expect a religion, any religion, to be otherwise. Research done thus far indicates that religious involvement is generally associated with better mental health and greater well-being, and there is growing evidence that religious interventions are efficacious in reducing distressing symptoms especially in religious clients. Although more systematic research is needed to better understand the relationship between religion and mental health and to identify and refine religious interventions, there is enough evidence today to proceed cautiously in utilizing clients' religious resources in treatment. Doing so sensibly and expertly is an art that all helping professionals should learn and practice.

Reference

Backus, W., & Chapian, M. (2000). *Telling yourself the truth*. Bloomington, MN: Bethany House.

Resources
Researchers, Clinicians, Educators, and Clergy

In this last section, educational and training resources are provided to help researchers, clinicians, educators, and clergy optimize the care of those with mental health problems and emotional issues, including the addressing of religious issues. Although there is considerable overlap in what a particular profession will get out of a particular resource, these resources are listed and described here by professional group. Each resource is annotated to provide the reader with a brief description of what it's about.

RESOURCES FOR RESEARCHERS

Measures of Religiosity

Belief Into Action Scale (Koenig et al., 2015a; Koenig, Wang, Al Zaben, & Adi, 2015)
Brief RCOPE (Pargament, Smith, Koenig, & Perez, 1998)
Duke Religion Index (Koenig, Meador, & Parkerson, 1997; Koenig & Büssing, 2010)
Intrinsic Religious Motivation Scale (Hoge, 1972)
Muslim Religiosity Scale (Koenig, Sehlo, Khalifa, & Zaben, 2013; Koenig, Al-Zaben, Khalifa, & Al Shohaib, 2014)
Religious Commitment Inventory (Worthington et al., 2003)
Religious Coping Index (Koenig et al., 1992)

(*Next page for full scales and psychometric properties*)

Religion and Mental Health. http://dx.doi.org/10.1016/B978-0-12-811282-3.00015-X

Belief into Action Scale (BIAC) (Koenig et al., 2015a,b)

Circle a *single* number for each question below:

1. Please *circle* the highest priority in your life now? (*most valued, prized*)

1 My health and independence
2 My family
3 My friendships
4 Job, career or business
5 My education
6 Financial security
7 Relationship with God
8 Ability to travel and see the world
9 Listening to music and partying
10 Freedom to live as I choose

2. How often do you attend religious services? (*circle* a number below)

Never	Rarely	Couple times/yr	Every few mos	About once/m	Several times/m	About every wk	Every week	More than	Daily
1	2	3	4	5	6	7	8	9	10

3. Other than religious services, how often do you get together with others for religious reasons (prayer, religious discussions, etc.)?

Never	Rarely	Couple times/yr	Every few mos	About once/m	Several times/m	About every wk	Every week	More than	Daily
1	2	3	4	5	6	7	8	9	10

4. To what extent (on a 1–10 scale) have you decided to place your life under God's direction?

Not at all (really haven't thought about it)				To a moderate degree					Completely, totally
1	2	3	4	5	6	7	8	9	10

5. What percentage of your gross annual income do you give to your religious institution or to other religious causes each year?

0%	Less than 1%	1%–2%	3%–4%	5%–6%	7%–8%	9%–10%	11%–12%	13%–14%	15% or more
1	2	3	4	5	6	7	8	9	10

6. On average, how much time each *day* (in 24 hours) do you spend listening to religious music or radio, or watching religious TV?

0 (never)	1–5 min	6–10 min	11–20 min	21–30 min	31–60 min	More than 1 hr, less than 2 hr	More than 2 hr, less than 3 hr	3–4 hrs	5 hrs or more
1	2	3	4	5	6	7	8	9	10

7. On average, how much time each *day* do you spend reading religious scriptures, books, or other religious literature?

0 (never)	1–5 min	6–10 min	11–20 min	21–30 min	31–60 min	More than 1 hr, less than 2 hr	More than 2 hr, less than 3 hr	3–4 hrs	5 hrs or more
1	2	3	4	5	6	7	8	9	10

8. On average, how much time each *day* do you spend in private prayer or meditation?

0 (never)	1–5 min	6–10 min	11–20 min	21–30 min	31–60 min	More than 1 hr, less than 2 hr	More than 2 hr, less than 3 hr	3–4 hrs	5 hrs or more
1	2	3	4	5	6	7	8	9	10

9. On average, how much time each *day* do you spend as a volunteer in your religious community or to help others for religious reasons?

0 (never)	1–5 min	6–10 min	11–20 min	21–30 min	31–60 min	More than 1 hr, less than 2 hr	More than 2 hr, less than 3 hr	3–4 hrs	5 hrs or more
1	2	3	4	5	6	7	8	9	10

10. To what extent (on a 1–10 scale) have you decided to conform your life to the teachings of your religious faith?

Not at all (really haven't thought about it)				To a moderate degree					Completely, totally
1	2	3	4	5	6	7	8	9	10

Scoring: Recode Q1 as follows: 7 = 10, all other answers = 1; sum recoded Q1 + Q2 through Q10 to arrive at total score (range 10–100). Higher scores indicate greater religious commitment.

Psychometric Properties

Internal consistency: alpha coefficient is 0.89 (95% CI = 0.86–0.91), and test-retest reliability is 0.92; *convergent/concurrent validity*: correlates with intrinsic religiosity (r = 0.77), organizational religiosity (r = 0.76), private religious activity (r = 0.60), religious support (r = 0.67), and RCI-10 (r = 0.67) and, as predicted, correlates inversely with negative religious coping (r = −0.20); *divergent/discriminant validity*: correlates weakly with depressive symptoms (r = −0.12), caregiver burden (r = −0.19), social support network size (r = 0.13), and physical health (r = 0.01); *construct/factor analytic validity:* single factor that explains 94% of the total variance (with factor loadings for individual items ranging from 0.55 to 0.80).

Brief RCOPE (Pargament et al., 1998)

For general stressors use the following introduction: "The following items deal with ways you coped with negative events in your life. There are many ways to try to deal with problems. These items ask what you did to cope with the negative events you have encountered."

For a specific stressor, use the following introduction: "The following items deal with ways you coped with the most significant negative event in your life. There are many ways to try to deal with problems. These items ask what you did to cope with this specific negative event."

The rest of the instructions here are for both general and specific stressors: "Obviously different people deal with things in different ways, but we are interested in how you tried to deal with it. Each item says something about a particular way of coping. We want to know to what extent you did what the item says. *How much or how frequently?* Don't answer on the basis of what worked or not-just weather you did it. Use these response choices. Try to rate each item separately in your mind from the others. Make you answers as true *for you* as you can. *Circle* the answer that best applies to you."

Not at all	0
Somewhat	1
Quite a bit	2
A great deal	3

1. I looked for a stronger connection with God
2. I sought God's love and care
3. I sought help from God in letting go of my anger
4. I tried to put my plans into action together with God
5. I tried to see how God might be trying to strengthen me in the situation
6. I asked forgiveness for my sins
7. I focused on religion to stop worrying about my problems
8. I wonder whether God had abandoned me
9. I felt punished by God for my lack of devotion
10. I wondered what I did for God to punish me
11. I questioned God's love for me
12. I wondered whether my church had abandoned me
13. I decided the Devil made this happen
14. I questioned the power of God

Scoring: Add up totals to 1–7 = Positive religious coping score. Add up totals to 8–14 = Negative religious coping score.

Psychometric Properties

Internal consistency: alpha coefficients are 0.90 for positive RC (PRC) subscale and 0.81 for the negative RC (NRC) subscale in a college sample, and 0.87 and 0.69 in an older hospitalized sample; *convergent/concurrent validity*: PRC subscale correlates positively with religious growth/outcome (r = 0.58–0.73); d*ivergent/discriminant validity*: PRC subscale correlates weakly with emotional distress (r = 0.01–0.04), GHQ (r = −0.10), and callousness (r = 0.08); NRC subscale has little/no correlation with religious growth/outcome (r = 0.09) and correlates weakly with emotional distress (r = 0.00–0.18), stress-related growth (r = 0.13), and GHQ mental distress (r = 0.13); *construct/factor analytic validity*: reveals two factors corresponding to PRC and NRC with component loadings ranging from 0.53 to 0.78 for PRC and 0.51 to 0.83 for NRC.

Duke University Religion Index (DUREL) (Koenig et al., 1997)

Please *circle* the number in front of the answer that most accurately describes your usual behavior or belief (*circle* only one answer for each question).

1. How often do you attend church or other religious meetings?
   1 More than once/week
   2 Once a week
   3 A few times a month
   4 A few times a year
   5 Once a year or less
   6 Never

2. How often do you spend time in private religious activities, such as prayer, meditation, or Bible study?
   1 More than once a day
   2 Daily
   3 Two or more times/week
   4 Once a week
   5 A few times a month
   6 Rarely or never

The following section contains 3 statements about religious belief or experience. Please mark the extent to which each statement is true or not true for you.

3. In my life, I experience the presence of the Divine (i.e., God).
   1 Definitely true of me
   2 Tends to be true
   3 Unsure
   4 Tends *not* to be true
   5 Definitely *not* true

4. My religious beliefs are what really lie behind my whole approach to life.
   1 Definitely true of me
   2 Tends to be true
   3 Unsure
   4 Tends *not* to be true
   5 Definitely *not* true

5. I try hard to carry my religion over into all other dealings in life.
   1 Definitely true of me
   2 Tends to be true
   3 Unsure
   4 Tends *not* to be true
   5 Definitely *not* true

Scoring: Reverse score all items; score range for ORA (1) is 1–6, NORA (2) is 1–6, and IR (3–5) is 3–15; total score range 5–27 (but should analyze each dimension separately).

Psychometric Properties

Internal consistency: alpha coefficients for the DUREL range from 0.78 to 0.91 (0.75 for 3-item IR subscale), and test-retest reliability (intraclass correlation) is 0.91; *convergent/concurrent validity*: overall scale correlates strongly with the Hoge intrinsic religious motivation scale ($r = 0.85$); *divergent/discriminant validity*: ORA, NORA, and IR subscales correlate weakly with depressive symptoms (r's = 0.03 to −0.15), severity of medical illness (r's = 0.04 to −0.20), physical function (r's = 0.02 to −0.09), and social support (r's = 0.08–0.24); *construct/factor analytic validity:* factor analysis indicates a single factor (Storch et al., 2004; Nurasikin, Aini, Syarinaz, & Ng, 2010; Koenig and Büssing, 2010).

Intrinsic Religious Motivation Scale (IRS) (Hoge, 1972)

The following section contains 10 statements about religious belief or experience. Please mark the extent to which you disagree or agree with each statement.

Strongly disagree	Disagree	Neutral	Agree	Strongly agree
1	2	3	4	5

1. My faith involves all of my life
2. In my life, I experience the presence of the Divine (i.e., God)
3. Although I am a religious person, I refuse to let religious considerations influence my everyday affairs
4. Nothing is an important to me as serving God as best as I know how
5. My faith sometimes restricts my actions
6. My religious beliefs are what really lie behind my whole approach to life
7. I try hard to carry my religion over into all my other dealings in life
8. One should seek God's guidance when making every important decision
9. Although I believe in religion, I feel there are many more important things in life
10. It doesn't matter so much what I believe as long as I lead a moral life

Scoring: Sum scores after reverse-scoring items 3, 9, and 10, with higher scores indicating greater intrinsic religiosity.

Psychometric Properties

Internal consistency: alpha coefficients for the IRS range from 0.87 to 0.90, and test-retest reliability is high (91.3% agreement at 6 weeks) (Hoge, 1972; Koenig, Smiley, & Gonzales, 1988); *convergent/concurrent validity*: correlates strongly with Allport–Ross's original intrinsic subscale (0.86) and Feagin's intrinsic scale (0.87); d*ivergent/discriminant validity*: correlates relatively weakly with psychological and social measures (Koenig, Kvale, & Ferrel, 1988; Koenig, Moberg, & Kvale, 1988; Koenig, George, & Titus, 2004); *construct validity*: high correlation between scale scores and ministers' judgments of intrinsic versus extrinsic individuals ($r = 0.59$); *factor analytic validity*: two factors (eigenvalues of 5.1 and 1.1) corresponding to intrinsic and extrinsic items (with extrinsic items reverse scored) (Koenig, 2017).

Muslim Religiosity Scale (Koenig et al., 2013)

1. How often do you attend *group* religious services for worship and prayer at mosque or in *small group* at work or in your home (obligatory prayers) (Fard)?
   1 5 Times/day
   2 1–4 Times/day
   3 Several times/week
   4 Several times/month
   5 Never

2. How often do you pray *alone* in private (Nawafl)?
   1 Never
   2 Rarely
   3 Occasionally
   4 Often
   5 Very often

3. Are you regular in prayer or do you sometimes sum two or more of your obligatory prayers (Fard) with each other or skip?
   1 Always skip prayers
   2 Often skip
   3 Sometimes skip
   4 Occasionally skip
   5 Never skip (regular)

4. How often do you read or recite the Qur'an or other religious literature (magazines, papers, books) in your home?
   1 Not at all or rarely
   2 During Ramadan only
   3 Occasionally, besides Ramadan, but less than several times per week
   4 Several times/week
   5 Once a day or more

5. How often do you listen to or watch religious programs on radio or TV?
   1 Not at all or rarely
   2 During Ramadan only
   3 Occasionally, besides Ramadan, but less than several times per week
   4 Several times/week
   5 Once a day or more

6. Do you give Zakat to poor each year?
   1 Never
   2 Rarely
   3 Occasionally
   4 Often
   5 Very often
7. Do you give money to poor as a free gift (not obligatory like Zakat)?
   1 Never
   2 Rarely
   3 Occasionally
   4 Often
   5 Very often
8. How often do you fast from food/water (Sawm)?
   1 Never
   2 During Ramadan (part of month)
   3 During Ramadan (all of month)
   4 During Ramadan (all of month) + occasionally other times (Nawafl)
   5 During Ramadan (all of month) + many other times (Nawafl)
9. How often do you make Hajj?
   1 Never
   2 Once
   3 Twice
   4 Several times, but not yearly
   5 Yearly
10. How often do you make Umrah?
    1 Never
    2 Once
    3 Several times
    4 Every year
    5 Several times per year
11. In my life, I experience the presence of Allah/God.
    1 Definitely true of me
    2 Tends to be true
    3 Unsure
    4 Tends *not* to be true
    5 Definitely *not* true

12. My religious beliefs are what really lie behind my whole approach to life.
    1 Definitely true of me
    2 Tends to be true
    3 Unsure
    4 Tends *not* to be true
    5 Definitely *not* true

13. I try hard to carry my religion over into all my other dealings in life.
    1 Definitely true of me
    2 Tends to be true
    3 Unsure
    4 Tends *not* to be true
    5 Definitely *not* true

Scoring: First, reverse code items 1, 11, 12, and 13. Second, add items 1 through 10 to create a religious practices subscale score (range 10–50). Third, add items 11 through 13 to create an intrinsic religiosity subscale score (range 3–15). Higher scores indicate greater religiosity.

Psychometric Properties

Internal consistency: alpha coefficient for full scale is 0.68 (religious practices subscale = 0.64, intrinsic religiosity subscale = 0.93), and test-retest reliability (intraclass correlation) is 0.96 for full scale (95% CI = 0.91–0.98); *convergent/concurrent validity*: has not been established; d*ivergent/discriminant validity*: MRS correlates weakly with depressive symptoms ($r = -0.08$), stressful live events ($r = 0.06$), physical function ($r = 0.18$), cognitive function ($r = 0.13$), and severity of medical illness ($r = 0.12$); *construct/factor analytic validity*: two major factors (eigenvalues of 2.58 and 1.63) corresponding to the religious practices and intrinsic religiosity subscales (Al Zaben et al., 2015a; Al Zaben, Sehlo, Khalifa, & Koenig, 2015)

Religious Commitment Inventory-10 (Worthington et al., 2003)

Read each of the following statements. Using the scale to the right, *CIRCLE* the response that describes how true each statement is for you.

Not at all true of me	Somewhat true of me	Moderately true of me	Mostly true of me	Totally true of me
1	2	3	4	5

1. I often read books and magazines about my faith	1	2	3	4	5
2. I make financial contributions to my religious organizations	1	2	3	4	5
3. I spent time trying to grow in understanding of my faith	1	2	3	4	5
4. Religion is especially important to me because it answers many questions about the meaning of life	1	2	3	4	5
5. My religious beliefs lie behind my whole approach to life	1	2	3	4	5
6. I enjoy spending time with others of my religious affiliation	1	2	3	4	5
7. Religious beliefs influence all my dealings in life	1	2	3	4	5
8. It is important to spend periods of time in private religious thought and reflection	1	2	3	4	5
9. I enjoy working in the activities of my religious affiliation	1	2	3	4	5
10. I keep well informed about my local religious group and have some influence in its decisions	1	2	3	4	5

Scoring: Add the scores on each item. If you want to use the two subscale scores separately (items 1, 3, 4, 5, 7, and 8 make up the Intrapersonal Religious Commitment subscale; items 2, 6, 9, in 10 make up the Interpersonal Religious Commitment subscale), add the items on each subscale.

Psychometric Properties

Internal consistency: alpha coefficient for full scale is 0.93 (intrapersonal subscale = 0.92, interpersonal subscale = 0.87), and test-retest reliability (intraclass correlation) is 0.87 for full scale; *convergent/concurrent validity*: correlates strongly with Rokeach religiosity ($r = 0.54$), participation in organized religion ($r = 0.70$), and frequency of religious activities ($r = 0.72$); *divergent/discriminant validity*: RCI-10 correlates weakly with morality ($r = 0.09$), exemplary human characteristics ($r = 0.18$); *construct/factor analytic validity:* revealed two major factors (eigenvalues 6.2 and 1.0) that explained 72% of the total item variance that corresponded to the intrapersonal and interpersonal subscales.

Religious Coping Index (RCI) (Koenig et al., 1992)

1. "How do you manage to cope with your situation? In other words, how do you keep yourself from getting depressed, sad, or discouraged, despite your current situation?"
   (*score 10 if religious, 0 if not religious*)
2. "Do your religious beliefs or activities help you to cope with or handle your situation? Here is a scale ranging from 0 to 10. On this scale, 0 indicates that you do not use religion at all to cope and 10 indicates that religion is the most important thing that keeps you going. Please mark on this scale the extent to which you use religious belief or activity to help you to cope with or handle your situation."
   (*subject marks on 0 to 10 scale the extent to which he/she uses religion to cope*)
3. In the third item, the interviewer rates the subject's degree of religious coping based on a discussion with the subject about how he or she uses religion to cope. When was the last time religion was used to cope? What exactly was done? How frequently is religion used to cope in this way? All responses are recorded verbatim.
   (*interviewer rates on a 0–10 scale the extent to which the interviewer perceives that the subject uses religion to cope*)

Scoring: Sum scores on three items; score range 0–30, with higher scores indicating greater religious coping.

Psychometric Properties

Convergent/concurrent: correlates (r = 0.84) with importance of religiosity (Meisenhelder & Chandler, 2002); d*ivergent/discriminant*: correlates with negative mental health states such as depressive symptoms (r = −0.14 to −0.16; *criterion/predictive*: correlates with older age (r = 0.05), Black ethnicity (r = 0.15), marital status (married) (0.06), alcohol use (−0.16), lack of religious correlation (r = −0.15).

Training Manuals and Books

- *Spirituality & health research: methods, measurement, statistics, & resources.* Conshohocken, PA: Templeton Foundation Press, (2011).
  This training manual/book summarizes and expands the content presented in the Duke University's 5-day Research Workshop on Spirituality and Health (see below), and is packed full of information on how to perform and publish research on this topic.
- *Handbook of religion and health* (2nd ed.). New York, NY: Oxford University Press, (2012).
  This Second Edition presents a systematic review of the original quantitative research on religion, spirituality, and health (more than 3300 studies published up through 2010).
- *Health and well-being in Islamic societies*. New York, NY: Springer, (2014).
  The core of the book focuses on research exploring religiosity, mental health, and physical health in Muslim populations, comparing research findings in Christians and other religious groups.
- 2017 *Religion and Mental Health Book Series*. Each book in this series contains a comprehensive review of religious beliefs/practices of the religious tradition, including historical background; a systematic review of research examining relationship between that religion and mental health before 2010, review of recent research since 2010, and for Hinduism and Buddhism, original research not published elsewhere; and a detailed review of clinical applications for mental health professionals and clergy or that specific religious tradition.
  - *Judaism and mental health: Beliefs, research and applications*. Amazon: CreateSpace Publishing Platform.
  - *Catholic Christianity and mental health: Beliefs, research and applications.* Amazon: CreateSpace Publishing Platform.
  - *Protestant Christianity and mental health: Beliefs, research and applications*. Amazon: CreateSpace Publishing Platform.
  - *Islam and mental health: Beliefs, research and applications*. Amazon: CreateSpace Publishing Platform.
  - *Hinduism and mental health: Beliefs, research and applications*. Amazon: CreateSpace Publishing Platform.
  - *Buddhism and mental health: Beliefs, research and applications*. Amazon: CreateSpace Publishing Platform.

Review Articles (Classic)

- Bonelli, R. M., & Koenig, H. G. (2013). Mental disorders, religion and spirituality 1990 to 2010: a systematic evidence-based review. *Journal of Religion and Health*, *52*(2), 657–673.
- Koenig, H. G. (2009). Research on religion, spirituality, and mental health: a review. *Canadian Journal of Psychiatry*, *54*(5), 283–291.

- Larson, D. B., Sherrill, K. A., Lyons, J. S., Craige, F. C., Thielman, S. B., Greenwold, M. A., & Larson, S. S. (1992). Dimensions and valences of measures of religious commitment found in the American Journal of Psychiatry and the Archives of General Psychiatry, 1978–1989. *American Journal of Psychiatry, 149,* 557–559.
- Larson, D. B., Pattison, E. M., Blazer, D. G., Omran, A. R., & Kaplan, B. H. (1986). Systematic analysis of research on religious variables in four major psychiatric journals, 1978–1982. *American Journal of Psychiatry, 143,* 329–334.

Measurement

- Koenig, H. G., Al-Zaben, F., Khalifa, D. A., Al Shohaib, S. (2014). Measures of religiosity, (Chapter 19). In G. J. Boyle, D. H. Saklofske, G. Mathews (Eds.), *Measures of personality and social psychological constructs* (pp. 533–564). San Diego, CA: Academic Press (Elsevier).
- Hill, P. C., Hood, R. (1999). *Measures of religiosity*. Birmingham, AL: Religious Education Press.
- Koenig, H. G., Meador. K. G., Parkerson, G. (1997). Religion index for psychiatric research. *American Journal of Psychiatry, 154*(6), 885–886.
- Koenig, H. G., Wang, Z., Al Zaben, F., Adi, A. (2015). Belief into Action Scale: A comprehensive and sensitive measure of religious involvement (review). *Religions, 6*(3), 1006–1016.

Websites

- *Duke University's Center for Spirituality Theology and Health.* Many resources and research updates available, along with archive of monthly e-newsletters (Crossroads) that provide an update on the latest research being published in the field (http://www.spiritualityandhealth.duke.edu/).
- *Harvard's Initiative on Health, Religion and Spirituality* (http://projects.iq.harvard.edu/rshm/home).
- *Religion & Public Health Collaborative at Emory University* (http://www.rhcemory.org/).
- *Centre for Spirituality, Health and Disability* (University of Aberdeen, Scotland) (http://www.abdn.ac.uk/cshad).

Workshops

- *5-Day Duke University spirituality and health research workshop* (Durham, North Carolina)
  Research workshop focused on conducting and evaluating the research on religion spirituality and health. Presenters are from Duke University School of Medicine, Emory University School of Nursing, Yale University School of Medicine, the Veterans Administration, and elsewhere. Participants from a wide range of religious faith traditions

and from all over the world come to this workshop that has been held yearly since 2004, and is the only place where training on design and methods, funding resources, academic publication, study management, and career development can be obtained from researchers active for more than 30 years in the field. Individual mentorship is also provided (http://www.spiritualityhealthworkshops.org/).

Conferences

Many conferences on religion, spirituality, and mental health are held yearly in countries all over the world. See Crossroads e-newsletter for dates and locations of these conferences (http://www.spiritualityandhealth.duke.edu/index.php/publications/crossroads).

References

Al Zaben, F., Khalifa, D. A., Sehlo, M. G., Al Shohaib, S., Binzaqr, S. A., Badreg, A. M., & Koenig, H. G. (2015a). Religious involvement and health in dialysis patients in Saudi Arabia. *Journal of Religion and Health*, *54*(2), 713–730.

Al Zaben, F., Sehlo, M. G., Khalifa, D. A., & Koenig, H. G. (2015b). Test–retest reliability of the Muslim religiosity scale: follow-up to "religious involvement and health among dialysis patients in Saudi Arabia". *Journal of Religion and Health*, *54*(3), 1144–1147.

Hoge, D. R. (1972). A validated intrinsic religious motivation scale. *Journal for the Scientific Study of Religion*, *11*, 369–376.

Koenig H.G. (2017). *Factor analysis of the Intrinsic Religious Motivation Scale*. Durham, NC: Duke University Center for Spirituality, Theology and Health [Unpublished data from 251 adult caregivers in North Carolina and Los Angeles County].

Koenig, H. G., Al-Zaben, F., Khalifa, D. A., & Al Shohaib, S. (2014). Measures of religiosity. In G. J. Boyle, D. H. Saklofske, & G. Mathews (Eds.), *Measures of personality and social psychological constructs* (pp. 551–553). San Diego, CA: Academic Press (Elsevier) [Chapter 19].

Koenig, H. G., & Büssing, A. (2010). The Duke University Religion Index (DUREL): a five-item measure for use in epidemiological studies. *Religions*, *1*(1), 78–85.

Koenig, H. G., Cohen, H. J., Blazer, D. G., Pieper, C., Meador, K. G., Shelp, F., Goli, V., & DiPasquale, R. (1992). Religious coping and depression in elderly hospitalized medically ill men. *American Journal of Psychiatry*, *149*, 1693–1700.

Koenig, H. G., George, L. K., & Titus, P. (2004). Religion, spirituality, and health in medically il hospitalized older adults. *Journal of the American Geriatrics Society*, *52*, 554–562.

Koenig, H. G., Meador, K., & Parkerson, G. (1997). Religion index for psychiatric research: a 5-item measure for use in health outcome studies. *American Journal of Psychiatry*, *154*, 885–886.

Koenig, H. G., Kvale, J. N., & Ferrel, C. (1988a). Religion and well-being in later life. *The Gerontologist*, *28*, 18–28.

Koenig, H. G., Moberg, D. O., & Kvale, J. N. (1988b). Religious activities and attitudes of older adults in a geriatric assessment clinic. *Journal of the American Geriatrics Society*, *36*, 362–374.

Koenig, H. G., Nelson, B., Shaw, S. F., Al Zaben, F., Wang, Z., & Saxena, S. (2015a). Belief into Action scale: a brief but comprehensive measure of religious commitment. *Open Journal of Psychiatry*, *5*(1), 66–77.

Koenig, H. G., Sehlo, M., Khalifa, D. A., & Zaben, F. (2013). *A 13-item scale assessing Muslim religious practices and intrinsic commitment*. Durham, NC: Duke University Center for Spirituality, Theology and Health [Unpublished manuscript].

Koenig, H. G., Smiley, M., & Gonzales, J. (1988c). *Religion, health and aging*. Westport, CT: Greenwood Press [pp. 171–187].

Koenig, H. G., Wang, Z., Al Zaben, F., & Adi, A. (2015b). Belief into Action Scale: a comprehensive and sensitive measure of religious involvement. *Religions*, *6*(3), 1006–1016.

Meisenhelder, J. B., & Chandler, E. N. (2000). Spirituality and health outcomes in the elderly. *Journal of Religion and Health*, *41*(3), 243–252.

Nurasikin, M. S., Aini, A., Syarinaz, A. A., & Ng, C. (2010). Validity and reliability of the Malay version of Duke University Religion Index (DUREL-M) among a group of nursing students. *Malaysian Journal of Psychiatry*, *19*(2), 68–72.

Pargament, K. I., Smith, B. W., Koenig, H. G., & Perez, L. (1998). Patterns of positive and negative religious coping with major life stressors. *Journal for the Scientific Study of Religion*, *37*(4), 710–724.

Storch, E. A., Roberti, J. W., Heidgerken, A. D., Storch, J. B., Lewin, A. B., Killiany, E. M., et al. (2004). The Duke Religion Index: a psychometric investigation. *Pastoral Psychology*, *53*(2), 175–181.

Worthington, E. L., Jr., Wade, N. G., Hight, T. L., Ripley, J. S., McCullough, M. E., Berry, J. W., Schmitt, M. M., Bursley, K. H., & O'Connor, L. (2003). The Religious Commitment Inventory-10: development, refinement, and validation of a brief scale for research and counseling. *Journal of Counseling Psychology*, *50*(1), 84–96.

RESOURCES FOR CLINICIANS

Clinicians include psychiatrists, psychologists, social workers, licensed counselors, and licensed pastoral counselors.

Training Manuals and Books

- *Religiously-integrated cognitive behavioral therapy* (RCBT) *manuals and workbooks* (2015).
  Christian, Jewish, Muslim, Buddhist, and Hindu therapy manuals for clinicians, along with workbooks for both client and therapist are available for download without cost (http://www.spiritualityandhealth.duke.edu/index.php/religious-cbt-study/therapy-manuals).
- *Spiritually-oriented cognitive processing therapy* (SOCP) manual for moral injury in PTSD, now in development.
- *Cognitive behavioral therapy for Christians with depression: a practical tool-based primer*. Templeton Press, (2016).
  This book is based on RCBT research specific to manual for Christian CBT above, authored by the researcher who helped develop the intervention and supervised clinicians during the Duke University clinical trial delivering RCBT.
- *APA handbook of psychology, religion, and spirituality*. American Psychological Association, (2013).
  This two-volume handbook has been marketed as the most comprehensive coverage of the current state of the psychology of religion and spirituality.
- *Spirituality in patient care* (3rd ed.). Templeton Press, (2013).
  The Third Edition provides the latest information on how health professionals can integrate spirituality into patient care. Chapters target physicians, nurses, chaplains and pastoral counselors, and mental health professionals.
- *Religion and spirituality in psychiatry*. Cambridge University Press, (2009).
  Edited textbook written primarily by European psychiatrists and mental health professionals that covers a wide range of clinical topics.
- *Handbook of religion and mental health*. Academic Press, (1998).
  Classic 26-chapter handbook provides clinical applications across various religious traditions by experts in these traditions.
- 2017 *Religion and Mental Health Book Series* (see above description; includes clinical applications for members of each major religious tradition).

Review Articles

- Koenig, H. G., Boucher, N. A., O'Garo, K. N., Pearce, M. J. (2016). Religiously-integrated cognitive-behavioral therapy for major

depression in chronic medical illness: review of results from a randomized clinical trial. *Health and Social Care Chaplaincy*, 4(2): 237–253.
- Koenig, H. G., Boucher, N. A., Oliver, J. P., Youssef, N., Mooney, S. R., Currier, J. M., Pearce, M. P. (2017). Rationale for spiritually-oriented cognitive processing therapy for moral injury in active duty military and veterans with post-traumatic stress disorder. *Journal of Nervous and Mental Disease*, 205(2):147–153.
- Pearce, M. J., Koenig, H. G., Robins, C. J., Nelson, B., Shaw, S. F., Cohen, H. J., King, M. B. (2015). Religiously-integrated cognitive behavioral therapy: a new method of treatment for major depression in patients with chronic medical illness. *Psychotherapy*, *52*(1), 56–66.
- Koenig, H. G. (2014). The spiritual care team: enabling the practice of whole person medicine. *Religions*, *5*(4), 1161–1174.

Video Presentations

- *Religious CBT training video*
  This is an introductory training video for clinicians wishing to use the religious CBT manuals described above in treating clients with depression (http://www.spiritualityandhealth.duke.edu/index.php/religious-cbt-study/training-video).
- *Integrating spirituality into patient care video series*
  Five professionally produced 45-minute videos on why and how to "integrate spirituality into patient care" available for free, unless CME/CE is desired. Videos are targeted at physicians, nurses, chaplains, and social workers in an effort to help them form spiritual care teams to provide "whole person" health care that includes the identifying and addressing of spiritual needs of patients (http://www.spiritualityandhealth.duke.edu/index.php/cme-videos).

Websites

- *APA Division 36: Society for the Psychology of Religion and Spirituality* (http://www.apa.org/about/division/div36.aspx).
- *World Psychiatric Association (WPA) Religion, Spirituality and Psychiatry* (http://www.wpanet.org/detail.php?section_id=11&content_id=541).
- *Royal College of Psychiatrists' Spirituality and Psychiatry Special Interest Group* (http://www.rcpsych.ac.uk/college/specialinterestgroups/spirituality.aspx).
- *Canadian Association for Spirituality and Mental Health* (http://www.spiritualityandmentalhealth.org/).
- *Columbia University Spirituality Mind-Body Institute* (http://spiritualitymindbody.tc.columbia.edu/).

Workshops

- *The center for anxiety training workshops* (http://www.centerforanxiety.org/training/)
  Provides training for mental health professionals and students in evidence-based spiritually oriented therapies targeting anxiety.

Conferences

- *Emerging tools for innovative providers* (ETIP), *Fuller theological seminary* (http://emergingtoolsforinnovativeproviders.com/).
- Many other conferences on religion, spirituality, and mental health for clinicians are held yearly in countries all over the world. See Crossroads e-newsletter for dates and locations of these conferences (http://www.spiritualityandhealth.duke.edu/index.php/publications/crossroads).

TABLE 1 Mental Health Spiritual History for Use in Clinical Assessment

1. "Do you consider yourself religious or spiritual person or neither?"
2. If religious or spiritual, ask: "Explain to me what you mean by that?"
3. If neither religious nor spiritual, ask: "Was this always so?" If no, ask: "When did that change and why?" [Then *end the spiritual history for now*, although may return to it after therapeutic relationship established.]
4. "Do you have any religious or spiritual beliefs that provide comfort?"
5. If yes, ask: "Explain to me how your beliefs provide comfort." If no, ask: "Is there a particular reason why your beliefs do not provide comfort?"
6. "Do you have any religious or spiritual beliefs that cause you to feel stressed?"
7. If yes, ask: "Explain to me how your beliefs cause stress in your life."
8. "Do you have any spiritual or religious beliefs that might influence your willingness to take medication, receive psychotherapy, or receive other treatments that may be offered as part of your mental health care?"
9. "Are you an active member of a faith community, such as a church, synagogue, or mosque?"
10. If yes, ask: "How supportive has your faith community been in helping you?" If no, ask: "Why has your faith community not been particularly supportive?"
11. "Tell me a bit about the spiritual or religious environment in which you were raised. Were either of your parents religious?"
12. "During this time as a child, were your experiences positive or negative ones in this environment?"
13. "Have you ever had a significant change in your spiritual or religious life, either an increase or a decrease?" If yes, ask: "Tell me about that change and why you think the change occurred."
14. "Do you wish to incorporate your spiritual or religious beliefs in your treatment?" If yes, ask: "How would you like this to be done?"
15. "Do you have any other spiritual needs or concerns that you would like addressed in your mental health care?"

Source: Spiritual history above is adapted from: Koenig, H. G. (2002). An 83-year-old woman with chronic illness and strong religious beliefs. Journal of the American Medical Association, *288(4), 487–493.*

RESOURCES FOR EDUCATORS AND TEACHERS

Manuals and Books

- *Spirituality in patient care* (3rd ed.). Templeton Press, (2013) (see description above) includes model curriculums for training programs.
- *Faith & mental health: religious resources for healing*. Templeton press, (2005).
- *Model curriculum for psychiatry residency training programs: religion and spirituality in clinical practice*. National Institute for Healthcare Research, (1996) [pdf available from Harold.Koenig@duke.edu].
- 2017 *Religion and Mental Health Book Series* (see above description).

Review Articles

- Koenig, H. G. (2012). Religion, spirituality and health: the research and clinical implications. *ISRN Psychiatry, 2012* [Article ID 278730].

Video Presentations

- *Integrating Spirituality into Patient Care Video Series* (see description above) (http://www.spiritualityandhealth.duke.edu/index.php/cme-videos).

Websites

- *Duke University's Center for Spirituality Theology and Health* (see description above) (http://www.spiritualityandhealth.duke.edu/).
- *UCLA's Spirituality in Higher Education Program* (http://www.spirituality.ucla.edu/).

Workshops

- *5-Day Duke University spirituality & health research workshop* (see description above). Although workshop is focused on researchers, much material for educators is also provided during these 5 days of intensive training.

Conferences

- Many other conferences on religion, spirituality, and mental health for educators are held yearly in countries all over the world. See Crossroads e-newsletter for dates and locations of these conferences (http://www.spiritualityandhealth.duke.edu/index.php/publications/crossroads).

RESOURCES FOR CLERGY

Clergy include both professional chaplains and community-based clergy.

Books

- *Spirituality in patient care* (3rd ed.). Templeton Press, (2013) (see description above).
- *Pastoral care of alcohol abusers*. Fortress Press, (2008).
- *Counseling persons with addictions: A handbook of pastors and other helping professionals*. Pilgrim Press, (2007).
- *Faith & mental health: Religious resources for healing*. Templeton press, (2005).
- *Counseling families across the life span: A handbook for clergy and other helping professionals*. Abingdon Press, (2002).
- *Pastoral care of older adults*. Augsburg-Fortress, (1998).
- *Counseling troubled older adults: A handbook for pastors and religious caregivers*. Abingdon Press, (1997).
- *Religion and Mental Health Book Series* (see above description).

Review Articles

- Weaver, A. J. (1995). Has there been a failure to prepare and support-based clergy in their role as front-line community mental health workers: a review. *Journal of Pastoral Care, 49*, 129–149.
- Weaver, A. J., Koenig, H. G., Ochberg, F. M. (1996). Post-traumatic stress, mental health professionals, and the Clergy: a need for collaboration, training, and research. *Journal of Traumatic Stress*, 9, 847–856.
- Weaver, A. J., Koenig, H. G. (1996). Elderly suicide, mental health professionals, and the clergy: a need for clinical collaboration, training and research. *Death Studies, 20*, 495–508.
- Weaver, A. J., Koenig, H. G., Larson, D. B. (1997). Marriage and family therapists and the clergy: a need for clinical collaboration, training, and research. *Journal of Marital and Family Therapy, 23*, 13–25.
- Weaver, A. J., Samford, J., Koenig, H. G. (1997). Depression awareness training and the clergy. *American Journal of Psychiatry, 154*, 717–718.
- Weaver, A. J., Samford, J. A., Kline, A. E., Lucas, L. A., Larson, D.B., Koenig, H. G. (1997). What do psychologists know about working with the clergy? An analysis of eight APA journals, 1991–1994. *Professional Psychology: Research and Practice, 28*, 471–474.
- Weaver, A.J.,Flannelly, K, Larson, D. B., Stapleton, C. L., Koenig, H. G. (2002). Mental health issues among clergy and other religious professionals: a review of the research. *Journal of Pastoral Care and Counseling, 56*, 393–403.
- Weaver, A. J., Koenig, H. G., Flannelly, L. (2004). Nurses and healthcare chaplains: natural allies. *Journal of Healthcare Chaplaincy, 14*(2), 91–98.

Video Presentations

- Integrating spirituality into patient care video series (see description above) (http://www.spiritualityandhealth.duke.edu/index.php/cme-videos).

Websites

- *Association of Professional Chaplains* (http://www.professionalchaplains.org/).
- *The HealthCare Chaplaincy* (http://www.healthcarechaplaincy.org/).

Workshops

- *5-Day Duke University spirituality & health research workshop* (see description above). Although workshop is focused on researchers, the majority of participants are often chaplains and many community clergy attend as well.

Conferences

- *Association of Professional Chaplains Annual Conference* (http://www.professionalchaplains.org/content.asp?contentid=452).

Index

FSC
www.fsc.org
MIX
Papier | Fördert gute Waldnutzung
FSC® C083411

Kolibri 360 GmbH
Ferdinand-Jühlke-Straße 7
99095 Erfurt, Deutschland
produktsicherheit@kolibri360.de